Criminal Reconciliation in Contemporary China

Criminal Reconciliation in Contemporary China

An Empirical and Analytical Enquiry

Jue Jiang

Visiting Scholar (honorary), Centre for Rights and Justice, The Chinese University of Hong Kong

Edward Elgar
PUBLISHING

Cheltenham, UK • Northampton, MA, USA

Published by
Edward Elgar Publishing Limited
The Lypiatts
15 Lansdown Road
Cheltenham
Glos GL50 2JA
UK

Edward Elgar Publishing, Inc.
William Pratt House
9 Dewey Court
Northampton
Massachusetts 01060
USA

A catalogue record for this book
is available from the British Library

Library of Congress Control Number: 2016938610

This book is available electronically in the **Elgar**online
Law subject collection
DOI 10.4337/9781785363115

Printed on elemental chlorine free (ECF)
recycled paper containing 30% Post-Consumer Waste

ISBN 978 1 78536 310 8 (cased)
ISBN 978 1 78536 311 5 (eBook)

Typeset by Columns Design XML Ltd, Reading
Printed and bound in the USA

Contents

Preface

Criminal reconciliation (*xingshi hejie*) is a special procedure in China's new Criminal Procedure Law, which came into effect in January 2013. It allows the alleged perpetrators and victims of certain crimes – here referred to as 'the parties' – to resolve criminal cases through reconciliation or mediation. It is officially understood as a mechanism to promote a 'harmonious society' (*hexie shehui*) through voluntary offender–victim reconciliation and bringing 'closure' (*an jie shi liao*) to criminal cases in a way that empowers the parties. It has been designed as a mechanism that can overcome perceived deficiencies of the ordinary, in principle adversarial criminal justice process.

This book, written while criminal reconciliation was being experimentally used in some locations, draws on case examples and interviews with prosecutors, judges, lawyers and parties who participated in this programme in pilot projects in three different regions of China. It critically describes and examines the purposes, successes and failures of this practice observed during fieldwork and argues that while the criminal reconciliation mechanism has contributed to improvements in enforcing compensation agreements between suspects/defendants and victims, it can enable abuses of power and influence and infringement of the parties' rights and fail to lead to just outcomes, as long as wider problems of the current criminal justice system remain unaddressed.

While the case files accessed for the purpose of this research purport to document a well-functioning process of criminal reconciliation in accordance with the rules and principles supposed to govern it, interviews provide a drastically different picture. In practice, in many cases observed, the criminal reconciliation process was not characterized by the principle of voluntariness supposed to be one of its main advantages; rather, the officials in charge dominated the process. In addition, the entire process focused largely on compensation, so it was potentially unfair to economically weak suspects and defendants. It was also found in some cases that the conflict between the parties still existed or had worsened at the end of the criminal reconciliation programme. Evidence of the fact that criminal reconciliation has been used in serious cases well beyond the intended scope of 'criminal reconciliation' as a formal mechanism raised further concerns about power abuses.

On the basis of these findings, it is argued that criminal reconciliation throws light on certain fundamental problems with the wider criminal justice system. First, officials in the criminal justice system routinely circumvented certain legal rules protecting the parties' rights and to some extent replaced these rules with 'hidden rules' (*qian guize*), whose content is largely shaped by politically driven performance assessment criteria, as well as in some cases by intervention from other entities such as the Political-Legal Committee. Second, the criminal proceedings in China reflect an authoritarian, paternalistic and educational (thought-reform-based) approach to criminal justice; the parties' rights are regarded as secondary to this political end. Third, the State does not take sufficient responsibility to protect the victim's right to get compensation in the civil litigation collateral to criminal proceedings.

In conclusion, this book argues that resolving criminal cases through reconciliation and mediation may aggravate the problems already affecting the ordinary criminal justice process, because it is a mechanism designed to weaken procedural rights protections and eliminate the adversarial character of the criminal justice process. Thus, the promotion of criminal reconciliation may be one of the several signs that, since the early 2000s, China is deviating from the path of rule of law development that was once the political leadership's clearly stated goal.

Acknowledgements

This book is essentially based on my PhD dissertation that I undertook at the faculty of law, the Chinese University of Hong Kong between 2007 and 2012. First and foremost, I wish to thank my mentor Eva Pils. Dr Pils assumed the supervision of my dissertation at the juncture when I was considering quitting, and has provided me with comprehensive academic training and illuminating guidance ever since. She has carefully read every chapter as well as every revised chapter of the dissertation and provided insightful comments, inspiring suggestions and detailed edits every single time. She was always available to discuss any issue I would like to raise or problem I came across, and advised wisely, which has been the most important support to me. It was also her constant encouragement that drove me to seek publication opportunities for my dissertation. Without her support and help, neither the dissertation nor the book would ever be possible.

I owe special gratitude to all the people who kindly agreed to talk to me for my dissertation. They were my interviewees, including the victims and suspects of criminal reconciliation cases as well as their parents and teachers, the lawyers, judges and prosecutors. I know that, at least for some of them, recalling or relating the experiences and feelings was not easy. Heartfelt thanks for their trust in me and their affable openness. Withdrawing their names in this book is mainly for the sake of avoiding potential troubles to them. I also wish to in particular thank Di Xiaohua, Ge Lin, Guo Zhiyuan, Joshua Rosenzweig, John Braithwaite and Kathleen Daly for their thoughtful and enlightening conversations with me on criminal reconciliation and restorative justice.

In addition, I would like to thank Mike McConville for patiently reading, commenting and editing most of the chapters, Chui Wing Hong for helping me obtain access to the first two empirical studies, Yu Xingzhong for providing the approach for the third empirical study and Hennessy Hayes for helping me get the chance of observing restorative justice meetings in Brisbane, Australia. I am equally grateful to Zhang Yaling and Ye Zhusheng. The regular discussion of my research with them was far beyond gaining critiques and fresh ideas for the research itself – it was one of the most convivial moments in the mostly tough and lonely days of writing a PhD dissertation.

I am very thankful to four anonymous reviewers of the book proposal for their valuable comments and suggestions. Parts of the empirical findings in this book were accepted for publishing in the *Journal of Comparative Law* – I am very thankful to Michael Palmer and Fu Hualing for their great comments and suggestions for the draft article. Another part was published in the joint chapter 'The 2012 PRC Criminal Procedure Law' of the book *Comparative Perspectives on Criminal Justice in China*. I wish to thank the editors Mike McConville and Eva Pils for their great comments and suggestions as well.

Last but not least, I am indebted to the Centre for Rights and Justice of the Chinese University of Hong Kong. I wish to thank the Centre for generously offering me the opportunities of giving talks on various parts of my PhD dissertation, where I obtained thoughtful suggestions from the audience, mostly professors and colleagues of the Centre. I also thank the Centre for offering me a visiting scholar position after I was awarded the PhD – during this period, I completed revising my dissertation for the publication of this book.

All errors are of course mine alone.

1. The criminal reconciliation (*xingshi hejie*) system in China: background, pilot projects and debates*

In August 2011, the People's Republic of China (China) launched the second major revision of its Criminal Procedure Law (CPL) after its first major revision in 1996. In the revision draft, which was later passed in the fifth meeting of the 11th National People's Congress in March 2012, Articles 277 to 279 provide a statutory basis for a new 'special procedure,' which allows the alleged victims and suspects/defendants of certain crimes to 'reconcile' (*hejie*) and thereby close criminal cases. This revised CPL has been in effect since 1 January 2013.

Article 277 stipulates the 'requirements' and 'scope' of cases eligible for this process. It *may* (but does not have to) be initiated in the case of a suspected crime under Chapters 4 and 5 of the Criminal Law[1] if the crime has 'arisen' from what is characterized as 'disputes among the people' (*minjian jiufen*) which could lead to sentences of no more than three years' imprisonment, and in the case of a negligent 'crime' with a potential sentence of no more than seven years' imprisonment.[2] In addition, in these cases, the suspect/defendant should have 'regretted sincerely' and 'obtained the victim's forgiveness through compensation, apology, and other methods'; the law also requires that mediation must be initiated on the basis of *the victim*'s (not both parties') voluntariness.[3]

* Some sections of this chapter and Chapters 4 to 5 were accepted for publishing in a forthcoming issue of the *Journal of Comparative Law* as an article entitled 'Buying "Leniency," Selling "Justice"? A Critical Discussion of "Criminal Reconciliation" (*xingshi hejie*) under China's Revised Criminal Procedural Law.'

1 Chapter 4 of the PRC Criminal Law is about 'crimes infringing upon citizens' rights of the person and democratic rights'; Chapter 5 is about 'crimes of property violation.'

2 There is an exception for 'malfeasance crimes'; and suspects/defendants who committed an intentional crime within five years prior to the case at hand are excluded from this process.

3 Ibid.

Article 278 articulates the public authorities' role in this process: the Public Security Bureau, the People's Procuratorate or the People's Court should hear the parties' and other relevant people's opinions, review the reconciliation with regard to its voluntary nature and compliance with the law, and produce reconciliation agreements.[4]

Article 279 is about the outcomes of this process. It provides that the police may make suggestions for a lenient disposition to the People's Procuratorate; the prosecutor may also make such suggestions to the People's Court or decide not to prosecute; and the judge may give a lenient sentence to the defendant according to the law following a successful criminal reconciliation process.[5]

Overall, this revision means that reconciliation, which under the 1996 CPL could only be used in 'private prosecution (*zisu*) cases'[6] and 'civil litigation collateral to criminal proceedings (*xingshi fudai minshi susong*),'[7] is now legally allowed in certain public prosecution cases.

Having a legal basis only since then, such a procedure, generally called 'criminal reconciliation' (*xingshi hejie*) and referred to as a 'procedure for voluntary reconciliation among the parties in public prosecution cases,' had been widely used by the Public Security Bureau, the People's Procuratorate and the People's Court nearly nationwide in China as 'pilot projects' from the beginning of the 2000s.

---

4 Article 278 CPL.

5 Article 279 CPL.

6 'Private prosecution (*zisu*) cases,' according to Article 170 of the 1996 CPL and Article 204 of the 2012 CPL, refers to cases 'to be handled only upon complaint,' cases 'for which the victims have evidence to prove that those are minor criminal cases' and 'cases for which the victims have evidence to prove that the defendants should be investigated for criminal responsibility according to law because their acts have infringed upon the victims' personal or property rights, whereas, the public security organs or the People's Procuratorates do not investigate the criminal responsibility of the accused.' According to Article 172 of the 1996 CPL and Article 206 of the 2012 CPL, 'the People's Court may conduct mediation in a case of private prosecution.' See the English translation of the 1996 CPL at http://www.cecc.gov/pages/newLaws/criminalProcedureENG.php (last accessed on 20 March 2011).

7 According to Article 77 of the 1996 CPL and Article 99 of the 2012 CPL, 'if a victim has suffered material losses as a result of the defendant's criminal act, he/she shall have the right to file an incidental civil action during the course of the criminal proceeding.' Article 96 of the Judicial Interpretation on CPL issued by the Supreme People's Court [最高人民法院关于执行《中华人民共和国刑事诉讼法》若干问题的解释] in 1998 further provides that 'the People's Court can conduct mediation in the civil litigation collateral to criminal proceedings, except for those cases lodged by the People's Procuratorate.'

The first section of this chapter provides a background of the introduction of criminal reconciliation in China, which is mainly a result of the authorities' changing perspectives on legal reform as well as on the criminal justice system in the early 2000s. Dating back to the late 1970s, after the revolutionary Mao era and the chaotic Cultural Revolution ended, China's legal reforms could largely be understood as taking the direction aimed at entrenching 'the rule of law' conceived in liberal terms. By contrast, since the early 2000s, the Chinese authorities began to emphasize concepts such as 'people's judiciary,' 'harmonious judiciary' and 'big mediation (*da tiaojie*),' dozens of which were actually adopted in the Mao era, under the 'ultimate goal' of 'establishing a harmonious society.' Designed as a process mainly based on the parties' (namely, the victim and the suspect/defendant) voluntary reconciliation, criminal reconciliation has been officially valued as overcoming the shortcomings of the normal criminal procedure, which is set as an adversarial system in the 1996 CPL, thereby bringing about the effects of 'satisfying the parties,' 'bringing "closure" (*an jie shi liao*) to criminal cases' and 'preventing petitioning related to judicial cases (*she fa shangfang*),' a phenomenon denounced by the authorities as a manifestation of 'disharmony' and 'instability.'[8] And, as stated by the Chinese authorities, such an explosion of petitioning is the judicial system's failure in fulfilling its political tasks, which significantly include maintaining social stability and harmony.[9]

---

8 'Petitioning' (*shangfang* or *xinfang*) is a system established in the 1950s in China by which a citizen, legal person or any other organization reports facts, submits suggestions or files complaints to the Xinfang (literally: 'Letters' and 'Visits') offices, which are established at all levels of administration and in all branches of the Party and State. 'Petitioning related to judicial cases' (*she fa shangfang* or *she su shangfang*) in a broad sense refers to the petitioning that concerns cases handled by the People's Courts, the People's Procuratorates and the Public Security Bureaus. In a narrow sense, it only refers to petitioning concerning cases handled by the People's Courts (in some instances, what petitioners complain about is inaction on the part of these authorities, i.e. they complain that a case has not been handled properly). See: Carl F. Minzner 'Xinfang: An Alternative to Formal Chinese Legal Institutions' (2006) Vol. 42 *Stanford Journal of International Law*; Li Yinfang [李银芳] Li Jinfu [李金富] 'Reasons and Strategies of Petitioning Related to Judicial Cases [涉法上访案件的成因及对策]' at http://www.dffy.com/fayanguancha/sh/200409/20040916085512.htm (last accessed on 8 February 2012).

9 Wu Aiying [吴爱英] 'Sparing No Effort to Make Judicial Organs Maintain Social Stability [全力做好司法行政机关维护社会稳定工作]' at

This change of perspectives has triggered much debate and criticism in academia domestically and abroad – in general, one group of scholars appreciates this shift as the authorities' careful adjustment of the judicial system towards 'Chinese characteristics and Chinese people's real needs.' According to them, mediation, or reconciliation, embeds China's traditional culture, which is still prevailing today, whereas liberal reforms of the judiciary and litigation, which are 'transplanted from western jurisdictions,' are not feasible in China. To them, the legal reform in the direction of the rule of law is the root of the upsurge of petitioning to government since the early 2000s. Meanwhile, some liberal-minded scholars, questioning the assertion of the prevalence and preference of mediation in China today, criticize this shift as an obvious retrogression of the Chinese judiciary, in particular in terms of judicial independence and judicial professionalism. Through discussing the resemblance of the current judicial reform with the judiciary in the Mao era, they argue that this shift has demonstrated the ruling Party (i.e. the Communist Party of China)'s intensifying and authoritarian control of the judiciary when it faces increasing crises and threats to its rule from society.

A comprehensive examination of criminal reconciliation, a major programme introduced against such a background, can shed some light on the current legal reform as well as the debates over it. The second section of this chapter provides a historical review of the Chinese mediation systems that have been in place since the Mao era, connecting mediation to the official design as well as practices of criminal reconciliation. The critical review shows that the mediation system in China is always connected closely with the Party's policies and is a tool of the Party to serve its political goals, such as *suppressing* disputes, instead of empowering the parties in *resolving* disputes. Such a programme can seriously infringe upon the parties' rights and voluntariness. The problems with the Chinese mediation systems raise doubts and concerns over criminal reconciliation regarding its real influences and ends.

The final section of this chapter critically overviews the existing discussions over criminal reconciliation practices. A literature review shows that the positive appraisals mainly focus on its effectiveness of smoothing compensation, satisfying the parties, educating the perpetrators, and thereby bringing 'closure' to disputes. And the criticisms surround the problems of unfairness (to economically weak suspects/defendants), coercion by public power, and violations of the current legal

---

http://www.gov.cn/gzdt/2012-10/23/content_2249495.htm (last accessed on 9 July 2015).

regulations governing this programme. Despite the plausibility of critical arguments, there are essential deficiencies with the existing literature discussing criminal reconciliation. For one thing, most of the appraisals are based on 'second-hand information,' some of which are even directly derived from official websites; for another, since the authors producing most of the empirical studies are usually officials implementing this programme themselves or scholars cooperating with these officials, the credibility of the empirical assessment is suspect. In this sense, information on the actual functioning of criminal reconciliation is of great significance in examining whether or not, or to what extent, the interaction between public power and individuals in this process resembles that in mediation since the Mao era, and importantly, whether this programme is helpful to promote a 'harmonious society' or doing harm to rights and justice. The author's empirical study discussed in the ensuing chapters responds to these concerns critically.

1.1 LEGAL REFORMS IN CHINA: FROM BUILDING THE RULE OF LAW SYSTEM TO ESTABLISHING A HARMONIOUS SOCIETY

An account of the introduction of 'criminal reconciliation' in China must first address the concept of 'harmonious society' (*hexie shehui*), a political goal embedded in the ideology of this process.

This political goal was formulated when the Party found that there had been increasing 'social unrest' ('unrest' in the Party-state's definition) in China since the early 21st century. The 'Central Commission of Comprehensive Governing' (*zhongyangzonghe zhili bangongshi*) stated that 'currently, China is at the very point of social and economic transition, so contradictions among the people (*renmin neibu maodun*)[10] are sharp,

[10] 'Contradictions among the people (*renmin neibu maodun*)' was a concept initially advanced by Mao Zedong in 'On the Correct Handling of Contradictions among the People' in 1957. In this article, conflicts in society were categorized into two different types – 'contradictions among the people (*renmin neibu maodun*)' and 'contradictions between the people and the enemies (*di wo maodun*),' which, according to Michael Palmer, also resembled the distinction made by Lenin as 'antagonistic contradictions' (*duikangxing maodun*) and 'non-antagonistic contradictions' (*fei duikangxing maodun*). Such a distinction was mainly for mobilizing people in class struggle. Contradictions among the people are 'the everyday disputes between people that arise in the course of work,

criminal offences are frequent, and fights against enemies[11] are complicated.'[12] Consequently, in 2004, the Party formally announced a policy of 'establishing a socialist harmonious society' at the fourth plenary session of the 16th Central Committee of the Chinese Communist Party (CCP). According to the 'Decision' published after this meeting, there were six main requirements or features of 'socialist harmonious society.' They were 'democracy and rule of law' (*minzhu fazhi*), 'fairness and justice' (*gongping zhengyi*), 'integrity and friendship' (*chengxin you'ai*), 'stability and order' (*anding youxu*), 'great dynamism' (*chongman huoli*) and 'men living in harmony with nature' (*ren yu ziran hexie xiangchu*).[13] Apparently, the first two requirements ('democracy and the rule of law' and 'fairness and justice') were directly targeting the legal system.

Announcing the establishment of a 'socialist harmonious society,' the Party seemed to follow its political discourse in the 1990s of establishing 'socialist rule of law' – for instance, as noted by Leïla Choukroune and Antoine Garapon, the Party stressed that 'a harmonious society is a society governed by law'; 'a harmonious society depends on the rule of law'; 'a harmonious society needs a stronger legal system that wields

---

production, and domestic life.' 'Contradictions among the people' are 'non-antagonistic' so they are best handled through non-coercive ways such as mediation. See: Michael Palmer 'The Revival of Mediation in the People's Republic of China: (1) Extra-judicial Mediation' in W.E. Butler (ed) *Yearbook on Socialist Legal Systems* New York, Transnational Publishers 1987, 227–8.

[11] According to Mao Zedong's expression in 'On the Correct Handling of Contradictions among the People' in 1957, the 'contradictions between the enemy and the people are antagonistic contradictions.' See: the English translation of this work at http://www.peopleofcolororganize.com/wp-content/uploads/pdf/poco/contradictions.pdf (last accessed on 9 July 2015). Enemies are mainly 'former exploiting classes and counterrevolutionaries' and conflicts between the enemy and the people should be handled through coercive methods, including 'punishment according to law.' See: Stanley Lubman 'Mao and Mediation: Politics and Dispute Resolution in Communist China' (1967) Vol. 55 No 5 *California Law Review* 1302; Fu Hualing 'Access to Justice in China: Potentials, Limits, and Alternatives' (draft) at http://papers.ssrn.com/sol3/papers.cfm?abstract_id=1474073 (last accessed on 9 July 2015).

[12] The Central Commission of Comprehensive Governing [中央社会治安综合治理委员会办公室] (ed) *Strategies for the Long-term Peace and Stability* [*长治久安之策*] Beijing, Chang'an Press [中国长安出版社] 2009, 295.

[13] See relevant reports on Xinhua Net at http://news.xinhuanet.com/politics/2006-08/09/content_4939383.htm (last accessed on 4 January 2011).

greater authority.'[14] However, if looking further into judicial documentation and practices under this political blueprint of a 'harmonious society,' a patent and essential shift can be spotted – reforms in the Chinese judiciary under the policy of 'promoting a socialist harmonious society,' ranging from guidelines to practices, have shown that mediation and reconciliation have been recognized by the authorities as the most effective way to address perceived 'factors of instability' in the judicial process, such as petitioning, appeals and protests by dissatisfied parties to a legal dispute.

As widely acknowledged, Mao Zedong's death and the end of the chaotically lawless ten-year Cultural Revolution in 1976 ushered in a new era of limited liberalization in China.[15] The leadership of Deng Xiaoping, announcing that 'the principal contradiction in China today is no longer class struggle but between the growing material and cultural needs of the people and the backwardness of social production,' started to construct a steady and formal legal system in an attempt to create a 'stable and orderly' domestic environment as well as to earn international cooperation for China's economic developments.[16] The following nearly three decades have witnessed long strides by the legal system – China has built a formal legal framework composed of abundant legislation, including those conceiving individual rights in liberal terms and constraints of state behaviours.[17] The Party-state also devoted enormous resources to legal education and professional training.[18] Legal professionalism has since gained substantial developments – the number of judges, prosecutors, lawyers and law schools have amounted evidently; professionals with formal legal training have gradually filled in the legal system and replaced revolutionary cadres.[19] So does legal formalism – adjudication according to law, rather than mediation, has been emphasized by

---

[14] Leïla Choukroune, Antoine Garapon 'The Norms of Chinese Harmony' (2007) 3 *China Perspectives* 37.

[15] Leng Shao-chuan, Chiu Hungdah, *Criminal Justice in Post-Mao China: Analysis and Documents* Albany, State University of New York Press 1985, 35.

[16] Randall Peerenboom, *China's Long March Toward Rule of Law* Cambridge, Cambridge University Press 2002, 55; supra note 15, 35–6.

[17] Supra note 15.

[18] Jerome A. Cohen 'China's Legal Reform at the Crossroads' at http://www.cfr.org/china/chinas-legal-reform-crossroads/p10063 (last accessed on 17 May 2015).

[19] Fu Hualing, Richard Gullen 'From Mediatory to Adjudicatory Justice: The Limits of Civil Justice Reform in China' in Margaret Y.K. Woo and Mary E. Gallagher (eds) *Chinese Justice: Civil Dispute Revolution in China* Cambridge, Cambridge University Press 2011, 30.

the authorities as the priority of the judicial system in addressing disputes.[20] Judicial reforms launched in the late 1990s embodied clearer intentions of advancing procedural fairness and justice.[21] Even in the conduct of mediation, legitimacy has been officially stressed, which is, as set in laws, tested based on voluntariness and lawfulness.[22] A domestic leading law professor Guo Daohui summarized that in the past three decades there were three prominent landmarks in China's path towards the rule of law:[23]

> The first one is the Party's third plenary session of the eleventh central committee held in 1978, which launched the policy and principle that 'there must be laws to go by (*you fa ke yi*), the laws must be observed and strictly enforced (*you fa bi yi, zhifa bi yan*), and law-breakers must be held accountable (*weifa bi jiu*)' – it is the sign of terminating the lawlessness in the Cultural Revolution and starting to build a 'rule by law' system. The second landmark is the promulgation of 'ruling the country according to law (*yi fa zhiguo*) and building a socialist rule by law country' in 1997 – since then, rule by law became the Party's political basic line, and debates over 'rule by law' and 'rule of law' had been expanding and flourishing. The third breakthrough happened in 1999, when for the first time the concept of 'rule of law' was entrenched in the Constitution. The Party stated that 'the premise of rule of law is ruling in accordance with the Constitution, and the premise of governing in accordance with law is governing in accordance with the Constitution.'

Yet in 2004, the year when 'harmonious society' was underscored by the Party as its central policy, mediation was expressly re-emphasized in the Chinese judicial system. In that year, the Supreme People's Court (SPC) promulgated 'Provisions on Several Issues Concerning the Civil Mediation Work of the People's Court.' In explaining the background and function of these 'Provisions,' Huang Songyou, the then vice-president of the SPC, said:[24]

---

20 Ibid.

21 Supra note 19, 39.

22 Supra note 19, 38.

23 Jiang Ping [江平] Guo Daohui [郭道晖] Li Buyun [李步云] 'Review: Further Discussions on Rule of Law and Rule of Man [温故：再谈法治与人治大讨论]' at http://www.aisixiang.com/data/80806.html (last accessed on 3 November 2011).

24 'Huang Songyou Answered Journalists Questions Regarding "Provisions of the Supreme People's Court about Several Issues Concerning the Civil Mediation Work of the People's Court" [黄松有就《关于人民法院民事调解

> Mediation (in litigation) is a significant means of the People's Court to enforce judicial authority and has its unique advantages in resolving disputes. It was called 'oriental experience' by the international jurisdiction. However, in recent years, some courts have over-emphasized 'announcing verdicts in court hearings,' and failed with paying sufficient attention to mediation. They did not mediate when they should or they can [mediate], which has resulted in the reduction of mediation rate and rising of appealing rate. The pressure of petition has been augmenting as well.

> Mediation (in litigation) has four main advantages: first, it makes litigation more 'humanized' (*renxing hua*). Since it resolves disputes through the parties' voluntary negotiation, rather than the judge's adjudication, the parties can understand and accept it more easily. Second, mediation highlights friendly negotiation and compromise and facilitates the parties' mutual understanding and cooperation, which can largely weaken the antagonism between the two parties and thereby promotes social harmony and stability. Third, mediation is more flexible and efficient, so it can not only alleviate the parties' burden but also save judicial resources. The fourth and also the most important advantage is that, resolving a case through mediation meets the substantial requirement of judicial fairness. Only the result opted by the parties themselves can mostly meet their needs and interests, which is the substantial justice the parties pursue. So it can facilitate the parties' fulfilment [of the agreement reached in mediation] on their initiatives.

Afterwards, in 2005, by announcing the principle of 'fusing trials and mediation, bringing "closure" (*tiao pan jiehe, an jie shi liao*),' the SPC stressed that both mediation and adjudication were means of the courts to address disputes, and should serve a common end of reducing social contradiction and promoting social harmony to the furthest extent.[25] Yet we can observe that until then, although mediation gained the central judicial authorities' promotion, it was not prioritized over adjudication. Some commented that at that time the SPC had not 'given up on the direction of judicial reforms towards formal adjudication and procedural justice.'[26] Nevertheless, in February 2009, the SPC explicitly changed

---

工作若干问题的规定》答记者问]' at http://www.china.com.cn/chinese/PI-c/661957.htm (last accessed on 12 May 2015).

[25] In Chinese, '能调则调，当判则判，调判结合，案结事了.' See: Xinhua News Agency 'Mediate When It Can, Adjudicate When It Should, Fuse Trials and Mediation, Bring Closure [新华社] '能调则调，当判则判，调判结合，案结事了]' at http://www.gov.cn/2007lh/content_549985.htm (last accessed on 3 November 2011)

[26] Wu Yingzi [吴英姿] '"Mediation First": Reform Pattern and Legal Interpretation ["调解优先": 改革范式与法律解读]' at http://article.chinalawinfo.com/ArticleHtml/Article_78723.shtml (last accessed on 20 June 2015).

this principle to 'prioritizing mediation, fusing trials and mediation (*tiaojie youxian, tiao pan jiehe*),' and started to promote mediation at all the stages of processing a case as well as in all kinds of cases including criminal and administrative litigation.[27] The judicial system in which mediation plays a dominant role aimed at addressing contradictions is officially called 'harmonious judiciary' (*hexie sifa*).[28]

Actually, in the criminal justice system, mediation had been promoted several years earlier. In 2006, in order to provide, as it were, a more detailed 'guide' to the reform of the legal system towards establishing a 'harmonious society,' the Party announced the policy of 'combining severity with leniency (*kuan yan xiangji*) in dealing with criminal cases' at the sixth plenary session of the 16th National CCP Congress. This policy is understood as the Party's reflection over its 'striking hard' (*yanda*)[29] policy implemented since the early 1980s when it realized that the tendency of (pure) harsh punishment could produce social instability and disharmony.[30] Requiring 'striking hard' against serious crime but leniency towards 'first offence, causal offence, juvenile crimes and

27 Ibid.

28 See more information on this concept of 'harmonious judiciary' at Xinhua Net [新华网] 'The Supreme People's Court Raised Idea of "Harmonious Judiciary" for the First Time [最高法院首次提出"司法和谐"理念]' at http://news.163.com/07/0107/11/347SD32N000122EH.html (last accessed on 9 March 2012).

29 The 'strike hard' campaign, or *yanda*, was originally launched in 1981 as a policy to deal with emerging social order crimes, particularly crimes committed by juveniles and 'hooligans' (*liumang*). In 1983, it developed into an anti-crime campaign that lasted for three years, which resulted in a 'brutalizing effect' as described by Børge Bakken. The 'strike hard' campaign was defined as a political struggle in which the whole society must participate; the death penalty and imprisonment were rampantly used. Afterwards, there were two other 'strike hard' campaigns in 1996 and 2001. See: Børge Bakken, *The Exemplary Society: Human Improvement, Social Control and the Dangers of Modernity in China* New York, Oxford University Press 2000, 394; Susan Trevaskes, *Courts and Criminal Justice in Contemporary China* U.K., Lexington Books 2007, 1 and 83–7. In June 2010, the fourth 'strike hard' was launched nationwide resulting from 'the mass's drop of sense of security.' See: *Southern Weekend* [*南方周末*] 'The Fourth Strike Hard: Can It Be Like the Previous Ones? [第四次严打：能像过去一样打吗?]' at http://nf.nfdaily.cn/epaper/nfzm/content/20100701/ArticelB10005FM.htm (last accessed on 29 November 2010).

30 Susan Trevaskes 'The Shifting Sands of Punishment in China in the Era of "Harmonious Society"' (2010) Vol. 32 No. 3 *Law & Policy* 333; Benjamin L. Liebman 'Leniency in Chinese Criminal Law? Everyday Justice in Henan' (2014) *Columbia Public Law Research Paper* 19.

crimes where the suspects/defendants' subjective culpability was not serious,' 'combining severity with leniency' was enshrined by the Party as 'an underlying criminal policy' in an attempt to sustain social stability and establish a 'socialist harmonious society.'[31]

The People's Procuratorates and People's Courts then devoted their efforts to concretize this policy and spell out what it meant for their work. On the 'severity' side, for instance, after three 'strike hard' campaigns in 1983, 1996 and 2001, China launched the fourth one in 2010;[32] on the 'leniency' side, one prominent sign is that reconciliation and mediation were especially highlighted by the Supreme People's Procuratorate (SPP) and the SPC in resolving cases involving 'disputes among the people' (*minjian jiufen*).

In 2006, the SPP issued the 'Opinions of the Supreme People's Procuratorate on Implementing the Criminal Policy of Combining Severity with Leniency in Procuratorial Work'[33] (hereafter the '2006 SPP Opinions'). This document states that 'the criminal policy of "combining severity with leniency" is an important policy of the Party and the State, and is an essential guide of the People's Procuratorate to implement the

---

[31] See the interpretation of the 'Decision' by Xinhua Net [新华网] 'Interpret Decisions of the Sixth Plenary Session: Implement Criminal Justice Policy of Combining Severity with Leniency [解读六中全会决定：实施宽严相济的刑事司法政策]' at http://news.xinhuanet.com/legal/2006-12/09/content_5459413.htm (last accessed on 7 April 2011).

[32] See: *Southern Weekend* [*南方周末*] 'The Fourth "Strike Hard" Campaign: The More We Gain, the More Horrible It Is [第四次全国"严打"成果越大越可怕]' at http://news.qq.com/a/20100702/000470.htm (last accessed on 21 March 2012); in June 2010, the fourth 'strike hard' was launched nationwide resulting from 'the mass's drop of sense of security.' See: *Southern Weekend* [南方周末], supra note 29.

[33] Article 20 of the 'Opinions of the Supreme People's Procuratorate on Implementing the Criminal Policy of Combining Severity with Leniency in Procuratorial Work' [最高人民检察院关于在检察工作中贯彻宽严相济刑事司法政策的若干意见] states that 'we shall stress conflict resolution in dealing with criminal cases. The Procuratorate shall strengthen resolution of the conflict and mediation of the dispute related to the crime, shall take the outcome of dispute resolution and the implementation of any agreement [related to the dispute] as a significant factor in considering a lenient disposition. In a case where there is a direct victim, the People's Procuratorate may request the suspect to apologize to the victim and compensate the victim if it gives a lenient disposition or decides not to prosecute. The People's Procuratorate shall also well explain the decision to the victim to avoid any further petitioning to the judicial authorities [on the part of the victim in this case].'

laws of the State.'[34] Therefore, 'the Procuratorates shall strengthen resolution of the conflict and mediation of the dispute related to the crime, shall take the outcome of dispute resolution and the implementation of any agreement [related to the dispute] as a significant factor in considering a lenient disposition.'[35] 'The People's Procuratorates shall adopt the promotion of social harmony as a major criterion in the examination of procuratorial work.'[36]

Article 12 of the '2006 SPP Opinions' further sets out the 'scope' of cases suitable for 'reconciliation' and 'lenient dispositions.' According to this Article, the People's Procuratorates 'shall be lenient in cases of crime triggered by conflicts among the people (*minjian jiufen*).'[37] 'In the case of a minor crime arising from disputes among relatives, neighbours or schoolmates, we [the People's Procuratorates] shall correctly handle case based on the spirit of "better making friends than enemies" and from the angle of conflict resolution.'[38] 'In the case of a minor crime in which the suspect has admitted guilt, repented, apologized, actively compensated the loss and obtained the victim's forgiveness or where the two parties have reached and implemented a reconciliation agreement, and where the harm done to society is not serious, we shall make the decision not to arrest or prosecute in accordance with the law.'[39] 'If prosecution is necessary, we may suggest a lenient sentence to the People's Court.'[40]

Later in 2010, the SPC also issued its 'Opinions on Implementing the Criminal Policy of Combining Severity with Leniency' (hereafter the '2010 SPC Opinions'). Article 40 of the '2010 SPC Opinions' says that 'in the case of a minor crime such as minor injury crime arising from disputes among the people (*minjian jiufen*), if the parties reach reconciliation after public prosecution has been initiated and the case been transferred to the Court, the Court shall (*yingdang*) approve [the reconciliation agreement] and keep it on record.'[41] 'The People's Court may

---

[34] Article 2 of the 'Opinions of the Supreme People's Procuratorate on Implementing the Criminal Policy of Combining Severity with Leniency in Procuratorial Work' [最高人民检察院关于在检察工作中贯彻宽严相济刑事司法政策的若干意见].

[35] Ibid, Article 20.

[36] Ibid, Article 1.

[37] Ibid, Article 12.

[38] Ibid.

[39] Ibid.

[40] Ibid.

[41] Article 40 of the 'Opinions of the Supreme People's Court on Implementing the Criminal Policy of Combining Severity with Leniency in Procuratorial Work.'

(*keyi*) also try to conduct work to facilitate reconciliation in such cases as long as doing so would not violate any legal provisions.'[42] Article 23 provides that 'if the defendant compensates the victim promptly, admits guilt and shows repentance after committing the crime, this may (*keyi*) be taken into consideration according to law as circumstances affecting the discretionary sentencing considerations (*zhuoding liangxing qingjie*).'[43] 'In a crime arising from disputes among the people (*minjian jiufen*) such as marriage or family disputes, if the victim and his family have forgiven the defendant, this shall (*yingdang*) be considered as circumstance under which discretional sentencing is allowed.'[44] Additionally, 'the People's Court shall mediate as much as possible to eliminate disputes and facilitate both parties' reconciliation in private prosecution cases' and in 'civil litigation collateral to criminal proceeding.'[45]

According to the '2006 SPP Opinions,' the emphasis on reconciliation serves three ends. It aims to resolve conflicts between suspects and victims, to 'prevent new "petitioning related to judicial cases" (*she fa shangfang* or *she su shangfang*),' and thereby to be helpful for establishing a 'harmonious society.'[46] The '2010 SPC Opinions' also characterize as desired outcomes of reconciliation or mediation that it should bring a sense of 'closure' (*an jie shi liao*) and promote a harmonious society.[47]

New criminal justice practices, which, in brief, address criminal cases through reconciliation or mediation between the parties, developed in the context of these 'Opinions'; these practices were given a name of 'criminal reconciliation' (*xingshi hejie*)[48] by domestic Chinese scholars and practitioners.

Such an evident shift of judicial reforms has triggered much debate. Some characterize these judicial reforms as the Chinese judicial system's adjustment in accordance with 'Chinese characteristics.'[49] To people holding this opinion, mediation and reconciliation in the form now increasingly practised in China are based on the people's real needs and

---

42 Ibid.

43 Ibid, Article 23.

44 Ibid.

45 Ibid, Articles 40 and 41.

46 Ibid, Article 20.

47 Ibid, Article 41.

48 He Yongjun [何永军] 'On Legitimacy and Legalization of Criminal Reconciliation [论刑事和解的合法性与合法化]' (2009) 3 *Journal of Kunming University of Science and Technology (Social Science)* [*昆明理工大学学报（社会科学版）*] 83.

49 Xia Min [夏敏] 'Closure: A Not Easy Task in Trial [案结事了：一个不轻松的审判课题]' (2007) 2 *China Trial* [*中国审判*] 13.

emotions, which are lacking in the formal legal system, so that they can resolve conflicts and bring about 'harmony.' For instance, Su Li has argued that the 'liberal reforms of the judiciary are not feasible in China – a country where more than half of the population live in rural places with stable relationships and a very strong tradition of mediation.'[50] According to Su Li, adjudication cannot resolve disputes, which might further cause difficulties with enforcement of the verdicts, in turn leading to the parties' petitioning.[51] In this context, mediation is mainly 'the Party's response to the Chinese people's needs and China's reality.'[52] Similarly, Fan Yu argues that 'litigation or law is transplanted from western jurisdictions, so they are somewhat conflicting with China's conditions and traditional culture.'[53] For instance, as maintained by Fan Yu, the value of 'procedural justice' is contradictory to the value of the Chinese traditional justice, which prefers efficiency and convenience, and is also contradictory to the Chinese people's pursuit of 'substantial justice.'[54] In addition, according to Fan, the problems of the judicial system, such as the difficulty with enforcement, judicial unfairness and corruption, which have led to 'disharmony' in society, are to a certain extent caused by the establishment of the 'modern' judicial system implemented in the past three decades; the increasing social unrest has actually shown the public's dissatisfaction with the current judicial system.[55] In the same vein, Xia Min especially praises mediation's positive effects to society (*shehui xiaoguo*) – as argued by Xia, 'in some cases, a modest mediation can have better social effects than a good verdict.'[56]

In contrast, some other scholars maintain that the judicial reforms under the policy of 'promoting a harmonious society' embody evident resemblances to the revolutionary judicial style adopted in the Mao era, because, as noted by these scholars, in the course of promoting mediation and reconciliation in dispute resolution, rather than referring to China's

---

[50] Su Li [苏力] 'Deliberative Justice and the Big Mediation System [关于能动司法与大调解]' at http://article.chinalawinfo.com/Article_Detail.asp?ArticleId=53760 (last accessed on 9 March 2012).

[51] Ibid.

[52] Ibid.

[53] Fan Yu [范愉] *The Theory and Practice of Dispute Resolution* [*纠纷解决的理论与实践*] Beijing, Tsinghua University Press [清华大学出版社] 2007, 295.

[54] Ibid, 297.

[55] Ibid, 294–5.

[56] Supra note 49.

traditional or cultural elements in mediation, the authorities re-embrace the concepts prevailing in the Mao era, mainly including 'the Ma Xiwu adjudication method,' calling for judicial activism in mediating disputes and 'people's judiciary' (*renmin sifa*), purportedly aimed at 'meeting the people's needs and emotions.'[57] Nevertheless, as the key ramifications of Mao's leading policy of 'mass line,' the essential feature of 'the Ma Xiwu adjudication method' is 'disregard of law and the rule of law,'[58] and the 'people's judiciary' is, in fact, the Party's intense and comprehensive control over the judiciary.[59] The underlying features of the mediation system implemented in the Mao era and how it departs from the rule of law are elaborated in detail in the next section, and in this sense, scholars holding these points have assessed the current judicial reforms towards 'a harmonious society' as an obvious retrogression of the Chinese judiciary, especially in the aspects of judicial independence and judicial professionalism, and they signal the Party's more direct and tight control over the judiciary. For example, as argued by Carl Minzner, the judicial reform 'return the judiciary to its Party-led, populist roots,' and is 'China's turn against law.'[60] Similarly, Jerome Cohen comments on the judicial reform as the Party's 'renewal of the simple "mass line,"' which had 'discouraged most professional progress' the Chinese legal system made towards 'the rule of law' since the late 1970s.[61] Leïla Choukroune and Antoine Garapon point to the trick of the authorities' claim of 'the people' as the orientation of the current judicial reforms – according to them, the idea of 'One People' is virtually the 'softer version of something common to totalitarian systems,' because it is impossible to say that there exists something like 'One People.'[62]

---

57 Benjamin L. Liebman 'Legal Reform: China's Law-Stability Paradox' (2014) Vol. 143 No. 2 *Daedalus Spring* 99.

58 Li Site [李斯特] 'The Context of the People's Judiciary and the Mass Line [人民司法群众路线的谱系]' in Su Li [苏力] (ed) *Law and Social Science* [*法律和社会科学*] *Vol. 1* Beijing, Law Press [法律出版社] 2006, 289, 302.

59 See relevant discussions in e.g. Gao Qicai [高其才] Zuo Ju [左炬] Huang Yuning [黄宇宁] *Political Judiciary: The People's Court of Hua County in 1949–1961* [*政治司法：1949–1961年的华县人民法院*] Beijing, Law Press [法律出版社] 2009.

60 Carl F. Minzner 'China's Turn Against Law' (2011) Vol. LIX No. 4 *The American Journal of Comparative Law* 944–7, 951.

61 Jerome A. Cohen 'The PRC Legal System at Sixty' at http://www.eastasiaforum.org/2009/10/01/the-prc-legal-system-at-sixty/ (last accessed on 9 March 2012).

62 Supra note 14.

According to these scholars, such a turn cannot be viewed as serving for 'the Chinese people's needs and China's reality.' Li Site holds that rather than a mostly 'acquaintance-based society' or a 'close-knit' society as described by Su Li, today Chinese society has changed to a 'society of strangers' based on a market economy.[63] Hence, a formal and independent judicial system that can address disputes efficiently and fairly would be more suitable than mediation in resolving (most) disputes.[64] Li Jianshu argues that the values underlying traditional Chinese culture that support mediation and reconciliation have largely collapsed in China today along with China's opening up and adoption of the market economy, which resulted in significant changes in society, inter alia, a more and more mobile population and increasingly sharp contradictions.[65] Importantly, scholars have noted that legal reforms promulgated by the Chinese leadership in the 1980s and 1990s in a liberal direction have given rise to 'rights consciousness' in Chinese society. As maintained by Stanley Lubman, the contemporary Chinese society relies more and more on contracts, which 'suggests increasing acceptance of concepts of law-based rights' as well.[66] Eva Pils argues, based on observations of citizen-state confrontations in China's 'letters and visits' (*xinfang*) system, that in contemporary China '*yuan* and rights discourse are inextricably connected.'[67] As noted by Teng Biao, the year of 2003 has been widely acknowledged as the hallmark of China's 'rights defence (*weiquan*) movement.'[68]

Empirical evidence and statistics which show that, after 30 years' developments of the legal system towards the rule of law, mediation and reconciliation are not preferred by the Chinese people compared with

---

63 Supra note 58.

64 Ibid.

65 Li Jianshu [李剑书] 'Three Bottle-necks in the Establishment of the Criminal Reconciliation System in China [中国刑事和解制度构建的三重瓶颈]' in Bian Jianlin [卞建林] and Wang Li [王立] (eds) *Criminal Reconciliation and an Alternative Procedure* [*刑事和解与程序分流*] Beijing, The Chinese People's Public Security University Press [中国人民公安大学出版社] 2010, 175–8.

66 Stanley Lubman 'Bird in a Cage: Chinese Law Reform after Twenty Years' (2000) *Northwestern Journal of International Law & Business* 388.

67 Eva Pils 'Taking Yuan Seriously: Why the Chinese State Should Stop Suppressing Citizen Protests against Injustice' (2011) No. 2 *Temple International and Comparative Law Journal* 306.

68 Teng Biao 'Rights Defence (*weiquan*), Microblogs (*weibo*), and the Surrounding Gaze (*weiguan*): The Rights Defence Movement Online and Offline' (2012/3) CEFC 29.

litigation when disputes arise provide further support for these arguments. For instance, in 2008, a domestic Chinese scholar Liang Ping undertook a survey concerning the various dispute resolution mechanisms in China today, including negotiation with the other party privately, mediation under the village or residence committee, mediation under the basic-level judicial office, mediation under the local-level police, the town government of street office (*jiedao banshichu*), bringing complaints to the relevant administrative department for mediation, and directly bringing lawsuit and petitioning in urban, suburban and rural places.[69] The result of Liang's survey shows that although 'negotiation with the other party privately' is still the first choice for the respondents in all the studied areas, 'litigation' has been the second choice for the respondents in both urban and suburban areas (only, mediation under the village committee is the rural respondents' second choice).[70] Also, by examining the ways to conclude civil cases, Fu Hualing and Richard Cullen found that, since 1997, both the number and percentage of mediated cases in the courts nationwide had been declining.[71] The mediation rates in big cities were dramatically low – for example, in Shenzhen, this rate was only 12 percent in 2001.[72]

Liang Ping's research further argues that the judicial system built since the 1970s in the liberal direction may not be the reason for the increasing social unrest and the parties' dissatisfaction. As shown in Liang's research, in total 63.1 percent of the respondents expressed themselves 'satisfied' or 'generally satisfied' with litigation and the percentage of 'satisfied' or 'generally satisfied' respondents is just slightly higher for mediation, which is 67 percent.[73] Concerning the effectiveness of the various mechanisms for resolving disputes, 69.9 percent of the respondents has assessed 'litigation' as 'useful' or 'generally useful' (though the researcher did not explain the meaning of 'useful' in the report), and such percentage was 64.4 percent in mediation.[74] On the basis of these

---

[69] Donald C. Clarke 'Choice of Dispute Resolution Mechanisms in China' at http://lawprofessors.typepad.com/china_law_prof_blog/2011/08/choice-of-dispute-resolution-mechanisms-in-china.html (last accessed on 11 September 2011).

[70] Ibid.

[71] Supra note 19, 42.

[72] Ibid.

[73] Liang Ping [梁平] 'The Establishment of a Diverse Dispute Resolution System [多元化纠纷解决机制的制度构建]' (2011) 3 *Contemporary Law Review* [当代法学] 122.

[74] Ibid, 124.

statistics, Liang contends that 'litigation has played a leading role in the whole dispute resolution system.'[75]

All this research shows that the so-called 'Chinese characteristics' cited by scholars like Su Li and Fan Yu as the justification of the increasingly extensive use of reconciliation and mediation by the judiciary may actually not correspond to the reality in China today – instead, there is a greater social need for well-functioning litigation as well as for a judicial system protecting rights and facilitating access to justice.

The authorities may be to some extent aware of these changes as well. Therefore at the central level, as noted above, the policy of 'establishing a socialist harmonious society' is advocated together with the notion of 'rule of law,' even if, as shown above, there exist obvious contradictions in these conceptions, and the practices have indicated a departure from the rule of law. The significant changes in Chinese society brought about by legal reforms towards the rule of law may also imply that a 'simple renewal' of or 'retrogression' to the conception or style of judiciary in the Mao era would not be appropriate to understand the recent judicial reforms under the policy of 'promoting a harmonious society.' For example, Fu Hualing argues that despite political difficulties, public interest lawyers in China have become 'more demanding and more challenging.'[76] Eva Pils also observes that even though there are increasing 'dilution and hostility to rights' under the current legal reforms, the rights movements in China show new features of more alignments and refined practices of rights defence (*weiquan*).[77] Hence, the real influences of these recent legal reforms in China may be more complex. In-depth studies on the systems launched in the recent judicial reforms under the policy of 'promoting a harmonious society', such as criminal reconciliation, are of great importance to understand the impacts and connotations of the current judicial reforms.

---

75 Ibid, 123.

76 Fu Hualing 'Challenging Authoritarianism Through Law' in Jean-Philippe Beja, Fu Hualing, Eva Pils (eds) *Liu Xiaobo, Charter 08, and the Challenges of Political Reform in China* Hong Kong, Hong Kong University Press 2012, 186.

77 Eva Pils 'The Dislocation of the Chinese Human Rights Movements' in Stacy Mosher, Patrick Poon (eds) *A Sword and a Shield: China's Human Rights Lawyers* Hong Kong, China Human Rights Lawyers Concern Group 2009, 159.

1.2 THE MEDIATION SYSTEMS: FROM THE MAO ERA TO CRIMINAL RECONCILIATION TODAY

As discussed above, some scholars have commented on the overall re-promotion of mediation in the current judicial reform as China's retrogression to the Mao era and a turn against the rule of law. An examination of the mediation systems implemented since the Mao era, in particular in terms of the role of public power and the relationship between public power and individuals in this process, helps to further understand this proposition as well as the connotation of the current judicial reform. The author argues that the historical experience with Chinese mediation practices since the Mao era shows that the parties' rights are likely to be infringed, and that parties are likely to be subject to coercion in a variety of ways.

1.2.1 Mediation in the Mao Era: Suppressing Disputes in an Attempt to Serve the Party's Policies

In 1957, along with Mao Zedong's article of 'On the Correct Handling of Contradictions,' contradictions in society were divided into two kinds – 'contradictions within the people' and 'contradictions between the people and the enemies.'[78] According to Mao, conflicts within the people can be resolved through the use of 'democracy' such as mediation, whereas conflicts between the people and the enemies should only be resolved through the methods of dictatorship such as 'punishment according to law.'[79]

Nevertheless, mediation in the Mao era had other functions apart from dispute resolution.[80] Stanley Lubman has argued that mediation in the Maoist time mainly served to 'articulate and apply the ideological principles, values, and programmes of the Chinese Communist Party and help mobilizing China's people to increase their commitment to Party policies and goals.'[81]

---

[78] Stanley Lubman 'Mao and Mediation: Politics and Dispute Resolution in Communist China' (1967) Vol. 55 No. 5 *California Law Review* 1306.

[79] Stanley B. Lubman *Bird in a Cage: Legal Reform in China after Mao* Stanford, Stanford University Press 1999, 42.

[80] Supra note 78, 1339.

[81] Ibid.

This function characterized mediation as a process suppressing rather than settling disputes between individuals.[82] Because, according to Lubman, disputes that the disputants themselves regarded as personal matters were imbued with political significance.[83] The resolution of disputes is thus seen as assisting the implementation of the Party's policies ranging 'from national unity [and] collective living to increased production.'[84] In mediation, the parties' intentions and grievances were likely to be overwhelmed by those political goals, and this could easily happen due to the power mediators possessed, which came from their 'belonging to the State and Party apparatus' and their close relation to the police.[85] As a result, disputes could not be really settled and the original problems remained after the end of the mediation.[86]

1.2.2 Mediation in the post-Mao Era: 'Plastering over' Disputes and Serving the Party's Policies

During the Cultural Revolution (1966–76), the mediation system was viewed as a method of 'harmonizing classes' (*jieji tiaohe*), and so it was abolished.[87] The end of the Cultural Revolution led to an era of reform, in which 'law has risen to greater prominence in the governance of Chinese society than ever before in Chinese history.'[88] In this era, mediation developed in parallel with the legal system and was integrated into the legal framework dispute resolution.[89] However, according to Stanley Lubman, mediation in the post-Mao era was still 'sporadically linked to specific policies,' only this connection was 'less noticeable than in the Maoist era.'[90] This continuing connection with the Party's policies

---

[82] Ibid.
[83] Ibid, 1342.
[84] Ibid.
[85] Ibid.
[86] Ibid.
[87] Liu Guangan [刘广安] Li Cunpeng [李存捧] 'People's Mediation and Rights Protection [民间调解与权利保护]' in Xia Yong [夏勇] (ed) *Towards an Age of Rights* [*走向权利的时代*] Beijing, China University of Political Science and Law Press [中国政法大学出版社] 1995, 290.
[88] Stanley Lubman 'Dispute Resolution in China after Deng Xiaoping: "Mao and Mediation Revisit"' (1997) Vol. 11 No. 2 *California Law Review* 235.
[89] Michael Palmer 'The Revival of Mediation in the People's Republic of China (1): Extra-judicial Mediation' in W.E. Butler (ed) *Yearbook on Socialist Legal Systems* New York, Transnational Publishers 1987, 220.
[90] Supra note 88, 294.

characterized mediation as a programme in which addressing conflicts remained subordinate to abstract and larger political goals.[91]

In a similar vein, Michael Palmer has shown that mediation in the post-Mao era was used to resolve novel problems and conflicts triggered by the Party's new policies in order to maintain social stability and unity, under the expectation of 'nipping trouble situations in the bud' and 'preventing civil cases and minor criminal cases to upgrade to be serious crimes.'[92] Mediation was also used to popularize law (*pufa*) as the Party's goal.[93] Mediation was used by the Party to educate disputants with relevant laws and policies.[94] However, according to Palmer, the propagation of laws and policies and legal education were actually mostly for 'encouraging social conformity' and conformity with the Party's goals.[95]

Mediators still had the power to coerce the parties to 'mediate' because, according to Palmer, they were 'nominated' by the chairman of local residents' and village committees and were controlled and supervised by the Party.[96] In mediation, as further argued by Palmer, 'the democratic principles such as voluntary participation, are subordinate to the political priority of maintaining order and discipline,' now that it was much more important for the Party's governance.[97]

1.2.3 Mediation Today: A (Still) Coercive Process

In the 1990s, although the function of people's mediation was lessened,[98] in cities the People's Mediation Committee was still positioned as the 'eyes of the government.'[99] This means that besides mediating disputes, it was also expected to undertake work relating to almost all the aspects of

---

91 Ibid, 293.

92 Supra note 89, 246.

93 Ibid, 247.

94 Ibid.

95 Ibid, 248.

96 Ibid, 249–51.

97 Ibid.

98 Fan Yu [范愉] *Research on Alternative Dispute Resolution* [*非诉讼纠纷解决机制研究*] Beijing, Renmin University of China Publishing [中国人民大学出版社] 2000, 505.

99 Kang Huaiyu [康怀宇] 'The Current Situation and the Future: An Investigation on People's Mediation from the Microscopic Perspective [现状与前瞻：人民调解的微观考察]' in Zuo Weimin [左卫民] (ed) *Dispute Resolution in the Age of Transformation* [*变革时代的纠纷解决*] Beijing, 北京大学出版社 [Peking University Press] 2007, 135.

a person's ordinary life.[100] In rural China, mediation remained popular and strong.

In his study of dispute resolution in a Chinese county, Fu Hualing discusses the popularity of mediation and the strong power of mediators in rural China. According to Fu, with the goal and principle of 'stability overwhelming everything,' the Chinese Communist Party required that 'all the conflicts should be controlled and solved within the localities where the conflicts arise.'[101] Otherwise, officials of that place would be disciplined and their future promotion would be adversely affected.[102] Mediators, appointed by the local government, therefore had strong motivation deriving from their tasks in politics, to 'quarantine conflicts in the locality.'[103]

In this context, they made every effort to 'persuade' (*zuo gongzuo*) the disputants to accept their suggested settlement and not to take their case to the courts or the higher levels of governments.[104] Benefiting from their status as 'state agents' with power, mediators in rural China could easily put pressure on the disputants.[105]

Power and coercion are (even) more evident in judicial mediation conducted by the courts. As argued by Wu Hongyu, judicial mediation in China is neither an alternative to trial, nor an independent system.[106] Rather, its operation is 'backed up by Courts, and the possible initiation of trial any minute,' so that 'it almost shares everything with the formal proceedings in Courts,' yet lacks the protection of rights required in the trial procedure.[107] Among all the shared characteristics, the judge's power or authority in the trial, since it stems from his/her function as a state official exercising public power, is most influential for the parties during mediation.[108] In addition, according to Wu, as 'closure' or 'closing the case' (*an jie shi liao*), not 'closing the case in accordance with law' is made as the ultimate goal of judicial mediation, judges may sacrifice the

---

[100] Ibid.

[101] Fu Hualing 'The Politics of Mediation in a Chinese County: The Case Study of Luo Lianxi' (2003) Vol. 5 No. 2 *Australian Journal of Asian Law* 110.

[102] Ibid, 111.

[103] Ibid, 122.

[104] Ibid, 117.

[105] Ibid, 123.

[106] Wu Hongyu [武红羽] *The Process of Judicial Mediation: From the Perspective of the Relationship Between Judicial Mediation and Judicial Realm* [*司法调解的生产过程：以司法调解与司法场域的关系为视角*] Beijing, Law Press [法律出版社] 2010, 59.

[107] Ibid.

[108] Ibid, 146–7.

fairness and voluntariness stipulated by law in order to achieve this ultimate end.[109] Wu argues that in fact, 'blurring right and wrong in disputes,' 'plastering over' disputes and 'oppressing the comparatively weak or "tractable"' party are all commonly adopted ways in mediation to suppress disputes and to reach 'closure.'[110] As a result, judicial mediation is actually controlled and dominated by judges, and the parties' rights are easily infringed.[111]

From the discussion above, it is clear that the Chinese mediation system since the Mao era has always been connected closely with State power and the Party's policies. Mediators also always have power coming from their status as state agents or their status in the Party organization.

Donald Clarke argues that once a system is institutionalized, it is almost impossible for it to avoid being controlled by State power, because, according to Clarke, Chinese authorities are 'uncomfortable with the existence of any organization.'[112] Hence, as argued by Clarke, it is actually not possible for the Chinese government to allow the parties to dominate truly in mediation, to 'revoke rules as they like,' or to come to an agreement that does not conform to state norms.[113] Stanley Lubman argues that as long as 'mediation remains available to the Party-state as an instrument of policy, mediators may subordinate the parties' rights to some larger political objectives.'[114]

The features of the mediation system in China since the Mao era raise the question as to whether or not, or to what extent, criminal reconciliation could reach the officially purported aims, in particular those concerning the rights and interests of the parties. These aims, as discussed in the following, range from empowering the parties and protecting the parties' rights to giving them a voice in the criminal justice process, to repairing the victim's (psychological) harm and satisfying the parties' expectations. It is also unclear whether or not criminal reconciliation could operate on the basis of voluntariness, and whether or not this process could reach 'harmony' in the Confucian sense, or it is still mainly a tool the Party uses to suppress visible conflicts. All these questions call for an examination of criminal reconciliation practices in China.

---

[109] Ibid, 149.

[110] Ibid, 150.

[111] Ibid, 38.

[112] Donald C. Clarke 'Dispute Resolution in China' (1991) Vol. 5 No. 2 *Journal of Chinese Law* 295.

[113] Ibid.

[114] Supra note 88, 293.

1.3 THE IMPLEMENTATION AND DEVELOPMENT OF CRIMINAL RECONCILIATION IN CHINA

What the author discusses in this section is not limited to practices explicitly called 'criminal reconciliation' (*xingshi hejie*), because at the point when 'criminal reconciliation' programmes started to be used in some localities in China around 2004, names given to such practices varied from place to place.[115] According to Song Yinghui, most places called it '*xingshi hejie*' (i.e. Hunan province, Beijing municipality, Shanghai municipality and Hainan province);[116] some called it '*pinghe sifa*' ('peaceful judiciary') (i.e. Yantai city in Shandong province);[117] also some called it '*huifuxing zhengyi*' or '*huifuxing sifa*,' translating from a popular concept in western jurisdictions – restorative justice (i.e. Wuxi city in Jiangsu province).[118] Nevertheless, according to the author's observation, along with the development of this practice, '*xingshi hejie*' (criminal reconciliation) has become the most widely accepted and used name for this mechanism, as well as one later entrenched in the revised Criminal Procedure Law.

When it emerged in China, criminal reconciliation was mainly conducted at the stage of examination for prosecution (*shencha qisu*) by the

---

[115] Song Yinghui [宋英辉] 'Empirical Analysis on Criminal Reconciliation in Public Prosecution [公诉案件刑事和解的实证分析]' at http://www.sqxb.cn/blog/blog.aspx?id–309&zuozeid–83 (last accessed on 27 July 2010).

[116] Research Group of 'Empirical Study of Restorative Justice and the Reform of the PRC Criminal Procedure Law' ['恢复性司法与中国刑事诉讼法改革实证研究' 课题组] 'An Overview of the Current Implementation of Criminal Reconciliation in China [我国刑事和解适用现状之概览]' in Song Yinghui [宋英辉] Yuan Jinbiao [袁金彪] (eds) *The Theory and Practice of Criminal Reconciliation in China* [*我国刑事和解的理论与实践*] Beijing, Peking University Press [北京大学出版社] 2009, 35.

[117] Wang Chengduo [王成铎] 'Yantai: On the Way of "Peaceful Judiciary" [烟台：走在"平和司法"的大道上]' at http://www.jcrb.com/n1/jcrb904/ca477942.htm (last accessed on 24 October 2011).

[118] The People's Procuratorate of Wuxi City in Jiangsu Province [江苏省无锡市人民检察院] 'A Summary of Restorative Justice Work in The People's Procuratorates of Wuxi City [无锡市检察机关恢复性司法工作总结]' in Song Yinghui [宋英辉] Yuan Jinbiao [袁金彪] (eds) *The Theory and Practice of Criminal Reconciliation in China* [*我国刑事和解的理论与实践*] Beijing, Peking University Press [北京大学出版社] 2009, 97.

People's Procuratorate.[119] Gradually, it came to be conducted at the stage of filing a case for investigation (*li'an zhencha*) by the Public Security Bureau and the trial stage by the People's Court.[120] And, this programme was first and experimentally conducted by the People's Procuratorate of Chaoyang district in Beijing from 2002.[121] Following this so-called 'pioneer' programme,[122] and especially after obtaining support from the Party's policy of 'promoting a harmonious society' and from the Supreme People's Procuratorate and the Supreme People's Court, more and more places in China started to conduct this programme.

Subsequently, numerous internet reports emerged in China about the growth of this programme. To give some examples, it was reported that from November 2006 to October 2011 that the People's Procuratorates in Hunan province had resolved 4,232 cases through criminal reconciliation; that 6,000 suspects had reached reconciliation with victims; and that 99.5 percent of the agreements reached in criminal reconciliation programmes had been 'smoothly enforced.'[123] In Hebei province, the police had successfully mediated 3,438 minor injury cases in one year since 2008.[124] The People's Court of Chaoyang district in Beijing had started to use criminal reconciliation mainly in the civil litigation proceedings collateral to criminal proceedings since 2005 and formulated its rules for this programme.[125] In 2006, the No. 1 Criminal Court

---

119 Cai Guoqin [蔡国芹] *Research on Criminal Mediation System* [*刑事调解制度研究*] Beijing, The Chinese People's Public Security University Press [中国人民公安大学出版社] 2010, 233.

120 Ibid.

121 Feng Liqiang [封利强] Cui Yang [崔杨] 'Experience and Problems of Criminal Reconciliation: An Investigation on the Implementation of Criminal Reconciliation in Chaoyang District in Beijing [刑事和解的经验与问题：北京市朝阳区刑事和解现状]' at http://article.chinalawinfo.com/Article_Detail.asp?ArticleID=42834 (last accessed on 24 October 2011).

122 Ibid.

123 Chen Xuan [陈暄] '4243 Cases Resolved "Privately": The Enforcement Rate of Criminal Reconciliation in Hunan Reached 99.5% [4243件案子"私了"：湖南刑事和解案件赔偿履行率达99.5%]' at http://hn.rednet.cn/c/2009/12/13/1871544.htm (last accessed on 27 July 2010).

124 Ma Jing [马竞] Cao Tianjian [曹天健] 'Hebei Police Successfully Mediated 3438 Minor Injury Cases in Nearly One Year [河北警方试水轻伤害案件调解处理，近一年成功调解3438起]' at http://www.criminallaw.com.cn/article/default.asp?id=2146 (last accessed on 27 July 2010).

125 Sun Yu [孙瑜] Chen Lei [陈磊] 'Solving Criminal Cases Privately: Moving on in Debates [刑事案件私了：在争议中前行]' at http://news.sina.com.cn/c/l/2007-03-21/160612576540.shtml (last accessed on 26 August 2008).

Division[126] of the People's Court of Chaoyang district resolved 327 cases through criminal reconciliation, and 60,000 yuan of compensation had been enforced in these cases.[127] In 2009, the People's Court in Chun'an county, Zhejiang province solved 302 criminal cases, accounting for 68.42 percent of all the criminal cases, and the number ascended to 553 in 2012, accounting for 87.14 percent of all the criminal cases.[128]

Reports from different places also indicate somewhat imbalanced developments of this programme, while this imbalance shows no direct connection with the degree of economic development of these different regions. For example, in the People's Courts of Aletai city in Xinjiang Uyghur Autonomous Region, criminal reconciliation was used in only 5 out of a total of 16 private prosecution (*zisu*) cases the Courts heard in 2011.[129] The People's Procuratorate of Chaoyang district in Beijing, according to the statistics provided by Feng Liqiang and Cui Yang, used criminal reconciliation in less than 3 percent of all the (suspected) minor

---

[126] According to the Organic Law of the People's Courts of the People's Republic of China, the People's Courts may set up a criminal division, a civil division and an economic division, each with a chief judge and associate chief judges. Normally, in the basic People's Courts and intermediate People's Courts, the criminal division is often divided into No. 1 and No. 2 criminal divisions with division of work. For example, in the No. 2 intermediate People's Court of Tianjin municipality, the No. 1 criminal division is mainly in charge of the first instance trial, and the No. 2 criminal division is mainly in charge of the second instance trial and counter-appeal cases and cases for 'instructions' (*qingshi*) sent by the lower level People's Courts. See: 'Work Allocation in Tianjin No. 2 Intermediate People's Court [天津市第二中级人民法院审判庭业务划分]' at http://www.huanglawyer.net/Article/ShowArticle.asp?ArticleID=435 (last accessed on 27 October 2011).

[127] Ouyang Fang [欧阳芳] 'The Police of Ji'an City in Jiangxi Province Experimentally Conducted Criminal Reconciliation to Promote Social Harmony [江西吉安公安局试行刑事和解制度,促社会和谐]' http://www.chinapeace.org.cn/zhzl/2009-08/24/content_82878.htm (last accessed on 27 July 2010).

[128] Chun'an Court Research Group [淳安法院课题组] 'Fieldwork on the Application of Criminal Reconciliation Procedure: Using Chun'an Court's Judicial Practice as a Sample [关于刑事和解程序适用问题的调研：以淳安法院司法实践为样本]' at http://www.hzcourt.cn/art/2015/6/3/art_51_12392.html (last accessed 2 October 2015).

[129] Zhang Guochen [张国臣] 'The People's Courts in Our City Implemented Criminal Reconciliation Actively to Resolve Social Conflicts [市法院充分运用刑事和解：积极化解社会矛盾]' at http://www.alt.gov.cn/Article/ShowArticle.aspx?ArticleID=44190 (last accessed on 27 October 2011).

injury cases in 2006.[130] From 2007 to 2008, the People's Procuratorates in Hunan province adopted criminal reconciliation programmes in merely 3.55 percent of all the cases dealt with by these Procuratorates.[131] The police of Ji'an county in Jiangxi province reportedly resolved 89 minor intentional injury cases through criminal reconciliation in three years between 2006 and 2009.[132]

Although for a long period there were no procedural regulations or guidelines on the operation of criminal reconciliation at the central level, as is common in Chinese legal practice, a number of regulations or guidelines were issued by local authorities, most often the People's Procuratorates and in some places jointly by the Public Security Bureau, the People's Procuratorate, the People's Court and the Justice Bureau.[133]

Some local regulations or guidelines can be accessed on the internet[134] or have been appended to monographs or books.[135] Yet some of them are still not publicly available, and are not permitted to be made publicly available. Taking the author's experience by way of example, in two fieldwork locations, the officials approached for copies of their local guidelines on criminal reconciliation simply declined to make them available, even for the purpose of anonymous research. The author was informed that 'these are internal documents' (*neibu wenjian*) so that they should be 'kept secret' (*baomi*). However, according to Article 2 of the 'Law of the People's Republic of China on Guarding State Secrets,' state secrets are defined as 'matters that have a vital bearing on state security and national interests and, as specified by legal procedure, are entrusted to a limited number of people for a given period of time.' It is hard to

---

130 Supra note 121.

131 Tan Zelin [谭泽林] Zhao Qiusheng [赵秋生] 'Problems and Improvements of Laws Accordingly in Implementing Criminal Reconciliation in China [我国刑事和解实施中的问题与相应实体、程序法完善]' (2009) 9 *Politics and Law* [*政治与法律*], 149.

132 Supra note 127.

133 Supra note 115, 35–9.

134 For instance, the Regulation issued by Zhuhui district People's Procuratorate of Henyang city in Hunan province can be found at http://www.hyzhq.gov.cn/ZWXX/StandAuthorityColumInfo.aspx?id=475 (last accessed on 1 November 2011).

135 For instance, the Procedural Regulations on the Implementation of Criminal Reconciliation issued by Chaoyang district and Haidian district People's Procuratorates in Beijing were enclosed as an appendix of the book *Criminal Reconciliation* [*刑事和解*] by author Wang Yijun [王一俊] and published by the China University of Politics and Law Publishing [中国政法大学出版社] 2010.

believe that guidelines for criminal reconciliation can be said to fall within these 'matters.' On the contrary, procedural regulations for the criminal reconciliation process, as a regulation over a legal process, should be open.[136] This belongs to 'access to all relevant information,' which is one of the minimum requirements for the 'right to a fair trial' as confirmed in the Universal Declaration of Human Rights and International Covenant on Civil and Political Rights.[137] In practice, given the abovementioned restrictions, it is likely that the parties participating in this process may have detailed knowledge and no way of obtaining information about the procedure of criminal reconciliation, as well as their rights to this process. This raises questions as to the process and effect of criminal reconciliation concerning the parties' roles and rights.

Based on their knowledge of available regulations and guidelines on criminal reconciliation in various locations across China, many Chinese scholars have interpreted the procedure as following a similar style and including four steps – initiation, criminal reconciliation meeting, the officials' decision and follow-up programmes (optional).[138] These steps or stages in the procedure are now also reflected in the Supreme People's Procuratorate's 'Opinions of the Supreme People's Procuratorate on the Handling of Minor Criminal Cases when the Parties Have Reached Reconciliation' issued in December 2010.[139] These four steps are set out

---

[136] Xu Bin [许斌] 'Laws and Regulations Should Be the Products of Open Game [法律法规应该是公开博弈的产物]' at http://www.china.com.cn/news/comment/2010-07/30/content_20607709.htm (last accessed on 6 March 2012).

[137] See: Equality and Human Rights Commission 'The Right to a Fair Trial' at http://www.equalityhumanrights.com/advice-and-guidance/before-the-equality-act/guidance-for-service-users-pre-october-2010/criminal-justice-system/the-right-to-a-fair-trial/ (last accessed on 6 March 2012).

[138] At present, almost all the places with the practice of criminal reconciliation have stipulated local regulations governing the procedure of this practice. See: Song Yinghui [宋英辉] Yuan Jinbiao [袁金彪] (eds) *The Theory and Practice of Criminal Reconciliation in China* [*我国刑事和解的理论与实践*] Beijing, 北京大学出版社 [Peking University Press] 2009, 35–9. Some of them can be searched on the internet like the 'Regulation on the Implementation of Criminal Reconciliation in Hunan Province' at http://www.fgw.czs.gov.cn/jcy/lwxjcy/wjfb/content_988.html (last accessed on 6 March 2012). Some are shown in academic work like the Regulations in Nanjing and Changzhou city, which are enclosed in Di Xiaohua [狄小华] Liu Zhiwei [刘志伟] (eds) *The Theory and Practice of Restorative Justice in Juvenile Cases* [*恢复性少年司法理论与实践*] Beijing, People Publishing [群众出版社] 2007.

[139] See the interview with Bai Quanmin, the spokesman of the Supreme People's Procuratorate about the 'Opinions' at http://www.lianghui.org.cn/2011/2011-03/12/content_22119264_2.htm (last accessed on 15 March 2011).

below where the term 'party' refers to the suspect/defendant and the victim (or alleged victim) in a case.

1.3.1 The Stage of Initiation

Criminal reconciliation can be initiated in three situations. First, the Public Security Bureau/People's Procuratorate/People's Court initiates it based on examining the circumstances of the case and asking both parties whether they agree to participate in criminal reconciliation.[140] This means that *both parties* should voluntarily participate in this process.[141] This type, mainly dependent on official initiation, is the one currently implemented in most places in China and also the one laid down in the 2012 CPL (except that the 2012 CPL requires only the *victim*'s voluntary participation).

Second, the Public Security Bureau/People's Procuratorate/People's Court initiates it according to either party's application. Upon this application, the police/prosecutors/judges should examine the case and make sure that *the other party* (in other words, it also requires that criminal reconciliation should be based on both parties' voluntary participation) also agrees to participate voluntarily.[142] An example of this situation is the one adopted in Shanghai municipality.[143]

Third, the parties have reached an agreement themselves, and submit the agreement to the Public Security Bureau/People's Procuratorate/People's Court for examination.[144] In this third case, initiation is not really triggered by the authorities; they merely confirm the result of a negotiation process carried out by the parties themselves. An example of this situation is the one adopted in Hunan province.[145]

Not all cases qualify for criminal reconciliation. Official examination of cases centres on:

---

140 Supra note 119, 232.

141 Supra note 115.

142 Li Ping [李萍] Liu Yu [刘宇] 'Discussion on the Establishment of Criminal Reconciliation System in Juvenile Cases in the People's Procuratorate [检察机关构建未成年人刑事和解制度探讨]' at http://www.shjcy.gov.cn/njcgyd2007/llsj/t20070809_33593.htm (last accessed on 12 February 2011).

143 Ibid.

144 Supra note 119, 232.

145 *San Xiang Municipal Newspaper* [*三湘都市报*] 'Hunan Tried Criminal Reconciliation: Minor Criminal Cases Can Be Reconciled Privately [湖南试行刑事和解制: 轻微刑事案件可私下和解]' at http://www1.china.com.cn/policy/txt/2006-11/22/content_7393033.htm (last accessed on 11 February 2011).

1. Whether or not the case is suitable for reconciliation. Normally, the case ought to concern a suspected 'minor crime' according to the PRC Criminal Law[146] and the suspect/defendant should not be a recidivist (in the event of conviction of the crime of which she/he is suspected).[147] It could be seen that the 'scope' of the cases eligible for criminal reconciliation stipulated in these local regulations or guidelines is wider than that in the 2012 CPL. Usually, criminal reconciliation is preferred in juvenile cases and cases in which the parties have some relationship established before the 'crime,' for instance because they are classmates, neighbours or relatives;[148]
2. Whether or not the parties' application or personal agreement is legitimate, namely it should be both parties' true intentions;[149] and
3. The suspect/defendant has to admit guilt (*renzui*) before entering a criminal reconciliation programme.[150] In some places, the suspect/

---

[146] According to Article 1 of the Judicial Interpretation on CPL issued by the Supreme People's Court [最高人民法院关于执行《中华人民共和国刑事诉讼法》若干问题的解释] stipulated in 1998, eight categories of crimes are 'minor crime.' They are: intentional injury crime according to Section 1, Article 234 of the PRC Criminal Law; illegal intrusion into others' residence according to Article 245 of the PRC Criminal Law; infringement of other citizens' right of communication freedom according to Article 252 of the PRC Criminal Law; bigamy according to Article 258 of the PRC Criminal Law; abandonment according to Article 261 of the PRC Criminal Law; manufacturing and selling fake and shoddy goods according to Section 1, Chapter 3 of the PRC Criminal Law (except those that seriously undermine social order and state interest); infringement of intellectual property rights according to Section 7, Chapter 3 of the PRC Criminal Law (except those that seriously undermine social order and state interest); crimes stipulated in Chapters 4 and 5 of the PRC Criminal Law which could be sentenced with a punishment lighter than three-year imprisonment.

[147] But in some places, criminal reconciliation has been also applied to felonies like serious intentional injury crimes and even death penalty cases. See: Song Yinghui [宋英辉] 'An Empirical Analysis of Criminal Reconciliation in China [我国刑事和解实证分析]' (2008) 5 *China Legal Science* [*中国法学*], 124–5.

[148] Ibid.

[149] Supra note 119, 233.

[150] Supra note 119, 232. In practice, it was required in some local regulations or guidelines (i.e. the one stipulated by the People's Procuratorate of Chaoyang district in Beijing and the one stipulated by the People's Procuratorate of Yuhua district in Shijiazhuang). See: the empirical research reports collected in Song Yinghui [宋英辉] *Empirical Research on Criminal Reconciliation* [*刑事和解实证研究*] Beijing, Peking University Press [北京大学出版社] 2010, 25, 219, 237. It can also be found as the premise of initiating a criminal

defendant has also to show remorse (*huizui biaoxian*) for the accused crime.[151]

1.3.2 Criminal Reconciliation Meeting

When criminal reconciliation is initiated by one of the State institutions, a criminal reconciliation meeting is expected to be held (arranged for and presided over) by the official.[152] Most of the regulations or guidelines explicitly emphasize that the criminal reconciliation meeting should proceed on the basis of fairness and voluntariness.[153] The potential tension arising from official roles and the principle of voluntariness turned out to be a major issue in the empirical study whose results are discussed in later chapters.

The criminal reconciliation meeting can be presided over by the responsible official (i.e. the police/prosecutor/judge concerned with handling this case) or by a people's mediator assigned by the responsible official.[154]

The main work of the official or mediator is to *guide* and *facilitate* the parties to reach an agreement. The official or mediator is forbidden to interfere with the parties' own wishes in criminal reconciliation meetings.[155] The criminal reconciliation meeting can be attended by both parties (*or* their agents[156]); it can also be attended by their relatives and

---

reconciliation programme in the Guidelines on the Implementation of Criminal Reconciliation in Wuxi city. See the full text of this Guideline in Bian Jianlin [卞建林] Wang Li [王立] (eds) *Criminal Reconciliation and an Alternative Procedure* [*刑事和解与程序分流*] Beijing, The Chinese People's Public Security University Press [中国人民公安大学出版社] 2010, 452.

151 An example is the Regulation on the Criminal Reconciliation Programme in Changzhou city enclosed in Di Xiaohua [狄小华], Liu Zhiwei [刘志伟] supra note 138.

152 Xiao Shiwei [肖仕卫] '"The Third Realm" in Criminal Justice: An Analysis of the Structural Position and Function of Criminal Reconciliation in China [刑事法治的"第三领域": 中国刑事和解制度的结构定位与功能分析]' (2007) Vol. 19 No. 6 *Peking University Law Journal* [*中外法学*], 724–5.

153 Supra note 119, 236.

154 Chen Ruihua [陈瑞华] 'Private Cooperation in Criminal Proceedings: The Emergence of Criminal Reconciliation in China [刑事诉讼的私力合作模式: 刑事和解在中国的兴起]' (2006) 5 *China Legal Science* [*中国法学*], 16–18.

155 Ibid.

156 'Agents' means persons entrusted by victims, or victims' legal representatives or near relatives.

other people (i.e. other officials and the parties' friends, teachers, employers, neighbours, or *lingdao* ('leadership')[157]).[158]

Generally, a criminal reconciliation meeting is expected to be conducted according to the following four steps.[159] First, the official or mediator briefly introduces the case to the participants. Second, the suspect/defendant states his/her attitudes to and feelings on the alleged offence, and then admits guilt, expresses regret, apologizes and expresses his/her willingness to compensate the victim *voluntarily*. Often, as indicated by some scholars, the official would also ask the suspect/defendant to indicate his/her resolutions for the future in the meeting. Third, the victim expresses his/her feelings and describes the harm and loss caused by the accused crime and then shows forgiveness and the *voluntary* acceptance of the compensation offered by the suspect/defendant. Finally, the parties sign an agreement that reflects the oral agreement reached in the meeting (or that may factually have been reached prior to the formal criminal reconciliation meeting).

It appears that the pre-revision criminal reconciliation processes for criminal reconciliation meetings as designed in the local regulations or guidelines were much more detailed and stressed both parties' participation and communication based on their voluntariness, yet these were missing in the 2012 CPL.

1.3.3 The Official's Decision

After the suspect/defendant has paid up, the officials in question have different options, depending on the stage at which criminal reconciliation was carried out. The police (Public Security Bureau) can 'dismiss' (*chexiao*) the case.[160] The People's Procuratorate *may* make a decision not to prosecute and to erase the suspect's criminal record, or suggest to the Public Security Bureau that it 'dismiss' the case, or suggest a lenient

---

157 The phrase 'leadership' (*lingdao*) is closely related to another phrase '[Party] cadre' (*ganbu*). The Chinese call people donating leadership skill and capability (or more precisely it is expected that *lingdao* are skilled/capable persons) in an organizational setup. 'Leader' (*lingdao*) or 'cadre' (*ganbu*) is the functionary who staffs the various Party and government bureaucracies and has authority to conduct Party or government affairs. In general, there are three categories of 'leader' (*lingdao*) or 'cadre' (*ganbu*): State, local and military. See: James C.F. Wang, *Contemporary Chinese Politics* New Jersey, Prentice Hall 1995, 119–20.

158 Supra note 119.

159 Supra note 119, 235–6.

160 Ibid.

sentence to the People's Court.[161] The People's Court can give the defendant a lenient sentence.[162] The 2012 CPL follows these options, except that the police are not allowed to directly 'dismiss' the case.

If the parties cannot reach or comply with the criminal reconciliation agreement, the case is transferred back to the normal criminal procedure.[163]

1.3.4 Follow-up Programmes

After the criminal reconciliation meeting, the official in charge *may* arrange for some follow-up work. This may consist in a programme called 'community correction' (*shequ jiaozheng*) or in a programme called 'help and teaching' (*bangjiao*) for the suspect/defendant.[164] In the follow-up work, the official continues to gather information about the suspects/defendants' conduct in daily life, for instance by visiting or calling them or their families regularly.[165]

'Community correction,' according to the 'Opinions on the Nationwide Trial Implementation of Community Correction' issued jointly by the Supreme People's Court, the Supreme People's Procuratorate, the Ministry of Public Security and the Ministry of Justice, is a type of non-custodial criminal punishment.[166] According to these Opinions, it means 'correcting the criminals in their respective community[167] with the

---

[161] Ibid.

[162] Supra note 116, 38–9.

[163] Supra note 119, 236.

[164] Song Yinghui [宋英辉] 'An Empirical Analysis of Criminal Reconciliation in China [我国刑事和解实证分析]' (2008) 5 *China Legal Science* [*中国法学*], 134.

[165] Supra note 119, 310.

[166] According to Article 1 of the 'Opinions on the Nationwide Trial Implementation of Community Correction' [最高人民法院、最高人民检察院、公安部、司法部关于在全国试行社区矫正工作的意见]. See the English translation of the 'Opinions' at LawInfoChina: http://www.lawinfochina.com/display.aspx?lib=law&id=8265&CGid= (last accessed on 6 May 2016).

[167] In China, although there are still debates on the criteria to divide community, ordinarily, a certain number of residences that subordinate to a residence committee (*juweihui*) or sub-district office (*jiedao banshichu*) can be viewed as a community. See: Xia Jianzhong [夏建中] 'The Concept of Community and the Establishment of Community in Urban China [社区概念与我国城市社区建设]' at http://www.ccpg.org.cn/Article/ShowArticle.asp?ArticleID=272 (last accessed on 8 December 2010). According to the 'Opinions on Improving the Establishment of Urban Community' issued by the

assistance of social organizations (*shehui tuanti*),[168] non-governmental organizations (*minjian zuzhi*)[169] and volunteers to correct their criminal

Ministry of Civil Affairs [民政部关于在全国推进城市社区建设的意见] promulgated in 2000, 'community' refers to the area under a residence committee (*juweihui*). According to Article 7 of the 'Organic Law of the Urban Residences Committees of the People's Republic of China' [中华人民共和国城市居民委员组织法], a residents committee shall be established for an area inhabited by 100–700 households on the basis of the distribution of residents and the principle of facilitating their self-government. The definition of sub-district office (*jiedao banshichu*), however, is unclear at present. The 'Organic Law of the Sub-District Office' [城市街道办事处组织条例] issued in 1954 provides that 'sub-district office (*jiedao banshichu*) is set in order to strength residential work in cities and the connections between the government and the residents.' And 'the municipality with more than one million population and city without districts should establish sub-district office.' 'The municipality with more than fifty thousand but less than one million population can establish sub-district office if necessary.' Yet this regulation expired in 2009 and there has been no new regulation on sub-district offices ever since. See: *Kunming Daily* [*昆明日报*] 'The Organic Law of the Sub-district Office over "50 Years Old" Was Banned, yet New Responsibility Has Not Been Clear yet: The Sub-district Office Is More and More Embarrassed ["50多岁" 的《城市街道办事处组织条例》已被废止, 但新职责依然不明确: 街道办身份越来越尴尬]' at http://szcg.km.gov.cn/ggxx/news.aspx?id=5371 (last accessed on 28 March 2011).

168 According to the 1998 Regulations on Registration and Administration of Social Organizations [社会团体登记管理条例], 'social organization' (*shehui tuanti*) means 'non-profit groups voluntarily organized by Chinese citizens in order to realize a shared objective according to their rules.' 'All organizations other than state organs may join social organizations as institutional members.'

169 Non-governmental organization (*minjian zuzhi*) means a non-profit non-government organization. It includes social organization (*shehui tuanti*), non-governmental non-enterprise entity (*minban fei qiye danwei*) and foundation. See: Hong Dayong [洪大用] 'An Initial Research on the Poverty Relief Work by Chinese Non-governmental Organizations [中国民间组织扶贫工作的初步研究]' (2002) 2 *Jianghai Academic Journal* [*江海学刊*] 100. Non-governmental non-enterprise entities (*minban fei qiye danwei*), according to the 1998 'Temporary Regulations on Registration and Administration of Non-profit Non-government Organizations' [民办非企业单位登记管理暂行条例], are 'non-profit social organizations established by social organizations, citizens, enterprises and other institutions by means of non-state owned property in order to conduct non-profit social service activities.' Foundation, according to the 2004 'Regulation on Foundation Administration' [基金会管理条例], is 'non-profit legal person established according to this Regulation and through making use of the property donated by persons, legal persons, or other organizations with the purpose of pursuing welfare undertakings.'

minds and bad behavior within the period determined by the judgment or decision, and to help them return to the society.'[170]

'Help and teaching' programmes are arranged by the responsible official using various resources in society (like volunteers and community workers) to 'educate, help, and supervise' the suspect/defendant.[171] In the programme, the suspect/defendant is often required to do some voluntary work and keep communicating with the people responsible for the programme.[172] The person undertaking the programme needs to report on the suspect/defendant's performance to the official.[173]

The time stipulated for these follow-up programmes varies from place to place. Usually, it lasts for several months. If the suspect/defendant gets favourable assessments at the end of this period, the decision made after the criminal reconciliation meeting may be confirmed; otherwise, the decision will be revoked.[174]

Although this stage is designed as an option (decided by the officials) for the procedure of criminal reconciliation in these local regulations or guidelines, it is not mentioned at all in the 2012 CPL. Whether this omission could affect the future conduct of follow-up programmes and its effect and importance on the process is further discussed in Chapters 4 and 5.

Overall, the procedure designed for criminal reconciliation as shown in the local regulations or guidelines is much more detailed and complicated than in the 2012 CPL. Articles 277 to 279 did not even ask for the suspect/defendant's voluntary participation in this 'reconciliation' process, which is stressed in these local regulations or guidelines and may be the foundation of a genuine reconciliation process.

These regulations or rules on criminal reconciliation also outline some essential differences between this process and the normal criminal

---

170 Article 1 of 'The Supreme People's Court, the Supreme People's Procuratorate, the Ministry of Public Security, the Ministry of Justice: Opinions on the Nationwide Trial Implementation of Community Correction' [最高人民法院、最高人民检察院、公安部、司法部关于在全国试行社区矫正工作的意见]. See the English Translation at LawInfoChina: http://www.lawinfochina.com/display.aspx?lib=law&id=8265&CGid= (accessed on 6 May 2016).

171 Supra note 164, 134.

172 Zhang Jie [张洁] '"Restorative Justice, Criminal Reconciliation, Community Correction": Three Crucial Systems in Juvenile Justice System ['恢复性司法、刑事和解、社区矫正': 少年司法中的三项重要制度]' at http://www.yffz.org/E_ReadNews.asp?NewsId=1249&page=2 (last accessed on 13 February 2011).

173 Ibid.

174 Ibid.

proceedings. The normal criminal procedure in the Chinese legal framework, according to the PRC Criminal Procedure Law, includes five stages, namely 'filing a case,' 'investigation,' 'prosecution,' 'trial' and 'execution.' According to the procedure designed for criminal reconciliation, except for the last stage of execution, criminal reconciliation can be initiated at each of the four stages of the normal criminal procedure. It has the effect of ending the normal procedure at one stage (i.e. the police can 'dismiss' the case at the stage of 'filing a case' or 'investigation'; the prosecutor can decide not to prosecute). It can also continue with the normal procedure after the end of the criminal reconciliation process (i.e. the police/prosecutors make suggestions about lenient dispositions to the prosecutor/judge; the judge gives a lenient sentence).

More essentially, the process of criminal reconciliation is different from the normal criminal procedure because the 1996 PRC Criminal Procedure Law has set the normal procedure as an adversarial system (or a more adversarial system compared with the inquisitorial system as set out in the 1979 PRC Criminal Procedure Law).[175] This design as an adversarial system has also been on principle preserved by the new CPL, to become effective in January 2013. In designing an adversarial system, the 1996 CPL imposes restrictions on public power and provides protection for the suspect/defendant's rights. Fu Hualing summarizes the multiple main advances the 1996 PRC Criminal Procedure Law had made towards an adversarial system:[176]

> In many aspects, the [CPL] Amendment introduces important changes to the previous procedures and significantly redistributes the existing division of powers within the criminal justice system. It restricts police power and the prosecution's discretion. It enhances the position of the court and differentiates the role of judges. It also offers more protection for the rights of the accused and enhances the position of defence lawyers in the criminal process in substantive and procedural aspects. Consequently criminal lawyers are expected to play a more active and meaningful role in criminal defence.

Also, at trial, in contrast to the very active role to 'pursue truth' (through pre-trial investigation, and so on) under the generally inquisitorial system

---

[175] Randall Peerenboom 'What Have We Learned about Law and Development? Describing, Predicting and Assessing Legal Reforms in China' (Spring 2006) Vol. 27 *Michigan Journal of International Law* 844.

[176] Fu Hualing 'Criminal Defence in China: The Possible Impact of the 1996 Criminal Procedural Law Reform' (Mar. 1998) No. 153 *The China Quarterly* 31.

laid down in the 1979 CPL,[177] judges under the current (more) 'adversarial system' serve a 'more neutral and independent role' during the process.[178]

However, as showed above, criminal reconciliation is essentially based on the two parties' communication and negotiation. That is to say, the two parties are not supposed to stand in 'adversarial' positions in criminal reconciliation processes. As a 'reconciliation' process, voluntariness (from both parties, or only the victim as problematically stipulated in the 2012 CPL) is the basic and core principle underlying criminal reconciliation. The officials' role is also very different: they still have power (i.e. in initiating this process, presiding over criminal reconciliation meetings and deciding the case), so that rather than restricting their discretion as required in the normal procedure, the proceeding of criminal reconciliation heavily relies on their discretion. Furthermore, criminal reconciliation is based on the suspect/defendant's admission of guilt (or showing remorse) beforehand, which is the key issue to establish in the normal procedure.

Although there remain crucial deficiencies in the design of an adversarial system in the 1996 CPL (e.g. no 'presumption of innocence'), and judicial practices in China have been disappointing (or even displaying a reverse picture) in enforcing the CPL (as an adversarial system),[179] such differences in the designation of these two procedures may still have two further implications: first, it seems that the roles of the official and the parties are distinct from those in the normal criminal procedure. Then, what exactly are their roles in criminal reconciliation processes and what are the interactions between their roles? Second, without the mechanisms involved in the adversarial system serving to restrict the public power and protect the rights of the accused, can the suspect/defendant's (and the victim's) rights be protected in criminal reconciliation processes? Especially, could the most basic principle of voluntariness be guaranteed in criminal reconciliation when public power is supposed to take an active role? These questions indicate the need to look into the operation of this procedure in practice.

---

[177] Mike McConville *et al*, *Criminal Justice in China: An Empirical Inquiry* Cheltenham, UK and Northampton, MA, USA, Edward Elgar Publishing 2011, 10–11.

[178] Jennifer Smith, Michael Gompers 'Realizing Justice: The Development of Fair Trial Rights in China' at http://www.law.upenn.edu/journals/ealr/articles/volume2/issue2/SmithGompers2ChineseL.&Pol%E2%80%99yRev.108(2007).pdf (accessed on 10 January 2010).

[179] Supra note 167, 10–12.

1.3.5 Recent Developments of Criminal Reconciliation

In 2007, the Party staged 'big mediation' (*da tiaojie*) in the judicial system. According to the 'Opinions on Deeply Promoting the Resolution of Social Conflicts, the Innovation of Social Management, and the Fairness and Integrity of Law Enforcement' issued by the CCP Central Political and Judicial Committee (*zheng fa wei*) and the CCP Central Leading Group of Stability Maintaining Work in 2010, '*da tiaojie*' refers to mechanisms 'established by Party Committees and governments at all levels' to 'coordinate political, legal, comprehensive governance (*zonghe zhili*), stability maintenance, petitioning departments for involving the participation of society, and thereby to allow people's mediation, administrative mediation and judicial mediation fully to play their roles and cooperate with each other.'[180] Accordingly, 'big' in this mechanism refers to the mobilization of all elements and resources in society with the aim of using mediation to resolve as many cases as possible.[181] This asks for an even wider coverage of mediation in the Chinese judicial system.[182]

In this context, criminal reconciliation has three further developments – although, none of these developments were provided in laws and are *prima facie* in tension with constitutional principles. First, it has been used in suspected cases of 'serious crimes' including even death penalty cases. For instance, official media reported that in Jiangsu province, criminal reconciliation had been used to deal with serious intentional injury crimes occurring among inmates in prison.[183] It was also reported that Dongguan city in Guangdong province, Jinhua city in Zhejiang

---

180 中央政法委员会、中央维护稳定工作领导小组关于深入推进社会矛盾化解、社会管理创新、公正廉洁执法的意见 [Opinions of the Central Political-Legal Committee, the Central Leading Group of Maintaining Stability On Promoting Social Conflicts Resolution, Innovating Social Management and Fair and Incorrupt Legal Enforcement], See the full text (Chinese version only) at http://www.dffy.com/faguixiazai/ssf/201105/22812.html (last accessed on 8 November 2011).

181 Wu Zhiming [吴志明] Lin Huabin [林化宾] Wu Junying [吴军营] (eds) *The General Mediation System: The Eastern Experience of Responding to Social Conflicts* [*大调解: 应对社会矛盾凸显的东方经验*] Beijing Law Press [法律出版社] 2010, 30–31.

182 Ibid.

183 Jiang De [蒋德] Wan Zhong [万众] 'Criminal Reconciliation Has Been Introduced into Prison: The Judge Says that It Is Not Illegal Leniency [狱内伤害案引入刑事和解: 检察官称绝非法外施恩]' at http://news.sohu.com/20090721/n265364272.shtml (last accessed on 22 July 2009).

province and Shanghai municipality had all used criminal reconciliation in death penalty cases, in which the judges gave the defendants lighter sentences due to their reconciliation with the victim's families and prompt payment of compensation.[184] Between 28 July and 4 August in 2009, the official newspaper *Legal Daily* reported five death penalty cases released by the Supreme People's Court – although none of them expressly referred to the phrase '*xingshi hejie*,' it could be found that criminal reconciliation, in particular, compensation, had played a significant role in the Supreme People's Court's decision of not approving the death penalty.[185]

Second, there has been a '*duijie*' or '*liandong*' (collaboration or coordination) mechanism in conducting criminal reconciliation, which refers to mechanisms whereby different state authorities collaborate in implementing criminal reconciliation programmes. In one form of *duijie* or *liandong*, the Public Security Bureau, the People's Procuratorate and the People's Court work together in conducting criminal reconciliation. This means that a case may be mediated by the police, the prosecutors and the judges throughout the criminal process from investigation and prosecution to trial and execution. If reconciliation cannot be reached by one organ or in one phase, efforts to achieve reconciliation will be continued after the case proceeds to another phase. According to the saying of the Public Security Bureau/the People's Procuratorate/the People's Court implementing this form of *duijie* or *liandong*, this collaboration aims to provide the parties concerned with every opportunity to reach a reconciliation agreement at any point during the criminal procedure.[186] In the other form of *duijie* or *liandong*, the Public Security

---

[184] Sun Wanhuai [孙万怀] 'Do Death Penalty Cases Need Reconciliation and Can They Be Reconciled? [死刑案件可以并需要和解吗?]' (2010) 1 *China Legal Science* [*中国法学*] 180–81.

[185] Wang Dong [王栋], Zhao Bin [赵斌] 'Main Problems Facing Criminal Reconciliation and Strategies [刑事和解面临的主要问题与对策]' at http://www.hongfan.org.cn/projects.php?optionid=377&auto_id=29 (last accessed on 7 August 2015).

[186] Ouyang Fang [欧阳芳] 'The Police of Ji'an City in Jiangxi Province Experimentally Conducted Criminal Reconciliation to Promote Social Harmony [江西吉安公安局试行刑事和解制度,促社会和谐]' at http://www.chinapeace.org.cn/zhzl/2009-08/24/content_82878_2.htm (last accessed on 27 July 2010); The People's Procuratorate of Wuhua District in Kunming City [昆明市五华区检察院] 'Cooperation Among Departments and Between the People's Procuratorate and the People's Court Promotes Criminal Reconciliation in Our Court [我院'部门联动检调对接'积极促进刑事和解]' at http://www.kmwh.gov.cn/kmwh/web/jwb/j5/jcy/showdoc.jsp;jsessionid=Ot51m9BDkebtjnp8

Bureau/the People's Procuratorate/the People's Court coordinate with the People's Mediation Committee (*renmin tiaojie weiyuanhui*), an entity that exists outside the formal court system and is generally used to mediate civil disputes, in conducting criminal reconciliation. Normally, the official informs the parties of the choice of criminal reconciliation if he/she thinks that the case concerned is eligible for this programme. If the parties agree, the case will be transferred to the People's Mediation Committee (this may be the one where the case occurred, or where the victim/suspect is based[187]). The Mediation Committee will conduct mediation in a certain period; wherever an agreement can or cannot be reached within this period, the case concerned will be transferred back to the state authorities for review and decision.[188]

Third, it has involved participation from an increasingly wider circle of persons in the criminal reconciliation meeting. For instance, the People's Court in Foshan city in Guangdong province invited prosecutors, members of the National People's Congress, and public media to attend criminal reconciliation meetings.[189] This wide participation in criminal reconciliation meetings, according to an official of this Court, was to oversee (the judges' conduct) in criminal reconciliation.[190] It was also reported that the People's Procuratorate in Suining city in Sichuan province authorized victims to select and nominate members of the

---

RzU7mU9Qmv9bnuDjlMTimcwXMvfFgfOVXroz!742181009?docid=D105138&fieldid=F3792 (last accessed on 25 October 2011).

[187] The Justice Bureau of Haishu District [海曙区司法局] 'Haishu District Has Reached Perfect Collaboration Between Criminal Reconciliation and the People's Mediation [海曙区实现刑事和解与人民调解工作无缝对接]' at http://www.zjsft.gov.cn/art/2011/8/8/art_61_31321.html (last accessed on 25 October 2011).

[188] Fei County of Linyi City in Shandong Province [山东省临沂市费县] 'Measures on Establishing Collaboration Between Criminal Reconciliation and People's Mediation [关于建立刑事和解与人民调解对接机制的实施办法]' at http://fxzfw.cn/News_View.asp?NewsID=438 (last accessed on 25 October 2011).

[189] Yan Xiaoguang [闫晓光] 'Criminal Reconciliation Conducted by the People's Court of Foshan City of Guangdong Province Triggered Debates: It Was Criticized as "Avoiding Punishment with Money" [广东佛山法院刑事和解引争议：被指"以钱买刑"]' at http://news.163.com/10/0730/00/6CQ5UU5R0001124J.html (last accessed on 23 July 2010).

[190] Ibid.

People's Congress they trusted as supervisors in their criminal reconciliation programmes.[191] This was done, according to the official reports, also for the purpose of supervising (*jiandu*) the official's use of power in criminal reconciliation processes. The prosecutors in charge in Suining said that the involvement of members of the People's Congress could 'expose their work and power to the sunshine' and 'connect work of the People's Procuratorate with the People's Congress's oversight,' which was 'helpful to obtain the parties' as well as the public's support and trust in implementing criminal reconciliation.'[192] According to some media reports, such extensive participation in criminal reconciliation might also serve the purpose of education. For instance, it was reported that in Xuzhou city in Jiangsu province, the responsible prosecutor, Prosecutor Ming, had held meetings attended by the juvenile offender, members of the People's Congress, the offender's teachers and parents in order to 'better educate the juvenile suspect.'[193]

1.4 THE SCHOLARLY DEBATES SURROUNDING CRIMINAL RECONCILIATION PROGRAMMES

Scholarly debates on criminal reconciliation practices in China mainly surround the effects of this programme, namely whether it is a programme helpful for promoting a 'harmonious society' in accordance with officially set aims or beneficial in other ways, or whether it is actually an unfair and involuntary programme doing harm to the parties' rights and justice in the criminal justice processes. This part discusses these debates, and suggests that they fail fully to address the problems with criminal reconciliation.

---

[191] Liu Dehua [刘德华] Wang Li [王莉] Jian Hua [简华] 'The Victim Can Nominate National People's Congress Deputy to Participate in the Criminal Reconciliation Process [哪位代表介入刑事和解？ 被害人点名]' at http://news.china.com.cn/rollnews/2010-07/05/content_3023494.htm (last accessed on 28 July 2010).

[192] Ibid.

[193] Xu Chi [许驰] Liu Xiaohan [刘晓晗] 'Ming Guangchao: Lighting Up the Light in Juvenile Delinquent's Heart [明广超：点亮失足少年心中的灯]' at http://js.jcrb.com/rwgs/201010/t20101014_454600.shtml (last accessed on 19 March 2012).

1.4.1 Positive Appraisals

Praise in the scholarly work mainly revolves around criminal reconciliation's tangible benefits to all the three parties to the criminal procedure, namely the suspect/defendant, the victim and the officials or state authorities. For instance, according to Ge Lin, criminal reconciliation has effectively allowed the victim to obtain satisfactory (monetary) compensation, largely eased the tension between the parties and raised efficiency in dealing with criminal cases.[194]

In order to support these positive assessments, Ge Lin draws on some data from studies sponsored by state authorities;[195] some of her information was taken from media reports.[196] For example, according to Ge, a study of seven basic-level People's Procuratorates in Beijing indicates that the average amount of compensation in criminal reconciliation cases is 18,200 yuan, far more than the amount in minor injury cases decided by the courts, which is only 6,300 yuan.[197] Ge praises the larger amount of compensation in criminal reconciliation cases as the main reason leading to 'victim satisfaction' and as reducing the tension between the suspect/defendant and the victim.

Moreover, Ge says that according to a study conducted by a Procuratorate of Yima city in Henan province, a minor injury case normally takes 115 to 135 days at the prosecution stage of the criminal process, while it only takes about 90 days in criminal reconciliation if the People's Procuratorate decides not to prosecute, and on average 30 days if the Public Security Bureau decides to withdraw the case directly after it has been mediated successfully.[198]

Some other scholars have also addressed these two aspects of criminal reconciliation. For example, Chen Qi applauds the smooth 'enforcement' of compensation in criminal reconciliation cases (i.e. the fact that suspects/defendants will not get lenient treatment until they have paid the

---

194 Ge Lin [葛琳] *On Criminal Reconciliation* [*刑事和解研究*] Beijing, The Chinese People's Public Security University Press [中国人民公安大学出版社] 2008, 301–2.

195 Ibid. As noted, Ge Lin used the information and data provided in the surveys conducted by Beijing Dongcheng district People's Procuratorate and Beijing Chaoyang district People's Procuratorate and the People's Procuratorate of Yima City in Henan Province.

196 Ibid. Ge Lin provides examples taken from the *Procuratorial Daily* [检察日报] and *Chongqing Evening News* [重庆晚报].

197 Ibid. The study used by Ge Lin here is conducted by Beijing Dongcheng district People's Procuratorate.

198 Ibid.

compensation they have promised as part of the compensation agreement) as leading to a resolution of the difficulty with enforcing sentences.[199] Also addressing the raising of efficiency in dealing with criminal cases, Chen Ruihua says that in some minor criminal cases, like intentional injury 'crime,' evidence is usually very hard to collect, and collecting it requires a great many resources.[200] Limited resources and the increased number of criminal cases require a more reasonable allocation of existing resources.[201] A system that could alleviate the prosecutor's and the judge's workload and allow them to put more effort into more serious cases is therefore needed.[202] Criminal reconciliation, which is able to close minor criminal cases in a shorter period (and with less effort spent), according to Chen Ruihua, is a system serving this end.[203]

Ge Lin further praises criminal reconciliation's effect of educating and rehabilitating the suspect/defendant,[204] a point also supported by many other scholars.[205] For example, Sun Qin says that in criminal reconciliation cases handled by the People's Procuratorate, the suspect could get

---

199 Chen Qi [陈颀] 'The Incentive Mechanism of "Reducing Punishment with Money" ["赔钱减刑" 的激励机制]' in Su Li [苏力] (ed) *Law and Social Sciences* [*法律和社会科学*] Beijing, Law Press [法律出版社] 2009, 30.

200 Chen Ruihua [陈瑞华] *Criminal Proceedings: The Chinese Model* [*刑事诉讼的中国模式*] Beijing, Law Press [法律出版社] 2008, 17–19.

201 Ma Mingliang [马明亮] *Negotiated Justice: A New Procedural Idea* [*协商性司法：一种新程序主义理念*] Beijing, Law Press [法律出版社] 2007, 1–5.

202 Supra note 200, 16–17.

203 Ibid.

204 Supra note 194, 302.

205 This viewpoint can be found in much domestic work discussing the values of criminal reconciliation. See: e.g. Sun Qin [孙勤] *An Analysis of the Values of Victim–Offender Reconciliation* [*刑事和解价值分析*] Beijing, The Chinese People's Public Security University Press [中国人民公安大学出版社] 2009, 154; Ge Lin [葛琳] *On Criminal Reconciliation* [*刑事和解研究*] Beijing, The Chinese People's Public Security University Press [中国人民公安大学出版社] 2008, 45; Wu Xiaofeng [武小凤] *Conflict and Compromise: On Criminal Reconciliation* [*冲突与对接：刑事和解刑法制度研究*] Beijing, The Chinese People's Public Security University Press [中国人民公安大学出版社] 2008, 180–81; Miu Weihui [缪伟辉] '刑事和解的价值提取 [The Values of Criminal Reconciliation]' (2010) 10 *Legal System and Society* [*法制与社会*] 20; Xiang Chaoyang [向朝阳] Ma Jinghua [马静华] 'The Establishment of the Values of Criminal Reconciliation and Its Chinese Pattern [刑事和解的价值构造及中国模式的构建]' (2003) 6 *Chinese Legal Science* [*中国法学*] 115.

the official's decision not to prosecute and thus avoid a criminal record. In cases that have already been transferred to the People's Court, the defendant could normally get a non-custodial sentence if criminal reconciliation is successful.[206] This, according to Sun, means that the suspect/defendant could be rehabilitated in society whereas, by contrast, time in prison would make rehabilitation tough.[207] Zhou Shixiong observes that according to follow-up interviews with juvenile suspects after the conclusion of criminal reconciliation programmes in Hunan province, 100 percent of the juvenile suspects were assessed as 'performing well' in school and 86 percent of them had made obvious progress in study.[208]

Based on the above, Xiang Chaoyang and Ma Jinghua suggest that criminal reconciliation serves the 'value of justice' (*gongzheng jiazhi*).[209] This 'value of justice,' according to Xiang and Ma, means that criminal

---

[206] Ordinarily, in a case with the prosecutor's decision not to prosecute, the suspect will still have a criminal record which will affect his/her employment and education, and so on. Also, a person with a criminal record is not qualified for the civil service examination and army enlistment. Article 100 of the PRC Criminal Law stipulates that 'when people join the military, or seek employment, those who received criminal punishments according to law should honestly report the punishments they received to the relevant units and should not conceal them.' See the English translation at: http://chinalawtranslate.com/%E4%B8%AD%E5%8D%8E%E4%BA%BA%E6%B0%91%E5%85%B1%E5%92%8C%E5%9B%BD%E5%88%91%E6%B3%95%EF%BC%882015%E5%B9%B4%E4%BF%AE%E6%AD%A3%EF%BC%89/ (last accessed on 6 May 2016). Article 24 of the Civil Servant Law of the People's Republic of China stipulates that 'anyone who has been imposed on a criminal punishment shall not be employed as a civil servant.' 'Criminal record system is long deemed as to be helpful for recidivism prevention.' See the English translation at: http://www.pkulaw.cn/fulltext_form.aspx?Db=chl&Gid=58050 (last accessed on 6 May 2016). But in criminal reconciliation, the suspect's criminal record will be expunged together with the decision of non-prosecution, so that the suspect's future life will not be influenced by the record/his past wrongdoing. See: Sun Qin [孙勤] *An Analysis of the Values of Victim–Offender Reconciliation* [*刑事和解价值分析*] Beijing, The Chinese People's Public Security University Press [中国人民公安大学出版社] 154.

[207] Sun Qin [孙勤] ibid.

[208] Zhou Shixiong [周世雄] 'On Criminal Reconciliation: Taking the Exploration of Criminal Reconciliation in Hunan Province as an Analytic Sample [也论刑事和解制度：以湖南省检察机关的刑事和解探索为分析样本]' (2008) 3 *Law Review* [*法学评论*] 21.

[209] Xiang Chaoyang [向朝阳] Ma Jinghua [马静华] 'The Establishment of the Values of Criminal Reconciliation and Its Chinese Pattern [刑事和解的价值构造及中国模式的构建]' (2003) 6 *Chinese Legal Science* [*中国法学*] 114.

reconciliation 'has balanced the protection of the interests of the [participants in] three roles in criminal procedure, namely the [interests of the] victim, the suspect and the state authorities. This is different from the normal criminal procedure in which the victim is often ignored.'[210]

In addition to the benefits to the parties and the state authorities, criminal reconciliation is also praised by scholars for meeting the expectations articulated by the Supreme People's Procuratorate and the Supreme People's Court, namely the expectations of bringing 'closure' to criminal cases and preventing 'petitioning related to judicial cases.' Scholars like Chen Ruihua argue that the traditional core goals of the PRC Criminal Law, which he identifies as combating crimes and punishing criminals, cannot resolve the conflict between the victim and the suspect/defendant caused by the crime.[211] Under the traditional goals, the conflict still exists after the case has been closed, so the parties may be dissatisfied with the judicial system.[212] The victim would feel more dissatisfied facing a long-standing problem with the Chinese judicial system, namely, it is extremely hard to enforce the court's sentence in cases where a civil dispute about compensation has been joined to the criminal litigation.[213] These two elements, according to Chen, are the main cause leading to 'petitioning related to judicial cases' (*she fa shangfang* or *she su shangfang*), which has been viewed by the government as a symptom of lack of 'harmony' in society and therefore a phenomenon that needed to be tackled.[214] Criminal reconciliation, possessing the aforementioned advantage of 'enforcing' compensation obligations, is then praised by these scholars for having the function of closing cases and preventing the parties (mainly the victim) from petitioning.[215] In practice the statistics seem to support this argument – for example, in 2014, the Procuratorate of Huangmei county in Hubei province had conducted criminal reconciliation in 43 cases at the stage of examination for arrest, and there was no appeal or petitioning in those 43

---

210 Ibid.

211 Supra note 200, 19.

212 Ibid.

213 Article 77 of the 1996 PRC Criminal Procedural Law provides that 'if a victim has suffered material losses as a result of the defendant's offence, he shall have the right to file an collateral civil appeals during the course of the criminal proceeding.' However, due to various reasons, usually the victim with the court sentence concerning 'civil compensation' cannot get the sentence enforced. See: Chen Ruihua [陈瑞华] ibid.

214 Ibid.

215 Ibid.

cases after the Procuratorate decided not to arrest the suspects.[216] On the eve of the promulgation of the revised Criminal Procedure Law, Chaoyang District People's Procuratorate published their survey on 100 criminal reconciliation cases they had conducted between 2002 and 2012, which showed that 100 percent of the parties (including the victim and the offender) reported satisfaction with criminal reconciliation's justice, and criminal reconciliation had achieved the effectiveness called 'four zeros,' namely, zero recidivism, zero new dispute between the parties, zero lawsuit lodged by a victim out of poor protection of his/her interests, zero appeal and petitioning.[217]

Based on this effect, Chen Ruihua suggests that criminal reconciliation serves 'the value of harmony' (*hexie jiazhi*), which, according to Chen, comes from its function of restoring relationships in society.[218] As interpreted by Chen, the 'value of harmony' has nothing to do with either the procedure or outcome of the criminal process; rather, 'it is a wholly new value in addition to, as well as "challenging" the traditional two values of procedural fairness and justice of outcomes.'[219]

Without further elaboration, however, such a view of a new value is too vague to understand. As a 'challenge' to the values of procedural fairness and justice of outcomes according to Chen Ruihua, is this third value of 'harmony' in contradiction with the other two values (or can it be)? If this is the case, how should we understand the relationship between criminal reconciliation and a rights-centred conception of justice?

Xiao Shiwei and Ma Jinghua argue that criminal reconciliation has shown 'communication between State law and customs in society' by

---

216 Xiao Zhiyun [肖之云] 'Huangmei: "Two Fast One Trial" Criminal Reconciliation Are Effective [黄梅：'两快一审'刑事和解显成效]' at http://www.hbjc.gov.cn/ssjd/201509/t20150907_714579.shtml (last accessed on 1 November 2015).

217 Yang Mengchen [杨孟辰] Zhang Shuyang [张舒阳] '北京朝阳检察院十年刑事和解工作当事人满意率100% [Beijing Chaoyang Procuratorate Implemented Criminal Reconciliation for Ten Years 100 Percent of Parties Satisfied]' at http://legal.people.com.cn/n/2012/0926/c42510-19110709.html (last accessed on 1 November 2015).

218 Excerpted from Chen Ruihua [陈瑞华]'s talk collected in Criminal Reconciliation: A Conversation Between Legal Experts and Legal Scholars [刑事和解: 法律家与法学家对话录] at http://www.procedurallaw.cn/xsss/zdwz/200807/t20080724_51763.html (last accessed on 24 October 2011).

219 Ibid.

absorbing the practice of 'resolving crimes privately' (*xing'an si liao*), which is common in Chinese society, into the legal framework.[220]

'Resolving crimes privately' refers to situations in which 'issues of alleged criminal responsibility that should be processed by judicial organs are simply sorted out by the parties privately.'[221] Many scholars, including Xiao and Ma, view this as an ultimately problematic practice. For instance, according to Xiao and Ma, '*xing'an si liao*,' even if it could in some cases satisfy both parties, has harmed the interests of the State, since it 'excludes the State's participation in (suspected) criminal cases.'[222] Li Lianfeng and Shang Shumin characterize such 'exclusion' of the State in handling criminal cases as a '[sign of] disregard for and a challenge to the State law and legal policies.'[223] Chen Yufan and Qu Guangchen express the concern that '*xing'an si liao*' may lead to 'hidden trouble' for society by leaving unpunished 'offenders' in society.[224] Some other scholars note the potential harm of '*xing'an si liao*' to the individual parties. For example, Chen Yufan and Qu Guangchen say that coercive 'reconciliation' is very likely to happen in '*si liao*' (i.e. when one party has more power and influence).[225] Zhang Shuqin claims that it has been found that in practice, officials, in particular the police, also play some role in '*si liao*,' which might result in rent-seeking, judicial corruption and encourage coercive 'reconciliation.'[226]

Yet scholars acknowledge that '*xing'an si liao*' is very popular in China. According to Zhang Shuqin, it has been found that, in 2001, 70 percent of the intentional injury cases, theft cases and bigamy cases in

---

220 Xiao Shiwei [肖仕卫] Ma Jinghua [马静华] 'The Unique Function of Criminal Reconciliation in China: From the Perspective of Resolving the Problem of "Solving Criminal Cases Privately" [中国刑事和解的独特功能：以刑事案件"私了"问题之解决为起点的分析]' (2010) 2 *Criminal Science* [*中国刑事法杂志*] 63.

221 Chen Yufan [陈玉范] Qu Guangchen [屈广臣] 'Thoughts on "Private Resolution" ["私了"问题的法律思考]' (1995) 1 *Modern Legal Science* [*当代法学*] 24.

222 Supra note 220, 65.

223 Li Lianfeng [李连峰] Shang Shumin [尚淑敏] 'On the Construction of Criminal Reconciliation System: On the Basis of "Private Resolution" among the People [论我国刑事和解制度的构建：以民间"私了"传统为基础的构建模式]' (2009) 12 *Academic Exchange* [*学术交流*] 83.

224 Supra note 221, 24.

225 Ibid.

226 Zhang Shuqin [张书琴] 'Treating Criminal Reconciliation Rationally [理性对待刑事和解]' (2007) 3 *Hebei Law Science* [*河北法学*] 120.

Leping city in Jiangsu province were solved privately.[227] Another study conducted by a law firm in Shandong province in 2003 indicates that 25 percent of 'crimes' in rural China have been resolved through this way.[228] It should be noted, however, that neither of these studies mentions the way in which they collected their data.

Xiao Shiwei and Ma Jinghua do not attribute the popularity of '*xing'an si liao*' to the Chinese citizen's ignorance of or disregard for the law, as is often done; they argue that it is due to what they view as incoherence between the State law and social customs, and this needs to be addressed.[229] The way to address it, according to Xiao and Ma, is for the State law to 'critically acknowledge this custom,' which is reached by criminal reconciliation.[230]

Some other scholars praise the value of criminal reconciliation from the perspective of traditional Chinese culture. For example, Li Lianfeng and Shang Shumin say that 'the popularity of "*xing'an si liao*" reflects a value of Chinese culture and embodies Confucian ideas of "no litigation" (*wu song*) and "valuing peace" or "valuing harmony" (*he wei gui*),' so it is worthwhile to have a system like criminal reconciliation in the legal framework to address such practices.[231] Several scholars even suggest learning from what they describe as a customary Tibetan law:[232]

> After offences like murder and intentional injury, the parties do not resort to any judicial authority; they would invite agencies with [high social] standing to help them communicate with each other and invite members of their families to discuss and assess the loss in the case, and then to resolve the cases through reconciliation and compensation.

This compensation is aptly called '*pei ming jia*' ('赔命价' or literally 'the price for [a] life') or '*pei xue jia*' ('赔血价' or literally 'blood price') in the work just cited.[233]

Therefore, in these scholars' opinions, criminal reconciliation is a system showing the State law's adoption of customs that have always existed in Chinese society, while at the same time 'overcoming the

---

227 Ibid.

228 Ibid.

229 Supra note 220, 24.

230 Ibid.

231 Supra note 223, 83.

232 Ma Congcong [马丛丛] 'An Examination of the Idea of Restorative Justice Embodied in the Customary Tibetan Law [藏族习惯法之现代恢复性司法理念审查]' (2011) 7 *Business Culture* [*商业文化*] 17.

233 Ibid.

shortcomings of *xing'an si liao*' with participation from and oversight by state authorities.[234] It is, according to them, of great significance to the establishment of 'the socialist rule of law with Chinese characteristics' and the 'increase of State's capacity of ruling society at the grassroots.'[235]

Nevertheless, there might be three problems with this praise. First, as noted in the previous part, criminal reconciliation was initially implemented in comparatively developed locations in China such as Beijing and Jiangsu province, not rural China where the State law is much weaker and customs are much stronger. This calls into question this purported function of 'connecting the State law and customs in society' through criminal reconciliation. Second, criminal reconciliation is conducted in cases handled by the Public Security Bureau/People's Procuratorate/People's Court, namely in cases that have already come into the hands of state authorities. These scholars did not indicate whether this mechanism was able to attract matters potentially to be resolved privately into the state authorities. Therefore, it might be far-fetched to appraise criminal reconciliation as helpful to address the problem of '*xing'an si liao*.' Third, the enthusiasm for adopting 'customs' such as '*pei ming jia*' or '*pei xue jia*' without careful and in-depth examination of these customs and the context in which these customs emerged and existed might be too facile. Also, it might be too facile to assert the value of traditional culture, namely Confucian ideology in the legal framework.

In addition, there is a crucial problem with all these positive appraisals expressed by the scholars – they all build their praise largely on information provided in the Procuratorate/Court's reports. The heavy reliance on official sources raises doubts as to the reliability of the factual basis upon which they make such assessment, given especially that these data were collected at a time when the Procuratorates/Courts in question were expected to participate in the promotion of the Party's 'harmonious society' policies through their contribution to criminal reconciliation.[236]

1.4.2 Concerns and Criticisms

In general, criticism and concerns over criminal reconciliation focus on two issues – fairness and voluntariness. Concerning whether or not criminal reconciliation is unfair to economically weak suspects/

---

[234] Supra note 220, 67.

[235] Ibid.

[236] Further discussion of the issue of reliability of official sources can be found in Chapter 3.

defendants, perhaps the most serious problem has been that the main focus of this process is on the amount of compensation to be paid to the victim.

For instance, Ge Lin observes that in practice the payment of compensation has been normally adopted by the official as the most important, or even the only, standard to assess whether or not the parties have achieved mutual understanding, the suspect/defendant is remorseful and has obtained the victim's forgiveness.[237] According to Ge, rarely could we find that a criminal reconciliation programme ends without the payment of compensation.[238]

Therefore, some comments on criminal reconciliation are along the lines of 'if you have money, you will get a lenient sentence; if you are poor, you will go to prison.'[239] Criminal reconciliation programmes have accordingly been criticized as unfair to the poor, since 'the rich can pay money to avoid punishment' (*yi qian shu xing* or *pei qian jian xing*).[240] Compensation agreed upon in the context of criminal reconciliation has tellingly been called 'reconciliation fee' (*hejie fei*), and criminal reconciliation has been characterized as a 'trade-off between money and [the victim's] rights' (*quan qian jiaoyi*).[241] Further, some scholars have warned that criminal reconciliation like this is actually harmful to the establishment of a 'harmonious society,' since it is likely to sharpen contradictions and trigger discontent in society.[242]

Li Ming characterizes criminal reconciliation as a mechanism 'all about money.'[243] And, according to Li, those who like it most are officials, since it could 'largely facilitate rent-seeking and corruption.'[244]

---

237 Ge Lin [葛琳] 'An Analysis of the Practical Predicament of Criminal Reconciliation [刑事和解的现实困境解析]' (2010) 5 *Justice of China* [*中国司法*] 19.

238 Ibid.

239 Li Hongjiang [李洪江] 'The Implementation of Criminal Reconciliation Should be Slowed Down' [刑事和解应缓行] (2006) 5 *Chinese Prosecutors* [*中国检察官*] 13.

240 Ibid.

241 Shan Shibing [单士兵] 'The "Illusion of Harmony" behind Criminal Reconciliation [刑事和解背后的 "和谐幻觉"]' at http://gb.cri.cn/9083/2006/11/23/2165@1317252.htm (last accessed on 24 February 2012).

242 Ibid.

243 Li Ming [黎明] 'The "All-about-Money" Criminal Reconciliation Is Damage [要钱的刑事和解是祸水]' at http://news.ifeng.com/opinion/society/detail_2009_08/18/1303072_0.shtml (last accessed on 5 November 2011).

244 Ibid.

Yet in the meantime, scholars are arguing that there is no such problem of unfairness in criminal reconciliation. For instance, Zhang Fuxiong says that an exclusive focus on compensation in criminal reconciliation is similar with '*shuxing*' (赎刑), a practice which had been adopted in laws in ancient China since the Qin and Han dynasties.[245] *Shuxing* translates roughly as 'redemption of punishment' and it was always closely connected to the making of payments by the culprit. Although '*shuxing*' is different from criminal reconciliation since it only allows certain privileged categories of persons to 'pay money to avoid punishment,' Zhang argues that the exclusive focus on compensation in criminal reconciliation could be justified by this ancient system in China for its 'absorption of the traditional system.'[246] Yet by saying this, Zhang does not discuss whether '*shuxing*' is a fair and just system. The simple 'absorption' of a traditional system cannot justify the (potential problem of) unfairness of criminal reconciliation.

Du Yu also defends criminal reconciliation as a fair process by arguing that 'equality in the sense of law refers to equality of opportunity' and 'criminal reconciliation actually provides this equality of opportunity to all the suspects/defendants.'[247] Besides, the outcomes in criminal reconciliation cases (i.e. withdrawing the case, non-prosecution or suspended sentence) are 'the results of compensating the loss, which indeed shows the suspect/defendant's attitudes and inclination to be good, not of the wealth he/she possesses.'[248]

Likewise, Wang Zhixiang and Zhang Weike argue that in criminal reconciliation 'money is no more than a signal to show the suspect/defendant's attitudes and "harmfulness to society" (*shehui weihaixing*).'[249] And 'whether or not the suspect/defendant can get a lighter sentence is absolutely up to the judge,' who will 'oversee not only the

---

245 Zhang Fuxiong [张孚雄] 'Thoughts on the Use of Criminal Reconciliation in Serious Crimes [重罪案件刑事和解的理论思考]' (2011) 2 *Law and Economy* [*法制与经济*] 185.

246 Ibid.

247 Du Yu [杜宇] '"Criminal Conciliation": Critics and Preliminary Response ["刑事和解"：批评意见与初步回应]' 8.

248 Ibid.

249 Wang Zhixiang [王志祥] Zhang Weike [张伟珂] 'On the Legitimacy of Criminal Reconciliation in Capital Cases [死刑案件中刑事和解的正当性探究]' (2011) 4 *Northern Legal Science* [*北方法学*] 52.

criminal reconciliation process, but also the other facts and evidence in the case concerned to guarantee the legality of criminal reconciliation cases.'[250]

In the author's view, however, these justifications are far-fetched and unacceptable. For one thing, it is hard to assert that the suspect/defendant who is too poor to compensate does not truly feel regretful (or even that the poor suspect/defendant is less 'inclined to be good') or has more 'harmfulness to society,' and vice versa. For another, the argument concerning the 'outcome' in compensation is hard to understand – how to make the link between the wealth the suspect/defendant possesses and the amount of compensation he/she ought to pay?

The second main concern with criminal reconciliation is the public power's infringement upon the parties' voluntariness in this process. For instance, Du Yu claims that there are two forms of 'coercion' in criminal reconciliation – one is defined by him as 'obvious coercion,' which means that 'one party with advantages in status, influence or economic conditions may pressurize the other party to "reconcile" through threatening or intimidating [the other party], or buying [them] off etc.'[251] Yet Du thinks that this form of coercion could be effectively addressed through the supervision (*jiandu*) and examination of the parties' real intentions by the officials.[252]

The other form of coercion the parties may be confronted with in criminal reconciliation is named by Du as 'subtle coercion.'[253] This 'subtle coercion,' according to Du, may first come from the 'harsh treatment the suspect/defendant thinks may be imposed in the normal criminal procedure' such as arrest and incarceration.[254] It may also come from the (negative) comments from other people living around the parties or the public opinion.[255] The third form of 'subtle coercion' in criminal reconciliation processes, according to Du, comes from the officials' 'inducement' (i.e. through exaggerating the risk and adverse impact of the normal procedure, and fabricating information).[256]

Du Yu further contends that the first two forms of 'subtle coercion' could not be said to violate the parties' voluntariness in criminal reconciliation. Because 'in the first case, the parties make their decisions

250 Ibid, 44.
251 Supra note 248, 12.
252 Ibid.
253 Supra note 248.
254 Ibid.
255 Ibid.
256 Ibid.

based on a balance of costs and benefits' (i.e. 'how much reconciliation is worth for me to avoid criminal record and punishment'); and in the second case, Du argues that 'although the parties may be influenced, after all they can still make decisions freely.'[257] Only the third form of 'subtle coercion,' according to Du, has violated the parties' voluntariness.[258] Because, 'the officials possess absolute advantages in knowledge, information and experience etc. in comparison with the parties in criminal reconciliation,' and in practice, 'the parties are facing the same official if they refuse the officials' "suggestions" in criminal reconciliation,' which is very likely to make the parties feel worried about any adverse outcomes in the criminal case.[259] Therefore, as argued by Du, it is very hard for the parties to resist the officials' intentions in criminal reconciliation processes, even though they do not want to accept them.[260]

Other scholars also suggest reasons to worry about public power's infringement upon the parties' rights in criminal reconciliation. For example, Chen Weidong observes that criminal reconciliation has actually given 'added power to the officials,' which 'may provide the officials with another opportunity of rent-seeking.'[261] Xu Yang expresses concern that this infringement upon the parties' rights and voluntariness by public power is very likely to happen in criminal reconciliation, because 'this programme is now promoted vigorously by the government and has been connected with so many political goals.'[262] These, according to Xu, are strong incentives for the officials to abuse their power in criminal reconciliation that would harm the parties' voluntariness and rights.[263]

In order to address this problem, scholars are keen on an adequate supervision (*jiandu*) mechanism to curb the officials' power in criminal reconciliation.[264] For example, Ge Lin writes:[265]

---

257 Ibid.

258 Ibid.

259 Ibid.

260 Ibid.

261 Chen Ruihua [陈瑞华] 'Criminal Reconciliation: A Conversation Between Legal Experts and Legal Scholars [刑事和解：法律家和法学家的对话]' at http://www.procedurallaw.cn/xsss/zdwz/200807/t20080724_51763.html (last accessed on 24 October 2011).

262 Xu Yang [徐阳] 'Harmfulness of and Safeguard Against Power Abuse in Criminal Reconciliation [刑事和解中权力过度推进之危害及其防范]' (2009) 6 *Legal Review* [*法学评论*] 134.

263 Ibid.

264 Chen Weidong [陈卫东] 'Several Opinions on Criminal Reconciliation [关于刑事和解的几点看法]' (2009) 3 *Chinese Laws* [*中国法律*] 12.

265 Supra note 194, 303.

> Criminal reconciliation leads to particular needs of checks (on the officials' power) and the passive role (of the officials' role in this programme). The initiative in criminal reconciliation programmes should be on the parties' side. Even so, public power has been so strong in criminal reconciliation, now that officials can decide to initiate this programme entirely by themselves. Therefore, checks from inside and outside of this system are of great significance to curb the abuse of power and prevent judicial corruption.

Yet such a supervision system to curb public power in criminal reconciliation processes is not addressed in the 2012 CPL. Furthermore, it would be difficult to create an effective supervision system in the Chinese criminal justice system taking into account the problems and 'malfunctioning' of the current supervision system stipulated in the Criminal Procedure Law. Indeed, the very idea of 'supervision' in the Chinese context may be in itself problematic. These points are discussed in detail in Chapter 6.

As described above, although neither the local regulations or guidelines nor the 2012 CPL allows it, the use of criminal reconciliation in practice has been extended from suspected minor crimes to felonies and capital cases. This 'development' has triggered much debate and concern in Chinese academia. Scholars who are generally supportive of the practice may still be critical of what they see as its excessive uses.

The primary justification for the use of criminal reconciliation in capital cases is concerned with its intended function of implementing the Party's policy of 'killing less, killing with restraint' (*shao sha, shen sha*) and an effective way to restrict the use of the death penalty in China. Nevertheless, it has been heavily criticized by the scholars. Scholars such as Liang Genlin and Sun Wanhuai argue that 'the control of [uses of the] death penalty should not rely on criminal reconciliation which almost upgrades compensation as the unique element in judges' consideration in capital sentence.'[266] That is to say, if the payment of compensation by the victim can lawfully become a major consideration affecting the judge's sentence in capital cases, this might reinforce the impression that life could also be 'bought' with money, and if you were too poor to afford compensation, you would have to face the death penalty.

Is criminal reconciliation in capital cases and suspected serious crimes legitimate, then, if it does *not* focus on compensation? Liang Genlin sees this 'extension' as an 'erosion of the State's power to impose criminal

---

[266] Liang Genlin [梁根林] 'Ten Falsification in Using Criminal Reconciliation in Death Penalty Cases [死刑案件被刑事和解的十大证伪]' (2010) 4 *Legal Science* [法学] 18; supra note 184.

punishment,' because it has 'privatized the Criminal Law to an extreme,' and is actually an 'excuse for the state to evade its responsibility in addressing the damage caused by crime.'[267] According to Liang, compensating the victim's loss caused by the crime should not only be the offender's responsibility; rather, the state should also take this responsibility through, for instance, establishing a national compensation system (to redress the loss of the victim).[268] Moreover, Liang claims that the use of criminal reconciliation in capital cases has seriously violated the 'passive nature of the judiciary' (*sifa de beidong xing*) due to its great reliance on the officials' discretion, which is very likely to cause judicial corruption.[269]

Another scholar, Sun Wanhuai, also criticizes the use of criminal reconciliation in homicide cases on the grounds that the implementation of criminal reconciliation in these cases makes the victim's lost life part of a bargaining process, in which the victim's relatives, who bargain for compensation, have necessarily replaced the (direct) victim.[270] This is, according to Sun, 'also a violation of [the principle of] criminal reconciliation in itself, since this process calls for communication and negotiation between the (direct) parties themselves in resolving the case.'[271]

The arguments advanced by Liang and Sun seem more persuasive and may not be limited to criminal reconciliation used in death penalty cases and suspected serious crimes. As already mentioned, Liang criticizes the official's discretion in this process as a violation of the 'passive nature of judiciary' that potentially harms the parties' rights. However, as mentioned earlier, this might also be a problem with the use of criminal reconciliation in suspected minor crimes and Liang offers no reason for why this problem exists only in major cases. Likewise, Sun's argument may have ignored the point that in traffic accident related crime cases (which belong to 'minor crime'), the (direct) victim may also be dead when criminal reconciliation is initiated so there is also no communication between the direct parties. In sum, Liang and Sun's criticisms sound as though criminal reconciliation is justifiable in suspected minor crimes (as provided in the local regulations or guidelines governing criminal reconciliation as pilot practices and the 2012 CPL). Yet they do

---

267 Ibid 15–17.
268 Ibid.
269 Ibid 19.
270 Supra note 184, 185.
271 Ibid.

not explain why these concerns around criminal reconciliation in serious 'crimes' and death penalty cases can be set aside in minor criminal cases.

The support for the availability of criminal reconciliation otherwise (concerning its outcome of a lenient sentence), in particular by defendants and their lawyers, is understandable considering what a severe criminal justice system they are facing,[272] and their support might be more the result of China's flawed criminal justice system. Yet given these abovementioned problems with criminal reconciliation, this goal, while understandable in individual cases, should not blind us to the potential injustice of this system. The injustice will be further elaborated in the ensuing chapters.

[272] See, e.g. Dui Hua, a nonprofit humanitarian organization, estimates that there are around 4,000 executions of death penalty in China every year, 'Dui Hua Estimates 4,000 Executions in China, Welcomes Open Dialogue' https://sna.etapestry.com/prod/viewEmailAsPage.do?databaseId=DuiHuaFoundation&mailingId=22213781&personaRef=11073.0.152691&jobRef=2967.0.31681565&memberId=789166155&erRef=11073.0.152697&key=e2eacaff46787bfeefcaa24cf35264c7 (last accessed on 1 March 2012).

2. A comparative look at criminal reconciliation: a transplant of restorative justice?

What has been accompanying the pilot practices of criminal reconciliation is the heated debate among domestic Chinese scholars over the 'nature' (*xingzhi*) of this programme. In general, domestic professionals suggest two ways of understanding this programme: the first one may be simplified as 'looking outside' – domestic Chinese scholars of this school have focused themselves on restorative justice – keen on presenting the resemblances between criminal reconciliation and restorative justice, and the merits of restorative justice, they were seeking justification for its adoption in the Chinese criminal proceedings. On the other hand, another school of scholars, such as Su Li and Fan Yu, stick to their aim of 'looking inside' – as elaborated in Chapter 1, they maintain that criminal reconciliation is a purely indigenous Chinese practice which develops from as well as fits Chinese history, culture, custom, and importantly, the Chinese people's preference and demands. In his article 'China's Turn Against Law,' Carl Minzner compares China's national shift towards mediation since the 2000s with such a shift happening in other developing countries, which primarily results from the (deemed failure) of the law-and-development and the (emergence) of the law-and-society movement.[1] Su Li and Fan Yu are acknowledged as leading scholars in China's law-and-society study field.[2] However, as also critically discussed in the previous chapter, with the rise of rights consciousness in Chinese society, what the scholars like Su Li and Fan Yu maintain is debatable and serves the authorities' political ends. Consequently, public power or coercive force is almost bound to take a critical role in criminal reconciliation in

[1] Carl F. Minzner 'China's Turn Against Law' (2011) Vol. LIX No. 4 *The American Journal of Comparative Law* 964.

[2] A comprehensive overview of China's society-and-law research and the development of the sociology of law in Liu Sida and Wang Zhizhou 'The Fall and Rise of Law and Social Science in China' (2015) Vol. 11 *Annual Review of Law and Social Science* 373–85.

China. In fact, in the author's fieldwork, multiple interviewees, including the parties, the lawyers, as well as the judicial officers, have expressed a strong desire to comply with the (normal) procedure provided by law. This constitutes the essential difference from the 'backlash' against the law-and-development movement in other developing countries which takes a 'bottom-up' approach and is driven by the dissatisfaction with the shortcomings of 'black letter law' in society, for example in some cases, adhering to the 'black letter law' will lead to an unfair or unjust result, or an ignorance of the wider social context.[3] The shift in China, as pointed out by Minzner, is an 'indigenous rejection of the judicial reforms [towards the rule of law] by Chinese leaders' and is 'tied to a broader politicized takedown' of the judicial institutions.[4] This chapter is not further elaborating on this comparison based on the discussion of scholarly debates surrounding China's veer of judicial reforms towards reconciliation and mediation in Chapter 1. Rather, since the domestic Chinese scholars holding the standpoint of 'looking outside' stare at a broader trend of the popularity of ADR (alternative dispute resolution), in particular restorative justice, this chapter concentrates on a comparison between these two mechanisms.

Viewing criminal reconciliation as China's transplant of restorative justice (translated as '*huifuxing sifa*' or '*huifuxing zhengyi*' in China), scholars define criminal reconciliation with reference to 'Victim-Offender-Reconciliation,' one of the typical forms of restorative justice. Scholars taking this view say that 'criminal reconciliation' equals 'Victim-Offender-Reconciliation' in restorative justice, which means that crimes and contradictions are resolved through negotiation and reconciliation in an attempt to 'restore relationship and social order, repair harm and rectify offenders.'[5] Criminal reconciliation is then highly valued by these scholars with reference to the advantages of 'Victim-Offender-Reconciliation,' including restoring relationship, repairing harm and

[3] Brian Z. Tamanaha 'The Primacy of Society and the Failures of Law and Development' (2009) Vol. 44 *Cornell International Law Journal* 241.

[4] Supra note 1, 968–72.

[5] See e.g. Liu Lingmei [刘凌梅] 'Introduction and Assessment on Criminal Reconciliation in Western Jurisdictions [西方国家刑事和解理论和实践介评]' (2001) Vol. 23 No. 1 *Modern Law Science* [*现代法学*] 152–3 and Ma Jinghua [马静华] 'The Theoretical Basis of Criminal Reconciliation and the Construction of this System in China [刑事和解的理论基础及其在我国的制度构想]' (2003) 4 *Legal Science* [*法律科学(西北政法大学学报)*] 81.

rectifying offenders, and so on.[6] These advantages, it is said, address deficiencies of the Chinese criminal justice system and ultimately help to promote a harmonious society.[7] By characterizing it as a form of 'Victim-Offender-Reconciliation,' these scholars also suggest that the use of criminal reconciliation conforms to 'the global trend of restorative justice.'[8]

Yet some other scholars have claimed that there are a few differences between restorative justice and criminal reconciliation. For example, Zhang Zhaoxia and Xie Caineng argue that restorative justice is an alternative to the normal criminal justice system, while criminal reconciliation is conducted in the context of the normal criminal justice system and also supported by the normal criminal justice system.[9] Chen Ruihua observes that restorative justice stresses *real* communication and exchange between the victim and the suspect/defendant in order to reach restoration, in particular psychologically, while criminal reconciliation mainly focuses on (financial) compensation.[10] Ge Lin notices the

---

6 Zhang Huihua [张辉华] Wang Yuan [王媛] 'On the Introduction and Implementation of Criminal Reconciliation in China from the Perspective of Restorative Justice [从恢复性司法看刑事和解在我国的引入和应用]' at http://www.chinacourt.org/html/article/200411/02/137288.shtml (last accessed on 22 July 2008).

7 *The People's Court Daily [人民法院报]* 'From Controversy to Harmony: The Transplant of Restorative Justice to China [从对抗走向和谐：恢复性司法的本土移植]' at http://news.xinhuanet.com/legal/2007-05/10/content_6080026.htm (last accessed on 2 March 2012).

8 See e.g. Wu Jianxin [吴建新] 'Confusions and Thoughts during the Transplant of Restorative Justice in China [恢复性司法中国化中的困惑与思考]' in Wang Ping [王平] (ed) *Forum on Restorative Justice* [*恢复性司法论坛*] *Vol. 2007* Beijing, China Procuratorial Press [中国检察出版社] 85; Di Xiaohua [狄小华] 'Restorative Justice and Criminal Mediation [复合正义和刑事调解]' in Wang Ping [王平] (ed) *Forum on Restorative Justice* [*恢复性司法论坛*] Vol. 2005 Beijing, Qunzhong Publishing [群众出版社] 126–9.

9 Zhang Zhaoxia [张朝霞] Xie Caineng [谢财能] 'Criminal Reconciliation: Misunderstanding and Clarification [刑事和解：误读与澄清]' in Bian Jianlin [卞建林] and Wang Li [王立] (eds) *Criminal Reconciliation and an Alternative Procedure* [*刑事和解与程序分流*] Beijing, The Chinese People's Public Security University Press [中国人民公安大学出版社] 2010, 202–3.

10 Chen Guoqing [陈国庆], Chen Ruihua [陈瑞华], Wang Jiangcheng [汪建成], Zhang Zhiming [张志铭] *et al* 'Theoretical Basis of Criminal Reconciliation [刑事和解的理论基础]' in Song Yinghui [宋英辉] and Yuan Jinbiao [袁金彪] (eds) *The Theory and Practice of Criminal Reconciliation in China* [*我国刑事和解的理论与实践*] Beijing, Peking University Press [北京大学出版社] 2009, 6.

significance of the community in restorative justice, which, according to Ge, is often missing in criminal reconciliation programmes in China.[11]

Based on discussing the distinctions between restorative justice and criminal reconciliation, these scholars criticize the understanding of criminal reconciliation as a transplant of restorative justice as '[displaying] unnecessary enthusiasm for transplanting systems from western jurisdictions without seriously considering the domestic reality,' which in their view indicates 'some Chinese scholars' lack of confidence in native judicial practices.'[12] In general, these scholars hold that criminal reconciliation emerged entirely due to the Chinese judicial system's striving to resolve its problems by itself, a movement unconnected to any theory or practice, such as restorative justice, in western jurisdictions.[13] In their view, criminal reconciliation, as an indigenous practice, is also able to draw on the problems with the Chinese criminal justice system and thereby help to promote a 'harmonious society.'

The author agrees that criminal reconciliation in China is different from restorative justice and argues below that there are three further major discrepancies between these two systems, which previous scholarly debate has neglected. Importantly, these discrepancies are likely to account for some of the failures of criminal reconciliation, and make it impossible for criminal reconciliation to possess the advantages of restorative justice.

2.1 A SKETCH OF RESTORATIVE JUSTICE

The traditional criminal justice system, with retributive justice as its spiritual core, has dominated in human history for a long time. It is valued as efficient, fair and just with the guarantee of a rigorous procedural system. Yet in the eyes of the restorative justice scholars, it is a 'top-down' approach where decisions are imposed according to strict

---

[11] Ge, Lin [葛琳] *On Criminal Reconciliation* [*刑事和解研究*] Beijing, The Chinese People's Public Security University Press [中国人民公安大学出版社] 2008, 26–7.

[12] Xiao Shiwei [肖仕卫] '"The Third Realm" in Criminal Justice: An Analysis of the Structural Position and Function of Criminal Reconciliation in China [刑事法治的"第三领域": 中国刑事和解制度的结构定位与功能分析]' (2007) Vol. 19 No. 6 *Peking University Law Journal* [*中外法学*] 721–2.

[13] Chen, Ruihua [陈瑞华] 'Private Cooperation in Criminal Proceedings: The Emergence of Criminal Reconciliation in China [刑事诉讼的私力合作模式：刑事和解在中国的兴起]' (2006) 5 *China Legal Science* [*中国法学*] 19.

rules, but leaves very restricted room for offenders and victims as well as those indirectly affected by crimes (summarized as 'stakeholders' of an offence by restorative justice scholars).[14] Although it seems that the offender is the centre of the traditional criminal justice system, retributive justice mainly concerns the punishment imposed on him/her, rather than his/her real need, his/her reintegration and ways to 'make good what [he/she] has done.'[15] As for victims, according to these scholars, they usually play the role of witness serving the overall goal of punishing the offender by the State.[16] Community is rather often missing in the traditional criminal justice system in which the interests of the abstract notion of 'public' or 'state' are the key.[17]

Scholars enthusiastic about restorative justice also criticize retributive justice as both ethically questionable and instrumentally inefficient.[18] For one thing, according to them, punishment asks for the debt to be paid from the offender to the State, whereas in most of the crimes the interests of the State are abstract and hard to define.[19] Hence, the crucial principle of 'proportionality' in deciding punishment is problematic – it is actually very hard to measure how much pain or punishment the offender should be subjected to, to align with the crime he/she has committed.[20] Restorative justice further objects to the deliberate infliction of pain, which is, as maintained by the restorative justice scholars, unethical.[21] For another, the deliberate infliction of pain through punishment is concerned with the offender's past misconducts while it neglects the consequence of punishment.[22] During such a 'backward-looking' process, the offender could be labelled as a morally blameworthy 'bad person' and therefore be rejected by the context he/she lives in. This rejection from the community or

---

[14] Lode Walgrave 'Imposing Restoration Instead of Inflicting Pain: Reflection on the Judicial Reaction to Crime' in Andrew von Hirsch, Julian Roberts, Anthony E. Bottoms, Kent Roach and Mara Schiff (eds) *Restorative Justice & Criminal Justice: Competing or Reconcilable Paradigms?* Oxford, Hart Publishing 2003, 70.

[15] Ibid.

[16] Ibid.

[17] Tony F. Marshall, *Restorative Justice: An Overview* Minnesota, Centre for Restorative Justice & Mediation 1998, 2.

[18] Lode Walgrave 'On Restoration and Punishment: Favorable Similarities and Fortunate Differences' in A. Morris and G. Maxwell (eds) *Restorative Justice for Juveniles* Oxford, Hart Publishing 2001, 17–37.

[19] Ibid.

[20] Ibid.

[21] Supra note 18, 66.

[22] Ibid.

society may further deter the offender's reintegration after punishment.[23] This constitutes hidden perils for future conflicts or recidivism – this is viewed as the 'instrumentally inefficient' part of retributive justice.

Then, in what sense does restorative justice differ from retributive justice? First of all, restorative justice views crime as a violation of people's interests and interpersonal relationships.[24] As claimed by Howard Zehr:[25]

> Crime is a violation of people and relationships. It creates obligations to make things right. Justice involves the victim, the offender, and the community in a search for solutions which promote repair, reconciliation, and reassurance.

Although a wide range of values has been suggested by restorative justice scholars, the core values of restorative justice acknowledged mostly include mutual respect, empowerment of all parties except the facilitator,[26] the neutrality of the facilitator, accountability, consensual, non-coercive participation and decision-making, and the inclusion of all the relevant parties in meaningful dialogue.[27] Divergence on the values of restorative justice also exists. The most debatable one may be the value of non-coercion. Some of the scholars view non-coercive participation and decision-making as an important value of restorative justice, while some others argue that it should not be included as a value of restorative justice.[28] These scholars maintain that, in many cases, the offender chooses to accept the restorative justice programme just to escape from harsher treatments in the formal, retributive criminal justice system, and in some cases, the final agreement is reached under the somewhat

---

[23] Ibid.

[24] Howard Zehr and Harry Mika 'Fundamental Concepts of Restorative Justice' in Declan Roche (ed) *Restorative Justice* England, Dartmouth Publishing Company 2004, 77.

[25] Howard Zehr *Changing Lenses* Ontario, Herald Press 1990, 181.

[26] This means that in the restorative justice process, participants are given power to have a saying, communicate and decide the consequence and agreement reached at the end of the whole process. The facilitator does not have power to influence or give any pressure to the participants during the process but just guide or safeguard the process with their professional knowledge.

[27] Carolyn Hoyle and Richard Young 'Restorative Justice: Assessing the Prospects and Pitfalls' in Mike McConville and Geoffrey Wilson (eds) *The Handbook of the Criminal Justice Process* Oxford, Oxford University Press 2002, 527.

[28] Ibid.

coercive power of the officials, whereas in all these cases the apologies and amendment measures are still voluntarily conducted.[29]

Aiming at this divergence, Howard Zehr proposes a 'restorative continuum' from 'fully restorative' through 'partially restorative' to 'non-restorative.'[30] He suggests six key questions to help judge how restorative a programme or model is: (i) Whether the programme or model addresses harms, needs and causes or not; (ii) To what extent is it victim-oriented; (iii) Whether offenders are encouraged to take responsibilities or not; (iv) Are all the stakeholders of the offence involved? (v) Is it a process involving dialogue and participatory decision-making? (vi) Is it respectful to everyone involved? But this idea of classifying the degree of restorative justice according to different embodied values is not accepted by the mainstream of the research on restorative justice. Most of the scholars insist that coercion should be absent from the restorative justice process.

The first restorative justice practice took place in 1974 in Canada.[31] It took the form of victim-offender-mediation and was used as an alternative to probation for young offenders.[32] In this programme, with the facilitation of a probation officer, two young men apologized to 22 victims whose houses had been vandalized by them.[33] This programme was replicated by Mennonites in the US in 1978 in Elkhart, Indiana.[34] Then it was taken up more and more in Canada and America, leading to the establishment of the Victim-Offender-Reconciliation (VOR) programmes.[35] VOR is recognized as the earliest form of restorative justice programme. It is also what some Chinese scholars mostly refer to as the 'origin' of criminal reconciliation. Victim-offender mediation (VOM) stems from the VOR.[36] It involves bringing together victims and offenders along with a mediator who coordinates and facilitates the face-to-face

---

29 Ibid.

30 Marian Liebmann, *Restorative Justice: How it Works* London and Philadelphia, Jessica Kingsley Publishers 2007, 31.

31 Ibid, 38.

32 Daniel W. Van Ness, Allison Morris, Gabrielle Maxwell 'Introducing Restorative Justice' in Allison Morris and Gabrielle Maxwell (eds) *Restorative Justice for Juveniles* Oxford, Hart Publishing 2003, 4.

33 Supra note 31.

34 Ibid.

35 Ibid.

36 Jennifer Gerarda Brown 'The Use of Mediation to Resolve Criminal Cases: A Procedural Critique' in Declan Roche (ed) *Restorative Justice* London, Ashgate Publishing 2004, 209.

meeting.[37] Most VOM programmes involve face-to-face meetings although some do not require face-to-face meetings by allowing the parties to 'meet' with the mediator by phone, or allowing the mediator to act as a go-between to caucus with each party individually to work out a restitution agreement.[38] In the meeting process, victims describe their experiences of the crime and the effect it has had on them and offenders explain what they did and the reason, answering questions the victim may have.[39] After that, the mediator will help them seek ways to make things right and then reach an agreement.[40] However, this agreement is 'secondary to the initial dialogue between the parties.'[41] VOM emphasizes building relationships between parties and establishing trust with the mediator.[42] Gradually, VOM also involves others who have been affected by the offence or who are present to provide support to the principal parties.[43] Nowadays, restorative justice has become a worldwide trend. Lots of countries have adopted restorative justice theory in their legislation and implemented the practice widely. Over 1,000 programmes worldwide are now viewed as restorative justice.[44]

In 2006, along with the global popularity of restorative justice, the United Nations came up with a definition in its 'Handbook on Restorative Justice Programmes,' which says, 'restorative justice refers to a process for resolving crime by focusing on redressing the harm done to the victims, holding offenders accountable for their actions and, often also, engaging the community in the resolution of that conflict.'[45] And, a restorative justice process is 'any process in which the victim and the offender and, where appropriate, any other individuals or community members affected by a crime participate together actively in the resolution of matters arising from the crime, generally with the help of a facilitator,' and a restorative outcome is 'an agreement reached as a result

---

[37] Supra note 32, 7.

[38] Supra note 36, 212.

[39] Supra note 32, 7.

[40] Ibid.

[41] Paul McCold 'Primary Restorative Justice Practice' in Allison Morris and Gabrielle Maxwell (eds) *Restorative Justice for Juveniles*, 44.

[42] Ibid.

[43] Supra note 32, 7.

[44] Lü Gang [闾刚] 'The Analysis of the Judicial Function and Process of Restorative Justice [恢复性司法功能和过程分析]' (2005) 1 *Journal of Anhui Vocational College of Police Officers* [*安徽职业警官学院学报*] 55.

[45] United Nations Office on Drugs and Crime 'Handbook on Restorative Justice Programmes (2006)' at http://www.unodc.org/pdf/criminal_justice/06-56290_Ebook.pdf (last accessed on 24 January 2008).

of a restorative process, which may include referrals to programmes such as reparation, restitution and community services, aimed at meeting the individual and collective needs and responsibilities of the parties and achieving the reintegration of the victim and the offender.'[46]

On the basis of restorative justice briefly introduced in this part and criminal reconciliation in the previous chapter, below the author discusses three core differences between restorative justice and criminal reconciliation, namely the different roles of community or society, the role of 'reintegrative shaming' and the ultimate goals of the two systems.

2.2 DIFFERENCES BETWEEN CRIMINAL RECONCILIATION AND RESTORATIVE JUSTICE

2.2.1 The Different Roles of Community

Since the 1970s, there has been a trend of 'diversion,' which is to move the offender away from the formal criminal process including prosecution and imprisonment.[47] One of the reasons for this trend is the ideology of 'community treatment' or 'community control' of crime and delinquency, which was advanced by Donald Black as a 'social control' theory.[48] 'Social control' theory views the origins of crime in social conditions (i.e. family, community, school and economic system), so crime prevention and cure must also depend on communities taking responsibility for remedying the conditions causing crime.[49] This theory of 'social control' also arose in the context that the State-centred control (i.e. prison) has been found to be ineffective, and the 'community alternative is viewed as less costly and more humane.'[50] Restorative justice theory is built on the theory of 'social control.'

---

[46] Ibid.

[47] Preston Elrod and R. Scott Ryder *Juvenile Justice: A Social, Historical, and Legal Perspective* Sudbury, Massachusetts, Jones and Bartlett Publishers 2005, 180.

[48] Allan V. Horwitz 'Diversion in the Juvenile Justice System' in Gunter Albrecht and Wolfgang Ludwig-Mayerhofer (eds) *Diversion and Informal Social Control* Berlin, Walter de Gruyter 1995, 17.

[49] Tony F. Marshall, *Restorative Justice: An Overview* Minnesota, Centre for Restorative Justice & Mediation 1998, 2.

[50] Ibid.

Accordingly, in restorative justice not only the offender but also the community has the responsibility for the loss caused by the crime.[51] Accordingly, restorative justice asks not only the offender but also the community to 'remedy the conditions leading to crime,' to 'support the offender's reintegration,' and to 'provide general welfare in an attempt to redress the (victim's and offender's) harm caused by the crime,' and to 'strengthen the community to prevent re-offending.'[52]

Moreover, in restorative justice, community members are recognized as 'indirect victims,' who are harmed by the crime and need reparation as well.[53] So they are also invited to participate in restorative justice programmes to resolve the problem together with those 'direct parties' (namely, the victim and the offender in the case concerned) and to get reparation.[54]

It seems that this theory can be found in criminal reconciliation in China: the decisions officials suggest lenient decisions to the suspect/defendant if they can comply with the reconciliation agreements – at the most, non-custodial sentences will be given, or there will be a decision to withdraw the case, not to prosecute, or to give a suspended sentence. Besides, criminal reconciliation values rehabilitating and correcting offenders in society through follow-up programmes. Therefore, it seems that community and society also play a vital role in criminal reconciliation programmes.

Nevertheless, the author argues that in fact there are tremendous differences in the roles of community in criminal reconciliation and restorative justice. In criminal reconciliation, society is mainly set as a place to (help the officials) educate and correct the suspect/defendant. Technically, concerned members of the community are expected to help the officials with the resolution of the case concerned, for example by persuading the immediate parties to the process to accept a solution suggested by the official (see further Chapters 4 and 5 *infra*). All the other accountabilities of the community or of wider society addressed above in restorative justice are missing in criminal reconciliation. Members of the community are also not viewed as 'indirect victims' seeking reparation in criminal reconciliation programmes.

---

51 Ibid.

52 Supra note 48.

53 Susan Sharp *Restorative Justice: A Vision for Healing and Change* Alberta, Edmonton Victim Offender Mediation Society 1998, 7–12.

54 Supra note 24, 78.

2.2.2 'Reintegrative Shaming' is Missing in Criminal Reconciliation

'Reintegrative shaming' was put forward by John Braithwaite in his book '*Crime, Shame and Reintegration.*' Braithwaite defines 'reintegrative shaming' as an 'expression of community disapproval, which may range from mild rebuke to degradation ceremonies, followed by gestures of reacceptance into the community of law-abiding citizens.'[55]

'Reintegrative shaming' is distinguished from the ideology of 'stigmatic shaming' and 'labelling' in retributive justice. According to Braithwaite, from the perspective of 'stigmatic shaming' and 'labelling' theories, the offender is 'bad' and 'evil.'[56] Retributive justice aligned with these theories imposes shame on the offender's personality.[57] Yet such shame is a barrier for the offender to reintegrate into society afterwards.[58] Moreover, as argued by Braithwaite, under the ideas of 'stigmatic shaming' and 'labelling,' 'the offender's sense of shame may be further lost and animosity may be created,' which is likely to cause re-offending.[59]

On the contrary, in 'reintegrative shaming' as proposed by Braithwaite, the object for 'shaming' is only the offender's *bad action.*[60] That is to say, the offender is still viewed as a 'good person worth respect' by the victim and other members of the community.[61] Because of this, according to Braithwaite, the offender can return to the community again much more easily.[62]

The author argues that this rationale of 'reintegrative shaming' is not embodied in criminal reconciliation in China either. This could be reflected in criminal reconciliation's different attitude towards the suspect/defendant compared to that in restorative justice.

---

55 John Braithwaite *Crime, Shame and Reintegration* Cambridge, Cambridge University Press 1989, 55.

56 John Braithwaite 'Crime, Shame and Reintegration' at http://www.ciaj-icaj.ca/english/publications/DP1999/braithwaite.pdf (last accessed on 20 January 2008).

57 Ibid.

58 Ibid

59 Ibid.

60 Barbara Hudson 'Restorative Justice and Gendered Violence: Diversion or Effective Justice?' (2002) Vol. 42 No. 3 *The British Journal of Criminology* 619.

61 Ibid.

62 John Braithwaite and Stephen Mugford 'Conditions of Successful Reintegration Ceremonies: Dealing with Juvenile Offenders' in Declan Roche (ed) *Restorative Justice* England, Dartmouth Publishing Company 2004, 5.

As noted in the preceding chapter, in criminal reconciliation programmes, the suspect/defendant is mainly viewed as an object to be educated and corrected, which is one of the officially purported goals for this programme. The biggest benefits the suspect/defendant could obtain in criminal reconciliation programmes, as stated by officials and many academics, are lenient dispositions such as non-prosecution or a suspended sentence. Although suspects/defendants, according to the officially claimed aims, are granted power and a voice in the process of criminal reconciliation, without the support of 'reintegrative shaming,' this process may still be 'stigmatic' for them. Moreover, the particular stress on 'education' may not only focus on the suspect/defendant's past wrongdoings, but also on their personalities. This problem is not addressed in the domestic literature on criminal reconciliation; it is shown and discussed in Chapters 4 and 5 when the author describes the findings in the empirical study of criminal reconciliation practices in China.

2.2.3 'Political Goals' Set for Criminal Reconciliation Are Not Involved in Restorative Justice

Tony Marshall defines five objectives for restorative justice. These objectives include benefits to the victim, the offender, the community as well as the criminal justice system. To the victim (including both direct and indirect victims), restorative justice is to 'fully attend' to their needs, which may involve 'expression, information, participation, empathy, reparation of the sense of security.'[63] With regard to the offender, it is to 'facilitate their undertaking of accountabilities caused by crimes and their reintegration into the community afterwards.'[64] With regard to the community, it is to 'prevent recidivism through rehabilitating the victim and the offender.'[65] With regard to the criminal justice system, restorative justice 'aims to raise its efficiency through resolving cases by an alternative means.'[66]

It seems that many similarities could be seen between the claimed aims of criminal reconciliation and those of restorative justice. For example, they both aim to protect the parties' rights as to voice and participation in

---

[63] Tony F. Marshall 'Restorative Justice: An Overview' at http://library.npia.police.uk/docs/homisc/occ-resjus.pdf (last accessed on 16 February 2008).

[64] Ibid.

[65] Ibid.

[66] Ibid.

criminal justice processes; they are both purported to redress the victim's material loss and psychological harm through the parties' communication and discussion and the suspect/defendant/offender's apology and compensation.

Nevertheless, it appears that some of the officially stated goals of criminal reconciliation in China, such as eliminating petitioning, and promoting a 'harmonious society' in the sense of the political theory developed by the CCP are not involved in restorative justice. This may indicate another critical difference between these two systems: in contrast to restorative justice, which pays absolute attention to the parties (and other people who are also affected by crime), criminal reconciliation has been 'imposed' on many 'large (or greater) goals,' or actually political goals, that mainly serve the interests of the authorities.

Most importantly, as also noted by Chen Ruihua, compensation plays quite different roles in these two systems. Compensation neither displays any special status nor is particularly stressed in restorative justice. Although it is also characterized by restorative justice as a way of making the offender accept accountability and reach restoration, it is not the only way or a way more important than other ways (i.e. apology, communication, and community service) in reaching these goals. It is even viewed as secondary to the process of restorative justice, which includes the parties' dialogue and relationship.[67] Yet in criminal reconciliation in China, compensation is officially stated to be a very significant element to address the long-standing problem of enforcing the sentence in the normal criminal procedure. This is officially viewed as a way to satisfy the victim, to prevent their petitioning and to achieve 'closure,' which are all for establishing a 'harmonious society.' As a result, compensation is ultimately crucial in criminal reconciliation programmes.

2.3 RESTORATIVE JUSTICE IN PRACTICE: A GLIMPSE FROM THE AUTHOR'S OBSERVATIONS IN BRISBANE, AUSTRALIA

The above analysis shows that criminal reconciliation in China may not be simply parallel with restorative justice. In the following three chapters, the author will discuss her empirical work and findings on criminal

[67] Ibid.

reconciliation practices in three cities in mainland China, which illustrates the gap between criminal reconciliation 'on paper' and 'in practice.' Hence, a description of restorative justice practices may merit a further understanding of the differences between these two systems. In early 2010, also for the sake of this comparative research, the author observed two VOR meetings in Brisbane, Australia. Below, the author provides the observation notes to show how VOR is implemented.

Victim-Offender-Reconciliation takes the form of 'conferencing for juvenile offenders' in Queensland, Australia.[68] It is a diversion programme compared to the normal criminal proceedings. Participants 'normally include the young person, a family member or caregiver, the victim or their representative together with a victim supporter, the referring police officer and two conference conveners.'[69] The victim's consent to this programme is necessary, though he/she could opt not to attend the conference in person.[70] As shown below, it could be assessed that the practice at large complied well with the procedure designed in the two cases which were based on the author's own random selection.

First Observation

Time: 9:30am–10:10am, 7 April 2010

Place: Department of Communities, Queensland Government

I arrived at the conference room about 15 minutes earlier, the convener, Sean, was preparing some paperwork for the upcoming conference. I chatted with him – he had graduated from Griffith University with a Criminology degree in 1996 and worked as a VOR convener since then. In Brisbane, the qualification of being a convener is based on one week's training, mainly on the restorative justice process and speaking skills, as well as on long-time observation and learning under a senior convener.

Then he started to arrange the seats: they were arranged in a circle, and Sean told me that it was for the juvenile offenders' feeling of safety. There were four chairs: one for the juvenile offender, one for the offender's supporter (the young man's father in this case), and the convener would sit next to the offender. The fourth chair was for the

---

[68] Heather Strang 'Restorative Justice Programs in Australia: A Report to the Criminology Research Council' at http://www.criminologyresearchcouncil.gov.au/reports/strang/qld.html (last accessed on 7 April 2015).

[69] Ibid.

[70] Ibid.

police officer. There was no victim in this case as it was an unregistered driving charge. I, as an observer, would sit back, around one metre from the circle. After Sean had arranged the seats, the police officer working at the traffic branch, John, stepped into the room. Sean introduced the process of VOR briefly to John and gave him a sheet of paper detailing the charge against the young offender, Nicolas, who was 17 years old. Sean told John that he could read out the charge written on the paper at the conference and Sean would ask Nicolas whether or not he admitted guilt at the beginning of the conference. Later, the young offender and his father arrived. Sean introduced everyone in the room to each other (this was also for the offender's feeling of safety, according to Sean). There were tea and coffee in the room and Sean entertained Nicolas and his father with it in a very friendly manner. The room was a quiet and comfortable space with nice paintings on the wall. Then we all sat down and the conference formally began.

First, Sean announced the procedure of the conference and the confidentiality clauses. Then, he turned to Nicolas, asking, 'What happened?' Nicolas started to relate the story (the offence) – this young man flushed and looked very remorseful for what he had done – his voice was quite low, sometimes he only murmured. During the whole process of his relation, everyone there was very concentrated and patient, sometimes echoing with a nod. When Nicolas finished talking, the police officer read out the charge on the paper and asked him whether or not he admitted guilt. Nicolas said yes. Sean asked how he felt about it. Nicolas talked about his regret and embarrassment. Sean also asked Nicolas's father about his feelings – he did not blame his son at all; instead, he expressed that he was not upset with Nicolas, and in fact, he was rather glad that Nicolas had told him all this immediately after the incident. Nicolas listened carefully and further lowered his head. After that, John talked about why unregistered driving constituted an offence and how harmful it could be. Sean also asked Nicolas for his feedback and feelings on this. Nicolas said he had never thought about the potential harm of his conduct and the conference had brought different experiences to him. The conference then moved to the last stage to discuss an agreement. The conference convener first consulted the police officer, who mentioned his shift of attitude too – as a senior police officer working in the traffic branch for years, he actually did not like those people violating the law and wanted to send them to court, but after this conference, he thought it was worthwhile to give juveniles one more chance – the requirement proposed by John was just Nicolas's promise of not driving until he obtained a licence. Nicolas agreed. The focus of the whole conference was apparently not the final agreement as it took really little time. As an observer, my impression was that they really cared about the young offender, about his feelings and how this process could help him. Lastly, Sean told Nicolas that if he failed to comply with this agreement, he would face the formal procedure and harsher punishment.

After the participants had left, I chatted with Sean for a while. Sean told me that he supported restorative justice as he believed this process could change the offender and the victim, as well as the police officer. He spoke highly of getting to know the offender's 'underneath' story and making it known to the victim and the police officer – for example, in the case I had just observed, Nicolas's mother had left him when he was little and his father was very busy earning money, so Nicolas's action might be largely out of attracting his father's attention. Also, in some theft cases, the offender committed crimes just due to extreme poverty – for instance, Sean told me, in one case, a girl stole as she wanted to have more money for her very sick mother in hospital. Yet Sean also mentioned that his workload was massive. On average he had 40 cases per month and he had to do a lot of preparation work for each of the conferences – such as, he needed to conduct pre-conference interviews with the offender and his/her family. Sometimes, during the meeting, the offender did not speak at all (though agreed to attend the meeting voluntarily) – the offender, the victim and the police officer just stared at each other angrily. In this case, Sean also needed to get them to speak. But that was not the most difficult part for him – Sean told me that the most challenging thing was to get the participants' feelings swiftly and reacted to appropriately. He said he would ask the victim and offender more questions about their feelings and stimulated the offender to talk more about his thoughts on the offence in order to detect fake remorse. Sometimes, if the offender pretended remorse, the victim would not be satisfied with the offender's apology and they would not reach any agreement. Sometimes, the offender would not perform the agreement afterwards and would go to court.

Second Observation

Time: 10:00–11:10am, 8 April 2010

Place: Department of Communities, Queensland Government

When I arrived at the conference room (the same as where I observed the previous meeting), the conveners, Jack and Melissa, were discussing the case with the police officer, Angela. Also, the police officer was given a piece of paper about the charges. Seeing me arriving, they briefed me about the case and the participants in our upcoming meeting – the juvenile offender we would meet soon, Eden, was 16, and her parents died several years ago. Her only relative was her very old grandfather, who would also be Eden's supporter for the conference. Yet Eden and her grandfather did not live together so they rarely met and communicated with each other in daily life. Eden had quitted school some time ago and been working part-time in a pub. One night after getting drunk, she and her three friends kicked another girl's head heavily, which would very likely cause permanent damage to that girl's brain. Jack told me that as the victim was still in hospital, she would not come to the conference, and Melissa, who had been communicating a lot with the victim, was here on behalf of the victim and would pass on the victim's words to Eden.

After Eden and her grandfather arrived, the conference began. The procedure was not very different from that of yesterday. At first, Jack asked Eden to tell us what happened after a brief introduction of the process and the confidentiality clauses. Then Jack asked questions about her feelings, the victim's feelings in her imagination and her thoughts on the impact of her conduct. Eden also looked quite regretful, and spoke quite low too. The police officer then read the charges and Eden admitted them. As cultural difference (between Maori and Fijian) was one chief reason for their conflict, Jack, who had Maori origins as well, told Eden that actually there were many similarities in the two cultures. Then Melissa talked about the victim – the girl of the same age as Eden had been hurt a lot by Eden; now she was inclined to isolate herself – she feared to go out at night as she did not feel safe, she was a dancer and may not be able to dance in the future. Eden looked even more sorry and remorseful hearing all this. Melissa then told Eden that although the victim as well as her family and friends were all upset about this, they were trying their best to forgive her and to move on. What they wanted from Eden was her sincere apology, her 'underneath' story and her promise of never doing that again. Then Jack asked Eden, 'Did all this surprise you?'; 'What would you think and feel if that happens to you?' – Eden said she now could really feel for the girl who was badly hurt by her and she would never do that again. Angela, the police officer, then said that Eden's act would also negatively affect her, for example, a criminal record which would make job hunting tougher. The young lady was all ears and admitted that she had never thought about these consequences before. Eden's grandfather said he was upset and felt sorry for the victim and the victim's family; he even wanted to apologize to them himself too. Then Jack asked Eden about her feelings and thoughts regarding her relationship with her grandfather, including, 'Do you feel that your grandfather cares about you?'; 'Is there anything you wish to say to your grandfather?'; 'Why your grandfather wanted to apologize even though he did not do anything wrong?' I sensed that both of them realized that they needed more communication. Also, throughout the meeting, Jack remained sensitive to all the participants' emotions and reactions. He also regularly asked if anyone wanted to say something or add something. At the final stage of reaching an agreement, Angela first proposed an apology letter including Eden's resolutions, such as giving up drinking and returning to school. Eden agreed, and her grandfather would be her supervisor, which also meant more interaction and communication between them. Finally, Jack confirmed again if everyone there was happy with the conference before they signed the agreement. When the whole process ended, Jack had a further informal chat with Eden, and as Jack told me, he would stay in touch with Eden and check on how she was (and this case) from time to time as a follow-up.

2.4 SUMMARY

Following the scholarly debates over criminal reconciliation in Chapter 1, this chapter further addresses the academic divergence on the 'nature' of this programme by comparing it with restorative justice. The comparative study shows the essential differences between these two systems. These differences will be further bolstered by the empirical findings in Chapters 3 to 5. The implication this comparison carries is that to justify the implementation of criminal reconciliation without legal basis in China by referring to the trend and merits of restorative justice is far-fetched. The understanding of criminal reconciliation requires a down-to-earth examination of this system itself in China, in the context of China's political-legal system. However, as argued in Chapter 1 and the beginning of this chapter, a law-and-society approach, as maintained by scholars such as Su Li and Fan Yu, turns a blind eye to the reality as well. All this embodies the significance of an empirical study of criminal reconciliation practices in China.

3. Criminal reconciliation in practice: evidence from official case files

3.1 THE MOTIVATION FOR THE EMPIRICAL STUDY

In addition to the description, analysis and debate around criminal reconciliation based on second-hand information shown in Chapter 1, there have been fieldwork reports describing the processes, outcomes and problems of criminal reconciliation practices in selected locations in China. Some of these reports have been produced by prosecutors or judges purporting to describe criminal reconciliation practices in their procuratorates or courts. Some have been conducted jointly by scholars and prosecutors or judges. Very few have been conducted solely by scholars.

In general, these reports have covered the procedure designed for criminal reconciliation (in some selected procuratorates or courts) as shown in Chapter 1. Some of the reports also provide statistics concerning the number of criminal reconciliation cases in the institutions studied. Such data are in accordance with the analysis in Chapter 1 – as shown in these reports, criminal reconciliation, in pilot projects before the revision of the CPL in 2012, was not often used by the State authorities.

For instance, a report produced by the research office based in the People's Procuratorates of Wuxi city in Jiangsu province showed that in 2006, in the People's Procuratorates of Wuxi city, only 8.8 percent of the minor criminal cases had been resolved through criminal reconciliation.[1] Two prosecutors, Tan Zelin and Zhao Qiusheng revealed in their report that from 2007 to 2008, among all the cases solved by the People's Procuratorates in Hunan province, only 3.55 percent had been

[1] The Research Office of the People's Procuratorate in Jiangsu Province [江苏省检察院研究室] The Research Office of Wuxi City People's Procuratorate [无锡市检察院研究室] 'Innovating Judicial Ideas and Exploring Criminal Reconciliation [创新司法理念探索刑事和解]' in Bian Jianlin [卞建林] and Wang Li [王立] (eds) *Criminal Reconciliation and an Alternative Procedure [刑事和解与程序分流]* Beijing, The Chinese People's Public Security University Press [中国人民公安大学出版社] 2010, 447.

resolved through criminal reconciliation.[2] Even in the People's Procuratorate of Chaoyang district in Beijing that started this programme early in 2002, criminal reconciliation was found to have been used in only 2.9 percent of all the minor criminal cases.[3] A survey mainly presided over by scholar Song Yinghui and undertaken in eight cities in China implied that in the basic level People's Procuratorates studied, on average only nine cases had been resolved through criminal reconciliation each year, which amounted to about 17 percent of all cases dealt with by these procuratorates.[4]

Empirical reports showed that criminal reconciliation was rarely initiated by courts as well. For example, a judge stated in his report that in the studied court in Foshan city in Guangdong province, only 1.6 percent of the cases under the first instance trial had been resolved through criminal reconciliation from 2008 to 2009.[5]

The empirical studies conducted by these officials and scholars also inclined to show the success or satisfactory effects of criminal reconciliation practices. For example, Song Yinghui, who held and conducted fieldwork on criminal reconciliation practices in the People's Procuratorates in four provinces in mainland China from 2006 to 2008, claimed in his report that criminal reconciliation produced three main effects in practice.[6] First, it resolved the conflicts between the parties.[7] According to Song, the questionnaires distributed to the parties of criminal

---

2 Tan Zelin [谭泽林] Zhao Qiusheng [赵秋生] 'Problems and Improvements of Laws Accordingly in Implementing Criminal Reconciliation in China [我国刑事和解实施中的问题与相应实体、程序法完善]' (2009) 9 *Politics and Law* [*政治与法律*] 149.

3 Song Yinghui [宋英辉] 'An Empirical Analysis of Criminal Reconciliation in China [我国刑事和解实证分析]' (2008) 5 *China Legal Science* [*中国法学*] 124–5.

4 Ge Lin [葛琳] 'An Analysis of the Practical Predicament of Criminal Reconciliation [刑事和解的现实困境解析]' (2010) 5 *Justice of China* [*中国司法*] 19.

5 Wang Xuetang [王学堂] 'Popular Identification on Criminal Reconciliation: An Empirical Analysis Based on Three News Reporting [刑事和解的民众认同： 基于三起新闻事件的实证分析]' at http://www.dffy.com/faxuejieti/ss/201101/20110110150022.htm (last accessed on 19 December 2011).

6 Song Yinghui [宋英辉] 'Empirical Report on the Implementation of Criminal Reconciliation by the People's Procuratorates in Four Provisions [四省检察机关适用刑事和解调查报告]' in Song Yinghui [宋英辉] (ed) *Empirical Research on Criminal Reconciliation* [*刑事和解实证研究*] Beijing, Peking University Press [北京大学出版社] 2010, 72.

7 Ibid.

reconciliation cases showed that all the parties were satisfied with criminal reconciliation programmes and there was no petitioning, appealing or 'ravelment' (*jiuchan*) after the end of criminal reconciliation programmes.[8]

Second, criminal reconciliation, according to Song, better protected the victim's rights. For one thing, Song's study showed that the victims had obtained a larger sum of compensation and more swiftly.[9] In the criminal reconciliation cases in Song's empirical study, the largest amount of compensation was 60,000 yuan, with the average standing at 78,029.2 yuan.[10] Some 88.1 percent of the compensation had been paid immediately the criminal reconciliation programmes ended, and 91.4 percent of the compensation agreements were enforced; this enforcement rate was much higher than that in normal criminal procedure, which ranged from 33.2 percent to only 0.5 percent in the studied locations.[11]

Third, Song concluded that criminal reconciliation was more beneficial in educating offenders, helping them return to society and thereby reducing re-offending.[12] According to Song's visit to some offenders in criminal reconciliation cases, only 11.2 percent of them failed to find a new job after the end of criminal reconciliation programmes and none offended again.[13] In this sense, Song further argued that although criminal reconciliation would cost more time and effort on the part of the officials in individual cases, it could promote judicial efficiency in a general way, since it could reduce recidivism.[14]

Another report produced by two prosecutors from their field study in the procuratorate they worked at has shown similar beneficial effects of criminal reconciliation. For instance, they found in their study that none of the victims and suspects expressed dissatisfaction with the *outcome* of criminal reconciliation programmes.[15] Their reports also mentioned that, normally, the victims said that they viewed criminal reconciliation as a

---

8 Ibid, 73.

9 Song Yinghui [宋英辉] 'Empirical Analysis on Criminal Reconciliation in Public Prosecution [公诉案件刑事和解的实证分析]' at http://www.sqxb.cn/blog/blog.aspx?id=309&zuozeid=83 (last accessed on 27 July 2010).

10 Ibid.

11 Ibid.

12 Supra note 6, 73.

13 Ibid.

14 Ibid.

15 Supra note 2, 150.

'very humanistic' process; the juvenile suspects found it a 'fair programme,' which made them 'realize their faults and the victims' feelings.'[16] Also, in the studied procuratorate, 96 percent of the compensation agreements had been enforced in 2007 and the rate even reached 98 percent in 2008.[17] Meanwhile, the recidivism rate of the criminal reconciliation cases in 2007 and 2008 was zero.[18]

Accordingly, in these empirical reports, criminal reconciliation practices have been praised as successfully achieving the officially stated goals and benefiting the establishment of a harmonious society.[19]

However, the author is sceptical of the findings and conclusions for three principal reasons. First, the researchers carrying out these projects had some stake in the reports. Often, such reports were conducted collaboratively by scholars and judges/prosecutors, or wholly carried out by officials. The possibility that the officials, as the ones responsible for criminal reconciliation at the point it was vigorously promoted as successful by the Supreme People's Court and Supreme People's Procuratorate, were biased in favour of these programmes cannot be precluded.

Second, the methods these researchers adopted to collect data and information are problematic. According to the accounts in these reports, most of the researchers collected data and information by means of panel discussions which were attended by officials, parties and the researchers. In such settings, it is likely that the parties were reluctant to deliver negative information or comments on a programme which had already secured official endorsement. Moreover, the panel members are likely to have withheld any criticisms that they might have had considering the fact that they were likely to have been informed that what they said would be published.

Third, these researchers failed to provide important information regarding the methods they adopted. For instance, they did not mention the circumstances in which they had distributed their questionnaires, how they identified parties in their surveys and what questions were included in their questionnaires. Such information is crucial to assessing the contribution that the studies might make as decisions taken by the researchers in this regard might affect the findings of the study. For

[16] Ibid.

[17] Ibid.

[18] Ibid.

[19] Zhang Xingchuan [张星川] 'An Initial Analysis of the Problems and Strategies for the Current Criminal Reconciliation Work [浅议当前刑事和解工作中存在的问题及对策]' at http://www.jcrb.com/jcpd/jcll/201008/t20100803_394537.html (last accessed on 12 December 2011).

example, the parties' attitudes and answers to the question 'Are you satisfied with the *outcome* of criminal reconciliation?' could be quite different from their response to the question 'Are you satisfied with criminal reconciliation?'

These problems suggest that the conclusions of the researchers cannot properly be assessed because the impact of the undisclosed methods on the findings is unknowable. This alone calls for further examination and independent verification. In order to test the official accounts and publicly available resources, and for the reasons explained above, the author conducted fieldwork in three selected places in China, namely: Changzhou in Jiangsu province; Chongqing Municipality; and Xi'an in Shaanxi province. This study has two distinct aspects: (i) the examination of case files; and (ii) interviews conducted with the public officials, the parties and other people participating in the criminal reconciliation programmes.

The first two empirical studies were conducted in two district People's Procuratorates in Changzhou and Chongqing in May and June 2008, at a time when criminal reconciliation started expanding in China and when its practice was extended from several cities in eastern China such as Changzhou to western cities such as Chongqing.[20] The two cities were chosen as representative of places with varying degrees of experience with criminal reconciliation, in order to get a better picture of criminal reconciliation in China.

Another consideration motivating the choice of research sites was ease of access. Criminal justice is one of the most sensitive fields in the area of Chinese law, because of its close relationship with politics and the interests of the State.[21] Given that criminal reconciliation had been heralded as a beneficial reform, it is unsurprising that those who are

---

[20] The People's Procuratorates in Changzhou were among the first groups in China to implement criminal reconciliation. It had implemented this practice for almost five years before 2008. Chongqing Municipality was a place which initiated criminal reconciliation in the procuratorates on an experimental basis in 2006.

[21] According to Article 2 of the 1996 PRC Criminal Law, the tasks of the PRC Criminal Law are 'to use punishment to crack down crime and to defend national security, the political power of the people's democratic dictatorship, and the socialist system.' 'It is to protect state-owned property, property collectively owned by the laboring masses, and citizens' privately owned property.' 'It is also to protect citizens' individual rights, democratic rights, and other rights to maintain social and economic order, and to safeguard the smooth progress of the socialist construction.' Article 1 of the 1996 PRC Criminal Procedural Law provides that 'this law is enacted in accordance with the Constitution and for the purpose of ensuring correct enforcement of the Criminal Law, punishing crime, protecting the people, safeguarding State and public security and maintaining

entrusted with promoting it, namely the prosecutors and judges, tend to repel outsiders' investigations. Securing access to sites which were hospitable to the idea of research was, accordingly, a critical factor in choice of location notwithstanding that, in other circumstances, different considerations would be more influential in determining where the research would be undertaken and despite the limitation that interviews with the parties had to be conducted in the presence of prosecutors. Regarding the latter, the examination of case files was undertaken as a cross-check and as a means of identifying bias introduced by the presence of officials at the interviews.

The third empirical study was conducted in August and September 2010 in courts and procuratorates of two districts in Xi'an, the capital city of Shaanxi province in northwestern China. In contrast to the first two studies, the author set out to contact participants personally to arrange interviews without the presence of officials in order to avoid any potential interference. This research method provided a means to eliminate the direct influence of officials on the parties in this site and provided a basis for comparison with the two other sites in which the presence of officials at interviews had to be tolerated.

3.2 AN OVERVIEW OF CRIMINAL RECONCILIATION PRACTICES IN THE THREE FIELDWORK LOCATIONS

The author started this empirical work through the examination of case files. The purpose of this was to understand criminal reconciliation as set down on paper in the places selected, and to see if criminal reconciliation practices in these locations met the ends it was expected and claimed to serve. The case files allow us to see what the officials and authorities concerned with the criminal reconciliation process regard as important for official documentation purposes. They are not public and are often, as explained, designated 'internal' or 'secret.' They provide us with what might be called an official picture of criminal reconciliation which has been prepared for official not research purposes.

---

socialist public order.' See the English translation at http://www.chinalawedu.com/new/23223a23228a2011/2011311ifei16451.shtml (last accessed on 6 May 2016).

Accordingly, the author first provides an overview of the basic statistical facts, processes and outcomes of criminal reconciliation programmes in these three locations, based on the information gathered from the case files. Following it, the author analyses the findings of the case files in an attempt to address the questions raised in the first part of this chapter. Meanwhile, the author points out several questions that were implied in the case files studied but cannot be answered by those files.

3.2.1 Selection of Cases

One limitation of this study is that the author was unable to secure permission to randomly select cases to study for the purpose of this project. It is therefore possible that officials provided access only to case files selected as 'the best examples' of criminal reconciliation. Indeed, it is a fair inference that this was the case since the officials were supposed to be promoting reconciliation as a successful innovation. In Changzhou, the prosecutors allowed the author to read 10 out of the 50 available case files. All ten cases shared one characteristic: the parties were local residents (i.e. people who possessed local *hukou*).[22] The author was told by the chief prosecutor that the choice of files was made on the basis that it would be more convenient to contact parties who had local *hukou* registrations for interview. Of course, while acknowledging the logic of this official explanation and its apparent understanding of the needs of the researcher, it cannot preclude the possibility that the choice was

---

22 The residence registration system or *hukou zhidu* was established in China in the 1950s. It is an administrative system by which the government manages citizens through recording almost all the information about each citizen including name, birth date, dwelling place, occupation, education, marriage, death, movement, and so on. Although population management is widely implemented by governments worldwide, China's *hukou* system is characterized by its close connection with a person's rights concerning education, career, medical treatment and welfare as such resources are distributed in an unbalanced fashion to different areas, and its essential function is to divide urban residence and rural residence and thereby to control or restrict rural residence's migration to cities. So it is actually a system the government used to effectively control the citizens and the distribution of resources within the country. Although long criticized and undergoing various reforms, this system has not been cancelled or changed essentially until now. See: Wang Feiling [王飞凌] 'The Transformation of China's Hukou System [中国户口制度的转型]' at http://www.chinaelections.org/newsinfo.asp?newsid=185108 (last accessed on 6 December, 2010); Chen Chunlong [陈春龙] 'The Current Situation and Reform of China's Hukou System [中国 "户口制度" 的现状与改革]' http://www.iolaw.org.cn/showArticle.asp?id=1729 (last accessed on 6 December 2010).

actually made on other grounds, for example because the officials thought that those ten cases were the most successful in the criminal reconciliation programme.

Likewise, in Chongqing, it was hard to get the prosecutors' permission to examine case files since the files were all labelled 'secret' (*mimi*). After negotiation and promising to limit the author's use to academic purposes in an anonymous fashion, the author was given eight files to examine. The author was not allowed to choose files at random. Again, it seems possible, indeed likely, that those eight cases were selected by the prosecutors as 'the best ones' in their opinion.

Access to case files was even harder in Xi'an. The 'secret' nature of the files was given by the officials as the refusal ground as well. Access to judges and prosecutors was also harder in comparison with the previous two studies.

There were iron gates on the first or second floor of the Court and Procuratorate in Xi'an. After registration at the main gate, which the procuratorates in Changzhou and Chongqing also required, any outsider who wanted to go upstairs to visit the officials had to call them through a phone supplied by an officer guarding that gate. Personal permission from the officials confirmed by that gatekeeper was necessary to go any further. From anecdotal evidence the author collected while in Xi'an, it appeared that, sometimes, even citizens who had appointments with the officials behind the gate could not get them to answer the guard's call. Although there were offices on the first floor of the courts and procuratorates and each judge or prosecutor was scheduled to receive petitioners every day, according to the author's observation, usually those offices for receiving petitioners were closed. Moreover, petitioners had to wait outside for long periods (sometimes they were waiting at the point when the author arrived, and still waiting when the author finished a day's work). Through chats with several of them, the author learned that they were all here with appointments with the judges/prosecutors. It was even absurd that the author was once introduced to a judge who was just the one a petitioner was waiting for beside the iron gate and always got the reply from the gatekeeper that 'he is not around.' As to the reason of petitioning, all the persons the author chatted with referred to the judges'/prosecutors' delinquencies during prosecution, sentence enforcement or litigation. Yet according to the author's interviews with the officials, many of them said that the petitioners were just making trouble and being bad (*taoyan*). So they might want to use the iron gate and gatekeeper to get rid of the petitioners. It seemed that the officials intended to get rid of trouble and avoid risk. This had the effect of blocking access by citizens who were trying to exercise their rights to appeal, petition or to meet the presiding prosecutors/judges of their cases.[23] This also illustrates the somewhat tense atmosphere at the time of the visit, which was probably caused by the large number of petitioners waiting in and outside the Court and Procuratorate, and some extremely sharp conflicts between judges and individual parties that had occurred recently elsewhere.[24]

In this situation, negotiation with judges and prosecutors for case file examination was especially difficult. Finally, in Y district, the author got to examine three traffic accident related crime cases in the People's Court, and one juvenile robbery case in the People's Procuratorate; in B district, the author examined two juvenile robbery cases in the People's Court, together with four traffic accident related crime cases and one juvenile robbery case in the People's Procuratorate. Those cases were selected by the prosecutors, so the possibility that they were picked out as 'the best criminal reconciliation cases' still could not be excluded. Moreover, it seemed that case files the author was given in the People's Procuratorate of Y district were incomplete as there was only the suspects' contact information in the files.

---

23 Article 32 of the PRC Judges Law says that 'judges are forbidden to meet the party concerned or his/her agent privately and attend dinners or accept presents given by the party concerned or his/her agent.' However, the vague phrase of 'meeting privately' (*sizi huijian*) is debatable. There is an argument that this provision only forbids the judge's meeting with the party or his/her agent beyond the judge's working place, time and responsibility. See: Sun Ming [孙明] 'My Views on the Judge's Private Meeting with the Parties and Their Lawyers [法官私自会见当事人及委托律师之我见]' at http://www.dffy.com/sifashijian/sw/200601/20060104221654.htm (last accessed on 9 April 2011). Besides, Article 35 of the PRC Prosecutors Law also only forbids the prosecutors' meeting with the party or his/her agents privately (*sizi huijian*).

24 As to recent conflicts between individual parties and judges, a very notable one was an incident in Yongzhou city in Hunan province. In June 2010, an unsatisfied victim who had won the litigation but could not get the sentence enforced shot three judges to death and seriously wounded three other judges. See: *Southern Weekend* [*南方周末*] 'A Shooting Case Resulting in Three Judges' Death in Yongzhou, Hunan Province: The Murder Has an Incurable Disease [湖南永州致三法官死枪击案： 凶手身患绝症]' at http://www.infzm.com/content/45861 (last accessed on 15 November 2010).

3.2.2 The Basic Statistical Facts

Criminal reconciliation was rarely used in the three locations

Even though the People's Procuratorate of X district in Changzhou had been implementing the criminal reconciliation programme for over five years, only about 50 cases were handled through criminal reconciliation from 2003 to 2008.[25] According to the yearbook (*nianjian*) of X district,[26] the Public Security Bureau transferred 864 cases to the People's Procuratorate of X district for examination before prosecution and of which 851 were prosecuted from 2003 to 2005; the Public Security Bureau transferred 1,179 cases, of which 1,120 cases were prosecuted from 2006 to 2008.[27] It is unclear what happened to the remaining cases. Some of them may have been handled through criminal reconciliation. In others, the Procuratorate may have decided that charges should be dropped altogether. Direct statistical information on how many cases were handled through criminal reconciliation in Changzhou is not available in the yearbook.

In the People's Procuratorate of D district in Chongqing, fewer than 20 cases were resolved through criminal reconciliation from 2006 to 2008.[28] The total number of cases transferred and prosecuted in 2006 was not available from public sources. However, according to the statistical bulletin of D district, the People's Procuratorate of D district prosecuted 199 cases in 2007 and 327 cases in 2008.[29]

---

[25] According to the introduction by the chief prosecutor of the People's Procuratorate of X district in Changzhou.

[26] Yearbook, or *nianjian*, according to '现代汉语词典' [*Modern Chinese Dictionary*] published by 商务印书馆 [the Commercial Press] (the 1977 edition), is 'the publication of the collection of the information and data that cover economy, technology, education, politics etc. or only one area of a place in the last year.'

[27] See: Almanac of X District, Changzhou City 2003–2005 at http://www.cznd.gov.cn/nj2005/zfrw/4.htm (last accessed on 15 November 2010); Almanac of X District, Changzhou City 2006–2008 at http://www.cznd.gov.cn/nj2008/Templates/zhengfa/html5-6.html (last accessed on 15 November 2010).

[28] According to the introduction by a prosecutor in the People's Procuratorate of D district in Chongqing.

[29] See the 2007 Statistical Bulletin of the National Economic and Social Development of D District in Chongqing at http://www.ddktj.gov.cn/wwweb/sjck/tjgb/20091223/1950.html (last accessed on 7 February 2011); the 2008 Statistical Bulletin of the National Economic and Social Development of D District in Chongqing at http://www.ddktj.gov.cn/wwweb/sjck/tjgb/20091223/1951.html (last accessed on 7 February 2011).

In Xi'an, as criminal reconciliation had only been practised since 2008, the judges and prosecutors of the two districts studied told the author that no statistics on criminal reconciliation were available at that time. The author was unable to obtain information on how many cases out of the cases transferred by the Public Security Bureau for examination before prosecution had been handled through criminal reconciliation.

This data suggests that although criminal reconciliation was promoted by the Supreme People's Court and the Supreme People's Procuratorate as a system embodying the idea of 'combining severity with leniency' (*kuan yan xiangji*) and was described in the publicly available literature as developing rapidly in China, it was in fact rarely implemented in practice in the locations studied. Except for the discussion of the performance assessment system and wrongful conviction and decision investigation system proposed by Ge Lin in Chapter 1, the reasons for this will be further analysed in Chapter 5 based on interviews.

3.2.3 The Cases Eligible for Criminal Reconciliation

All the case files involved suspected 'minor crimes' and juvenile crimes

In all the cases the author was allowed to study, the alleged crimes in criminal reconciliation cases were limited to 'minor crimes' including traffic accident related crimes and minor intentional injury crimes, and some juvenile crimes such as robbery and theft.

Of the ten cases the author examined in Changzhou, there were four traffic accident related crime cases, four theft cases and two intentional injury cases. All eight cases in Chongqing were also suspected 'minor crimes' including seven intentional injury cases and one traffic accident related crime case. Yet these files represented only the minority of all criminal reconciliation cases, there being 50 criminal reconciliation cases in Changzhou and 20 in Chongqing. In Xi'an, the author was told that cases of suspected traffic accident related crime and juvenile robbery constituted the 'absolute majority' of criminal reconciliation cases there; and the case files the author was given access to, as shown above, were all concerned with such crimes.

3.2.4 The Suspects/Defendants Eligible for Criminal Reconciliation

No preference for juvenile suspect/defendants was evident

Suspects in half of the cases the author examined in the People's Procuratorate of X district in Changzhou were between 18 and 29 years old. The others, namely suspects in the four traffic accident related crime cases and one theft case, were between 30 and 50 years old. In the

People's Procuratorate of D district in Chongqing, suspects in seven of the eight cases examined were aged over 30. In Xi'an, only 4 among the 11 cases concerned juvenile suspects/defendants.

3.2.5 The Procedure of Criminal Reconciliation and Follow-up Programmes

The criminal reconciliation procedure in the fieldwork locations followed the pattern summarized by Chinese scholars
A typical criminal reconciliation programme without follow-up supervision progressed as follows:[30]

> 14 February 2007: a woman allegedly knocked down two pedestrians at night in her car. One of the pedestrians died on the way to hospital; the other received serious injuries.[31]
>
> 5 March 2007: the case was filed for investigation by the Public Security Bureau.
>
> 15 January 2008: the case was transferred to the People's Procuratorate for examination before prosecution.
>
> 10 March 2008: the prosecutor informed the parties of their rights and obligations in criminal reconciliation.
>
> 12 March 2008: the parties signed statements to the effect that they agreed to participate in criminal reconciliation 'voluntarily.'
>
> 21 March 2008: a criminal reconciliation meeting was held in the People's Procuratorate and an agreement was achieved; the prosecutor reported the case to the procuratorial committee.[32]

---

[30] From the case file of case no. 2, a suspected traffic accident related crime case, in location A.

[31] The PRC Criminal Law only stipulates traffic accidents giving rise to serious injuries, deaths, or great losses of public or private property as crimes. Otherwise, they can only be recognized as traffic accident related behaviours and be given administrative punishment by traffic management department of the Public Security Bureau according to the 1996 Law of the People's Republic of China on Public Security Administration Punishments, 2003 Law of the People's Republic of China on Road Traffic Safety, and 2009 Provisions on the Procedure of Handling Traffic Accidents. Traffic accident related crime was thought to involve negligence and hence to be a 'minor crime.'

[32] The 1983 Organic Law of the People's Procuratorates of the People's Republic of China stipulates that 'the People's procuratorate at any level shall set up a procuratorial committee (检察委员会).' 'The procuratorial committee shall apply the system of democratic centralism and, under the direction of the chief

15 April 2008: the procuratorial committee worked out a discussion report expressing agreement with the presiding prosecutor's proposal not to prosecute.

18 April 2008: the prosecutor announced the decision not to prosecute the suspect.

A typical criminal reconciliation process and its follow-up supervision are described below:[33]

27 November 2006: a 20-year-old young man was suspected of having stolen a crime prevention team (*zhi'an lianfangdui*) member's motorbike.[34] Later the case was filed for investigation by the Public Security Bureau.

---

prosecutor, hold discussions and make decisions on important cases and other major issues. In the case where the chief prosecutor disagrees with the majority's opinion on the decision concerning an important issue, this matter may be reported to the standing committee of the People's Congress at the corresponding level for final decision.' See the English translation at http://www.pkulaw.com/fulltext_form.aspx?Db=chl&Gid=10942 (last accessed on 20 December 2010). The 2008 Organic Regulation of the Procuratorial Committee of the People's Procuratorate [检察委员会组织条例] further stipulates that 'the procuratorial committee of the people's procuratorate at any level shall comprise the chief-prosecutor, deputy chief-prosecutor, specialized members of the procuratorial committee, and persons in charge of the relevant internal bodies of the same procuratorate.' See the English translation at http://www.lawinfochina.com/display.aspx?lib=law&id=6742&CGid= (last accessed on 20 December 2010).

33 From the case file of case no. 6, a suspected theft case, in location A.

34 A crime prevention team (*zhi'an lianfangdui*) is a citizens' self-management and self-service public security organization that is subordinate to the villagers' committee (*cunmin weiyuanhui*) and urban residents' committee (*chengshi jumin weiyuanhui*). According to Article 2 of the 2010 Organic Law of the Villagers' Committees of the People's Republic of China [村民委员会组织法], a villagers' committee is a mass organization for self-government at the grass-roots level, in which villagers administer their own affairs, educate themselves and serve their own needs, and in which elections are conducted, decisions are adopted, administration is maintained and supervision is exercised democratically. See the English translation at http://www.lawinfochina.com/display.aspx?lib=law&id=8445&CGid= (last accessed on 20 December 2010). According to Article 2 of the 1989 Organic Law of the Urban Residents' Committees of the People's Republic of China [城市居民委员组织法], an urban residents' committee is a mass organization for self-government at the grass-roots level, in which the residents manage their own affairs, educate themselves, and serve their own needs. The Organic Law of the Villagers' Committees of the People's Republic of China provides that 'a villagers committee shall, when necessary, establish sub-committees for people's mediation, public security, public health, etc.' The Organic Law of the Urban

19 October 2007: after investigation, the case was transferred to the People's Procuratorate for examination before prosecution.

24 October 2007: the prosecutor informed the victim and suspect of their rights and obligations with regard to criminal reconciliation; the victim and suspect provided signed statements indicating their willingness to participate in criminal reconciliation; the prosecutor heard the victim's opinions about the case.

28 October 2007: the prosecutor wrote a report about the decision to use criminal reconciliation in the case.

8 November 2007: a criminal reconciliation meeting was held and achieved three 'agreements.' First, the suspect apologized to the victim. Second, the suspect paid compensation in the amount of 1,000 yuan to the victim. Third, there would be a rehabilitation programme undertaken by the community the suspect was living in.

9 April 2008: the prosecutor inquired about the suspect's performance with the community volunteers and the suspect's 'leadership (*lingdao*)' in work.

18 April 2008: the community volunteers and the suspect's leader submitted final reports about the suspect's performance during the rehabilitation period to the prosecutor. The suspect submitted a 'thought report' (*sixiang huibao*) to the prosecutor.

'Thought reports,' or, *sixiang huibao,* are supposed to be written, for instance, by the members of the Chinese Communist Party or people who intend to join the Chinese Communist Party.[35] The content often covers their opinions on the Party's policies and political events, and any problems in personal life, and so on. The Chinese Communist Party intends to thereby understand the political positions and thoughts of the writers of *sixiang huibao*. The phrase used here in criminal reconciliation indicates that what the suspects are asked to write is similar to thought reports written for the purpose of joining the Chinese Communist Party and Party members: the report will be about the writer's thoughts and

---

Residents' Committees of the People's Republic of China provides that 'a residents committee shall, when necessary, establish sub-committees for people's mediation, public security, public health and other matters.' See: Li Keji [李克杰] 'A Contradictory System of Quality and Task and Its Gap from the Reality [素质与任务的矛盾制度与现实的断裂]' at http://epaper.timedg.com/html/2010-07/12/content_492444.htm (last accessed on 20 December 2010).

[35] See 'An Introduction of the Thought Report System in the Chinese Communist Party [党员思想汇报制度]' at http://www.whci.gov.cn/whjszx/shownews_dj.asp?newsid=20 (last accessed on 27 January 2011) and 'An Introduction of the Thought Report System in Universities in China [学生党员思想汇报制度]' at http://www.csust.edu.cn/pub/wfxy/xsgz/xsdj/t20081121_83308.htm (last accessed on 27 January 2011).

experience, and it is written for the People's Procuratorate's acknowledgement and review. More in-depth analysis of 'thought report' can be found in Chapter 6.

As a consequence of the follow-up period having been successfully concluded, the prosecutor made the decision not to prosecute the suspect.

It could be seen that the criminal reconciliation procedure in the fieldwork locations had also gone through the stage of initiation, criminal reconciliation meeting and a criminal reconciliation agreement at the end of the meeting, the official's decision (e.g. not to prosecute) and in some cases, a subsequent 'follow-up' programme. In the following, the author shows each stage with the documents enclosed in the case files to elaborate the criminal reconciliation procedure in the three locations as depicted by the case files.

At the initiation stage of the criminal reconciliation programme

In all three locations, the author saw statements written by the victims or suspects/defendants in which they stated that they had participated in criminal reconciliation programmes voluntarily. In Chongqing, the author also saw statements signed by both parties about their voluntary acceptance of criminal reconciliation. It is important to remember here that 'the parties' to a criminal reconciliation case were not necessarily the suspect and victim, but might be their representatives, such as the juvenile parties' parents.

Immediately before the meeting, the procedure was that the prosecutor/judge would merely ask the parties if the statements reflected their true intentions, and their replies would be written down by the prosecutor/judge and enclosed in the case files. If the parties confirmed that those statements reflected their true intentions, a criminal reconciliation meeting would be held and a compensation agreement might be reached.

In a few cases, before a criminal reconciliation meeting could be initiated, the suspect/defendant had also been required by the official to provide a written apology, addressed to the victim, in advance of the meeting. The victim or victim's family had also been required by the official to provide a statement expressing acceptance of the suspect/defendant's apology and criminal reconciliation. These documents showed that much negotiation (undocumented or documented but not available to the author) must have gone on before the formal criminal reconciliation procedure was initiated. Below the author provides an example of such a document written by the victim of a suspected theft case in Changzhou.[36] Actually, it was a form that had been supplied by

[36] Translated from the form enclosed in the case file of case no. 6, a suspected theft case in location A.

the Procuratorate. The victim only needed to fill in the suspect's name and the suspected crime.

> To the People's Procuratorate of X district in Changzhou:
>
> As to the case being examined for prosecution by you, I accept the apology extended by and agree to the use of criminal reconciliation in this case.
>
> The party: Date:

The very existence of such forms no doubt assists the bureaucratic management of this process but also raises questions as to the 'voluntariness' of the participating parties and as to whether such pro formas capture the real feelings and motivations of the participants.

The criminal reconciliation meeting

In Changzhou, the case files showed that except for one case, the prosecutors had held one or more criminal reconciliation meetings in each of the nine cases. Those participating in these meetings varied, as shown in Table 3.1. Some meetings were attended by one party in the sense defined above, some by both, and some also by other persons who could not be regarded as parties to the conflict that was at issue in the reconciliation process. In the tenth case, the parties had reached an agreement solely through the prosecutor's persuasion in separate meetings with the suspect and the victim (and their representatives), and these parties had in fact never met.[37]

As for the meeting place, six of the meetings were held in the Procuratorate (often in the responsible officials' offices); three were held in the parties' schools; one was held in the Justice Bureau, as is shown in Table 3.1.

In Chongqing, each of the eight cases studied had one criminal reconciliation meeting presided over by the prosecutor and attended by both parties, or one party, or some other participants, as can be seen in detail from Table 3.2. All the meetings were held in the prosecutors' offices.

In all the cases examined in Xi'an, one criminal reconciliation meeting had been held by the prosecutors/judges in their offices. Some meetings were attended by both parties, some by the parties' families, and some also by other participants such as the parties' teachers or employers or the officials from the Justice Bureau. The detailed information is presented in Table 3.3.

---

[37] From the conversation with the presiding prosecutor of this case.

Table 3.1 Criminal reconciliation meetings in the People's Procuratorate of X district, Changzhou (hereafter cited as location A)

Case	Participants of the first meeting	Participants of the second meeting (if any)	Meeting place
Case no. 1: suspected traffic accident related crime	The prosecutor; the suspect; the victim's family; the police officers concerned with the case; officials of the Justice Bureau	No second meeting	The People's Procuratorate of X district
Case no. 2: suspected traffic accident related crime	The prosecutor; the suspect; the victim's family	The prosecutor; the suspect; the victim's family; officials of the Justice Bureau; official of the Community Correction Office of Jiangsu province[1]	The People's Procuratorate of X district (both meetings)
Case no. 3: suspected traffic accident related crime	The prosecutor; the suspect; the victim's family	No second meeting	The People's Procuratorate of X district
Case no. 4: suspected traffic accident related crime	The prosecutor; the suspect; the victim's family; the police officer concerned with the case; officials of the Justice Bureau	No second meeting	The People's Procuratorate of X district
Case no. 5: suspected theft crime	The prosecutor; the suspect; the victim; both parties' parents; the suspect's teachers and some students' representatives from the parties' school; the police officer concerned with this case	No second meeting	The suspect and the victim's school (they are from the same school)
Case no. 6: suspected theft crime	The prosecutor; the suspect; the victim; the officials of the Justice Bureau	No second meeting	The Justice Bureau of X district

Table 3.1 (continued)

Case	Participants of the first meeting	Participants of the second meeting (if any)	Meeting place
Case no. 7: suspected theft crime	The prosecutor; the suspect	No second meeting	The People's Procuratorate of X district
Case no. 8: suspected theft crime	No criminal reconciliation meeting	No criminal reconciliation meeting	N/A
Case no. 9: suspected intentional injury crime	The prosecutor; the suspect; the victim; both parties' parents	The prosecutor; the suspect; the victim; both parties' parents; both parties' teachers; student representatives	The first meeting: the People's Procuratorate of X district; the second meeting: the parties' school
Case no. 10: suspected intentional injury crime	The prosecutor; the suspect; the victim; both parties' parents; both parties' teachers	No second meeting	The parties' school

Note: [1] The Community Correction Office of Jiangsu Province (江苏省社区矫正办公室) is an organ established by and directly subordinate to the Department of Justice in Jiangsu province. Its main work includes: (i) formulating plans, rules and strategies for community correction work in Jiangsu province; (ii) supervising, overviewing and guiding the community correction work in Jiangsu province; (iii) organizing training and theoretical study of community correction in Jiangsu province; (iv) coordinating community correction work with other institutions in Jiangsu province. See the website of the Justice Department of Jiangsu Province at http://www.jssf.gov.cn/xxgk/jgsz/nsjg/200810/t20081028_18928.html (last accessed on 6 December 2010).

Table 3.2 Criminal reconciliation meetings in the People's Procuratorate of D district, Chongqing (hereafter cited as location B)

Case	Participants of the criminal reconciliation meeting	Meeting place
Case no. 1: suspected intentional injury crime	The prosecutor; the suspects; the victim	The People's Procuratorate of D district
Case no. 2: suspected intentional injury crime	The prosecutor; the suspect; the victim; the victim's family	The People's Procuratorate of D district
Case no. 3: suspected intentional injury crime	The prosecutor; the suspect	The People's Procuratorate of D district
Case no. 4: suspected intentional injury crime	The prosecutor; the suspect; the victim	The People's Procuratorate of D district
Case no. 5: suspected intentional injury crime	The prosecutor; the suspects; the victim	The People's Procuratorate of D district
Case no. 6: suspected intentional injury crime	The prosecutor; the suspects; the victim	The People's Procuratorate of D district
Case no. 7: suspected intentional injury crime	The prosecutor; the suspects; the victim; the suspects' parents; the victim's parents; both parties' teacher	The People's Procuratorate of D district
Case no. 8: suspected traffic accident related crime	The prosecutor; the suspect; the victim's son (the victim died in the alleged traffic accident related crime)	The People's Procuratorate of D district

Table 3.3 Criminal reconciliation meetings in the People's Courts and Procuratorates of Y and B districts in Xi'an (hereafter cited as location C)

Location	Case	Participants of the first meeting	Participants of the second meeting (if any)	Meeting place
The People's Court of Y district	Case no. 1: suspected traffic accident related crime	The judge; the defendant; the victim's family	No second meeting	The People's Court of Y district
	Case no. 2: suspected traffic accident related crime	The judge; the defendant; the victim's family	No second meeting	The People's Court of Y district
	Case no. 3: suspected traffic accident related crime	The judge; the defendant; the victim's family; the defendant's leader at his work unit	No second meeting	The People's Court of Y district
The People's Procuratorate of Y district	Case no. 4: suspected juvenile robbery	The prosecutor; the suspects' parents; the victim's parents	The prosecutor; the suspects' parents; the victim's parents	The People's Procuratorate of Y district
The People's Court of B district	Case no. 5: suspected juvenile robbery	The judge; the defendants' parents; the victim's parents	The judge; the defendants' parents; the victim's parents; an official from the Justice Bureau	The People's Court of B district
	Case no. 6: suspected juvenile robbery	The judge; the defendants' parents; the victim's parents	No second meeting	The People's Court of B district

Location	Case	Participants of the first meeting	Participants of the second meeting (if any)	Meeting place
The People's Procuratorate of B district	Case no. 7: suspected traffic accident related crime	The prosecutor; the suspect; the victim's family	No second meeting	The People's Procuratorate of Y district
	Case no. 8: suspected traffic accident related crime	The prosecutor; the suspect; the victim's family	No second meeting	The People's Procuratorate of Y district
	Case no. 9: suspected traffic accident related crime	The prosecutor; the suspect; the victim's family	No second meeting	The People's Procuratorate of Y district
	Case no. 10: suspected traffic accident related crime	The prosecutor; the suspect; the victim's family	No second meeting	The People's Procuratorate of Y district
	Case no. 11: suspected juvenile robbery	The prosecutor; the suspect; the victim; the parties' teacher and classmates	No second meeting	The People's Procuratorate of Y district

The meeting recorded in these three locations contained additional information or description: they stated, for instance, that there had been 'active communication between the parties in a peaceful atmosphere which focused on apology and compensation.' Some meeting records also stated that the prosecutors/judges were engaged in 'an effort to provide the suspects/defendants with legal knowledge.' For instance, in one robbery case, the prosecutor had read Article 264 of the 1996 PRC Criminal Law, which concerned robbery, in the meeting, and advised the suspect to treasure this opportunity and change his mistaken idea of 'reaping without sowing' and to strive to be a person contributing to society.[38]

The criminal reconciliation agreement

All the cases examined had a criminal reconciliation agreement enclosed. In terms of the content of the agreement, it was drafted in simple terms and mainly involved a requirement that the suspect/defendant provided an apology and compensation. Here is an example taken from Changzhou:[39]

> Party A: the suspect
>
> Party B: the husband and son of the victim (who died in the suspected traffic accident related crime)
>
> At 19:16 pm on 14 January 2007, a traffic accident happened on 332th street next to X Factory in which the suspect's car (with the licence plate number: xxx) hit the victim, who died the same night in hospital. Through negotiation, the two parties reached an agreement on compensation: the suspect is to pay 390,000 yuan to the victim's husband and son in one instalment. After the payment has been made, the two parties agree not to trouble each other any further. Since the suspect has taken care of the financial needs of the victim's family, the victim's family decided to request the judicial system not to investigate the suspect's criminal liability.
>
> Party A (signature): Party B (signature):

The official's decision after the criminal reconciliation programme

The outcome of all the criminal reconciliation cases examined in the three People's Procuratorates took the form of the prosecutor's decision not to prosecute and to expunge the suspect's criminal record. The

---

[38] From the report on the criminal reconciliation meeting of case no. 5, a suspected theft case in location A.

[39] From case no. 4, a suspected traffic accident related crime case in location A.

outcome of the three resolved cases conducted in the People's Courts in Xi'an was a suspended sentence. According to the records contained in the case files, such decisions were made by the presiding prosecutor or judge, which had to be discussed by the procuratorial committee/judicial committee[40] beforehand for approval.[41] Yet the record of the procuratorial committee/judicial committee discussion was, as noted earlier, 'secret,' which meant that the non-judicial parties themselves could not review it. The final decision was written and signed by the presiding prosecutor/judge alone with some reasons given to support it. The reasoning supporting the decision not to prosecute in all the observed cases was similar to the example below taken from the file of a suspected traffic accident related crime studied at the People's Procuratorate of B district in Xi'an:[42]

A decision not to prosecute was made based on the following reasons:

1. Traffic accident related crime was a delinquency, and the suspect had expressed regret and repentance to the victim's family.
2. In this case, the victim also had some faults.
3. The victim's family had forgiven the suspect. The two parties had reached an agreement which was fully complied with by them.
4. This decision was in accordance with the spirit of criminal reconciliation and judicial resources saving.

---

40 Article 11 of the 2006 Organic Law of the People's Courts of the People's Republic of China stipulates that 'the People's court at any level shall set up judicial committee [审判委员会] which adopts the principle of democratic centralism.' 'The tasks of the judicial committee are to summarize judicial experience and to discuss important or difficult cases and other issues relating to judicial work.' 'The president of the People's Court should preside over the meetings of the judicial committee.' The chief procurator of the People's Procuratorate at the corresponding level may attend such meetings but without voting rights.' See the English translation at http://www.pkulaw.cn/fulltext_form.aspx?Db=chl&Gid=81825 (last accessed on 7 December 2010).

41 Opinions on Reforming and Improving the Judicial Committee of the People's Court Issued by the Supreme People's Court [最高人民法院关于改革和完善人民法院审判委员会制度的实施意见] (2010). See the English translation at http://en.pkulaw.cn/display.aspx?cgid=127979&lib=law (last accessed on 7 December 2010). Article 4 of the 2008 Organic Regulation of the Procuratorial Committee of the People's Procuratorate [检察委员会组织条例] at http://www.lawinfochina.com/display.aspx?lib=law&id=6742&CGid= (last accessed on 7 December 2010).

42 From case no. 7, a suspected traffic accident related crime case in location C.

Follow-up programmes

Half of the ten cases in Changzhou included follow-up programmes. In Chongqing, there was only one intentional injury crime case with follow-up 'supervision work.' In Xi'an, the officials' reconciliation decisions for all the four juvenile robbery cases demanded that the suspects participated in follow-up programmes called 'help and teaching' (*bangjiao*).

A 'help and teaching' programme, or *bangjiao*, was effectively a supervision period, in most observed cases of half a year. It involved a series of activities arranged by the officials for the suspects/defendants. Usually, those activities were undertaken by volunteers from the universities or communities that the suspects/defendants dwelled in, or by the officials themselves. In the 'help and teaching' programmes, the suspects/defendants were asked to participate in some voluntary activities or activities organized by the courts/procuratorates like art performance or basic legal knowledge workshops. In addition, the people responsible for such a programme would visit the suspects'/defendants' families to have conversations with them, and take them for an outing. In the cases the author studied, two of the 'help and teaching' programmes (*bangjiao*) were undertaken by volunteers serviced by some university students, while the other two were handled personally by the presiding judges.

Figure 3.1 is a flowchart showing the envisaged stages of a 'help and teaching' programme (*bangjiao*) obtained from the People's Procuratorate of Y district in Xi'an.

In the follow-up programme, the official had to assess the suspect/defendant's 'rehabilitation' or 'correction situation' (*jiaozheng qingkuang*). What was meant by this was an account of the suspect/defendant's performance in the school or work unit after a criminal reconciliation meeting had been successfully held and the victim and suspect had formally agreed to 'reconcile.' It was made on the basis of the volunteer's reports, the suspect/defendant's teacher's or leader's reports, and the suspect/defendant's 'thought reports' which were all about the suspect/defendant's performance and made every month, or once every several months. If the suspect/defendant performed well according to those reports, a decision not to prosecute (or a lenient sentence in the Court) would be confirmed by the official and the case closed; otherwise, the suspect would be prosecuted again (or the lenient sentence for the defendant would be revoked).

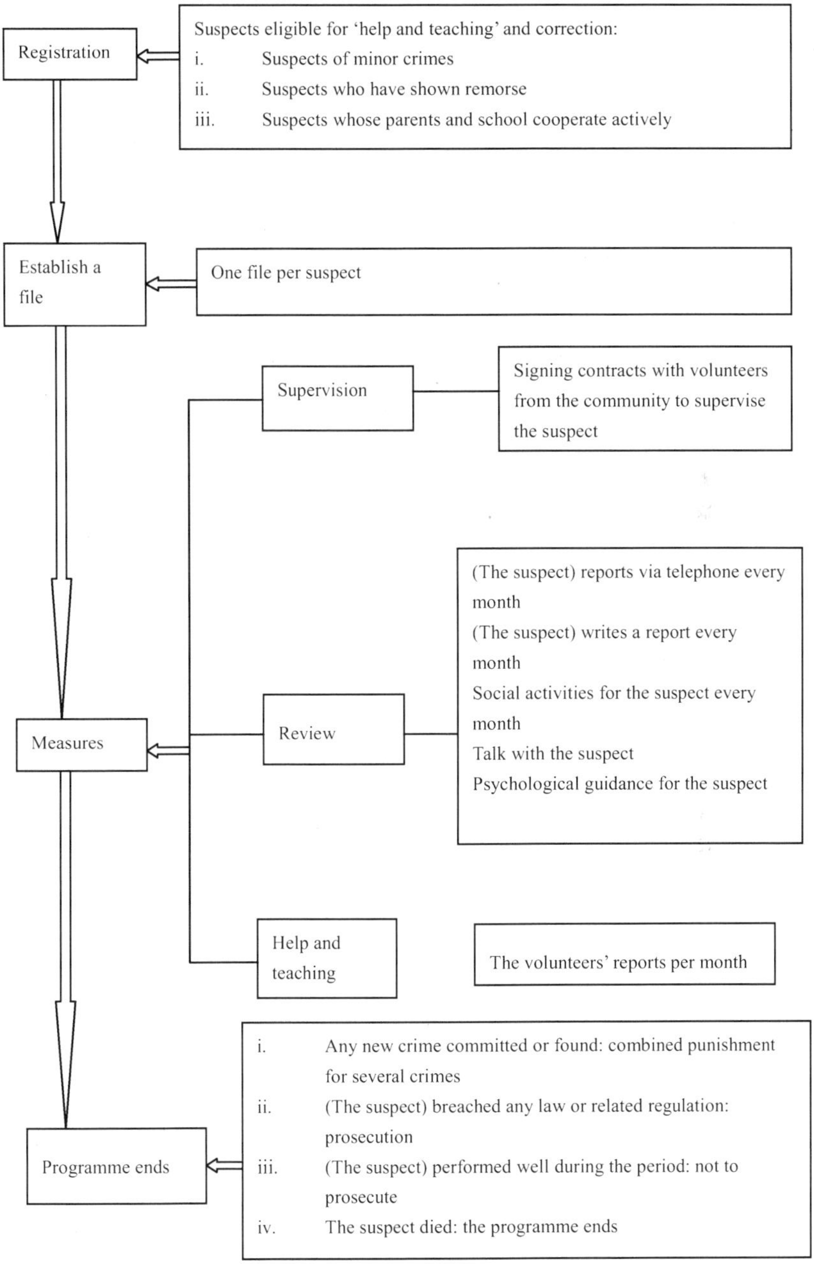

Figure 3.1 Correction procedure of the People's Procuratorate of Y district, Xi'an

According to the supervision reports reviewed in the context of this research project, whether supplied by the prosecutors/judges, or the volunteers from the communities and universities, or the juvenile suspects'/offenders' schools and parents, the suspects/defendants all performed well after criminal reconciliation meetings. The reports demonstrated a satisfactory 'correction' or 'rehabilitation situation' of the follow-up programme. Usually, such positive assessments took the form that 'X studied much harder than before,'[43] or 'X worked very hard and the superiors were now very satisfied,'[44] or 'X became more mature,'[45] or 'X helped doing housework and did not indulge in playing online games,'[46] or 'X stayed away from his "bad friends" and got along well with his classmates and teachers'[47] and so on. Furthermore, the suspects'/defendants' 'thought reports' always mentioned their gratitude for the officials and criminal reconciliation (as it gave them a chance to rectify their faults), their deep reflection, sincere regret, and positive resolutions for the future, together with a description of their satisfactory recent situation. According to the final reports enclosed in the case files, the prosecutors/judges evaluated all such information as criminal reconciliation's outcome of effective suspect/defendant rehabilitation.

3.2.6 Duration of Criminal Reconciliation Programmes

It was noted in the first chapter that criminal reconciliation was officially predicted to close a case more efficiently, compared to the normal criminal processes, in an attempt to save judicial resources. Yet the practices in the fieldwork locations as shown in the case files did not supply evidence of this.

---

[43] From the supervision work reports enclosed in the case files of case nos 5 and 9 in location A, case no. 7 in location B, and case nos 4, 6 and 11 in location C.

[44] From the supervision work report enclosed in the case file of case no. 6 in location A.

[45] From the supervision work report enclosed in the case files of case nos 7 and 10 in location A and case no. 7 in location B.

[46] From the supervision work report enclosed in the case file of case no. 6 in location A.

[47] From the supervision work reports enclosed in the case files of case nos 5, 6 and 11 in location C.

Counting from the point in time at which the alleged criminal offence had happened, half of the studied cases in Changzhou lasted for less than one year until the official announced the decision, while the rest lasted for up to two years, as can be seen from Table 3.4. What can also be noticed from this table is that criminal reconciliation processes in which two meetings were held lasted longer than processes with only one meeting or without any meeting. Processes with more participants attending the meeting or meetings lasted longer than those in which only one party and the prosecutor attended the meeting or meetings.

Table 3.4 Timetable of criminal reconciliation cases in the People's Procuratorate of X district, Changzhou

Case	Timeline
Case no. 1: suspected traffic accident related crime	Duration: one year 14 April 2007: the alleged criminal offence occurred; 24 March 2008: the criminal reconciliation meeting was held; 18 April 2008: the prosecutor announced the decision not to prosecute the suspect
Case no. 2: suspected traffic accident related crime	Duration: one year and two months 14 February 2007: the alleged criminal offence occurred; 11 March 2008: the first criminal reconciliation meeting was held; 21 March 2008: the second criminal reconciliation meeting was held; 18 April 2008: the prosecutor announced the decision not to prosecute the suspect
Case no. 3: suspected traffic accident related crime	Duration: three months 16 November 2006: the alleged criminal offence occurred; 26 January 2007: the criminal reconciliation meeting was held; 12 February 2007: the prosecutor announced the decision not to prosecute the suspect
Case no. 4: suspected traffic accident related crime	Duration: six months 14 January 2007: the alleged criminal offence occurred; 4 July 2007: the criminal reconciliation meeting was held; 9 July 2007: the prosecutor announced the decision not to prosecute the suspect
Case no. 5: suspected theft crime	Duration: one year 20 April 2007: the alleged criminal offence occurred; 8 April 2008: the criminal reconciliation meeting was held; 21 April 2008: the prosecutor announced the decision not to prosecute the suspect

Table 3.4 (continued)

Case	Timeline
Case no. 6: suspected theft crime	Duration: one year and five months 17 November 2006: the alleged criminal offence occurred; 8 November 2007: the criminal reconciliation meeting was held; 18 April 2008: the prosecutor announced the decision not to prosecute the suspect
Case no. 7: suspected theft crime	Duration: three months 8 December 2006: the alleged criminal offence occurred; 2 February 2007: the criminal reconciliation meeting was held; 8 February 2007: the prosecutor announced the decision not to prosecute the suspect
Case no. 8: suspected theft crime	Duration: six months 11 July 2006: the alleged criminal offence occurred; 8 February 2007: the prosecutor announced the decision not to prosecute the suspect
Case no. 9: suspected intentional injury crime	Duration: one year and four months 5 January 2006: the alleged criminal offence occurred; 18 July 2006: the first criminal reconciliation meeting was held; 9 May 2007: the second criminal reconciliation meeting was held; 19 May 2007: the prosecutor announced the decision not to prosecute the suspect
Case no. 10: suspected intentional injury crime	Duration: eight months 7 April 2007: the alleged criminal offence occurred; 28 November 2007: the criminal reconciliation meeting was held; 6 December 2007: the prosecutor announced the decision not to prosecute the suspect

Five of the eight cases the author examined in Chongqing lasted for less than one year from the initial incident until the prosecutor announced the decision not to prosecute. The rest lasted for one year and over, as shown in Table 3.5.

In Xi'an, except for one case that had not yet been resolved at the point the author conducted the fieldwork, those criminal reconciliation programmes with two meetings lasted for over a year, while those with one meeting closed within one year. The detailed information is presented in Table 3.6.

Table 3.5 Timetable of criminal reconciliation programmes in the People's Procuratorate of D district, Chongqing

Case	Timeline
Case no. 1: suspected intentional injury crime	Duration: four months 3 January 2006: the alleged criminal offence occurred; April 2006: the criminal reconciliation meeting was held; May 2006: the prosecutor announced the decision not to prosecute the suspects
Case no. 2: suspected intentional injury crime	Duration: one year and one month 24 June 2006: the alleged criminal offence occurred; July 2007: the criminal reconciliation meeting was held; July 2007: the prosecutor announced the decision not to prosecute the suspect
Case no. 3: suspected intentional injury crime	Duration: six months January 2007: the alleged criminal offence occurred; June 2007: the criminal reconciliation meeting was held; July 2007: the prosecutor announced the decision not to prosecute the suspect
Case no .4: suspected intentional injury crime	Duration: eleven months January 2007: the alleged criminal offence occurred; 19 November 2007: the criminal reconciliation meeting was held; 4 December 2007: the prosecutor announced the decision not to prosecute the suspect
Case no. 5: suspected intentional injury crime	Duration: one year and two months October 2006: the alleged criminal offence occurred; December 2007: the criminal reconciliation meeting was held; 21 December 2007: the prosecutor announced the decision not to prosecute the suspects
Case no. 6: suspected intentional injury crime	Duration: eleven months 23 June 2006: the alleged criminal offence occurred; May 2007: the criminal reconciliation meeting was held; May 2007: the prosecutor announced the decision not to prosecute the suspects
Case no. 7: suspected intentional injury crime	Duration: one year and two months 9 September 2006: the alleged criminal offence occurred; October 2007: the criminal reconciliation meeting was held; November 2007: the prosecutor announced the decision not to prosecute the suspect
Case no. 8: suspected traffic accident related crime	Duration: five months December 2007: the alleged criminal offence occurred; 25 April 2008: the criminal reconciliation meeting was held; 19 May 2008: the prosecutor announced the decision not to prosecute the suspect

Table 3.6 Timetable of criminal reconciliation programmes in the People's Courts and Procuratorates of Y and B districts in Xi'an

Spot	Case	Timeline
The People's Court of Y district	Case no. 1: suspected traffic accident related crime	Duration: five months May 2008: the alleged criminal offence occurred; September 2008: the criminal reconciliation meeting was held; October 2008: the judge announced the suspended sentence
	Case no. 2: suspected traffic accident related crime	Duration: ten months November 2008: the alleged criminal offence occurred; July 2009: the criminal reconciliation meeting was held; September 2009: the judge announced the suspended sentence
	Case no. 3: suspected traffic accident related crime	Duration: four months January 2010: the alleged criminal offence occurred; May 2010: the criminal reconciliation meeting was held; May 2010: the judge announced the suspended sentence
The People's Procuratorate of Y district	Case no. 4: suspected juvenile robbery	Duration: one year and three months February 2009: the alleged criminal offence occurred; January 2010: the first criminal reconciliation meeting was held; May 2010: the second criminal reconciliation meeting was held; May 2010: the prosecutor announced the decision not to prosecute
The People's Court of B district	Case no. 5: suspected juvenile robbery	Duration: one year August 2009: the alleged criminal offence occurred; May 2010: the first criminal reconciliation meeting was held; 28 July 2010: the second criminal reconciliation meeting was held; August 2010: the judge announced the suspended sentence
	Case no. 6: suspected juvenile robbery (unresolved)	Duration: one year and seven months (unresolved) February 2009: the alleged criminal offence occurred; February 2010: the criminal reconciliation meeting was held

Spot	Case	Timeline
The People's Procuratorate of B district	Case no. 7: suspected traffic accident related crime	Duration: four months January 2009: the alleged criminal offence occurred; April 2009: the criminal reconciliation meeting was held; April 2009: the prosecutor announced the decision not to prosecute
	Case no. 8: suspected traffic accident related crime	Duration: eleven months January 2009: the alleged criminal offence occurred; December 2009: the criminal reconciliation meeting was held; December 2009: the prosecutor announced the decision not to prosecute
	Case no. 9: suspected traffic accident related crime	Duration: ten months March 2009: the alleged criminal offence occurred; January 2010: the criminal reconciliation meeting was held; January 2010: the prosecutor announced the decision not to prosecute
	Case no. 10: suspected traffic accident related crime	Duration: six months February 2009: the alleged criminal offence occurred; July 2009: the criminal reconciliation meeting was held; August 2009: the prosecutor announced the decision not to prosecute
	Case no. 11: suspected juvenile robbery	Duration: ten months April 2008: the alleged criminal offence occurred; January 2009: the criminal reconciliation meeting was held; February 2009: the prosecutor announced the decision not to prosecute

The cases studied in the three locations indicated that most of the criminal reconciliation programmes lasted for less than one year from the initial incident to the officials' confirmation of the decision, while some, especially those with two criminal reconciliation meetings, took up to two years. As indicated by some officials, this was no shorter than the average time needed in the formal criminal justice procedure to dispose of such kinds of minor crimes, which ordinarily took three to six months. Most of the officials interviewed also commented that criminal reconciliation took much more of their time and energy compared to formal criminal justice processes. This situation is in contradiction to the official expectation that criminal reconciliation would take less time than the formal criminal justice processes.

3.3 AN ANALYSIS OF THE PRACTICE OF CRIMINAL RECONCILIATION RELYING ON THE EVIDENCE FROM OFFICIAL CASE FILES

The information provided in the case files, from the official perspective notwithstanding, sheds some light on the questions raised in the first part of this chapter that were concerned with the process and outcomes of this programme. In this part, the information described in the previous section is analysed to address those questions. We begin by looking into the procedure of this programme to see whether it operated in practice in accordance with its design as set out in Chapter 1. Since the author's access to the procedures and guidelines in Chongqing and Xi'an was denied, the procedure summarized by scholars, as shown in Chapter 1, is adopted as a criterion here.

3.3.1 The Procedure of Criminal Reconciliation in Practice

The initiation stage

As shown in the case files, the criminal reconciliation programme in all the three locations studied had adopted the mode that 'the People's Procuratorate/People's Court initiates criminal reconciliation based on examining the case and asking for the parties' opinions as regards if they agree to participate.'[48]

As to the requirements of eligible cases which should be examined by officials, it appears that all the cases studied in the three places comply with the stipulated requirements. With regard to the kind of suspected crime, all the studied cases concerned 'minor crimes.' With regard to the suspect/defendant, no preference for juvenile suspect/defendant could be found and this was not a compulsory premise of initiating this programme. With regard to the parties' voluntary participation, all the case files the author was given access to had enclosed documents such as letters written by the parties or forms filled out by the parties that explicitly provided such information. Additionally, all the interrogation records enclosed in the case files included the prosecutors'/judges' question to the suspects/defendants as to whether or not they admitted guilt, and the answer was invariably 'yes.'

---

[48] Cai Guoqin [蔡国芹] *Research on Criminal Mediation System* [*刑事调解制度研究*] Beijing, The Chinese People's Public Security University Press [中国人民公安大学出版社] 2010, 232.

The criminal reconciliation meeting

So far as the officials' presiding and the parties' attendance is concerned, the practices in the three places were generally in accordance with the requirements. As shown in the above tables, in most of the examined cases, the criminal reconciliation meeting was presided over by an official and attended by both parties or their agents (or also by other people such as the parties' leaders, bosses, teachers and classmates). Yet there is one case each in Changzhou and Chongqing in which only one party attended the meeting, and one case in Changzhou that did not hold any criminal reconciliation meeting.

It is also a requirement that in the meeting, the prosecutor/judge provides the parties with sufficient communication and negotiation without interfering with the discussion or commenting on any party's statements. In other words, it is required that the case should be fully discussed and primarily resolved by the parties themselves. As mentioned above, documents contained in the case files also showed that the communication in the criminal reconciliation meetings was sufficient, that it addressed all relevant questions and was conducted in a 'peaceful' atmosphere. Although a few presiding officials had delivered some 'educational comments' in the meetings, it would be far-fetched to say that they had interfered with the process. To that extent, participation in and contributions to the criminal reconciliation meetings could be characterized as voluntary.

In terms of the issue of 'fairness' stressed in the local regulations or guidelines as summarized by the scholars, although there was no document in the case files directly on this point, there was no hint of 'unfairness' in those files.

The official's decision

As required, in the People's Procuratorate, the prosecutor's decision for a case closed through criminal reconciliation could be non-prosecution, suggesting that the Public Security Bureau withdraw the case, or suggesting a lenient punishment for the suspect to the People's Court. In the People's Court, the judge's decision could be a lenient sentence for the defendant. As presented above, these possible outcomes were precisely what the case files demonstrated.

Moreover, as exemplified, in all the cases studied, the prosecutors'/judges' decisions were supported by many reasons and had been discussed by the procuratorial committee or judicial committee before being announced.

The procedural regulation also provided that in a criminal reconciliation programme if an agreement could not be reached, or either party regretted prior to signing the agreement, the case should be transferred to the normal procedure immediately, but no case file the author examined embodied that situation.

The follow-up programmes

As shown above, in the three fieldwork locations, a follow-up programme was conducted in some cases. Since this was not a compulsory requirement, the practice in these locations was in accordance with the procedural regulation or guideline.

In conclusion, by and large, the practice of criminal reconciliation in the places studied had complied with the procedure designed for criminal reconciliation. Yet as pointed out in the previous parts as well, there were still some circumstances in which the procedure was not followed (i.e. no criminal reconciliation meeting was held at all in a case in Changzhou). The reason for the incidental violations of the requirements is further discussed in Chapters 4 and 5, along with the description of the officials on their incentives and considerations of these violations.

The next question was concerned with the outcomes of the criminal reconciliation practices. Putting aside the situation in which the procedure was violated, can the practices complying with the procedure produce the purported outcomes or aims?

3.3.2 Achievements and Failures of the Official Goals in Practice

The Supreme People's Procuratorate and the Supreme People's Court, as shown in Chapter 1, have predicted some further outcomes for criminal reconciliation, namely reducing petitioning related to judicial cases (*she fa shangfang* or *she su shangfang*), providing closure (*an jie shi liao*) and promoting a harmonious society. Yet these outcomes cannot be observed through a study of the case files accessed.

As displayed in the case files, criminal reconciliation had addressed the problem with compensation enforcement which was viewed by the authorities as the main cause of petitioning related to judicial cases and the main obstacle to closure. Compensation, as the focus of the criminal reconciliation agreement, was provided by the suspect/defendant in full and usually on the spot. And it was also explicitly indicated in some agreements that the compensation amount was negotiated freely and autonomously by the parties, and that it involved some 'psychological compensation.' Nevertheless, the author thinks it is still hard to assert that such agreements or this programmme has given a final resolution to the conflict triggered by crime and satisfied the parties (or the victim at least), and thereby effectively tackled the issue of petitioning. Such messages were not provided in the official case files and could only be directly obtained from the parties.

As to better rehabilitating and correcting the suspect/defendant by means of non-prosecution or non-custodial punishments for the suspects/defendants, it appears to have been largely achieved in the cases with follow-up programmes. As shown above, all the reports provided by the officials and volunteers responsible for the follow-up programmes, and the 'thought reports' written by the suspects/defendants themselves, indicated a satisfactory situation of suspect/defendant rehabilitation. Nevertheless, such information could not be observed in the cases without a follow-up programme. In this regard, it can be said that a follow-up programme is of great significance for suspect/defendant rehabilitation. Yet cases without a follow-up programme constituted a very large part of the cases the author examined.

As also shown in Chapter 1, criminal reconciliation was also expected in academic work to promote the efficiency of the Chinese judicial system.[49] Judging from the cases studied, however, this process does not display much advantage in this aspect: most of the cases lasted for around one year (and some were up to two years). Only 4 among the 10 cases examined in Changzhou lasted for less than half a year; only 3 of the 8 cases examined in Chongqing lasted for less than half a year; and in Xi'an, except for 1 case that had not been resolved when the author conducted the empirical work, the equivalent figure is 4 out of 11 cases. Moreover, none of the suspected minor injury crime cases in those locations lasted less than 135 days. Hence, it seems that as compared with the normal criminal procedure, overall criminal reconciliation does not obviously promote judicial efficiency as commonly claimed.

Regarding the effects expected to be produced by the criminal reconciliation meeting, it seems that criminal reconciliation has made the parties participate and empowered them to resolve cases mainly by themselves. The criminal reconciliation meeting records showed that the victims and the suspects/defendants had been given sufficient opportunity to express their feelings and needs in the meetings and reached agreements based on their intentions.

It could also be seen from the case files studied that the educational effect of criminal reconciliation meetings was often highlighted by the officials. In the reports on criminal reconciliation meetings, which were

---

[49] Ma Mingliang [马明亮] *Negotiated Justice: A New Procedural Idea* [*协商性司法：一种新程序主义理念*] Beijing, Law Press [法律出版社] 2007, 1–5.

enclosed in the case files, the officials liked describing the suspects/defendants as having expressed their remorseful feelings, and then apologized to the victims (or their families and representatives) in the criminal reconciliation meetings. Yet no information concerning the criminal reconciliation meeting's long-term impact on suspects/defendants (especially recidivism prevention) can be observed from the case files.

For the victim, however, no message indicating this process's psychological reparation effect appears in the case files studied. Although the criminal reconciliation meeting records showed that the victims had expressed some negative emotions and communicated with the suspects/defendants actively in the meetings, and they had often obtained 'psychological compensation' as specified in the agreements, the effect of these arrangements on the victims cannot be assessed.

To sum up, it appears from the case files that the criminal reconciliation practices in the fieldwork locations have produced the purported effects of resolving the problem with compensation enforcement and empowering the parties to resolve the cases mainly by themselves. In the cases with a criminal reconciliation meeting, the communication between the parties is sufficient and voluntary, and the goal of educating the suspect/defendant is achieved. In the cases with follow-up programmes, the effect of correcting the suspect/defendant is positive. Yet the officially stated aims concerning the parties' feelings and those somewhat long-term goals like preventing recidivism and facilitating a 'harmonious society' cannot be evaluated from the case files. The goal of judicial efficiency promotion has generally failed in the three fieldwork locations.

It seems therefore that complying with the procedure does not guarantee the expected outcomes. Moreover, it is worth noting that the case files can only show how criminal reconciliation operated from the accounts on paper, and actually it was chiefly described by the officials who had conducted it and very likely was selected as 'the best practices' by them. That is to say, the actual practice might be very different from the information presented in this chapter.

3.3.3 Questioning the Official Design of the Criminal Reconciliation Procedure

Nevertheless, there arises the question that why did complying with the procedure not produce the predicted outcomes? In the author's opinion, this is first concerned with the procedure in itself. This is to say, many provisions in the local procedural regulations or guidelines have embodied the danger that some expected outcomes might fail in practice. Some of the failures had been shown in the cases the author was permitted to examine as listed above, while others might not be shown in the case files.

For example, it was stipulated in the regulations or guidelines that the criminal reconciliation meeting could be attended by the representatives of the parties. However, it was hard to expect such a meeting without the parties' presence to produce the outcomes expected through participation and sufficient communication between the parties. As analysed by some scholars like Cai Guoqin, the victim could feel relieved only or at best through expressing the feelings and emotions related to the alleged crime to the person causing it (in his/her mind) and through sufficient and free communication with the suspect/defendant.[50] Hearing the suspect/defendant's apology was also of great significance for psychological reparation to the victim.[51] The victim's expression as such in a face-to-face meeting, according to Cai, could better educate the suspect/defendant and make them reflect and feel remorseful.[52]

Furthermore, the regulation and guidelines provided that many other people like the parties' employers, their 'leadership' or their teachers could also attend the criminal reconciliation meeting. Yet it was likely that their presence would place pressure on the suspect or victim (depending on the case) or at least make them uneasy, yet they had to accept this, as they might be reluctant to offend the officials as well as those people. More importantly, in this situation, it might be difficult to prevent the communication and discussions between the parties being impaired by this pressure and those 'powerful' persons for them.

The meeting place was also problematic. Although it was not specified in the procedural regulations, the author found in the case files that most of the criminal reconciliation meetings were held in the prosecutors'/judges' offices. Such a meeting place might also create some pressure for the parties as it could give them the impression that the criminal reconciliation process was still dominated by the officials rather than themselves. In addition, since the parties knew that the prosecutors/judges played a key role in their cases, it was possible that they might subject themselves to the officials' wishes.

In all these situations, the parties' voluntariness or autonomy could be easily violated. If the parties were coerced into participating in the

---

50 Cai Guoqin [蔡国芹] *Research on Criminal Mediation System* [*刑事调解制度研究*] Beijing, The Chinese People's Public Security University Press [中国人民公安大学出版社] 2010, 247.

51 Ibid.

52 Ibid.

criminal reconciliation programme, the outcomes of satisfying the parties, psychological reparation, and closure were unlikely to be produced. More importantly, such a process driven by official pressure is difficult to view as a process that empowers the parties to resolve the cases by themselves.

3.3.4 Conflicting Official Goals

Another reason causing the failure of some officially stated aims as shown in the case files is that the official goals set for criminal reconciliation conflict with each other.

As demonstrated in this chapter, criminal reconciliation in these three fieldwork locations failed to promote judicial efficiency. Yet it was actually very hard to close a case in a short time if the official properly observed the procedure, which asked for his/her explanation of the programme to the parties for their voluntary participation, arrangements for a meeting or meetings that were expected to produce so many outcomes and some follow-up programmes. These claimed goals were in conflict with each other because it was impossible to complete so many tasks in a short period. Perhaps this was also one reason that most of the cases examined did not have any follow-up programme. This further helps to address a question raised in the first part of this chapter in terms of the resolution when the aims conflicted with each other. In cases of conflicted aims, very likely, officials would choose those immediately beneficial for themselves, such as closing the case quickly, rather than those beneficial for the parties, such as conducting follow-up programmes.

This point may be supported by the finding that much negotiation and communication between the parties that ought to be an essential part of the criminal reconciliation meeting were in fact done before this programme was formally initiated. This suggested that, in this case, criminal reconciliation programmes were purely formal, empty processes allowing the officials to confirm agreements reached previously by the parties. This raised a suspicion of further, more serious, problems such as coercion or unfair deals. Those problems were hard to discover because on paper officials entered the process at a rather late stage, even assuming that they were interested in investigating. In fact, the case files suggested that the officials concerned would simply ask the parties whether the letters of apology or forgiveness were their true intentions as recorded in the case files. It seemed possible that the officials did not wish to find out those potential problems, which stem from what has been identified as conflicting goals of efficiency and voluntariness.

The above analysis shows that some of the official goals of criminal reconciliation might impair the interests of the parties concerned in this programme. Because of this, criminal reconciliation may not produce the outcomes of satisfying the parties and 'closure.'

Nevertheless, many questions or the questions raised above, especially if the parties were satisfied and if they were really coerced by the officials, can only be addressed through understanding the parties' feelings. The doubts and further questions cannot be answered through further examination of the case files. Of course, it is unreasonable to expect the case files to include all the information. Moreover, as a picture chiefly drawn by the officials, the case files were likely to have concealed some problems with the practice of criminal reconciliation. Perhaps there were more deficiencies in the procedure and the claimed outcomes (especially from the rights' perspectives). Therefore, it is important to conduct interviews with persons who had experience of criminal reconciliation to understand from them how it operated in practice.

4. The process of criminal reconciliation programmes: evidence from interviews

In Chapter 3, the practice of criminal reconciliation designed according to local regulations or guidelines in Changzhou, Chongqing and Xi'an was described based upon the documents enclosed in the case files and the extent that these practices were in compliance with the procedures was analysed. Nevertheless, case files could only show the practice as described 'on paper' and from an official perspective which might be skewed towards a favourable picture. Further investigation seemed both justified and indeed necessary to gain a complete understanding.

Because of deficiencies involved in the case file examination, further inquiry necessarily involved the utilization of other research methods. One obvious way was to interview people who had experience of this programme, especially the parties (the victim and suspect/defendant of the criminal reconciliation case concerned). Their feelings and comments on this programme were important to answering the questions raised by the case file examination.

In addition, the process of criminal reconciliation as described by them might be different from the one shown in the case files.

Therefore, interviews with people who had experienced criminal reconciliation programmes were conducted subsequent to the case file examination. Specifically, interviewees included judges and prosecutors who had been involved in conducting this programme, victims and suspects/defendants ('parties') who had participated in this programme, lawyers who had represented their clients in this programme, and some other people like the parties' parents or teachers who had also attended criminal reconciliation meetings. Questions designed for the interview centred on their experience, feelings and general comments on this programme.

In the first two interview series conducted in Changzhou and Chongqing, all the parties of the criminal reconciliation cases were contacted by the prosecutors and the author mostly had to interview them in the prosecutors' offices under the prosecutor's observation. This necessarily had the limitation that other parties might not feel free to share their true opinions in the presence of the prosecutor or judge who had presided over the reconciliation agreement. That would be especially so if the other party's 'consent' had been in any way forced or involuntary. Nevertheless, it was considered that there might be advantages to conducting interviews even under such constraints. In the third interview series in Xi'an, all the parties were contacted, approached and interviewed by the author alone without any official being present. It was felt that it would be easier for parties to speak freely by interviewing them alone as it could convince them, under guarantees of confidentiality and anonymity, that what they said would not adversely affect the outcome of their cases or their relationship with the officials.

As it transpired, information obtained in the interview, whether it was conducted with an official present or alone by the author, depicted a picture of criminal reconciliation different from what the case files had shown. In this chapter, the author describes the process of criminal reconciliation arising out of the interviewees' accounts. Differences between it and the process shown in the case files are pointed out along with the description. This description shows that more violations of the official procedures occurred, and it provides some insight into the tension between conflicting goals of criminal reconciliation as discussed in the preceding chapter. At the end of this chapter, further questions, mainly concerned with the parties' feelings and motivations and the officials' feelings and motivations during this process are raised to be addressed in the following chapter.

The discussion of the process of criminal reconciliation programmes in this chapter also tracks four stages: initiation of criminal reconciliation; criminal reconciliation meeting; official decision; and follow-up programmes.

4.1 THE INITIATION STAGE

4.1.1 Violations of Eligibility Requirements

Local procedural regulations or guidelines stipulate that at the initiation stage of a criminal reconciliation programme, the responsible prosecutor/judge should examine the case to see whether it was eligible for criminal reconciliation. As regards an eligible case, it was further provided that criminal reconciliation could be initiated only in cases of 'minor crimes' according to the PRC Criminal Law, and was encouraged in juvenile crimes. In addition, in cases being considered for criminal reconciliation, the suspects/defendants had to admit guilt (*renzui*) or show remorse (*huizui*) (in the 'Changzhou Regulation').

The case files examined implied that these requirements were fully observed by the officials. This finding was substantiated by several officials' accounts in the interview. For example, prosecutor L from the People's Procuratorate of B district in Xi'an summarized the factors the officials would consider before initiating criminal reconciliation.[1]

> Basically, we are inclined to initiate criminal reconciliation in a case with the following factors: first, it should be a case of 'minor crime.' The contradiction between the parties in 'minor crime' cases is often not very sharp and deep and therefore can be more easily resolved through reconciliation. This is a compulsory requirement. Second, it is desirable for there to be some relationship between the parties existing before the 'crime,'[2] for instance, they are neighbours, classmates or colleagues. It would be easier for acquaintances to reach a reconciliation agreement. Third, the suspect is a juvenile. Criminal reconciliation is recommended as an effective means to educate and correct juvenile suspects. Fourth, criminal reconciliation is suitable in cases where the victim also had some fault in the 'crime.' Fifth, there is no deep-rooted animus between the parties. Yet the latter three are not compulsory requirements for criminal reconciliation. And finally, the suspect must show remorse (*huizui*).

Some officials particularly mentioned their preference for criminal reconciliation in juvenile cases. One of them was judge L from the People's Court of B district in Xi'an.[3]

> I always appreciate criminal reconciliation as I believe that it is especially beneficial for young defendants. Criminal reconciliation can grant them one more chance to rectify mistakes, whereas litigation or imprisonment would very likely ruin their future, and even their whole life. So I have the tendency to use criminal reconciliation in juvenile cases.

The interviews more than merely substantiated what the case files had shown. In the interviews, officials also talked about how they decided to initiate criminal reconciliation in some cases that did *not* meet the

---

1 Interview with prosecutor L in the People's Procuratorate of B district in Xi'an in September 2010.

2 Prosecutor L simply said 'crime' (*fanzui*) in the interview. However, since the case was just processed at the stage of examination before prosecution, it actually should be characterized as 'alleged crime' or 'suspected crime' in this context.

3 Interview with judge L in the People's Court of B district in Xi'an in September 2010.

stipulated (strict and soft) requirements. Prosecutor H told the author how he changed his mind to initiate criminal reconciliation at the point when the suspects neither admitted guilt nor showed any regret at all in case no. seven in location B (an intentional injury case).[4]

> The Procuratorate I worked at was encouraging criminal reconciliation in juvenile cases, so I got in touch with the suspects to see if there was any chance for criminal reconciliation in this case when I received the case.
>
> Yet I found that the suspects showed an indifferent attitude towards their conduct and the victim they had allegedly harmed. Moreover, they each sought to put the blame on the other person. They did not realize that they had done something wrong and harmed other people. The suspects' parents were also indifferent about the victim their children had allegedly hurt and the criminal charge that their children had violated the law. They insisted that their children were the perfect and best ones in their minds.
>
> Regarding the victim, his parents and he were furious with the suspects after the case happened. The parents even threatened to retaliate.
>
> In such a situation, it was not feasible to use criminal reconciliation since the suspects did not show any repentance or regret and the contradiction between the two parties was fairly severe and sharp. However, after obtaining more information about the family background of the suspects, I began to reconsider resolving this case through criminal reconciliation.
>
> There were six suspects aged between 16 and 18 in this case. The suspect A lost his mother when he was little and lived with his father all along. His father was disabled and earned a living by selling fruit in a street market. B's parents had divorced and his father had married again; his mother, father and stepmother did not look after him much. C's mother worked in another city and only went back home once every six months. His father had stomach cancer and could not work. D's parents were not educated and did not have stable jobs, so the family had to live on subsistence allowances from the government. E's parents had also divorced yet lived together again, but they were too busy earning money and had no time to take care of their child. F's father was a migrant worker working in a construction plant with a very low salary; his mother was 'too weak' to work.
>
> Taking into account the suspects' family background, I felt that, on the one hand, it was unfair solely to blame the young suspects for their conduct as it was largely due to their parents' negligence; on the other hand, as the suspects were juveniles, prosecution and litigation would undoubtedly have very bad effects on their future. I also thought that since they still did not realize their fault and the harm allegedly caused by their conduct, it was difficult to count

---

[4] Interview with prosecutor H in the People's Procuratorate of D district in Chongqing in June 2008.

> on the ordinary criminal procedure to resolve it, which was even more harmful to their future moral development. Considering all these issues, I finally decided to initiate criminal reconciliation in this case.

In prosecutor H's accounts, it seemed that he viewed the suspects' remorse or admission of guilt as a result of criminal reconciliation rather than as a requirement for this programme. It was somewhat reasonable since the claim was that criminal reconciliation also had the effect of educating and correcting suspects/defendants. However, if this requirement could be arbitrarily abandoned by the officials, there might be a danger that an official could pressurize a suspect/defendant who was innocent (or claimed to be innocent) to enter this programme. Despite being an alternative to formal criminal litigation procedure, this programme is still part of the wider criminal procedure and involves the coercive power of the State. It is noticeable in prosecutor H's accounts that actually he simply viewed the suspects as persons who had carried out the alleged crime, even though the suspects did not admit that. So he tried to use criminal reconciliation to make them 'recognize their faults' and 'feel regretful.'

The phenomenon that the official was so convinced that the suspect/defendant had committed the suspected crime before the case was heard and sentenced in court might also indicate that there was no 'presumption of innocence' in these officials' minds. This issue is further discussed in Chapter 5 along with the analysis of the officials' roles in this programme.

Another prosecutor, S, from the People's Procuratorate of B district in Xi'an mentioned in the interview that, in general, the suspect's remorse was in fact not taken into account when the officials considered initiating a criminal reconciliation programme.[5]

> It is required to consider the suspect's regret before we make the decision to use criminal reconciliation in a case. But in fact this (whether or not the suspect feels regret) is very difficult to ascertain in that it is really hard to read someone's mind, and you know that it is easy to pretend to be regretful. Moreover, often the suspect is still in detention at this stage, so that we do not see them regularly. Some people may reflect and feel remorseful in the detention house, yet others may become even 'worse' via learning 'bad examples' after staying there.

---

[5] Interview with prosecutor S in the People's Procuratorate of B district in Xi'an in September 2010.

What prosecutor S said indicated that the officials found it difficult to consider, and might in some cases have chosen not to consider the suspects' attitude out of convenience. Reflecting a similar attitude, prosecutor S simply described the suspects as 'criminals' and observed in the interview that they could reflect on their wrongdoing in the detention house.[6] Judge Z from the People's Court of Y district in Xi'an even frankly said to the author that, in fact, the judges would conduct criminal reconciliation in almost all the cases where a civil dispute about compensation had been conjoined to the criminal litigation, regardless of whether the stipulated requirements had been met.[7]

> Guided by the Supreme People's Court's policy of 'Giving Priority to Mediation and Combining Mediation with Judgment' (*tiaojie youxian, tiao pan jiehe*),[8] nowadays we judges would conduct mediation or reconciliation in all the criminal cases with civil disputes on compensation, and we would try our best to use it. That is to say, actually there is no special precondition for initiating criminal reconciliation or mediation; as long as we meet cases of this kind (cases in which civil proceedings about compensation had been affiliated, or *xingshi fudai minshi susong*), we will conduct it.

---

[6] According to Article 2 of the PRC Detention House Regulation (2012), 'detention house' is an organ to detain (1) a person who is given a penalty of administrative detention by the Public Security Organ or the State Security Organ; or (2) a person against whom a detention decision has been made by the People's Court in accordance with law.

[7] Interview with judge Z in the People's Court of Y district in August 2010.

[8] The policy of 'Giving Priority to Mediation and Combining Mediation with Judgment,' or in Chinese *tiaojie youxian, tiao pan jiehe* (调解优先调判结合) was raised by the President of the Supreme People's Court Wang Shengjun in 2008. The Supreme People's Court issued the Opinions on Further Implementing the Working Principle of 'Giving Priority to Mediation and Combining Mediation with Judgment' [《最高人民法院关于进一步贯彻"调解优先、调判结合"工作原则的若干意见》] in 2010. Section 2 of the Opinions stresses mediation in dealing with criminal cases in the People's Court as 'a criterion of high quality and high effectiveness,' and the Courts shall adopt 'mediation ability as a high level of judicial ability.' So 'the People's Courts at all levels shall deeply apprehend the unique advantages and important values of mediation in dispute resolution and in promoting social harmony and stability, practically transform the idea of valuing judgment but neglecting mediation, and take mediation as the first choice in handling cases.' See the full text (Chinese version) of this document at http://news.xinhuanet.com/legal/2010-06/28/c_12271040.htm (last accessed on 9 September 2011); see the English version at LawInfoChina at http://www.lawinfochina.com/display.aspx?lib=law&id=8397 (last accessed on 9 September 2011).

The above accounts from prosecutor H, prosecutor S and judge Z implied that the stipulated requirements of initiating a criminal reconciliation programme were not always observed by the officials in practice. Further discrepancies between stipulated requirements and actual practices are discussed in the following sections of this chapter.

Except for the situation that criminal reconciliation was initiated by the officials in cases where some stipulated pre-conditions were not met, it was also found in the interview that in some circumstances, the officials 'added' a few preconditions by themselves in practice when they considered the initiation of criminal reconciliation in a case. These 'additional pre-requirements,' as indicated in the officials' accounts in the interview, included the suspect/defendant's performance before he/she was alleged to have committed the suspected crime and the suspect/defendant's local residence. It was further noticed in the interview that these pre-requirements, although not provided in the procedural regulations or guidelines, were in fact used by the officials as compulsory determinants in initiating criminal reconciliation programmes.

For example, prosecutor F from the People's Procuratorate of X district in Changzhou told the author how much the suspect's usual performance weighed in his consideration of initiating criminal reconciliation in case no. six in location A (a suspected theft case).[9]

> When I received this case, I found that the suspect, as a 20-year-old young worker, had a good performance record in the factory throughout his employment period. Even his boss spoke for him and asked for a lenient disposition when the case was transferred to the Procuratorate. Then I began to consider that criminal reconciliation might properly be initiated in this case.

Moreover, the accounts provided by prosecutor Z from the People's Procuratorate of Y district in Xi'an indicated that actually non-local juvenile suspects were excluded from the criminal reconciliation programme.[10]

> Generally, the following situation would affect my decision whether or not using criminal reconciliation in juvenile cases: it should be suspected minor crime; the victim should have forgiven the suspects; the parents and the school should have the ability to cooperate with our work by supervising the

---

[9] Interview with prosecutor F in the People's Procuratorate of X district, Changzhou in June 2008.

[10] Interview with prosecutor Z in the People's Procuratorate of Y district in Xi'an in August 2010.

> children in order to guarantee the rehabilitation effect after the criminal reconciliation meeting finishes. So those non-local children or those whose parents are not in Xi'an will not be considered (for criminal reconciliation) since it was so hard for us to trace them, especially in the follow-up supervision period.

The officials' making the suspects'/defendants' previous good performance and residence as the pre-requirements of criminal reconciliation might largely service for their own convenience (i.e. to trace the suspect in the supervision period if it is true). Yet it also causes the problem of unfairness among the suspects/defendants in criminal reconciliation programmes. This issue is further discussed in the next chapter together with the officials' accounts on their motivations for adding these pre-requirements.

4.1.2 No Presumption of Innocence

The procedural regulations or guidelines required that the suspect/defendant had to admit guilt (*renzui*) or show remorse (*huizui biaoxian*) before entering criminal reconciliation. The case files studied showed that this requirement was complied with in the three locations, and it was plainly reflected from the short question and answer between the officials and suspects/defendants. In the interviews, except in the case of one suspect the author approached in Xi'an, all suspects/defendants indeed expressed their admission of guilt and remorse. The single suspect the author referred to was accused of a traffic accident related crime and he accepted criminal reconciliation not out of feeling regretful, but just out of very practical considerations. He said:[11]

> My job is driving for others. Concerning this matter, I drove a lorry delivering goods and suddenly my lorry and their car crashed. Their daughter sitting beside the driver in the car died. But I do not think the main responsibility for this traffic accident lies with me. I think that in fact it is their fault. It is because they drove carelessly and too fast, so that they bumped into my lorry. I tried to dodge, but their car was really too fast.
>
> After the accident had happened, I felt stressed since I did not know how to deal with this matter. I thought about hiring a lawyer; I also consulted some friends and they told me that I could surely win the suit if I could have a lawyer defending me. But I am really too poor. I could neither afford the

[11] Interview with C, the suspect of a traffic accident related crime case, in Xi'an in August 2010.

> money for hiring a lawyer, nor pay for the accommodation I would have had to find here for a long period of litigation.
>
> At that point, the prosecutor called me and offered a choice of criminal reconciliation. I also learned from the prosecutor that the other party was rich so that I did not need to pay much compensation to them in criminal reconciliation. I then considered that I could get rid of this matter and work to earn money soon. I have an old father of over 70 years old with serious problems with his legs to take care of. The prosecutor also persuaded me that I would not be prosecuted if I could reach a reconciliation agreement with the other party successfully. In addition, it would not be hard since the other party's attitude was fine. Then I considered not persevering with this matter any further as after all their daughter died in this accident. I discarded the idea of hiring a lawyer and accepted the offer of criminal reconciliation.

In this specific case, although the suspect did not mention whether or not he had told the responsible prosecutor his real thoughts and difficulties in the interview, it at least showed that what the official cared about most was trying all means to make the suspect accept criminal reconciliation. This might be because the official knew about it and decided to discount it, or because he/she did not find out that the driver considered himself innocent. Perhaps this was the reason that the case files had shown only formulaic engagement with the question of 'regret' or 'admission of guilt' – a very simple question by the official and the suspect/defendant's short answer concerning this issue, before the initiation of criminal reconciliation.

4.1.3 Violations of the Principle of Voluntariness

It was further stipulated that if the responsible prosecutor/judge intended to initiate criminal reconciliation, he/she should explain this programme in terms of its procedure, outcome and the parties' rights for obtaining their voluntary participation. The documents, especially the parties' statements on their voluntary participation enclosed in the case files, showed that this procedural requirement was fully observed in the three research sites. Yet how the official obtained the parties' voluntary participation was not shown in the case files. Information as to this question was complemented and provided in greater detail by the interviews. For instance, the interviews with the victim and suspect, respectively, of case no. five in location A (a juvenile theft case) at their school shed some light on the prosecutor's conduct during this process.

In the interview with the suspect G, he first told the author that even he himself did not know why he had stolen his classmate H's mobile phone. 'Maybe it was just something wrong I did on an impulse. You know that actually I was not short of money,' G said about his motivation.[12] He then said that he had greatly regretted what he had done and been worried about his future when he was found out by the police. He felt that he was lucky when the prosecutor F approached him to talk with him about resolving this case through criminal reconciliation rather than going to court. He learned from F that criminal reconciliation would resolve the case with the outcome of non-prosecution and no criminal record if he could obtain H's forgiveness and reach an agreement with H. That was indeed attractive for him and largely relieved his worry, so he accepted the offer of trying to reconcile immediately.[13]

In the interview with the victim H, he said to the author that he felt 'very surprised, lost and angry' when he found his mobile phone had been stolen in the dormitory for it was the third time he had lost his mobile phone.[14] He really wanted to 'teach the thief a lesson' at that time. However, after he knew that the suspected thief was his classmate G and he got back the phone later, he thought that maybe G had done this just on an impulse and he 'did not hate G since the phone was returned.' Thus, when the prosecutor F approached him and communicated with him about resolving this case through criminal reconciliation rather than sending G to court, H agreed immediately.

> He is my classmate. Prosecution or sentence would have led to his being sent down by the university and that would have affected his future badly. It would have been terrible for him. So I really wanted to give him a chance as this crime actually had no lasting impact on me, whereas the resolution of this matter was imperative for him.[15]

It could be seen from the parties' narrative that, in this case, the official in charge of this case (prosecutor F) did not have to try very hard to get the parties' agreement to participate in criminal reconciliation since the offer of criminal reconciliation coincided with the parties' own wishes. The suspect was anxious for some alternative way other than prosecution/litigation, and the victim had somewhat forgiven the suspect when he knew that the suspect was his classmate.

But this was not always the case, the interviews showed that more often. What the officials had done during this process was far more than what prosecutor H had done in his case. In some cases, such a process

[12] Interview with G in Changzhou in May 2008.
[13] Ibid.
[14] Interview with H in Changzhou in May 2008.
[15] Ibid.

involved great efforts on the part of many other people, such as the parties' teachers or employers, and the party (or parties) had been repeatedly 'persuaded' by the officials and these other people to accept criminal reconciliation.

For example, J, the victim of case no. nine in location A (an intentional injury case) mentioned the reason for his agreement to participate in the criminal reconciliation programme as 'my coach and prosecutor F spoke to me many times.'[16] 'They taught me to consider the relationship between me and the suspects as schoolmates, so that I should give them one more chance.'[17] K, the victim in case no. six in location A (a theft case), described such a process as 'the suspect's employer and the responsible prosecutor F approached me no fewer than five times separately to persuade me to engage in criminal reconciliation.'[18] 'I was also told by them that the suspect L felt very remorseful, and since L was very young, I should give him an opportunity given that prosecution would destroy his future.'[19]

Judge L from the People's Court of B district in Xi'an also talked about this process and her hard efforts to get the victim's voluntary participation in case no. five in location C (a juvenile robbery case).[20]

> At first, the victim M and his parents were all very insistent that they did not want to give the defendants one more chance through reconciling with them. The defendants had hurt them so deeply that they only wanted to see them sentenced according to law. Yet I was also very insistent: I approached M and his parents three times and told them that those young defendants indeed felt extremely remorseful, and that litigation would destroy the defendants' future. Moreover, through criminal reconciliation, M and his family could get a larger sum of compensation more promptly compared with the compensation that might be awarded in a court decision. At last, I got the victim's and his parents' agreement to participate in the criminal reconciliation programme. M was also required by me to provide a statement about his voluntary participation in the criminal reconciliation programme.

In sum, it appeared from the parties' and the officials' accounts that the officials would mainly refer to the benefits of criminal reconciliation to the parties respectively to get their 'voluntary participation.' It was not a problem to explain the benefits of criminal reconciliation to the parties.

---

16 Interview with J, the victim of an intentional injury crime, in May 2008.
17 Ibid.
18 Interview with K in Changzhou in June 2008.
19 Ibid.
20 Interview with judge L in the People's Court of B district in Xi'an in September 2010.

However, in the circumstance that such an explanation, or precisely persuasion, was repeatedly done by the officials and sometimes also by the parties' teachers or employers, even though the parties finally presented their voluntary participation in writing as enclosed in the case files, the voluntariness of their agreement was questionable, as is reasoned in the following.

As argued in Chapter 3, the influence of the teachers, employers, leadership (*lingdao*) and officials as 'powerful persons' should not be neglected. The parties must be aware that the officials concerned, for instance, had power and the final say in their cases. And the parties' teachers, employers or leadership (*lingdao*) were the people that had close connections with as well as crucial influences on the parties in their daily lives, especially considering the fact that 'relationships' (*guanxi*) took an extraordinarily significant role in China. It was therefore hard for the parties to reject these persons' suggestions. In this sense, the voluntariness of the parties' participation was easily impaired. What the parties really felt in such a situation is further discussed in the following chapter on the basis of their own accounts.

Except for the point that the parties were subjected to hard 'persuasion' to accept criminal reconciliation, the interviews also showed that sometimes the parties were not approached at all during this process. Instead, it was their parents or lawyers that the officials approached and talked to about the possibility of criminal reconciliation. Accounts from prosecutor H on case no. seven in location B exemplified how the juveniles as the real parties in this case were totally replaced by their parents during this process.[21]

> I first suggested to the suspects' parents that since all the suspects were very young, it was meaningful to make them realize their faults and to teach them some legal knowledge which could best be done through criminal reconciliation. More importantly, in this case, the evidence was sufficient to sentence the suspects in the Court, yet criminal reconciliation could close the case through non-prosecution, and there would be no criminal record for the suspects, which meant that their children could go back to school soon. It seemed that these benefits of criminal reconciliation were attractive for the suspects' parents as they agreed to participate immediately after hearing that.
>
> As to the victim's parents, it seemed that they were considerate and sensible. Although they told me that the whole family had been harmed deeply by the suspects, they could still understand the meaning of non-prosecution and a decision not to burden the suspects who had harmed their child with a

---

[21] Interview with prosecutor H in the People's Procuratorate of D district in Chongqing in June 2008.

> criminal record. They also expressed sympathy after knowing the suspects' family backgrounds from me. Hence, they also agreed to participate in the criminal reconciliation programme. And after that, both parties' parents were required to confirm such agreements in written form.

Another prosecutor, L, from the People's Procuratorate of B district in Xi'an talked about an intentional injury case in which he discussed the possibility of criminal reconciliation only with the suspect's lawyer and then the lawyer successfully persuaded the suspect who originally did not want to participate.[22]

> At first, the suspect N did not want to accept criminal reconciliation as he insisted that he was innocent. His lawyer did not want to participate either. But I approached his lawyer and said to him that since N was preparing for the college entrance examination at that point, it was most important for N to get rid of this case and then to go back to school as soon as possible. Criminal reconciliation could resolve the case in one week and N could get a non-prosecution decision and no criminal record.
>
> Learning this, the lawyer advised N to accept criminal reconciliation. The lawyer did this out of a desire to protect N's greatest benefits; he as an experienced legal professional knew very well that defending innocence would take too long because it needed very strong evidence, while N could not afford the time. In addition, he might know that it was almost impossible to get an acquittal in cases of this kind. Very likely, the result was going to be a suspended sentence which was not any better than a non-prosecution decision, and it also meant that there would be no criminal record, if N accepted criminal reconciliation. Hence, the lawyer explained this to N and suggested that the best choice was criminal reconciliation. Finally, N agreed to participate in the criminal reconciliation programme.

Prosecutor L's accounts implied as well that the suspect N showed remorse or admitted guilt just out of compromise, and the prosecutor in fact did not care whether the suspect had committed the alleged crime. He just wanted to get N to accept his offer of criminal reconciliation.

In the above circumstances, the parties were represented by their parents or agents although there was no legal basis for that. The 1986 General Principle of the Civil Law of the PR China provides that the responsibilities of the parents as the juveniles' guardians are only to 'protect the juveniles, manage the juvenile's property, act as the juveniles' legal agents in some civil activities and in compensation claims.'[23]

---

[22] Interview with prosecutor L in the People's Procuratorate of B district in Xi'an in September 2010.

[23] Article 18 of the 1986 General Principle of the Civil Law of the PR China.

The 2007 PRC Lawyers Law stipulates the responsibilities of lawyers mainly as 'providing legal consultation and participating in litigation or mediation to protect their clients' interests.'[24] Neither law provides that the parents' or agents' intention could replace the juveniles' or their clients' intention. Moreover, the very meaning of reconciliation, and the importance assigned to voluntariness in reconciliation, would appear to preclude the use of representatives in this process. This is shown also in the relevance of regret, which as a personal feeling on the part of a wrongdoer, could surely not be felt by a parent or teacher or lawyer on the wrongdoer's behalf.

Moreover, the procedure designed for criminal reconciliation required that during the process of getting the parties' (the victim and the suspect/defendant) agreements to participate in criminal reconciliation, the prosecutor/judge should communicate with the parties *directly*, rather than with the parties' legal agents/parents and so on. In this sense, criminal reconciliation was purported to empower the parties to deal with their own case mainly by themselves. If the parties had not been approached and if there was no communication with them at all during this process, how could the officials make sure of their voluntary participation? It was somewhat absurd to assert that the parties truly agreed to participate so long as their parents or agents agreed. To a certain extent, it might also imply that actually the officials did not really care much about the parties' intentions and voluntary participation.

In conclusion, interviews with the officials and parties indicated that in the three locations, the requirements for initiating criminal reconciliation had been violated, at least in some cases. And the officials' conduct was likely to have impaired the parties' voluntary participation in some cases. It seemed that the officials just tried their best to make the parties (the victim and the suspect/defendant or their agents) engage in criminal reconciliation, when they themselves had decided on that course. In addition, it was implied in some cases that the suspects/defendants were simply viewed as 'criminals' by the officials who needed to be 'educated' and 'corrected' through criminal reconciliation before the suspects/defendants themselves admitted guilt or showed remorse. However, why were officials able to neglect key requirements of criminal reconciliation in the cases examined? And how did the parties truly feel in these circumstances? These questions are addressed in Chapter 5. Next, let us see what happened in criminal reconciliation meetings.

---

[24] Article 28 of the 2007 PRC Lawyer Law.

4.2 THE CRIMINAL RECONCILIATION MEETING

4.2.1 Appropriate Communication between the Parties in Some Reconciliation Meetings

Criminal reconciliation meetings have been described by some scholars as the essential stage of criminal reconciliation. The reason for the centrality of these meetings, it has been argued, is that many goals of this programme such as reparation of damage to the victim (both financially and psychologically), education of the suspect/defendant, and dispute resolution were expected to be produced chiefly through free communication between the parties in the meeting. As shown in Chapter 3, the case files often stated that 'there was an active and sufficient discussion between the parties in the criminal reconciliation meeting' 'without any official interference.' Such descriptions were substantiated by a few officials in the interviews.

Prosecutor H's accounts of the criminal reconciliation meeting held for case no. seven in location B was an example. This meeting was held in H's office in the People's Procuratorate of D district in Chongqing and attended by the victim and his parents, six suspects and their parents, and both parties' teachers with H presiding.[25]

> In the meeting, a platform for face-to-face communication was built for the parties. Each party was asked to raise any question they wanted to the other party. I also arranged various activities like showing the victim's medical record and photos documenting the injury he had received, letting the victim and his parents relate their feelings and pain, and arranged for the teachers to make 'educational statements' in the meeting.
>
> When the victim and his parents narrated their worries and sufferings with tears, it could be observed from the young suspects' and their parents' looks that they were truly moved. After these communicative activities, I also read a letter entitled 'To the suspects' parents' in which I attributed the reason leading to this case mainly to the parents' negligence of their children and emphasized the great significance of family education and much more care and communication in the family for a young person. At that point, all the suspects cried and apologized sincerely and repeatedly to the victim and his parents at the end of the meeting. Some of the parents also could not help crying and promised better education and supervision of their children in the future. Finally, both parties signed an agreement on compensation in an amount of 100,000 yuan that covered the victim's medical charges, nutrition

---

[25] Interview with prosecutor H in the People's Procuratorate of D district in Chongqing in June 2008.

> fee and psychological loss after a peaceful negotiation. The whole meeting lasted for about three hours.

It sounded as though in this meeting, the parties were provided by the prosecutor with an opportunity to communicate sufficiently. Such expression and communication aimed to repair the victim and educate the suspect. The various activities arranged by the prosecutor, such as the teachers' statements and his reading of the letter, were expected to have some educational effect on the suspects. The prosecutor even took an active role in assigning blame mainly to the parents of the suspects. It seemed effective since the parties (as well as their parents) changed their attitudes and showed regret, according to the responsible prosecutor's description.

Yet the prosecutor's conduct was debatable in itself. First, the arrangement of showing the photos of the victim's wound might make the victim feel upset and hurt again. Then, those 'educational activities' might be shameful for the suspects, especially considering that they did not admit guilt at that moment. Last but not least, the prosecutor in charge attributed the main responsibility for the alleged crime to the parents in the meeting. This might be somewhat unfair to the parents even though they did not show discontent in the interview, since the reasons for a crime are complicated, ranging from the general context like society and school to the family and individual. In this case, whether this particular criminal reconciliation meeting really had produced those outcomes and satisfied the parties could only be addressed through learning their actual feelings and comments, which is discussed in Chapter 5.

Examples of a criminal reconciliation meeting with much communication between the parties were also provided by some parties in the interview. L, the suspect of case no. six in location A (a theft case) described the criminal reconciliation meeting he once attended as involving much communication between the parties.[26]

> This case was resolved through only one face-to-face meeting attended by me, my boss, the victim K and K's leadership and presided over by the prosecutor F.
>
> During the meeting that lasted for about two hours, I first related the reason I committed the suspected crime and my remorse over that. I then apologized sincerely to K. Following that, my boss talked about his assessment of me as an employee and asked K seriously to consider forgiving me and giving me another chance. Then K talked about his feelings and at last indicated his forgiveness.

---

[26] Interview with L in the People's Procuratorate of X district in Changzhou in June 2008.

> After that, I asked K to indicate how much compensation he asked for. Since his motorbike [taken away by the suspect] had been quickly retrieved, he put forward the requirement of compensation for a new lock and his loss of reputation caused by the theft of his motorbike. Given that the loss of reputation was hard to evaluate precisely and he knew that I was not rich, he only asked for two thousand yuan. F did not comment on this compensation requirement and only asked about my opinion on that. I accepted immediately. Then we signed an agreement and I paid the money on the spot. Then the whole process ended in a peaceful atmosphere.

The above descriptions from prosecutors H and L showed that criminal reconciliation meetings in these cases were truly a place for the parties to communicate sufficiently and freely, which meant that they could express whatever they wanted without the officials' interference or pressure. And such a meeting sounded as if it had produced the expected outcomes such as repairing the damage the victim suffered because of the alleged crime, educating the suspect/defendant, satisfying the parties and resolving the dispute.

In the author's view, however, their accounts might already indicate a problem with a criminal reconciliation meeting. The criminal reconciliation meeting in these two cases was characterized by extensive participation and observation, which might cause some negative impacts on the parties. As raised in the last section of Chapter 3, it might put pressure on the parties, which would impair the parties' voluntariness, satisfaction and the effect of dispute resolution. This problem is also addressed in Chapter 5 with the parties' accounts.

4.2.2 Focus on Bargaining over Compensation

Contrary to the character of the criminal reconciliation meetings described above, it was also found in the interviews that, in some cases, the parties did not communicate or even meet at all in the criminal reconciliation meeting.

Sometimes, the parties went to the criminal reconciliation meeting but did not communicate with each other. The criminal reconciliation meeting was thus just a place for their families to bargain over the amount of compensation. This most often happened in juvenile cases. For instance, J, the victim of case no. nine in location A (a juvenile intentional injury case) described the meeting he attended as follows.[27]

---

[27] Interview with J, the victim of an intentional injury crime, in May 2008.

> It was really a terrible thing, for I did not want to see the suspects and mention my hurt anymore actually. Accordingly, I did not say anything in the meeting. Moreover, I have not received any apologies from the suspects to this day. The only impression I had of the meeting was that it was a bargaining process about the amount of compensation between our parents. I did not even want to look at the agreement containing the compensation amount when it was finally reached.

Sometimes, the suspect and victim did not meet each other at all in the criminal reconciliation meeting. Examples were the two criminal reconciliation meetings held for case no. five in location C (a juvenile robbery case), which were attended only by the juvenile suspects' parents and lawyers. L, the judge responsible for this case, described this meeting as follows.[28]

> After both parties' written agreements to participate in the criminal reconciliation programme had been obtained, I presided over the first criminal reconciliation meeting in the People's Court of B district in May 2010. The victim and his parents, all the defendants' parents and their lawyers attended the meeting. Since all the defendants were still detained at that moment, they did not attend the meeting.
>
> In the meeting, the victim M first talked about his hurt and negative emotions after the case. Then the defendants' parents apologized to him and said that it was also their fault, as they did not educate their children well. They also presented statements I had required them to write before the meeting about guaranteeing better supervision over their children to prevent them from reoffending, and documents showing that there were schools willing to accept their children during the probation period if the defendants could get suspended sentences. As all the defendants were still in detention, their lawyers conveyed their regrets and apologies to the victim on their behalf. Subsequently, M expressed his forgiveness and acceptance of the apologies.
>
> Then they turned to bargaining about compensation. However, even after nearly one hour of bargaining, they could not reach any agreement. The defendants' parents and lawyers argued that the victim's proposition of fifty thousand yuan was too high and they really could not afford this sum. Yet the victim's parents were unwilling to make any concessions. I tried to mediate between them, but I failed since both parties were quite insistent at that time.

Two months later a second meeting was held also in the People's Court of B district.[29] This time in addition to all the participants of the first meeting (but the defendants remained in detention), L also invited an

---

[28] Interview with judge L in Xi'an in September 2010.

[29] Recorded in the case file.

official of the Justice Bureau to observe the meeting. L mentioned that the reason for inviting that official was merely that the official had once expressed to her some interest in criminal reconciliation meetings. L also described the second meeting.[30]

> The content of the second meeting was all about compensation. I further stressed to M and his parents that all the three families of the defendant-party were really poor; one of them even lived on a state subsistence allowance. Besides, what they asked for was indeed far higher than the court would normally award in damages in this kind of case. The official of the Justice Bureau also helped me with this mediation. Then, after another one hour's negotiation mainly between the two parties' parents, an agreement on a compensation sum of 30,000 yuan was finally reached. The money was paid to the victim by the defendants' parents on the spot at the meeting. After getting the money, I required M to provide a statement requesting a lighter sentence for the defendants.

To sum up, although criminal reconciliation agreements were still reached in these two examples, the criminal reconciliation meetings, either in the suspect/defendant's absence, or in his/her presence but without substantive contribution from him/her to the reconciliation process, could hardly be evaluated as having served the predicted outcomes. This is because all these objectives such as restoration of a good relationship, redress for harm done to the victim (except by payment of damages), or rehabilitation or education of the suspect/defendant were expected to be served by sufficient communication and discussion between the parties in the criminal reconciliation meeting. In addition, the criminal reconciliation meetings in these cases mainly appeared to focus on compensation, not on the parties themselves.

With regard to the defendant's reluctance to talk in the criminal reconciliation meeting, it might be because of the problem pointed out in the first section that the official merely asked for his parents' opinions on 'voluntary participation.' This was supported by the interview with the defendant J, and is shown in the following chapter. The reason for the defendants' absence in the second example was their being in detention according to the responsible judge's accounts. This was symptomatic of a problem with the Chinese judicial system, much criticized by Chinese scholars, namely the long period of custody (*jiya*) of the suspects/defendants.

---

30 Interview with judge L in Xi'an in September 2010.

Custody, *jiya,* including pretrial custody and custody during trial, is a situation resulting from detention (*juliu*) and arrest (*daibu*).[31] It is reinforced by the fact that detention centres (carrying out detention, *juliu,* and arrest, *daibu*) are under the responsibility of the Public Security Bureau, that is to say, the criminal investigation authority in most cases discussed in the present context.[32] A serious problem with the detention system, according to much literature, is that it is as a custom always extended for a long period. According to the 1996 PRC Criminal Procedure Law, criminal detention (*juliu*) can be extended to up to 37 days in exceptional cases; but the exception is widely thought to have become the norm in practice.[33] Criminal arrest (*daibu*), as stipulated in the Criminal Procedure Law, can be extended to five months.[34] In addition, there is almost no supervision or examination in deciding extensions, and detention will in some cases continue beyond such stipulated time limits as long as the case is not closed.[35] As disclosed by some reports, the suspects/defendants in some cases have even been detained for over ten years.[36]

It is very problematic that detention, as a measure to limit and deprive the individuals of their freedom, can be imposed before the court adjudicates a case almost in an arbitrary way. Even worse, suspects/defendants in detention are usually simply viewed as criminals, since there is no 'presumption of innocence' in the Chinese legal system. In this context, individual rights are easily subverted by public power, which has constituted a constitutional problem.

The origins of this problem have been discussed in academic work as well. Concerning custody, especially after a case is transferred to court, which is recognized as happening most often in practice and is shown in this case, there are two main causes. The first is the intimate cooperation

---

[31] Chen Ruihua [陈瑞华] 'Theoretical Reflection on Detention [未决羁押的理论反思]' in Chen Ruihua [陈瑞华] (ed) *An Empirical Study of the Detention System* [*未决羁押制度的实证研究*] Beijing, Peking University Press [北京大学出版社] 2004, 4–5.

[32] Ibid, 6–8.

[33] Ibid. See also McConville *et al*, *Criminal Justice in China: An Empirical Inquiry* Cheltenham, UK and Northampton, MA, USA, Edward Elgar Publishing 2011, Chapter 3.

[34] Supra note 31, 4–5.

[35] Ibid, 19.

[36] Hua Rui [华蕊] 'The "Fuqing Discipline Inspection Commission Explosion Case" Unresolved for Ten Years Will Be Heard Recently [十年不决的'福清纪委爆炸案'二审于近日开庭]' at http://blog.boxun.com/hero/201104/chrd/106_1.shtml (last accessed on 14 June 2011).

between the Public Security Bureau, the People's Procuratorate and People's Court in dealing with a case, which is described as a 'line process.'[37] In this context, these three organs are positioned as 'working together' to resolve a case. As a result, one organ, like the Court, would hardly challenge the decisions or conduct such as detention made by the other two organs.[38]

Furthermore, it is actually very difficult for the People's Court to challenge the Public Security Bureau's decisions or conduct. This is because the power of the Public Security Bureau, as both an investigative and administrative organ in China, is so strong. The position of the Public Security Bureau is widely viewed as higher than that of the People's Procuratorate and People's Court.[39] This is also reflected in the custody system. By means of custody, the Public Security Bureau holds the absolute power to limit and deprive the suspects/defendants of their rights and freedom before the Court hears or adjudicates a case.[40] This problem is aggravated by the structure of the Chinese criminal process, in which 'investigation dominates' and 'confession is the king,' so that what the People's Court (and the People's Procuratorate) do is mainly to 'confirm' the investigation outcome transferred by the Public Security Bureau.[41] This problem is further demonstrated in Chapter 5 and discussed in Chapter 6.

When judge L mentioned that she could not get the defendants out of the detention house for criminal reconciliation and refused to say more about this issue,[42] it was possible that her request had been refused by the detention house. Yet it was also possible that she did not make that request, in light of the problem pointed out above, namely that the officials cared most about achieving a compensation agreement that allowed them formally to conclude the case, irrespective of the genuine views and wishes of the parties.

In the case file examination, there was one case in Changzhou in which no criminal reconciliation meeting was held and the criminal

---

[37] Chen Ruihua [陈瑞华] *Leading Issues in Criminal Proceedings* [*刑事诉讼的前沿问题*] Beijing, China Renmin University Press [中国人民大学出版社] 2005, 525.

[38] Ibid, 526.

[39] Supra note 37, 527.

[40] Ibid, 532.

[41] Ibid.

[42] Interview with judge L in the People's Court of B district in Xi'an in September 2010.

reconciliation agreement was reached only through the official's discussion with the respective parties. Although the author could not find the parties of this case to interview, it was even harder to tell if a criminal reconciliation programme of this kind could serve the official goals of the system, goals of repairing the victim and educating the defendant since there was no encounter at all between the parties. This further strengthens the impression that what the officials cared about most or essentially pursued was only a compensation agreement to close the case.

4.2.3 Private Agreement Reached prior to the Formal Reconciliation Meetings

In this circumstance, the criminal reconciliation was quite simple as well. Prosecutor Y described such a criminal reconciliation meeting held for case no. eight in location B (a traffic accident related crime case).[43]

> The criminal reconciliation meeting proceeded in a peaceful atmosphere. It did not last for a long time since the parties had reached an agreement privately beforehand. In the meeting, the suspect O apologized to the victim's son P (the victim died in the traffic accident) sincerely which was accepted by P. Then, an agreement which was in accord with their private agreement was signed, and the meeting finished.

In fact, in this interview, the officials and parties often indicated that the compensation in the criminal reconciliation agreement reached at the end of the criminal reconciliation meeting was 'paid on the spot.' In this case, it was likely that much private negotiation had gone on prior to the official criminal reconciliation meeting, because compensation in those cases was not a small sum of money which one would normally bring to the meeting. In this sense, it was far-fetched to say that it was the criminal reconciliation meeting that reconciled the parties. They had virtually reconciled themselves. Hence, the formal criminal reconciliation meeting was simple and short. One would not expect such a criminal reconciliation meeting (formally confirming a prior compensation agreement) to produce the other outcomes such as victim reparation and suspect/defendant education.

The problem with private negotiation in these (minor) criminal cases, nevertheless, was somewhat complicated. In this circumstance, the (minor) criminal cases were resolved through civil means and the judicial

---

43 Interview with prosecutor Y in the People's Procuratorate of D district in Chongqing in June 2008.

authority merely confirmed the outcome. Discussion of the relationship between tort law and criminal law (or, tortious liability and criminal liability) has been much in domestic academic work. On the one hand, scholars criticize the traditional definition of crime as individuals' infringements upon the interests of the State and argue that crime is also an infringement upon individual interests.[44] On the other hand, these scholars maintain that tort law and criminal law are not detached, and have considerable overlap.[45] Some further contend that crimes stipulated in the criminal law are in essence also tortious, and that tortious liability should be prior to the criminal liability.[46] This indicates balance and allocation of power between judicial authorities and individuals in the criminal justice system. However, even though there is much overlap between tort law and criminal law and they are closely connected, there are differences between them.[47] The criminal law deals with those relatively serious offences that infringe relatively more widely and seriously.

In this sense, it is debatable and improper whether criminal cases (even if they are minor ones) should be essentially and mainly resolved privately by the parties. More importantly, in the private negotiation, it is likely that improper or illegal conduct or coercion would occur, especially considering the pressure the suspect/defendant faces in that situation, namely that he/she would confront the rigid criminal justice system if he/she fails to reconcile with the victim. In fact, either party with stronger power could impose pressure on the other party easily as the outcome of 'reconciliation' is preferable for himself/herself. This constitutes further harm to (the other, weaker) party's interests and may re-victimize the victim.

---

44 Liao Huanguo [廖焕国] Zeng Xiangsheng [曾祥生] 'The Interactive Between the Civil Law and Criminal Law: Conflicts and Coordination of the Tort Law and Criminal Law [民刑互动：侵权责任法与刑法的冲突与协调]' (2010) 3 *Wuhan University Journal (Philosophy & Social Science)* [*武汉大学学报(哲学社会科学版)*] 290.

45 Ibid, 291.

46 Ma Zhangmin [马章民] 'Combination and Conflict Between the Tort Law and Criminal Law [侵权责任法与刑法的衔接与冲突]' (2010) 9 *Legal System and Society* [*法制与社会*] 27–8.

47 But the differences are also debatable among scholars. See e.g. supra note 44, 291.

4.2.4 Pressure on the Parties to Reach Agreement

An impression that the officials would not interfere with the parties' intentions in reaching a criminal reconciliation agreement was obtained from the case file examination. This also emerged in the interviews. For instance, prosecutor L from the People's Procuratorate of B district in Xi'an stressed the official's respect regarding the parties' own intentions in reaching a criminal reconciliation agreement.[48]

> Criminal reconciliation is mainly done by the parties themselves. We will at most help them reach an agreement. For example, we will persuade the suspects to apologize and compensate for a better outcome, and we will tell the victims that getting a considerable amount of compensation efficiently is best for them. But we will absolutely respect the parties' willingness. We will not coerce them to reach an agreement. If they cannot reach an agreement, the case will just go back to the normal procedure.

However, the author did not come across one case in which no agreement was reached at the end of the criminal reconciliation meeting. Maybe this resulted from the officials' great passion and efforts to 'help' the parties to reach an agreement. It was found that the officials would repeatedly hold criminal reconciliation meeting(s) for the parties' further discussion on compensation amount (see the above example of case no. five in location C provided by judge L). Alternatively, perhaps those cases in which no agreement was reached were simply not filed as 'criminal reconciliation case,' especially given the possibility raised in Chapter 3 that the officials would select the 'best examples' for the author to examine.

This caused two potential problems. On the one hand, some officials stated that criminal reconciliation had taken too much of their time and energy. On the other hand, in such circumstances, the officials' manifest interest might put pressure on initially reluctant parties to make them reach an agreement. It could not be excluded that the parties were in some cases afraid of some worse outcome if they 'offended' the official who would still be the one in charge of their case in the event of it being transferred back to the normal procedure later.

---

[48] Interview with prosecutor L in the People's Procuratorate of B district in Xi'an in September 2010.

4.2.5 Compensation as the Main Content of Criminal Reconciliation Agreements

In terms of the content of the criminal reconciliation agreement, whether it was reached by the parties in the official criminal reconciliation meeting or privately prior to the official programme, the case files showed that compensation was the absolute focus and main component. This was also substantiated by accounts from the officials and parties interviewed. Interviewees often described the agreements as 'the amount was more than the court would sentence,' and 'they were performed promptly' or 'on the spot.'

4.2.6 Clauses Added by Officials into Criminal Reconciliation Agreements

In some cases, as disclosed in the interviews, the content of the criminal reconciliation agreement was really reached by the parties themselves. The agreement could also include a part not provided for in the current laws. For example, K, the victim of case no. six in location A, had asked for compensation on his 'loss of reputation because of theft' at the end of the criminal reconciliation meeting, which was agreed by the victim and written into their agreement.[49] Also, it was not a problem if the victim wanted to waive compensation. In case no. five in location A (a theft case), the parties signed an agreement without reference to any compensation requirement (but it was the only such case the author encountered in the three locations). The victim in this case told the author that 'I did not want any extra compensation; I only wanted to hear the victim's sincere apology.'[50] In these cases, the criminal reconciliation agreements were based on the parties' own wishes.

However, in some other cases, the officials had actively put some content into the criminal reconciliation agreement. There were two examples – the criminal reconciliation agreement reached in case no. five in location A and case no. eight in location B. They both contained a clause that 'the parties were not allowed to go back on their agreement reached in the criminal reconciliation meeting' and 'if there was any further dispute between the parties concerning this case after they signed the criminal reconciliation agreement, they were not allowed to appeal

[49] Interview with K in the People's Procuratorate of X district in Changzhou in June 2008.

[50] Interview with H, the victim of a theft case, in Changzhou in May 2008.

the case to Court.' The parties and prosecutors in these two cases told the author that such a clause was added to the agreements by the prosecutors.[51]

Such a clause infringed on the parties' procedural appeal rights as stipulated in the Criminal Procedure Law. Articles 145 and 146 of the 1996 PRC Criminal Procedure Law stipulate that both the victim and suspect have the right to present an appeal to the People's Procuratorate if they are against the decision of non-prosecution. Articles 180 and 182 provide the defendant with rights to appeal to the People's Court at the next higher level and the victim with rights to request the People's Procuratorate to present a protest when they refuse to accept a judgment or order of the first instance trial. Although there was still no legal basis for the validity of criminal reconciliation agreements reached by the parties when the author conducted the empirical work, it was still illegal for the officials to just simply put the clause impeding the parties' further appeal in the agreements. Yet why did the official do this? The motivation of the officials' conduct is addressed in the next chapter, which analyses the officials' roles in criminal reconciliation.

4.3 FACTORS AFFECTING OFFICIAL DECISIONS IN CRIMINAL RECONCILIATION PROCESSES

4.3.1 Focus on Fulfilment of Compensation Obligations

As noted in Chapter 1, as provided in the local regulations or guidelines, after the parties had performed the criminal reconciliation agreement, the responsible official should make a decision about the case. The prosecutor could make a decision of non-prosecution (with expunging the suspect's criminal record), or suggest that the Public Security Bureau drop the case, or suggest to the People's Court that it should impose a lenient punishment on the defendant; the judge could give a lenient punishment or a suspended sentence. The case files showed that all the cases examined were officially closed with one of those decisions. Interviews further supported this finding, and showed more details concerning the officials' conducts in practice at this stage. For instance,

---

[51] Interviews with G, the suspect of case no. five, in Changzhou in May 2008 and prosecutor Y in Chongqing in June 2008.

prosecutor S from the People's Procuratorate of B district in Xi'an talked about the prosecutors' conduct in decision-making.[52]

> Most of the non-prosecution cases in our public prosecution division concern traffic accident related crimes. Only a few are minor intentional injury cases. Actually, in the traffic accident related crime cases, often the police would mediate at first; it is a necessary procedure of their work.[53] If they succeed, they will transfer the case file enclosed with the parties' agreement to us. Then we will examine the case file and the agreement for decision-making. If the police fail, they will transfer the case to us for further reconciliation or mediation.
>
> In the traffic accident related crime case, if the suspect can get the victim's forgiveness and they can reach an agreement on compensation, we will make a decision not to prosecute or suggest a lenient sentence to the Court.
>
> Usually, we will not prosecute a suspect if he/she has paid a large sum of compensation (i.e. fully or overcompensate the victim) given that in this circumstance, the victim could be largely satisfied and we could say that the suspect's risk to society is somewhat minor. We will still prosecute a suspect if he/she can only partly compensate the victim, but meanwhile we will present a 'sentence recommendation report' to suggest a lighter punishment for the suspect to the Court. Then, there may be two kinds of result for the defendant in Court: a suspended sentence or a shorter period of custody. As far as I know, judges will always take our recommendation and most of the defendants will be given a suspended sentence.

It sounded as though the amount the suspect had paid to the victim was the most crucial or even the only consideration for the prosecutors in making their decision to prosecute or not, or in deciding about a 'sentence recommendation' (*liangxing jianyi*).[54] In prosecutor S's view, it

---

[52] Interview with prosecutor S in the People's Procuratorate of B district in Xi'an in September 2010.

[53] Article 74 of the 2003 Law of the People's Republic of China on Road Traffic Safety [中华人民共和国道路交通安全法].

[54] According to the Opinions on Several Issues concerning the Regulation of Sentencing Recommendation (Trial Implementation) (2010) [关于规范量刑程序若干问题的意见(试行)] issued by the Supreme People's Court, the Supreme People's Procuratorate, the Ministry of Public Security, the Ministry of State Security and the Ministry of Justice, the People's Procuratorate may put forward a recommendation with respect to sentencing in public prosecution cases. The sentencing suggestions shall generally have a certain range. A sentencing recommendation shall generally state the People's Procuratorate's suggestions on the classification, range and execution mode of criminal penalties to be imposed on the defendant and the reasons and basis thereof. See the English version of

also reflected the suspect's remorse and risk to society, and the victim's satisfaction. This situation also existed in the People's Court.

Judge D from the People's Court of B district in Xi'an provided a copy of an 'internal guideline' in his Court about cases in which a criminal reconciliation agreement had been reached. This rule read that 'in a case where the defendant has actively compensated the victim, the defendant *ought to* be considered for a lenient punishment.' 'The degree of the sentence reduction *should* take into account the circumstances of the crime, the compensation amount, and the victim's attitude towards the compensation (to what extent the compensation could satisfy the victim).'[55] 'In the event that the defendant has actively compensated the victim and obtained the victim's forgiveness, the sentence *could* be reduced by 20 to 50 percent of the sentence made according to the Criminal Law and the crime's risk to society (which was termed as *ji zhun xing* in the rule).'[56] 'In the circumstance that the defendant has fully compensated the victim, the sentence *could* be reduced by less than 20 percent of the *ji zhun xing*.'[57] 'In the circumstance that the defendant has partly compensated the victim, the reduction should be less.'[58] 'If the defendant has compensated more than the victim's loss, there should be a further reduction.'[59] Each judge needed to fill in a form formulated according to this rule to demonstrate how the sentence he/she adjudicated was 'calculated.' This form is translated and enclosed as the appendix of this book.

It could be seen from this 'internal rule' that the defendants' different economic circumstances, determining their ability to provide compensation, were directly linked to the distinct results they could secure in the criminal reconciliation programme. Hence, although all the official decisions made by prosecutors and judges were in accordance with the designed procedural regulations or guidelines, the mechanism leading to these different decisions was flawed in terms of the rules governing it, which violated the spirit of criminal justice, the idea of equality before the law.

---

this 'Opinions' at LawInfoChina: http://www.lawinfochina.com/display.aspx?lib=law&id=8375&CGid= (last accessed on 3 November 2011).

[55] Translated from the 'Sentencing Normalization Form of the Criminal Tribunal of B District People's Court [in Xi'an].' See Appendix I.

[56] Ibid.

[57] Ibid.

[58] Ibid.

[59] Ibid.

The problem of unfairness in criminal reconciliation has been heavily criticized by many scholars, as noted in Chapter 1. In this sense, criminal reconciliation was hotly debated as a system in which the rich can pay money to avoid penalties while the poor who cannot pay compensation were excluded from this programme.[60] Although some scholars argued for criminal reconciliation by saying that compensation was not the focus of this programme, the information obtained in the author's interviews indicated that at least in the three studied locations, compensation was indeed the absolute focus.[61]

As shown in prosecutor S's accounts, the prosecutors would make a decision of non-prosecution if the suspect fully or overcompensated the victim. In the People's Court, as provided in the 'internal guidelines,' the sentence the judge would impose was directly related to the amount of compensation the defendant had paid. Although it was also true that the officials would usually consider some other factors in decision-making, such as the suspects'/defendants' risk to society and the suspects'/defendants' remorse, it was more likely that they plainly identified these factors with how much the suspects/defendants were able to pay. A lawyer interviewed also mentioned this problem based on his own experience of being an agent in a couple of criminal reconciliation cases.[62]

> The biggest problem I ever met in the criminal reconciliation programme was that the suspect/defendant was too poor to pay the compensation the victim asked for. Then the parties could not reach an agreement and the suspect/defendant had no means to get the result of non-prosecution or a lighter or suspended sentence. In this sense, I think that criminal reconciliation is an unfair programme. Since money is the most important thing in this programme, it is easy to get the impression that the criminal law or criminal penalty is just for the poor people who cannot enter criminal reconciliation due to lack of money. As a lawyer, I do not know how to resolve this problem. Perhaps the poor people could only accept it. It is really disappointing.

---

60 Chen Qi [陈颀] 'The Incentive Mechanism of "Reducing Punishment with Money" ["赔钱减刑" 的激励机制]' in Su Li [苏力] (ed) *Law and Social Sciences* [*法律和社会科学*] Beijing, Law Press [法律出版社] 2009, 29.

61 Yan Jun [严峻] 'The Debates Triggered by "Avoiding Punishment with Money" ["赔钱减刑" 引发的是非争议]' at http://www.zj.xinhuanet.com/magazine/2007-05/08/content_9972222.htm (last accessed on 4 March 2011).

62 Interview with lawyer L in Xi'an in September 2010.

In sum, the interviews showed that compensation was the absolute focus in the officials' decision-making in the criminal reconciliation programmes. This finding to a certain extent supports the criticism that criminal reconciliation is unfair to suspects/defendants with different financial circumstances. It was also found in the interview that criminal reconciliation programmes that focused on compensation had caused difficulties even to the suspects/defendants who had paid compensation and obtained the prescribed outcomes. Moreover, compensation, as argued later in Chapter 5, did not necessarily have the desired effect of redressing or satisfying the victim as mentioned by the officials. These points are discussed in the next chapter along with the parties' accounts.

4.3.2 The Lack of Judicial Independence

It was also provided in the procedural regulation and guideline as shown in Chapter 1 that decisions on criminal reconciliation could not be made by the presiding prosecutor/judge alone and had to be sent for discussion by the procuratorial committee or judicial committee before the responsible officials announced them. This provision was in accordance with the Criminal Procedural Regulation of the People's Procuratorates and Opinions on Reforming and Improving the Judicial Committee of the People's Court.

The case files showed, with the exception of one case, that the responsible prosecutors'/judges' decisions in the criminal reconciliation cases examined were all smoothly approved by the procuratorial/judicial committee. Only in case no. five in location C (a juvenile robbery case), was the responsible judge L's suggestion for a suspended or lighter sentence for the defendant Q rejected by the judicial committee. Judge L talked about this situation in the interview.[63]

> In the first instance trial of this case, the defendant Q, as the leader in the suspected robbery case concerned, did not get a lighter sentence or a suspended sentence. In the judicial committee's discussion of this case, although I had tried very hard to present the reasons for a lighter sentence or suspended sentence for all the defendants, unfortunately they were not wholly accepted by the committee. The president and vice-president of the Court insisted that it was not appropriate to grant a suspended sentence or lighter sentence to the leader Q in the context of a 'strike hard' (*yanda*) campaign nationwide currently.

---

[63] Interview with judge L in the People's Court of B district in Xi'an in September 2010.

Judge L then mentioned that, in fact, this requirement had been her principal difficulty in conducting criminal reconciliation.[64]

> Actually, my 'leaders,' namely the president and vice-president of the Court, did not support criminal reconciliation, so my suggestions were often rejected. I feel confused and frustrated as my decision was based on a serious consideration of the defendants' situation, which could convince me that a suspended sentence was much better for their rehabilitation and future life. Yet in fact, those who did not quite understand the situation and the case had the final say. The leaders' decision ruined my hard work over long periods of time in one stroke.

Judge L's difficulty actually implied a long-standing problem attracting much criticism, namely the problem that there is no judicial independence in China.[65] As pointed out by many scholars, there is neither external nor internal judicial independence in the Chinese judicial system.

In terms of 'external' judicial independence, not only is the judicial system as a whole not independent from the Party and the People's Congress, but also the People's Court is subject to the government and the Party Committee at the same level.[66] The 2004 PRC Constitution only provides that the People's Courts are not subject to interference by any administrative organ, public organization or individual, while they have to be under the Party's leadership's and the People's Congress's supervision.[67] The Commission of Politics and Law (*zhengfa wei*) was established by the Party in the central and at all levels to manage and

---

[64] Ibid. See also: McConville *et al*, *Criminal Justice in China: An Empirical Inquiry* Cheltenham, UK and Northampton, MA, USA, Edward Elgar Publishing 2011, 365.

[65] He Weifang [贺卫方] 'Amendments on the PRC Court Organic Law and Judicial Independence [中国法院组织法的修改与司法独立]' at http://article.chinalawinfo.com/Article_Detail.asp?ArticleID=33871&Type=mod (last accessed on 28 October 2010).

[66] He Weifang [贺卫方] 'The Reform of the Chinese Court and Judicial Independence: Observation and Reflection of a Participant [中国法院的改革与司法独立：一个参与者的观察与反思]' (2003) 3 *Zhejiang Social Sciences* [*浙江社会科学*] 83–4.

[67] Li Buyun [李步云] Liu Zhiwei [柳志伟] 'Several Issues Relating to Judicial Independence [司法独立的几个问题]' (2002) 3 *Legal Research* [*法学研究*] 9.

control the work of the Public Security Bureau, the People's Procuratorate and the People's Court.[68] Besides, finance and staffing of the People's Court are controlled by the government and the Party's Committee at the same level.[69] The problem of the lack of judicial independence, and the intervention in the People's Court by the Party and local governments, will be discussed in greater detail in Chapter 6.

In terms of internal judicial independence, the judge as an individual decision-maker in the court cannot adjudicate a case independently. Judicial authority lies in 'the court' not in the individual judge. This problem is shown in judge L's account of a criminal reconciliation case. It is chiefly due to the internal structure of the Chinese courts, which is virtually an administrative or authoritative one.[70]

According to the 2001 PRC Judges Law, there are 12 ranks of judges in the Chinese courts and the hierarchy between judges with different ranks is very rigid.[71] The relationship between judges with different ranks is that of superior and subordinate.[72] Not only does the judicial committee have the final say in some kinds of case as stipulated in law, but it is also even normal in the Chinese courts that judges would simply ask for directives and instruction (*zhishi*) from their 'superiors' when they judge cases.[73] In this regard, the Chinese courts are described as having the characteristic that 'those who sentence the case did not hear it' (*pan er bu shen*).

In such an administrative and hierarchical system, the judges' aim in their daily work tends to pursue a higher rank (by achieving the task imposed by their 'superiors' and observing their superiors' indications and instructions), rather than judging cases justly and fairly according to law.[74] Even worse, due to the lack of transparency and the application of a challenge system in the *zhishi* system and the judicial committee, the 'superiors'' power is easy to abuse which produces possibilities of

---

68 Zhang Yinghong [张英红] 'The Commission of Politics and Law Impedes Judicial Independence [政法委妨碍司法独立]' at http://www.chinaelections.org/NewsInfo.asp?NewsID=26678 (last accessed on 22 April 2011).

69 Supra note 66, 83–4.

70 Supra note 68.

71 Yao Li [姚莉] 'An Analysis of the Essentials of Judicial Justice [司法公正要素分析]' (2003) 5 *Legal Research* [*法学研究*] 19.

72 Ibid.

73 Yu Jingyao [俞静尧] 'A Structural Analysis of Judicial Independence and Legal Reform [司法独立结构分析与司法改革]' (2004) 3 *Legal Research* [*法学研究*] 54.

74 Ibid, 53–4.

under-the-table trade and corruption.[75] This problem has also been criticized as being the origin of judicial injustice in the Chinese judicial system.[76]

Concerning the impact of this problem on criminal reconciliation specifically, as indicated by judge L, it made the criminal reconciliation programme fail to reach her expectations. It was indicated in the interview that this problem also made criminal reconciliation disappoint the defendant. This is further discussed and illustrated in the next chapter.

4.4 INSIGHTS INTO FOLLOW-UP PROGRAMMES

4.4.1 Limited Substantiation of Findings in Case File Examination

As provided in the procedural regulations or guidelines, after the criminal reconciliation meeting finished, a follow-up programme could be arranged by the official. It was an option decided by the official, and the case files showed that this programme was undertaken in some cases, especially involving juveniles, though they constituted the minority of the cases examined. The interviews mostly substantiated such findings, while adding more detail.

As also shown in the case files, the follow-up programmes took a variety of forms. It could be a 'supervision period' lasting for several months. During this period, the suspects/defendants had to do some voluntary work and to report on their life and their thoughts regularly to the officials, and the officials would liaise with the suspects'/defendants' teachers or employers or families for updates on how the suspects/defendants were doing. G, the suspect of case no. five in location A (a juvenile theft case) described the follow-up programme of this form in his case.[77]

> After the criminal reconciliation agreement was signed by me and the victim, the prosecutor F told me that there would be a five month period of 'supervision' for me. The decision of non-prosecution could only be confirmed if I was assessed as 'having performed well' during this period by F,

---

[75] Supra note 66, 86.

[76] Li Hong [李宏] 'On Judicial Justice and Independent Trial [论司法公正与审判独立]' (2010) 5 *Legal System and Society* [*法制与社会*] 107.

[77] Interview with G, the suspect of a juvenile theft case, in the People's Procuratorate of D district in Changzhou in May 2008.

> otherwise, the decision of non-prosecution would be revoked and I would still be prosecuted.
>
> During this period, my teacher would regularly communicate with me to help me make progress in terms of my studies, my life and the development of moral character. Moreover, F arranged some voluntary work for me (i.e. helping an advertising company to produce some public service advertisement). I was also required to submit a 'thought report' (*sixiang huibao*) to F every month, and F often called me and my teacher to ask about my progress and situation. I was even invited to participate in an activity organized by the X district People's Procuratorate on Tree Planting Day. All the activities really let me feel cared for. After five months, I got F's positive evaluation and confirmation of the decision of non-prosecution as expected.

In some cases, the follow-up programme merely consisted in the official's continuous contact with the suspects/defendants, their families and teachers over a period of several months. For example, in case no. seven in location B (a juvenile intentional injury case), after the criminal reconciliation meeting ended, the responsible prosecutor H kept in touch in this way for about three months.[78]

Prosecutor H told the author in the interview that, during this period, he traced the suspects' performance at home and in school by calling their parents and teachers regularly in order to satisfy himself that criminal reconciliation had produced what he termed a 'good correction effect' (*jiaozheng qingkuang lianghao*) on them. After continually getting positive comments on the suspects from the parents and teachers, such as 'they did not make any serious mistake' and 'they worked hard at school' during this period, H confirmed that the suspects would not be prosecuted.[79]

The follow-up programme could also take the form of a so-called 'teaching and help' programme (*bangjiao*) which could be conducted by volunteers or by the officials who had been in charge of the criminal reconciliation process. Documents enclosed in the case files, as discussed in Chapter 3, have served to give an understanding of the process of 'teaching and help' programme (*bangjiao*), but interviews provided more details. Prosecutor Z from the People's Procuratorate of Y district in Xi'an described the 'teaching and help' programme in her Procuratorate as follows:[80]

---

78 Interview with prosecutor H in the People's Procuratorate of D district in Chongqing in June 2008.

79 Ibid.

80 Interview with prosecutor Z in the People's Procuratorate of Y district in Xi'an in August 2010.

> The 'teaching and help' programme is arranged for juvenile suspects. It is conducted by the community the suspects lived in and often takes the form of legal education or volunteer work arranged for the suspects. We will also invite the suspects to participate in some activities organized by our Procuratorate such as the art show last month. They sang a song or read a poem in that show, which was really great. We have also cooperated with the Northwest University of Politics and Law to do the 'teaching and help' programme. We will arrange two college students to help one juvenile suspect during this period. The volunteers will have conversations with them, take them out to parks or museums, and visit their families regularly.
>
> At this stage, we will not interfere, because for one thing, we do not have so much time; for another, the young suspects would communicate better with those college students as they might still be kind of fearing us. The volunteers have to report on the suspects' performance to us every month. If their reports show that the suspects perform well, we will confirm the decision of non-prosecution.
>
> I think that the 'teaching and help' programmes were of great significance for young suspects. This programme could educate and correct them; they may get worse via following the 'bad examples' in the prison.

What prosecutor Z described with regard to the 'teaching and help' programme in her Procuratorate was similar to 'teaching and help' programmes the author learned about in the interview with judge L when she talked about this programme arranged for case no. five in location C (a juvenile robbery case).

In this case, L in her functions as judge in charge of the case and criminal reconciliation process, decided that the two suspects, S and T, who had received suspended sentences, were to participate in a 'teaching and help' programme for half a year after the criminal reconciliation agreement had been reached in their case.[81] Such an arrangement was not a part of the parties' criminal reconciliation agreement. It was absolutely up to the responsible officials' discretion and the suspects/defendants seemed to have no chance to object – the officials did not even ask for their opinions on it.

The 'teaching and help' programme in this case talked about by judge L was undertaken by volunteers who were college students. Two college students were assigned to be responsible for one defendant. Those volunteers were to chat with S and T, visit their families and teachers about once a week to get updates on how they were doing, and take them out for hiking and so on.

---

[81] Interview with judge L in the People's Court of B district in Xi'an in September 2010.

The volunteers had to provide reports on the situation of S and T to judge L. During this period, S and T were also required to write a 'thought report' about their study, life and thoughts every month to L. If L found from the reports that these two defendants had done something that violated laws or administrative regulations or regulations of the Public Security Departments of the State Council during this period, the suspension of the sentence would be revoked and the punishment would be enforced.[82]

4.4.2 The Effects and Problems of the Follow-up Programmes

Information and personal assessments provided during the interviews suggested that the follow-up programmes, no matter what form they took, had produced a good effect of suspect/defendant rehabilitation. For instance, the parents of the suspects in case no. seven in location B told the author that 'we felt that our children grew up rapidly after it and became more mature than before.'[83] 'They studied much harder and their teachers in the school often praised them now.'[84] L, the suspect of case no. six in location A, said to the author that 'this work lasting for half a year let me reflect deeply about myself and I feel that I have matured rapidly through this process.'[85] 'I will definitely not do such things in the future, and I really appreciate this chance the prosecutor and the victim gave me.'[86] These assessments were in accordance with the case file's materials.

Nevertheless, judge L from the People's Court of B district in Xi'an mentioned her worries about the 'teaching and help' programme in the interview.[87]

> In the normal criminal procedure, normally the juvenile case would not be heard in public according to the Criminal Procedure Law. That is to protect the juveniles. But in the 'teaching and help' programme, people living around the young suspects would all come to know about the case. I think this may have some negative influence on the young people.

---

[82] Articles 69 and 77 of the PRC Criminal Law.

[83] Telephone interviews with A's father, B's father and D's mother in Chongqing in June 2008.

[84] Ibid.

[85] Interview with L in the People's Procuratorate of X district in Changzhou in June 2008.

[86] Ibid.

[87] Interview with judge L in the People's Court of B district in Xi'an in September 2010.

Judge L's worries are reasonable; the discussion in Chapter 5 of the roles played by people in the parties' (suspects/defendants and victims) social environment may shed some light on her worries.

4.4.3 The Potential Failure of the Official Aim of Correcting the Suspect/Defendant in Criminal Reconciliation Cases without Follow-up Programmes

As noted in Chapter 3, one juvenile case (in Changzhou) and all the adult cases in the three studied locations did not include any follow-up programme. Since the follow-up programme was designed to be optional and its use was left to the responsible official's discretion, cases without a follow-up programme still followed existing procedural regulations or guidelines. But it remains to be asked, as we did in Chapter 3, how well criminal reconciliation worked in cases without follow-up programmes. The interviews provide some indication that in cases without follow-up programmes, the results achieved were not good. For example, Y, the coach of the juvenile parties of case no. nine in location A, described the young suspects' situations after the conclusion of the criminal reconciliation programme without any follow-up programme.[88]

> After the case was resolved, one suspect U performed well; and he has just been selected by the professional judo team of Jiangsu province; the other two suspects V and W, however, left the school shortly after the programme ended. They gave up sports training and now worked as bodyguards in an organization to earn money because they owed too much money and their parents were unlikely to be able to pay it off [without contributions from the juveniles]. It was difficult for them to find some other job due to their lack of education and diploma. I often heard that they were not doing well and fought with others in this work.

However, it appeared that the responsible prosecutor F of this case knew nothing about the suspects' situations since there was no follow-up programme arranged. Hearing the coach's account, F yelled:[89]

> Why did you not tell me about that situation? I have not contacted them for long. I will definitely find V and W and talk to them. I believe that I can persuade them to go back to the school or find another job! Do not worry.

---

[88] Interview with Y in Changzhou in May 2008.

[89] The author witnessed this during the interviews with Y and F in Changzhou in May 2008.

Given the smallness of the sample of cases studied for the purpose of this research project, it certainly remains possible that in other cases without follow-up programmes suspects/defendants still performed well. After all, the criminal reconciliation meeting was in itself designed to have the effect of 'correction' and 'education' of the suspect/defendant. Moreover, access to the parties of criminal reconciliation cases was limited and those parties who had participated in *bangjiao* programmes may have had additional reasons for assuring the author that the programmes had been effective.

However, the different situations of the suspects/defendants in the cases with and without follow-up programmes, as shown above, at least to a certain extent strengthened the point that a follow-up programme was crucial for suspect/defendant rehabilitation; the expected goal of rehabilitating the suspect/defendant might be hard to achieve if there was no follow-up programme. Concerning why there was no such programme in the majority of cases, although an assumption that it was due to the conflicting goals of correcting the suspect/defendant and promoting judicial efficiency was raised in Chapter 3, more causes are analysed in the following chapter along with the narratives from the officials.

4.5 SUMMARY

By and large, this chapter has drawn a picture showing that in the three studied locations, criminal reconciliation practices complied with the designed procedure less than suggested by the official case files. It might to a large extent support the assumption that the case files examined were selected as 'the best examples' by the officials, and it was likely that the officials might have artificially used the case files to make the criminal reconciliation practices look in accordance with the designed procedure.

The findings raise questions concerning the reasons for the procedural departures shown in this chapter. However, the reasons provided in Chapter 3 for the violations, namely the problematic provisions in the procedural regulations or guidelines and the conflicting goals of criminal reconciliation, cannot explain all the violations shown in this chapter, because most of the violations shown in this chapter concern the officials' conduct or arrangements not provided in the procedural regulations or guidelines. For example, the officials added some 'compulsory pre-requirements' like household registration (*hukou*) or ability to pay compensation as prerequisites for initiating this programme. They also added some clauses to the parties' criminal reconciliation agreements; these clauses impeded the parties' rights to appeal after the conclusion of criminal reconciliation meetings. The conflicting aims of criminal reconciliation might to a certain extent affect the officials' conduct in practice, while not all the violations can be simply attributed to the officials' preference for efficiency. More reasons lie in other incentives motivating the officials' conduct. Additionally, the questions raised in the last section of Chapter 3 concerning the voluntariness of the parties' participation and their satisfaction with the criminal reconciliation process have not yet been addressed in this chapter. Comments and feelings from the officials and parties are key to answering these questions, which are presented in the next chapter.

5. The participants of criminal reconciliation programmes: evidence from interviews

In this chapter, which continues to draw on the interviews conducted in this project, the officials' and the parties' motivations and feelings, their comments, concerns and difficulties in criminal reconciliation processes are discussed. Such information is also important to understand whether or not the purported goals of criminal reconciliation such as redressing the damage the victim suffered from the alleged crime, educating and correcting the suspect/defendant, satisfying the parties, and closure (*an jie shi liao*) are achieved. Accounts from the lawyers and other people participating in the criminal reconciliation programmes such as the parties' parents, teachers, employers and leadership (*lingdao*) interviewed are also shown in order to complement the picture of criminal reconciliation practices drawn through the accounts of the officials and parties.

As in previous chapters, the term 'participants' is used broadly in this chapter. It refers to a number of persons involved in criminal reconciliation processes with different roles. It includes the prosecutors/judges who conducted criminal reconciliation programmes, victims and suspects/defendants of the criminal reconciliation cases, lawyers who represented in criminal reconciliation cases, and other people such as the victims'/suspects'/defendants' parents, teachers, employers and other persons belonging to what in China is called 'the leadership' (*lingdao*), who also participated in the criminal reconciliation programmes. The term 'parties,' as defined in Chapters 3 and 4, also refers to the victim (or the direct victim's family if the victim died in the case concerned) or the suspect/defendant of the criminal reconciliation cases.

5.1 OFFICIAL INVOLVEMENT IN CRIMINAL RECONCILIATION PROGRAMMES

5.1.1 Officials' Leading and Dominant Role

According to the procedural regulations or guidelines, what the officials could do in the criminal reconciliation process mainly involved examining eligible cases, explaining this programme to the parties, organizing criminal reconciliation meetings, making decisions for the suspects/defendants after the criminal reconciliation programme was completed and arranging some follow-up programmes. Except for the decision-making and the arrangement of follow-up programmes, the officials' role at the stage of initiation and criminal reconciliation meeting was passive in confronting the parties' intentions. Moreover, since criminal reconciliation was promoted as a programme empowering the parties to resolve their cases mainly by themselves, it was also explicitly stressed in the regulations or guidelines that the initiation and proceeding of this programme ought to be entirely based on the parties' voluntariness, and the officials were forbidden from interfering with the parties' wishes.

Five officials interviewed (one in Changzhou, two in Chongqing, two in Xi'an) seemed to fully acknowledge this and explicitly stressed their 'passive role' in the criminal reconciliation programmes. For example, prosecutor L2 from the People's Procuratorate of B district in Xi'an mentioned the prosecutor's role especially in the criminal reconciliation meeting as follows:[1]

> We merely preside over the criminal reconciliation meeting, and must avoid talking about our own opinions in the meeting … well, actually during the entire process of criminal reconciliation.

But she attributed the prosecutor's passive role to the reason that 'otherwise, it might give others grounds to act on (*lao ren huabing*),'[2] which meant that the officials' conduct in criminal reconciliation might be used by the parties to complain since there was no legal basis for such conduct. This motivation was not the publicly claimed one of empowering the parties to resolve their cases mainly by themselves. It sounded as though this motivation was more for the interests of the officials themselves.

---

1 Interview with prosecutor L2 in Xi'an in September 2010.
2 Ibid.

However, it was found in the interview that in other circumstances, the officials were not passive in the criminal reconciliation process. It was first embodied in the officials' arbitrary disregard of the requirements (both compulsory ones and optional ones) of eligible criminal reconciliation cases. As described in Chapter 4, instead of complying with the stipulated premises of eligible cases, the prosecutors/judges often initiated criminal reconciliation in cases that did not fulfil the compulsory preconditions, or they 'invented' some compulsory requirements that were not provided in the regulations or guidelines (i.e. the parties' residence, performance before allegedly committing the suspected crime, psychological test, and so on) in examining cases for criminal reconciliation. In this sense, the officials played a fairly dominant role in the criminal reconciliation process as they could actually 'make' the procedure in practice and ignore the existing (formal) one.

But why did the officials do this? Interviews with them shed further light on their motivations. For example, judge N from the People's Court of Y district in Xi'an mentioned the reason he preferred criminal reconciliation as the internal task imposed by his Court.[3]

> It is required in our Court that three judges should resolve five hundred cases in one year,[4] plus there are strict requirements on the quality of each case – 'people-oriented judiciary' (*sifa weimin*), 'resolving disputes and satisfying parties' (*xi shi ning ren*) and 'closure' (*an jie shi liao*).
>
> But in fact, the investigation quality in a number of cases is unsatisfactory; especially there are often some problems with evidence. Moreover, our work burden has always been extremely heavy. Thus, it is very difficult for us to meet the requirements in terms of quality and quantity at the same time.
>
> In this context, we [judges] have a strong motivation to conduct criminal reconciliation in that it can resolve cases with deficiencies in investigation or evidence much more quickly. It can also comfort both parties more easily. You know that the defendant can get a lenient punishment and the victim can get a considerable sum of compensation promptly in criminal reconciliation, which is very hard to achieve in the normal litigation procedure.

Judge N's colleague, judge L2, attributed his motivation in initiating criminal reconciliation to the internal performance assessment system (*jixiao kaohe*). This system required the judge's superiors to take into

[3] Interview with judge N in Xi'an in August 2010.

[4] Judge N did not specify in the interview why the task was allocated to three judges. Yet it was possible that in Y district People's Court in Xi'an, three judges as a group were to be disciplined (*chufen*) if the task could not be fulfilled.

account a criterion called 'mediation rate' (*tiaojie lü*), as well as a criterion concerning the judge's success in resolving problems of petitioning (*shangfang*). Both criteria, according to this judge, had been imposed by the People's Court of Y district in Xi'an.[5]

> It is normal that the victims or their families cannot get a decision regarding the defendants' payment of compensation through court litigation enforced by the Court.[6] In some cases, it is because the defendants just do not want to pay. Yet more often, it is because the defendants (or their families) are really too poor to pay. Whatever the reason, the conflict between the two parties cannot be resolved in this situation. And the victim/victim's family would also be dissatisfied with us (judges), so that they might continue making trouble (*naoshi*) or go to petitioning (*shangfang*). In accordance with an internal rule, we will be disciplined (*chufen*) by the Court if they engage in petitioning. So we have to try our best to let the victim get compensation! I think, if the defendant really cannot afford the compensation, they should borrow money or take out a loan to pay it.
>
> Moreover, there is an item in our internal performance assessment system requiring that the 'mediation rate' among all the cases each judge handled has to be at least 50 percent. And 'marks' will be deducted if we fail to reach such a rate.

The problems with the performance assessment system in general have been discussed in Chapter 1. So far as criminal reconciliation is concerned, judges' accounts demonstrate that it has given officials direct incentives to bypass the procedural regulations or guidelines in consequence of which the parties' voluntariness might be impaired and distress caused. For example, it is clear from the accounts of two judges (above) that the internal task imposed by their court and the performance

---

[5] Interview with judge L2 in Xi'an in August 2010.

[6] Article 41 of the Organic Law of the People's Courts of the People's Republic of China provides that 'Local people's courts at various levels have marshals to carry out the execution of judgments and orders in civil cases and the execution, in criminal cases, of the parts of judgments and orders concerned with property.' It means that in China the People's Court also has the responsibility of execution (*zhixing*), other than adjudication. This is rather unique since courts in other jurisdictions do not have to take such administrative responsibility. The Chinese People's Court often becomes a party in the disputes concerning execution thereof. Such a 'mix' of administrative and judicial roles would cause the Court to lose its neutrality in such sorts of disputes and the difficulty in enforcement. See: Guo Songmin [郭松民] 'The Embarrassment of the Enforcement Agency [法院执行局的尴尬]' at http://news.sina.com.cn/c/2005-09-20/18087819132.shtml (last accessed on 18 June 2011). More discussion of this problem can be seen in Chapter 6.

assessment system were the main reasons for their breach of the regulations or guidelines in the initiation of criminal reconciliation. Such incentives were also shown in the interviews with the prosecutors.

An example was case no. seven in location B (a juvenile intentional injury case), as illustrated in Chapter 4, in which the responsible prosecutor H initiated criminal reconciliation when the defendants did not admit guilt or show any remorse towards the alleged crime. In the interview, prosecutor H further mentioned the internal task imposed by his Procuratorate as the reason for his initiation of criminal reconciliation in this case, except for the defendants' family backgrounds.[7]

> In the last year, the High People's Procuratorate of Chongqing issued a document[8] stating that in the context of promoting a harmonious society and the experimental practices of criminal reconciliation in other localities nationwide, all the Procuratorates in Chongqing should stress the work of criminal reconciliation. Accordingly, our Procuratorate has allocated a task of implementing at least three criminal reconciliation programmes in one year to each prosecutor. Such a requirement is also included in our performance assessment system.
>
> Yet actually, it is not easy to identify a case eligible for criminal reconciliation. I thought that in this case involving juvenile defendants, it should be rather easy to make the parties reach an agreement. So I tried criminal reconciliation in this case.

Another prosecutor, L, from the People's Procuratorate of B district in Xi'an frankly explained that he initiated criminal reconciliation in a case mainly out of a desire to avoid 'losing' – that is to say, to avoid an acquittal – as the outcome of a potential criminal litigation.[9]

> Honestly, I conducted criminal reconciliation in that case not because of some greater goal of social harmony, social stability or conflict resolution. It was principally because I had no confidence in winning the litigation of that case.
>
> It happened between youngsters and was charged as an intentional injury crime case. I found it very hard to prove the suspect's subjective intention, and the investigation did not provide enough evidence either. I knew that in this case, it was difficult to win in litigation, yet it was not a problem if I

---

7 Interview with prosecutor H in Chongqing in June 2008.

8 Prosecutor H did not specifically mention whether or not it was an internal document, but the author was unable to obtain this document from public sources.

9 Interview with prosecutor L in Xi'an in September 2010.

> could resolve the case through criminal reconciliation. In criminal reconciliation, the most important thing was to make the parties compromise and reach an agreement.

Although prosecutor L did not explicitly mention the phrase of 'internal task' or 'performance assessment system' as his motivation for initiating criminal reconciliation in that case, his strong desire to win the case implied that this might have some connection with the performance assessment system adopted in his Procuratorate. Under it, the prosecutors would try their best to avoid losing a case in court.

This, however, might produce two problems. For one thing, criminal reconciliation was more likely a tool for the officials to 'plaster over' cases, especially those with deficiencies in evidence, in an attempt to fulfil the various internal objectives and performance assessment system. For another, the officials would also simply view the suspects/defendants as 'objects' for them to accomplish the internal tasks set in the performance assessment system. Therefore, the officials would still initiate criminal reconciliation regardless of the circumstances of the cases, and repeatedly 'persuade' the parties, or ask the parties' lawyers, teachers, employers or leadership to 'persuade' the parties to make them participate in the criminal reconciliation programmes. Judge L2 from the People's Court of Y district in Xi'an said in the interview that the judges would normally 'catch an opportune moment to persuade the parties' or '*zuo gongzuo*' ('do some work' or 'do some thought work on the parties') to get the parties' 'voluntary participation' if they do not want to accept the offer of criminal reconciliation initially.[10]

Nevertheless, the officials' efforts to initiate criminal reconciliation would in some cases be at the cost of the parties' wishes and interests. This was verified by several victims' accounts in the interviews, which are discussed in the following section.

In addition to this hard 'persuasion,' officials may directly use illegal methods to make the parties 'reconcile' and pay compensation. For instance, a lawyer disclosed that in a death penalty case he had represented, the judge simply kept detaining the defendant to 'wait for' any payment of compensation.[11]

> The presiding judge was very actively conducting mediation between the two parties. He had actually implied that as long as my client could compensate,

---

[10] Ibid.

[11] From a lawyer's talk at the seminar held by the Centre of Rights and Justice, the Chinese University of Hong Kong in February 2012.

he would not give the death penalty. However, very unfortunately, my client was really too poor to afford that. As a result, no agreement was reached in the first instance trial and my client is still detained at present – the case is now in the second instance trial phase – due to this issue. Yet his current detention has already exceeded the legally prescribed time limits.

Moreover, as raised above, the officials' dominant role in criminal reconciliation was also reflected in the fact that the officials could add some requirements themselves as compulsory prerequisites for initiating criminal reconciliation. It sounded as though a suspect/defendant could not enter criminal reconciliation without these (additional) 'qualifications' even though he/she had met the compulsory requirements stipulated in the procedural regulations or guidelines.

As shown in Chapter 4, such requirements often concerned the suspect's/defendant's (or his/her family's) residence, performance prior to committing the alleged crime, and most important, their ability to pay compensation. Interviews showed that officials had incentives to create additional requirements, for instance because they wanted to avoid failure in the criminal reconciliation process. For instance, prosecutor N from the People's Procuratorate of B district in Xi'an mentioned the reason that non-local suspects were precluded from participation in criminal reconciliation.[12]

Nowadays, the floating population (*liudong renkou*)[13] is too large. It is dangerous and troublesome for us if we cannot find the suspects after making a decision not to criminally arrest them, or during the follow-up supervision period in criminal reconciliation. You know that police power is also limited.

So we will only initiate criminal reconciliation for the suspects who are registered as Xi'an residents (i.e. have a Xi'an *hukou*). We have also established some cooperation with residential communities (*shequ*) in Xi'an to supervise the suspects (who have gone through the criminal reconciliation

---

[12] Interview with prosecutor N in Xi'an in September 2010.

[13] The floating population or *liudong renkou* in China is largely caused by the current household registration (*huji*) system. The current household registration system in China divides the Chinese population into people with urban household registration and people with rural household registration. Such a division was originally for the purpose of controlling the population and restricting free migration of the people. But since the 1980s, more and more of the rural population has migrated to cities to earn their living, which raises a lot of questions about this system and many argue for the abolishment of this system in China. See: Wang Xiang [王向] 'An Analysis on the Social Welfare Policy to the Floating Population [流动人口社会保障政策分析]' (2003) 4 *Information of Economics and Law* [*财经政法资讯*] 33.

> process). So of course this programme is only applicable in cases involving local people.

Another prosecutor, Z, from the People's Procuratorate of Y district in Xi'an explained why criminal reconciliation was only applicable to local suspects in a similar way.[14]

> It is very hard for us to trace the suspects' situation in the follow-up programmes if they live in other locations rather than in Xi'an. That is really too inconvenient and we do not have that much time and energy.

If the suspects' household registration (*hukou*) was a consideration chiefly motivated by the desire to avoid trouble and save time and energy, according to the officials, the officials' considerations of the suspect's/defendant's performance prior to the alleged crime and ability to pay compensation were mainly motivated by the desire to avoid the potential failure of the criminal reconciliation programmes. Prosecutor C from the People's Procuratorate of Y district in Xi'an explained this.[15]

> A difficulty I once encountered in implementing a criminal reconciliation programme was that it still failed after a long time of reconciliation and after the conclusion of a 'teaching and help' programme. Some children really could not control themselves. Their parents and schools did not supervise them well either. So they found their 'bad' friends and committed some offence again. Then the criminal reconciliation programme had to end and fail. That was really a waste of our time and effort in conducting criminal reconciliation.
>
> In order to resolve this problem, now, for one thing, we have added psychological tests for juvenile suspects to test their ability to control themselves before making the decision to implement criminal reconciliation. If the result of this professional test is not satisfactory, we will definitely not initiate criminal reconciliation. For another, we will take the suspect's performance before the alleged crime into account before making the decision to initiate criminal reconciliation. I think a usually good performance can to a large extent guarantee a good correction effect and the success of criminal reconciliation.

The ability to pay compensation, as noted in Chapter 4, was a very critical element affecting the officials' initiation of criminal reconciliation. And the officials interviewed indicated that criminal reconciliation was rarely initiated if they found that the suspects/defendants were going

---

[14] Interview with prosecutor Z in Xi'an in August 2010.
[15] Interview with prosecutor C in Xi'an in August 2010.

to be unable to afford a sum of compensation. And this was also mainly to prevent the failure of criminal reconciliation due to the suspects'/ defendants' failure to implement the compensation agreements.

So, it emerged from the interviews that the prerequisites added by the officials in initiating criminal reconciliation such as the suspects'/ defendants' self-control, usual performance and ability to pay compensation, were related to the officials' desire for the success of criminal reconciliation programmes. Although the officials only mentioned the reason to avoid the waste of time and effort they had put into such programmes, it also had some relationship to the internal performance assessment system. Taking into account the internal tasks and requirements, such as the 'mediation rate' set down in the performance assessment system, it was hard to exclude the influence of such a system on the officials' conduct.

It is also likely that the internal tasks and the performance assessment system were also the reason that the officials played a dominant and active role in the criminal reconciliation meeting. As described in Chapter 4, the officials repeatedly held criminal reconciliation meeting(s) in order to allow the parties to bargain about the compensation sum and reach an agreement. And the officials added some clauses themselves into the parties' criminal reconciliation agreement which infringed upon the parties' rights of appeal. Considering the requirement on 'mediation rate' in the performance assessment system and perhaps some restriction on 'appeal rate,' it was not hard to understand the officials' conduct in criminal reconciliation meetings.

5.1.2 Officials' Positive Comments on Criminal Reconciliation

In the interview, 16 officials (two in Changzhou, six in Chongqing, eight in Xi'an) indicated their satisfaction with the criminal reconciliation meeting(s), or the follow-up programmes or the whole criminal reconciliation process. For example, prosecutor H expressed his satisfaction with the criminal reconciliation meeting held for case no. seven in location B (an intentional injury case) as follows.[16]

> In this criminal reconciliation programme, mutual understanding between the parties was achieved; the suspects and their parents realized their faults and changed their indifferent attitudes; the victim and his parents discarded hatred and forgave the suspects; the compensation agreement was enforced fully and

[16] Interview with prosecutor H in Chongqing in June 2008.

in a timely fashion. These outcomes could hardly be achieved in the formal criminal procedure.

Another prosecutor, F, from the People's Procuratorate of X district in Changzhou also gave a high evaluation to the criminal reconciliation meeting and the whole programme conducted by him in case no. nine in location A (a juvenile intentional injury case).[17]

> This case was resolved peacefully by the face-to-face criminal reconciliation meeting. Conflicting emotions between the two parties were also eliminated through dialogue and discussion in that meeting. Furthermore, the problem of compensation enforcement was effectively resolved in criminal reconciliation programmes. It is helpful to maintain harmony in society. Therefore, I think that criminal reconciliation is a great programme that needs to be expanded to the whole country as soon as possible.

He also praised the criminal reconciliation programme he conducted in case no. six in location A (a theft case).[18]

> I was quite satisfied with the outcome of this case closed through criminal reconciliation. For one thing, the victim gave up his anger and chose to be tolerant which was fairly appreciated by his leadership. For another, the suspect's work, life and future were not affected by the act he committed on impulse. It was really very important for a young man to have such a chance after making mistakes. Moreover, I got feedback information from the suspect's boss and parents to the effect that he performed even better than before the criminal reconciliation programme during his supervision period. I was informed that he worked much harder now and even proposed to work overtime; he rarely went to internet bar and often helped his parents to do some farming work.

It sounded as though the officials rated the criminal reconciliation meeting(s) and programmes highly mainly from the aspects of the officially predicted aims of this programme such as redressing the harm the victim suffered, educating the suspect/defendant, resolving the parties' disputes and establishing a 'harmonious society.' Moreover, four officials (one in Chongqing and three in Xi'an) particularly talked about the advantages of criminal reconciliation as compared with the normal criminal process. For example, prosecutor S from the People's Procuratorate of B district in Xi'an said that:[19]

---

[17] Interview with prosecutor F in Changzhou in May 2008.
[18] Ibid.
[19] Interview with prosecutor S in Xi'an in September 2010.

> The most impressive advantage of criminal reconciliation compared with the normal procedure is that the suspect would know that others may forgive them after they have done something wrong. I believe that this is good for the suspect's future performance and mental development.

Judge L2 from the People's Court of Y district in Xi'an mentioned the effect of legal knowledge popularization (*pufa*) as the main advantage of criminal reconciliation.[20]

> A very significant function of criminal reconciliation is legal knowledge popularization (*pufa*). In criminal reconciliation programmes, we (judges) have to do much work to persuade the parties to accept our offer of criminal reconciliation. In doing this, we have to patiently explain to them that the outcome of the case resolved through criminal reconciliation is in accordance with the law and therefore is fair to them. During such a process, we would give them much relevant legal knowledge. The normal criminal procedure does not have such a function.
>
> It is beneficial. Often, the parties are unsatisfied with the Court's adjudication and then petition. But it is largely out of their disregard of legal knowledge! Too many people in China do not understand law and do not trust law, so as a judge in China, I think it is my responsibility to help them know some legal knowledge. Criminal reconciliation is a good channel, as we can have much communication with the parties in this programme.

It seemed that it was hard to learn negative comments from the officials as the people conducting the criminal reconciliation programmes, especially considering the fact that criminal reconciliation was connected so closely with their marks in the performance system. Yet the benefit of 'legal knowledge popularization (*pufa*)' as raised by judge L2 was debatable. It was problematic to assert that the reason parties petitioned was largely their disregard of the law. As noted in Chapter 1, it was in many cases due to the judicial officers' violations of law. Second, considering the fact that criminal reconciliation was only participated in by a comparatively small number of people (often only the victim and the suspect/defendant of the case concerned) it was a bit far-fetched to say that it was a better way of legal knowledge popularization compared with the normal procedure. It was also questionable to assert that the normal criminal process did not embody this function; this will be further discussed in Chapter 6. Yet most importantly, was legal knowledge popularization really a proper goal that a legal process or a criminal process should pursue? Probably, it should not be over-stressed for a

---

20 Interview with judge L2 in Xi'an in August 2010.

legal process, compared to the values of fairness, justice and protecting the parties' rights. All in all, it might not be proper to rate legal knowledge popularization as an advantage of criminal reconciliation.

5.1.3 Officials' Negative Comments on Criminal Reconciliation

Two officials out of 18 who were interviewed expressed some negative views on the criminal reconciliation programmes and their likelihood of achieving the predicted outcomes. Prosecutor C from the People's Procuratorate of Y district in Xi'an was worried about social circumstances in terms of reaching the aim of correcting juvenile suspects.[21]

> Nowadays, the social context is terrible. Too little concern is put on the juveniles. Also, juvenile crime prevention work is far from enough. There has been much propaganda, while all what we have is merely propaganda. The function of propaganda is so superficial. It cannot touch the juveniles' mind.
>
> Concern for juveniles not studying in school is even less. Could we reckon on such a society to address the problem of juvenile crime and to correct juvenile criminals effectively? What we (prosecutors) can do, or what criminal reconciliation and the 'teaching and help' programme can do is so limited. I believe that either crime prevention or criminal correction should rely on long-term efforts and the general social context.

Another prosecutor, L, from the People's Procuratorate of B district in Xi'an, expressed his misgivings concerning criminal reconciliation's impact on the victim (or his/her family) as well as the whole society.[22]

> I think that criminal reconciliation would bring about some negative feelings to the victims (or their families). For example, in the traffic accident related crime cases, the victims' families would think that they get money because of their relatives' death. But they have no opportunity to express such a feeling. And in fact, it is useless for them to express it.
>
> It is bad for society too – other people would think that it is just a monetary exchange in criminal cases. Criminal law is unfair in that it only deals with the poor, or people living at the bottom level of society. They will be further dissatisfied with our society.
>
> Besides, I do not think that criminal reconciliation can have great influence on society. Criminal reconciliation cases are minor and usually would not attract public attention. The public cannot get any feedback from these criminal reconciliation cases either.

---

21 Interview with prosecutor C in Xi'an in August 2010.
22 Interview with prosecutor L in Xi'an in September 2010.

> Now we use reconciliation as a way of resolving civil cases to deal with criminal cases. I feel that such a method is very utilitarian since it is used in the context that conflicts in our society today are too sharp and too much. Yet this has made the People's Procuratorate more like an official 'debt-collection company.'

Prosecutor L's comments on the problems of unfairness and the negative influence on the victim in criminal reconciliation could be further shown by the parties' accounts in the following sections. But he might somewhat underestimate the influence of criminal reconciliation cases on society. As noted in Chapter 1, there have been many news reports and articles about criminal reconciliation and some of them have attracted wide attention and discussion in society.

5.1.4 Officials' Expressed Concerns about Criminal Reconciliation

In the interviews, the officials also expressed uncertainty about the legal basis for criminal reconciliation programmes, even though in some of the locations studied, procedural regulations for these programmes existed at the local level. For example, prosecutor S from the People's Procuratorate of B district in Xi'an mentioned such confusion in the application of this programme:[23]

> Criminal reconciliation is in accordance with the criminal policy of 'combining leniency with severity' (*kuan yan xiang ji*). Thus, apparently it cannot be used in all kinds of crimes. But for which kinds of crime is it applicable? I really feel a bit confused.
>
> We are now just exploring this programme in practice. The guideline issued in our Procuratorate is too general and vague. So when I conducted criminal reconciliation programmes, I often asked myself whether what I was doing was legitimate. I hope that there would be clearer regulations for this practice. Then we (prosecutors) would feel much more secure if there was a solid legal basis for our work.

This prosecutor even viewed this as the main problem of criminal reconciliation practices.[24]

> It is the major problem of criminal reconciliation practices. In some criminal reconciliation cases, the suspects [whose cases are handled through criminal reconciliation] may think that committing a crime is not serious and that they

23 Interview with prosecutor S in Xi'an in September 2010.

24 Ibid.

> may do that again in the future. That is awful, so we must control the use of criminal reconciliation.
>
> I think that the way to prevent this problem is to limit the use of criminal reconciliation in suspected minor crime conducted by young people or minor crimes completely on impulse. And we should consider the suspects' characteristics in making the decision to use criminal reconciliation.
>
> But there is no solid legal basis for the criteria now used to judge if a case should be handled through criminal reconciliation. So they rely too much on the responsible official's subjective judgement, which would produce too much uncertainty as various people may have various criteria.

Another prosecutor, L, from the People's Procuratorate of B district in Xi'an, also talked about some confusion coming from the lack of a clear and solid legal basis for criminal reconciliation practices:[25]

> The first unclear issue in criminal reconciliation is whether it only applies to juvenile crimes or also includes adult crimes. There is no clear legal regulation for this programme now. I myself have conducted this programme for about one year in both juvenile and adult crimes.
>
> Second, I always feel confused about its nature. Is it plea bargaining? No. Plea bargaining is related to the problem of evidence, while in criminal reconciliation, the requirement of its application is that the evidence is 'clear and sufficient' (*zhengju queshi chongfen*). Then, is it something merely related to the circumstances to be considered in sentencing? Obviously it is not the statutory sentencing circumstances (*fading liangxing qingjie*); it is something concerning the officials' discretionary power. Yet there is no legal basis for such a discretionary power either.
>
> There is also no definition of criminal reconciliation, so I am not sure whether it is just an idea or a system, or a method adopted at a certain period in the context of 'establishing a harmonious society' (*hexie shehui*)?

He further talked about the officials' actual conduct facing this confusion.[26]

> Since criminal reconciliation has not been provided in any legal regulation yet, you cannot find this phrase in any document in the People's Court, People's Procuratorate or the Public Security Bureau. We can only write down those systems that have legal basis in the documents. With regard to criminal reconciliation cases, we would write that 'there is compensation' or 'there are circumstances affecting sentence' in the documents, instead of '*xingshi hejie*.'

---

25 Interview with prosecutor L in Xi'an in August 2010.

26 Ibid.

> The leadership in the Procuratorate did not support this programme much due to the lack of a clear legal basis. We could avoid being criticized by observing legal procedure. In criminal reconciliation, however, our conduct easily attracts criticism (*shuo san dao si*) by the parties since there is no clear legal basis for it.

Prosecutor L's account also helps explain the phenomenon noted in Chapter 1 that the statistics on the implementation of criminal reconciliation delivered in the public resources showed that this process was rarely used by the state authorities. Altogether 10 out of 18 interviewed officials (one in Changzhou, four in Chongqing, five in Xi'an) mentioned their problems with conducting criminal reconciliation programmes on the grounds that 'this practice currently has no legal basis.'[27] This problem also gave rise to the officials' conduct of adding a clause into the criminal reconciliation agreement which impeded the parties' rights to appeal. The prosecutor who had done this, Y, explained his motivation in the interview:[28]

> It is for the efficiency and effectiveness of the criminal reconciliation programme. On the one hand, litigation after criminal reconciliation is a waste of judicial resources.[29] On the other hand, it would impair the effectiveness of the criminal reconciliation agreement and the prosecutor's image [if the parties could go back to a litigation process after concluding criminal reconciliation]. If the parties could renege on their agreements at their own will, what would be the difference between agreements reached in the People's Procuratorate through criminal reconciliation and private agreements?

It seemed that, in prosecutor Y's opinion, the criminal reconciliation agreement should have the effect of barring any further litigation. Yet the validity of the agreement reached in criminal reconciliation was also

27 Interview with prosecutor C in Xi'an in August 2010.

28 Interview with prosecutor Y in Chongqing in June 2008.

29 Nowadays, there is no legal provision in China governing the way to deal with the parties' repentance after they reach/sign the criminal reconciliation agreement. Hence, the legal force of the criminal reconciliation agreement is uncertain according to Chinese Law. There are also debates in academia over this issue. See e.g. Feng Renqiang [冯仁强] Xie Meiyin [谢梅因] 'Definition and Disposition of the Repentance in Criminal Reconciliation [刑事和解"反悔"行为的认定与处理]' at http://www.procedurallaw.cn/xsss/zdwz/200902/t20090227_185404.html (last accessed on 25 June 2011). Yet Article 188 of the 1998 Judicial Interpretation on CPL issued by the Supreme People's Court [最高人民法院关于执行《中华人民共和国刑事诉讼法》若干问题的解释] provides that the parties can initiate a lawsuit in the People's Court concerning the case reconciled.

unaddressed in the current legal system (even in Articles 277 to 279 of the 2012 CPL). Therefore, the situation that there was no legal basis for criminal reconciliation (before the 2012 CPL took effect on 1 January 2013) had given rise to two problems. Firstly, the officials felt insecure about the legal force of this programme, so they 'created' something (i.e. adding a clause into the parties' agreement that explicitly prohibited either party bringing about litigation after signing the criminal reconciliation agreement) in an attempt to give it stronger force.

Secondly, these additions were in fact in conflict with the existing laws and infringed upon the parties' rights, while there was also no restriction in the law concerning the officials' conduct in this regard in criminal reconciliation programmes. The problem caused by the lack of legal restriction on the official's power in criminal reconciliation might lead to further problems. This will be further elaborated in the next chapter. Prosecutor L from the People's Procuratorate of B district in Xi'an mentioned the problem of corruption.[30]

> The official's discretionary power in criminal reconciliation is too great. So it is easy to earn personal benefits in this programme, especially given that there is no judicial supervision of this programme.

5.1.5 Difficulties Faced by Officials in Charge of Criminal Reconciliation

An official, prosecutor S from the People's Procuratorate of B district in Xi'an, expressed some confusion regarding the performance assessment system. She talked about the contradiction between a requirement regarding high 'prosecution rate' (*gongsu lü*) in the performance assessment system of her Procuratorate and the policy of 'establishing a harmonious society.'[31]

> There is a requirement on arresting and prosecuting a certain number of cases each year in my Procuratorate's performance assessment system. In fact, this system directly impacts the number of cases in which we would make a decision of non-prosecution and conduct criminal reconciliation.
>
> Sometimes we will not initiate criminal reconciliation merely in order to meet the assessment requirement on 'prosecution rate,' even though the case in itself is suitable for this programme.

---

[30] Interview with prosecutor L in Xi'an in September 2010.
[31] Interview with prosecutor S in Xi'an in September 2010.

> There is also a competition about these (i.e. arrest and prosecution) rates among all the districts in Xi'an. We will lose in the competition if we do not prosecute a sufficient number of cases. But isn't there a contradiction? Now we are advocating the establishment of a harmonious society, but in the meanwhile we are pursuing a high prosecution rate, which is a sign of non-harmonious society. I really feel puzzled.

Prosecutor S's account highlighted again the close relationship between the performance assessment system and the officials' conduct in their work. They used this system as the real 'guideline' for their work, even though they might also consider the system itself unreasonable.

The kind of pressure indicated by prosecutor S may also explain the finding obtained through case file examination that in contrast to the message delivered by public sources, according to which criminal reconciliation was developing rapidly and widely nationwide, not many cases were resolved through this programme in the two People's Procuratorates in Changzhou and Chongqing (the number was not obtained for Xi'an). Since criminal reconciliation would normally lead to a decision of non-prosecution, the prosecutors might restrict the use of it in order to fulfil the requirement on 'prosecution rate' in the performance assessment system.

Almost all of the officials interviewed expressed the view that this programme took too much of their time and energy. For example, prosecutor L from the People's Procuratorate of B district in Xi'an said:[32]

> Criminal reconciliation programmes take too much of our time and energy. In fact, it requires us (prosecutors) to possess mediation skills, which we should not be supposed to possess as judicial officials. Aunts of the Resident's Committee (*ju wei hui*) are much more competent in this aspect. And they have much time to do such work.

Prosecutor H from the People's Procuratorate of D district in Chongqing also described a criminal reconciliation programme he once implemented as very time-consuming:[33]

> Compared with prosecution, criminal reconciliation consumed much more of my time and energy given that I had spent much time before the criminal reconciliation meeting to seek the parties' agreements to participate, to prepare for the various activities in the meeting, and to do the supervision work after the criminal reconciliation meeting. Since my work burden as a prosecutor of the People's Procuratorate at basic level has been already quite

32 Interview with prosecutor L in Xi'an in September 2010.
33 Interview with prosecutor H in Xi'an in August 2010.

> heavy, I am inclined not to initiate another use of criminal reconciliation in the future even if I come across a case that by itself is suitable, so long as there is no 'task requirement' for that.

Yet, the officials said that a worse situation for them was that even after such hard work over a long period, the parties still could not reach an agreement. For example, prosecutor S from the People's Procuratorate of B district in Xi'an indicated it as the main difficulty she encountered in the criminal reconciliation cases:[34]

> In conducting criminal reconciliation programmes, the most serious problem for me is that I feel embarrassed when the parties cannot reach any agreement after a long period of reconciliation. In this case, the victim would be concerned that it is because we (prosecutors) have taken some 'benefits' from the suspect, so that we did not want to prosecute the suspect.

Concerning why the parties could not reach an agreement, the officials attributed it to the victim's unreasonable requirements on compensation or the suspect's/defendant's likely inability to pay compensation. For example, prosecutor L2 from the People's Court of Y district in Xi'an said:[35]

> Sometimes victims were fairly unreasonable (*bu jiang li*). They asked for too much and could not be persuaded to compromise. As a result, the parties could not reach a criminal reconciliation agreement and we had to go back to the normal procedure. This wasted our time.

Judge L from the People's Court of B district in Xi'an also viewed the failure to reach a criminal reconciliation agreement as the victim's responsibility.[36]

> Criminal reconciliation relies too much on the parties' will. Some victims are too stubborn; they put their own interests above anything else. In some cases like minor injury, we (prosecutors) do not think a very serious harm has been done, while they insist that they have been harmed so badly that they deserve a colossal sum of compensation from the defendant. In this kind of case, it is almost impossible for us to persuade such victims to compromise and, as a result, the parties cannot reconcile.

---

34 Interview with prosecutor S in Xi'an in September 2010.
35 Interview with prosecutor L2 in Xi'an in August 2010.
36 Interview with judge L in Xi'an in September 2010.

Two officials (in Xi'an) thought that it was the suspect/defendant, rather than the victim, that should be blamed for the failure in reaching a criminal reconciliation agreement. For instance, Judge Z, also from the People's Court of Y district in Xi'an, mentioned the defendant's inability to pay compensation as the chief obstacle to reaching a criminal reconciliation agreement.[37]

> Generally, the success rate of mediation and reconciliation in our Court is about 50 percent to 60 percent. The chief element affecting the success rate is the defendant's ability to pay compensation. If the defendant cannot afford the compensation demanded by the victim, it is impossible for them to reach a criminal reconciliation agreement. In criminal reconciliation, we should mainly take into account the victims' difficulties and needs since they are the party without fault in the suspected crime.

As indicated above, criminal reconciliation was included in the Procuratorate's and Court's internal performance assessment system, so the officials would try their best to make the parties reach an agreement once they had initiated this programme. Yet in the sense that criminal reconciliation would take too much time, the task set in the performance assessment system concerning a certain number of criminal reconciliation cases baffled the officials. A judge, L2, talked about a dilemma he met in criminal reconciliation practice, which resulted from the contradiction between criminal reconciliation's time-consuming character and the internal task imposed by the Court he was based in.[38]

> Normally, criminal reconciliation would take us at least three months to close a case. It is longer than the time the formal procedure would take, since minor crimes are usually dealt with by the simplified procedure (*jianyi chengxu*) which takes less than one and a half months. So in my opinion, criminal reconciliation has increased our workload. And it has put us in a very difficult position – the Court requires that three judges resolve five hundred cases per year.

This indicated the problem with the performance assessment system again: regardless of whether the officials wanted to implement criminal reconciliation, or whether the case in itself was not suitable for this programme, the officials had to initiate it largely for the purpose of meeting the requirements set in the performance assessment system.

---

[37] Interview with judge Z in Xi'an in August 2010.
[38] Interview with judge L2 in Xi'an in August 2010.

5.2 THE PARTIES PARTICIPATING IN CRIMINAL RECONCILIATION PROGRAMMES

According to domestic scholars, an essential difference between criminal reconciliation and the normal criminal procedure was that criminal reconciliation empowered the parties to resolve their cases mainly by themselves. In this sense, it protected what was referred to as the parties' 'rights of participation (*canyu quan*)' in the criminal justice process.[39] During this process, the victim was expected to be redressed both financially and psychologically and the suspect/defendant was expected to be properly 'educated' and 'rehabilitated.'

It could be seen from those descriptions that the parties were expected to be at the core and play a leading role in the criminal reconciliation process, especially at the stage of initiating this programme and during the criminal reconciliation meeting itself. The parties' voluntariness and leading role at these two stages were also stressed in the procedural regulations or guidelines.

However, as already discussed, in practice, it was the officials that controlled and led the whole process of criminal reconciliation. They might also pressurize the parties in this programme. They had the incentive to do so considering the performance assessment system and the capacity to do so considering their almost unrestricted power in criminal reconciliation processes. In this section, the parties' accounts are provided to further support this point. And the accounts further indicate that the officials' dominance in criminal reconciliation can cause harm to the parties.

5.2.1 The Victim's Participation under Coercion

It was found in two cases (in Changzhou) that the victims did not want to accept the offer of criminal reconciliation but they still agreed to participate mainly because of the pressure exerted by the officials. An example was victim C in case no. nine in location A (an intentional injury case).

In the interview, C looked very shy and initially did not want to talk. He just responded that 'you can ask the prosecutor and my coach,' or 'I cannot remember,' or 'just so-so' to the questions concerning the case, the

---

[39] Ge Lin [葛琳] *On Criminal Reconciliation* [*刑事和解研究*] Beijing, The Chinese People's Public Security University Press [中国人民公安大学出版社] 2008, 198.

criminal reconciliation meeting and his feelings. When the author asked more questions aimed at probing further into these vague responses, he did not say anything and remained expressionless, giving an impression of resistance and reluctance. After the author had explained to him again that the only purpose of this interview was for the writing of a PhD thesis and that the interview had nothing to do with the prosecutor or the final disposition of his case, he looked more relaxed and started to talk. He talked about how the attack by the fellow students hurt him deeply.[40]

> I could be enrolled in a university on the condition that my performance in the 16th national sports meeting was good, but the injury caused by them (the three defendants) compelled me to give up the sports meeting and so I lost the opportunity of going to university. Even worse, I had to change the training course because of the wound to my legs. You know that it is not easy to exercise a new discipline, so the progress and the grade of my training are now unsatisfactory. And I am very uncertain about the future – I have no idea when I will ever get another chance to go to university. Therefore, I hate the suspects very much and even view them as the murderers of my bright future.

Asked why he agreed to participate in the criminal reconciliation programme if he 'hated' them that much, C confessed that he really wanted to see them tried in court, yet his coach and the responsible prosecutor F had spoken to him many times and taught him to 'consider the relationship between them as schoolmates, so he should give them one more chance as their schoolmate.'[41] He said that he was also told by prosecutor F that criminal reconciliation was beneficial for educating the suspects and letting them realize their faults. And for C himself, criminal reconciliation could resolve the case in a short time and he could continue training as soon as the case was resolved. Therefore, at last C chose to accept criminal reconciliation for he did not want to offend his coach and the prosecutor. Also, he wanted to restart training as soon as possible.[42]

Thus, it is clear that actually C (the victim) did not want to participate in the criminal reconciliation programme initially, but the repeated 'persuasion' from his teacher and the responsible prosecutor and the promised benefit that criminal reconciliation would bring led him to accept it eventually.

---

[40] Interview with C, the victim of an intentional injury case, in Changzhou in May 2008.

[41] Ibid.

[42] Ibid.

C's account, while merely one case, illustrated that 'persuasion' could diminish the meaningfulness of the parties' 'voluntary' participation. In such circumstances, the criminal reconciliation meeting could not be expected to produce the projected outcomes such as redressing harm done to the victim and restoring the parties' relationship. Victim C further described the criminal reconciliation meeting as follows:[43]

> It was terrible! Actually, I did not want to see the suspects and discuss my painful experience anymore. Accordingly, I did not say anything in the meeting. The only impression I had about the meeting was a bargaining over the compensation amount between the parents of both parties. I even did not want to see the agreement containing the compensation amount reached finally. And I have not heard the suspects' apologies yet.

It seemed that a criminal reconciliation meeting without the parties' or one party's genuinely voluntary participation was merely an arrangement for negotiating over compensation, and that such arrangement was not appreciated by the parties or one of the parties in this case. When the author further asked C whether he viewed it as a fair process, or whether he felt satisfied with it, he paused, as though did not know how to answer. Finally, he just murmured that all the bad things had passed away and he could feel better now by trying as best he could to forget the case and the suspects.[44]

The second example was case no. six in location A (a theft case). The victim of this case, Q, also said that he still could not forgive the suspect after the incident:[45]

> I felt outraged when I found my motorbike stolen as the theft made me lose face in front of my friends. I hated the thief very much and only wanted to 'teach the thief a lesson' (*jiaoxun ta*) when I caught the suspect, X.

Then the author asked him why he had agreed to participate in criminal reconciliation if he hated the suspect that much. He said that he did not want to participate but that his leadership (*lingdao*), X's boss and the prosecutor F approached him no fewer than five times separately to persuade him to engage in criminal reconciliation. He was also told by them that X felt very remorseful and that, since X was very young, he should give X an opportunity given that prosecution would destroy his future.

43 Ibid.
44 Ibid.
45 Interview with Q in Changzhou in June 2008.

Although Q really could not understand why in such circumstances X should be immune from prosecution and be given another chance, he finally agreed to participate in the criminal reconciliation programme. But obviously he was unhappy with this:[46]

> Motorbike theft happens very often in our village. Why was X different from others? And why was I chosen to be a different victim from other victims (who were not pushed into a criminal reconciliation process), and why should I give him another chance? I am afraid that such a programme is not helpful in terms of cracking down on offences in our village. Yet under the circumstances at that time, I had no other choice, as it was impossible to say no to my *lingdao* and the prosecutor. I did not want to offend them and make them unhappy. That [antagonizing them] would not have been good for me.

Then the author asked him whether he viewed criminal reconciliation as a fair and just programme. He laughed and said that only students at school (like the author) still cared about things like fairness and justice nowadays, while in society, a variety of issues (i.e. relationships, connections and your leadership's 'image' or *mianzi*) mattered more.[47] 'Compromise is necessary in life. That is the truth and you have to accept it,' said Q.[48] But when the author asked him whether he felt satisfied with the criminal reconciliation programme, he only commented, 'It's alright.' And he said that 'I don't want to see X and mention the case anymore because I still feel furious now' at the end of the interview.[49]

It could be seen that, in this case, the victim Q did not participate in the criminal reconciliation programme voluntarily either. He was actually participating because of pressure from the official and his leader. His emotions as a victim could not be addressed appropriately through such a coercive process, though he viewed the 'compromise' as vital. Moreover, his anger might show that actually he viewed the process as unfair and unjust though he did not want to state this explicitly.

In a case in location C (a juvenile robbery case), the victim, Z's father, explicitly expressed his discontent with the situation resulting from the responsible judge's repeated persuasive efforts to get their acceptance of criminal reconciliation:[50]

---

46 Ibid.
47 Ibid.
48 Ibid.
49 Ibid.
50 Interview with Z's father in Xi'an in September 2010.

> Actually I think what the judge did was really a waste of time. It is because of this that the case has not been decided until this moment! In such a situation (the case has not been resolved yet), how could we comment on our government and our judicial system?
>
> Moreover, Z's situation is awful now. All the students in his class heard about this matter, and some of them laughed at him. Especially considering that this case has not been resolved, my son and his classmates may think that there would be no consequences for the boys that had done something wrong. What is worse, some of the suspects once threatened my son since they are not detained and still continue to study with my son.
>
> So Z is under such great pressure now that his life and study have been greatly impaired. We, as parents, feel terrible and upset too. At present, we even have no idea on how to explain this situation to Z as a juvenile. So we wrote a letter to the Court. We can only ask for a fair and timely trial of this case. If we get that, we could convince Z that there is fairness and justice in our society and we could help him get out of this trouble as soon as possible.

5.2.2 No Presumption of Innocence

The procedural regulations or guidelines stipulated that criminal reconciliation could only be initiated if the suspect/defendant had admitted guilt (*renzui*) or expressed regret (*huizui*). It was the basis of the official goal of criminal reconciliation, namely to educate and correct the suspect/defendant. However, from the descriptions in Chapter 4 it appears that the officials virtually initiated criminal reconciliation ignoring this premise and initiated it when the suspect/defendant did not admit guilt. For example, in case no. seven in location B (an intentional injury case), the responsible prosecutor H talked about his initiation of criminal reconciliation when none of the juvenile suspects showed any regret regarding the case. Another prosecutor, S, mentioned that normally the prosecutors would not consider the issue if the suspects admitted guilt since the suspects were detained at that moment. In this sense, the suspect/defendant was simply viewed by the officials as a 'criminal' in need of education and correction through criminal reconciliation processes.

This attitude was also reflected in the officials' accounts when they talked about the suspects/defendants in detention when they considered initiating criminal reconciliation. Some, as set out below, even expressed the view that the 'education and correction' (*jiaoyu he jiaozheng*) of the suspects/defendants could be expected to start from the moment they were detained, and that the detention house was a suitable place for 'education and correction.' For example, prosecutor S from the People's Procuratorate of B district in Xi'an said that:[51]

> Some suspects may get better after being educated in the detention house, yet some may get worse after staying in that kind of place.

Such a description was popular for juvenile suspects/defendants as well. Another prosecutor, L2, from the People's Procuratorate of B district in Xi'an mentioned that:[52]

> The circumstances in the detention house are rather bad and that is a good education for those children. Then they would bear in mind the outcome of committing crime and would not dare to do that again in the future.

However, the problem with excessively long custody (*chaoqi jiya*), as shown in case no. five in location C (a juvenile robbery case) and as discussed in Chapter 4, was found to cause much hurt to the family of the people detained in the interview. The mother of the defendant in case no. five in location C (a juvenile robbery case) could not help crying during the interview when she talked about her son, S, in the detention house after the first instance trial.[53]

> I have not seen S for about half a year, except for his brief appearance in court during the first instance trial.
>
> Although according to an internal rule, detainees may be visited by their families every 10th and 20th of the month, I have not seen him since he was sent there. I was only permitted to write him notes which were said to be passed on to S by the people working there.
>
> I feel extremely worried and upset, but I do not know why I was not allowed to see him and what I can do about it. What worries me most is my son's condition in the detention house because I have been unable to find out how he has been doing for such a long time. The whole family is under very great pressure and S's father is sick now out of being too angry and worried. So we insist on appealing (*shangsu*) for a fair sentence for S. The presiding judge also supports our appeal.

The reason for S's detention and segregation from seeing his family was not obtained in the interview, but the account above, as a snapshot, showed the seriousness of the problem of excessively long custody

---

51 Interview with prosecutor S in Xi'an in September 2010.
52 Interview with prosecutor L2 in Xi'an in September 2010.
53 Interview with S's mother in Xi'an in September 2010.

(*chaoqi jiya*) during the criminal reconciliation process on the one hand, and its harm to the parties' family on the other hand.

So far as the officials of the system regarded the suspects/defendants as criminals in need of education and correction, it was likely that the suspects/defendants would be pressed by the officials to enter criminal reconciliation to accept education and rehabilitation. And it was really hard to say no to officials holding such strong views since the suspects/defendants would also know that the officials were the ones having great power in making crucial decisions in their cases. None of the suspects/defendants interviewed mentioned this point. But it must be remembered that in Changzhou and Chongqing, for the purposes of this research, all the parties were contacted by the officials and interviews took place under their observation.

Deriving from this view held by the officials (that the suspects/defendants were criminals) it became clear that the suspects/defendants were further used as 'examples' embodying educational meaning to their peers. Thus, as noted in Chapters 3 and 4, the criminal reconciliation meetings in four juvenile cases (three in Changzhou and one in Xi'an) were attended not only by the parties and the officials, but also by the parties' schoolmates. For example, the criminal reconciliation meeting held in case no. five in location A (a juvenile theft case) in the parties' school was attended by the responsible prosecutor, F, both parties, several teachers who had taught the parties and some student delegates selected from the parties' class (they were from the same class) and all the other classes of the school.[54]

The student delegates' observation, according to the responsible prosecutor interviewed, was for the purpose of 'making this meeting a good chance for the other students to learn more about law'; and the teachers' observation was to 'help the teachers know this matter more comprehensively which was good for their educational work in the future.'[55]

However, it was possible that such a set-up mainly served the purpose of putting pressure on the parties (the suspect especially) to behave according to the teachers' and the officials' expectations (i.e. to serve the end of 'education'). Such a criminal reconciliation meeting was more like a show that sacrificed the parties' needs or interests for the so-called larger good or other people's expectations (i.e. 'education' in this case).

---

[54] Interview with the victim of this case in May 2008.

[55] Interview with prosecutor F at the People's Procuratorate of X district in Changzhou in May 2008.

But it was not the end that criminal reconciliation was claimed to pursue and it had violated the goal of empowering the parties during this process.

Although both the suspect and victim expressed their satisfaction with such a criminal reconciliation meeting in the interview, the victim of this case still mentioned that the suspect 'was very nervous in the criminal reconciliation meeting.'[56]

In this sense, the suspect might be unhappy with this arrangement, while having agreed out of the teacher's or the prosecutor's pressure. After all, it was hard for him to offend these people who acted as 'powerful persons' for him. His extreme nervousness in the meeting mentioned by the victim might be a sign of his reluctance of that extensive observation. In this regard, to what extent the criminal reconciliation meeting focused on the parties and granted them real power to resolve their own cases was questionable, now that even they could not have the criminal reconciliation meeting in the way they really wanted.

Yet the responsible prosecutor, F, further commented on such a criminal reconciliation meeting as 'a vivid lesson on law for the other students observing the meeting.'[57] Such comments again indicated that, rather than empowering the parties to resolve the case by themselves, criminal reconciliation and the parties were actually controlled by the officials to serve their own ends, sometimes at the price of sacrificing the parties' intentions and needs. And it might echo the doubt on the benefit mentioned by a judge that criminal reconciliation was expected to have the function of legal knowledge propaganda (*pufa*). However, neither the suspects/defendants nor the programme itself should be a tool or a show which accorded some 'larger good' greater than the parties' interests. Otherwise, it might violate the predicted aim of this programme as 'empowering the parties' and cause hurt to the parties.

5.2.3 Active Roles for Parties only in Private Reconciliation

It was found in the interview that in the criminal reconciliation programmes, the parties were not always 'used' by the officials to serve their own interests. They also negotiated and reached an agreement privately prior to the criminal reconciliation programme, as happened in case no. eight in location B (a traffic accident related crime case). The accounts

---

[56] Interview with the victim of this case in May 2008.

[57] Interview with prosecutor F at the People's Procuratorate of X district in Changzhou in May 2008.

from the parties in the interview provided further important details allowing a better understanding of the parties' attitudes.

In this case, W died in a traffic accident caused by the suspect X's negligent driving under extreme fatigue after overnight work.[58] X talked about his feelings and thoughts after the accident:[59]

> I really felt very sorry and regretful. I also expressed such feelings to the prosecutor. Nevertheless, in my view, the most important thing, rather than sadness or regret, was to find a way best for him and the victim's family to resolve the problems resulting from the accident as soon as possible.
>
> So I commenced to search information on the way of handling traffic accident related crime cases on the internet, and then found out a number of news reports about dealing with this kind of case through criminal reconciliation in many other cities in China. I found criminal reconciliation to be a win-win choice for me and the victim's family – I might not be prosecuted and they could get a considerable sum of compensation promptly. These were tangible benefits! Then I found a friend who also knew T (W's son) to help me communicate with T. These efforts were successful and T agreed to meet and discuss the way of resolving the problems together with me.

The victim's son T described the change in his thoughts before his acceptance of X's offer of private negotiation and reconciliation.[60]

> After the accident happened, I was sorrowful and angry. I felt that it was impossible for me to forgive the person who 'had killed' my mother. My family was full of that kind of emotion too at that time. When I knew X's intention from my friend, at the beginning I thought that I could not accept this suggestion as I just wanted to see X sent to trial and fired from his job.
>
> However, my father was so tolerant that he persuaded me and my brother and sister to forgive X and to give the young man another chance after he heard X's situation and regret from the prosecutor. Since I and my brother and sister firmly disagreed with our father's opinion, family conferences attended by my father and all the children were held many times to discuss whether we should accept X's reconciliation proposal.
>
> At first, all the three children refused to listen to our father's views. But in the meantime, I learned from the internet that in traffic accident related crime cases, the suspect often did not pay compensation according to the sentence delivered in the Court, and the suspect would not be sent to prison anyway since it was a minor crime. Then I began to consider my father's reasons and X's suggestion.

---

58 On the basis of the case file.
59 Interview with X in Chongqing in June 2008.
60 Interview with T in Chongqing in June 2008.

> Finally, I thought that my mother cannot come alive again; it is correct to rationally pay attention to the method how to best address this matter. Therefore, I agreed to meet with X and negotiate with him.

However, T's account showed that the main reason leading to his change of mind and acceptance of X's suggestion of reconciliation was his realization of the frustrating reality that it was almost impossible to get X sent to jail as he wished, and that it was very likely that his family would not get any compensation if X was convicted and sentenced in a criminal trial process. In other words, if T had been convinced that X would be punished harshly in accordance with T's wishes and that his (the victim's) family could also get compensation according to the Court's adjudication, he would not have chosen criminal reconciliation.

Concerning the private meeting between X and T, T described it as follows in the interview:[61]

> In our private meeting, we mainly talked about compensation and reached an initial agreement on that. We later suggested to prosecutor Y that we wanted to resolve the case through an alternative way other than litigation, which was smoothly adopted by Y.

This process showed that in this case, criminal reconciliation was factually driven more by X, the suspect, and T, the son of the victim, rather than by the prosecutor. The prosecutor was involved informally prior to the resolution meeting; but the parties had, de facto, come to an understanding, if not full agreement, beforehand based upon their assessment of what could be achieved in the reconciliation process as against the criminal process. In addition, it is interesting to see in this case that information on the general issue was available from the internet which might become an increasingly important source of 'legal advice.'

Subsequently, as shown in Chapter 4, the formal criminal reconciliation meeting was held by the responsible prosecutor Y simply to confirm the private agreement. Such a simple criminal reconciliation meeting, which revolved around confirming the parties' private agreement, could hardly serve the claimed purposes such as redressing the victim's damage and educating or correcting the suspect. It was further noticed in T's account that it seemed that the dispute between the parties was not well addressed either:[62]

---

[61] Ibid.
[62] Ibid.

> In fact, my brother and sister could not understand my choice of reconciliation even now. My brother and sister argued that I was putting a price tag on our mother's life. My father and I would continue persuading my brother and sister. And I believed that they would eventually understand that.

In this sense, actually a potential dispute remained since T's brother and sister still firmly objected to criminal reconciliation and its outcome. This made it hard to accept the official position that criminal reconciliation brought about 'closure.'

The suspect X's account in the interview confirmed that the claimed goal of educating and correcting the suspect was not reached in such a criminal reconciliation programme (see further below).

As to why the official accepted the parties' proposal of criminal reconciliation and the parties' private reconciliation, this was attributed to the fact that the parties' proposal met his expectation of using criminal reconciliation in this case. Maybe the official also knew that there might be some problems in the parties' private negotiation and such a criminal reconciliation was hardly likely to produce the predicted outcomes such as repairing the harm of the victim and educating and correcting the suspect/defendant. Instead of implying the parties' dominance, this might actually show that in fact, driven by the performance assessment system, what the officials cared about most was that they could close the case as they wished, the sooner, the better. The parties were actually marginalized in this process.

5.2.4 The Parties' Comments on Criminal Reconciliation

It was found in the interviews that most of the parties expressed satisfaction with criminal reconciliation. For example, in case no. five in location A (a theft case), the suspect commented on the criminal reconciliation programme he participated in as necessary and fair.[63]

> I am satisfied with this programme. It first provided an outlet for the victim L to express his emotions, and second, during this process, both of us could say what we wanted. After the case was resolved, my life went back to what it had been before.
>
> I felt stressed at the time I was discovered by the police, but this pressure disappeared when I found that my classmates, especially the victim L, and my teachers did not look down upon me and I reintegrated into the group easily after the case was resolved through criminal reconciliation. Moreover, since

[63] Interview with C, the suspect of case no. five, in location A in Changzhou in May 2008.

> there was no criminal record, my future would not be affected by this case. I also felt good that I had learnt some useful legal knowledge from the prosecutor in the meeting; it could help me control myself better in future.

The victim in this case also briefly expressed his satisfaction with this criminal reconciliation programme in the interview.[64]

> I have got what I wanted in the criminal reconciliation meeting, which really met my expectation. So I was fully satisfied with this programme.

In case no. six in location A (a theft case), the suspect, X, also expressed his satisfaction with the criminal reconciliation programme.[65]

> The best point of criminal reconciliation was that my work and life were not adversely affected by my wrongdoing. And the criminal reconciliation meeting provided a place for me to say anything I wanted freely, and to express my remorse and extend an apology to the victim. Accordingly, I regard criminal reconciliation as a fair and just programme that meets all my expectations. As to the relationship between us (the parties) after criminal reconciliation, on my side, I am very willing to say hello to the victim Q if we meet some day, though we have not met again after the case was resolved.

Even in the case mentioned above in which the essential negotiation was conducted before the formal criminal reconciliation meeting, the suspect stated his satisfaction with the outcome of the formal criminal reconciliation programme.[66]

> I am very satisfied with this programme and the outcome. After the case was resolved, my work was not adversely affected, and my life went back to what it had been before.
>
> If the suspect's family had insisted on litigation, I would have tried my best to avoid paying the compensation awarded by the Court in the civil suit collateral to criminal proceedings, since litigation would make me lose a job and have a criminal record which would badly influence my future. In this sense, I would have hated the victim's family and would not have wanted to pay anything to them.

---

[64] Interview with L, the victim of case no. five, in location A in Changzhou in May 2008.

[65] Interview with X, the suspect of case no. six, in location A in Changzhou in June 2008.

[66] Interview with X2, the suspect of case no. eight, in location B in Chongqing in June 2008.

Indicating satisfaction with the criminal reconciliation programme notwithstanding, X2's account led to reasonable doubts about the sincerity of his regret and apology in this programme. It seemed that those were merely built on the positive outcome criminal reconciliation could bring to him; had the outcome not met his expectations, he would have abandoned his remorseful emotions and become resentful. This, however, was not noticed by the responsible prosecutor in the criminal reconciliation programme, which was in fact an official formality to confirm the parties' agreement reached in the private negotiation. Perhaps this was also due to the problem pointed out above that what the officials cared about most was having the parties sign a criminal reconciliation agreement to reach the requirement set in the performance assessment system.

In this case, the victim's son who participated in the criminal reconciliation also expressed satisfaction with this programme in the interview, facing his brother and sister's objection though.[67]

> Although I am still sombre too, I do not regret my choice. I am pleased to have given the young suspect another chance and to see that his career and life were not affected. Also, since my mother could not be brought back to life even if X were sent to court and fired, for my family, receiving a considerable sum of compensation promptly was rational and meaningful.

There are also 'direct' parties of the criminal reconciliation cases expressing their satisfaction in the interview. For example, in case no. seven in location B (an intentional injury case), the victim's mother expressed her positive evaluation of criminal reconciliation in the author's interview with her over the phone:[68]

> I felt relieved to participate in the criminal reconciliation meeting and viewed it as a win-win practice. On the one hand, we felt much better through having been able to speak of our distress and other feelings in the meeting, and getting a sincere apology from the suspects. On the other hand, we were happy to see the changes in the suspects and to give them this chance after they had done something wrong.

The suspects' parents in this case also positively commented on the effect brought about by the criminal reconciliation programme in the telephone interview as 'the children became more mature than before; they studied

---

[67] Interview with T in Chongqing in June 2008.

[68] Telephone interview with the suspect L's father in Chongqing in June 2008.

much harder and their teachers in the school often praised them now.'[69] Nevertheless, the author only got the juvenile parties' parents as the 'indirect' parties to grant interviews, because the author was informed by the parents that all the children were extremely busy with preparing for their final examinations at that time. Although all the parents used 'we' not 'I' in the interview, which meant that they spoke also for the 'direct' parties, namely their children, the possibility that the juvenile parties in fact would not have provided such positive comments on the criminal reconciliation programme cannot be precluded.

Concerning why these parties expressed satisfaction with criminal reconciliation programmes, it might be because they had participated in this programme voluntarily, and the outcome of the programme had met their expectations. Referring to the earlier analysis, the victims who had participated mainly under pressure from officials of the justice system or their teachers or leaderships expressed displeasure and irritation with this programme. Those distinct emotions, to a certain extent, demonstrated that voluntary participation was crucial to whether or not criminal reconciliation could satisfy the parties. But it was also possible that the parties just did not want to show their negative comments on this programme for fear of any potential negative consequences this interview might have for them, especially since the interviews with the parties were contacted and observed by the officials in Changzhou and Chongqing.

5.2.5 The Parties' Difficulties in Criminal Reconciliation Programmes

Although being satisfied with the criminal reconciliation programmes, the parties also met difficulties in this programme. One difficulty mentioned by the victims interviewed was that not much attention was paid to them, except for the monetary issue which had little influence sometimes (i.e. the victim did not care or need money very much; or the psychological harm was more important than the monetary loss in the victim's mind). An example was the account delivered by the victim M in case no. five in location C (a robbery case):[70]

> In the criminal reconciliation meeting, I could really feel the defendants' parents' upset and remorse from their sincere apologies. Some of the parents

[69] Telephone interview with the victim P's mother in Chongqing in June 2008.

[70] Interview with M, a victim of a juvenile robbery case, in Xi'an in September 2010.

> even cried, and they were positive towards compensation. So I changed my mind to be willing to give the juveniles one more chance and signed the agreement.
>
> However, actually I do not think such a programme helped me a lot and it did not alleviate my hurt feelings. My psychological harm cannot be relieved through money. Now I still feel bad. I became a very timid person after that. I am very scared of going somewhere alone. I always feel very insecure now but I do not know how to deal with it.

Although criminal reconciliation effectively resolved the problem of compensation enforcement, from these remarks, the function of compensation for the victim in criminal reconciliation might be overstated. As mentioned by the lawyers interviewed, in fact some victims in good economic circumstances would not accept criminal reconciliation. This point was substantiated by the account of the victim's father in case no. six in location C (a juvenile intentional injury case). In this case, the first criminal reconciliation meeting failed and the victim's father firmly insisted on refusing the responsible judge's proposal of another criminal reconciliation meeting. The family asked for a trial as soon as possible even though the responsible judge had communicated with him no fewer than three times.[71] The victim's father, Z, explained his insistence in the interview:[72]

> My son Z's wound was so serious that there was now symptoms in his brain. Yet after the attack, when Z was in hospital, none of the defendants (or their families) appeared to visit him, or to apologize to him. We felt infuriated about the defendants' indifference, so honestly we did not want to see the defendants anymore.
>
> However, later we still agreed to meet them as arranged by the judge L in the so-called criminal reconciliation meeting. We did so purely to show the judge some respect. But the meeting made me even angrier, as we could not see even a gleam of sincere apology or remorse or concern for Z from them.
>
> All of their talk concentrated on our forgivenesses being essential for their children. And the parents attending the meeting even found various excuses for their children, rather than apologizing to us sincerely. It was really ridiculous, and made us feel angrier.
>
> So what we hope now is that the case could be decided in court as soon as possible. Now we do not care about money. We have spent all the money

71 Interview with judge L in Xi'an in September 2010.
72 Interview with the victim Z's father in Xi'an in September 2010.

> needed for Z's cure and we can afford that. We just want to see them sentenced according to law even if we cannot get any compensation from them.

It could be seen from Z's father's account that, different from the opinion widely expressed by the officials that compensation was of paramount importance for the victims, not all victims actually view it as that important. But the frustrating fact that they could hardly get compensation could to a large extent force victims needing it to enter criminal reconciliation by sacrificing their other needs or voluntariness. In such a context, however, to what extent the criminal reconciliation programme could redress the victims and satisfy them was questionable.

Concerning the defendant's difficulty in criminal reconciliation, it mainly related to the compensation they had to pay. As mentioned in the preceding chapters, the sum of compensation the suspects/defendants needed to pay in criminal reconciliation was normally higher than a court would award in the same kind of case. And it needed to be paid in a timely fashion. Otherwise, the suspects/defendants could not get the expected outcome like non-prosecution or a lenient sentence.

This was attested to by the fact that all the suspects/defendants, even though they had paid the compensation in the agreements, talked about the difficulties in life caused by such payment, and rated compensation as the top difficulty in criminal reconciliation. For example, L, the suspect of case no. two in location C (a traffic accident related crime case), mentioned it as follows:[73]

> Although I have got the suspended sentence I appreciate most through criminal reconciliation, my life is still impacted by this matter. As a migrant working here, the compensation of thirty thousand yuan is indeed a large sum of money for me. But I know that I do not have any choice. On the one hand, I really did something wrong so that I owe them (the victim); on the other hand, it was the only opportunity for me to get a lighter sentence.
>
> So I think that overall, criminal reconciliation is a fair process and I am satisfied with it since I have got the suspended sentence. But my difficulty is that I have borrowed too much money to pay the compensation, so now I have to work very hard to pay back the debt. Actually I am worried about that and under tremendous pressure.

It seems from L's account that he rather justified the difficulty caused by the compensation in terms of receiving the suspended sentence and he viewed criminal reconciliation as the only way for him to get that

[73] Interview with L in Xi'an in September 2011.

outcome. Such a thought was very common among the suspects/defendants interviewed. In a juvenile intentional injury case in location A, all the juveniles' parents also said that, because of the amount of compensation, although they were heavily in debt after the case was resolved, it was still worth resolving the case through criminal reconciliation. It meant that their children had no need to go through the criminal trial process and could resume school quickly. And they were willing to earn money and work harder to pay off the debt.[74]

Nevertheless, it seemed that the suspects'/defendants' difficulty was because compensation was the absolute focus of criminal reconciliation, and the officials even connected it directly with the suspects'/defendants' remorseful attitudes, the victim's satisfaction and the decisions they would make. However, was it totally the suspects'/defendants' burden to address the problem of enforcement? Alternatively, was it mainly or only the suspect/defendant that was to blame for this problem? Besides, could or to what extent did this mechanism really address the problem of enforcement? These are elaborated in the following chapter.

As noted in Chapter 4, more than that, the idea that identifying the suspects'/defendants' remorseful attitudes and the victim's satisfaction with compensation was absurd. While the suspects/defendants could still pay a large sum of compensation mainly for a lighter sentence, the victim still felt hurt after being paid.

5.3 THE LAWYERS AS ACTORS (PARTICIPANTS) IN CRIMINAL RECONCILIATION CASES

5.3.1 Lawyers' Role as Mediators between Officials and the Parties

As demonstrated in Chapter 4, it was noticed in the interview that in two cases the officials only approached the lawyers during the process of getting the parties' agreement to participate, and then the lawyers successfully persuaded the suspect to accept the offer of criminal reconciliation. Judge L from the People's Court of B district in Xi'an described how the lawyer acted as a 'bridge' or 'go-between' between her and the defendants (and their parents) during this process in case no. five in location C (an intentional injury case).[75]

---

[74] The above description is based on the telephone interview with the suspect L's father, Y's father and M's mother in June 2008 in Chongqing.

[75] Interview with judge L in Xi'an in September 2010.

> I first communicated with the defence lawyers assigned by the Court about the possibility of criminal reconciliation.[76] In my communication with the lawyers, I chiefly mentioned as the advantageous outcome of criminal reconciliation a lighter sentence or a suspended sentence, which was conditional upon the victim's acceptance of their clients' apologies and compensation payment. Since all the defendants were in the detention house at that point, I did not approach them. Then the lawyers conveyed my intention to the defendants in detention and their parents.
>
> In the notes recording the meetings between the lawyers and the defendants which were also enclosed in the case file, all the defendants explicitly talked about their repentance and regret, and expressed their willingness to go through a criminal reconciliation process. The lawyers also told me that all the defendants' parents agreed to fully compensate the victim and participate in the criminal reconciliation programme. Then the parents were required by me to write a statement about their voluntary participation in criminal reconciliation.

In the criminal reconciliation meetings that followed, the lawyers also conveyed the defendants' remorse on behalf of the defendants and helped the defendants' parents with bargaining over compensation. In an interview, Judge L2 from the People's Court of Y district in Xi'an also mentioned that 'usually the lawyers would actively facilitate criminal reconciliation.'[77]

The stated reason the officials sometimes approached the lawyers, instead of the parties they represented, to talk about the offer of criminal reconciliation, was that this would make the process easier. Prosecutor S from the People's Procuratorate of B district in Xi'an explained this as follows:[78]

> Often, the relationship between the two parties is tense immediately after the case has happened. The victim (or his/her family), especially, is angry with the suspect. Thus, it is hard for us to get them to accept criminal reconciliation and make some compromise. Besides, the suspect is generally detained at that time and it is not very convenient for us to meet him/her.

---

76 Article 36 of the Judicial Interpretation on CPL issued by the Supreme People's Court [最高人民法院关于执行《中华人民共和国刑事诉讼法》若干问题的解释] provides that 'the People's Courts should assign defenders for the defendants under 18 years old and do not have defenders when trials proceed.' It is to protect the interests of the juvenile defendants and to make up their deficient abilities in litigation. In this case, since the juvenile defendants could not afford and did not appoint defence lawyers, the Court assigned the lawyers for them.

77 Interview with judge L2 in Xi'an in September 2010.

78 Interview with prosecutor S in Xi'an in September 2010.

> In this kind of case, we would normally seek out their lawyers. It is much easier to communicate with the lawyers, as legal professionals, and they would know that criminal reconciliation is beneficial for their clients. Then they would persuade their clients, and it is also easier for the parties to accept their lawyers' advice.

It seemed that the officials had made working with their lawyers a 'strategy' to get the parties' participation in criminal reconciliation. Lawyer L interviewed in Xi'an also described this role played by lawyers in criminal reconciliation:[79]

> At first, the judge/prosecutor/police would tell us about the possibility of criminal reconciliation and the benefits of it. At this stage, the individual parties will not meet each other. I feel that the conflict between them still exists. So in fact they do not want to see each other.
>
> Normally, we will give our clients suggestions on accepting criminal reconciliation as it is really beneficial for them. The suspect/defendant could get some lenient punishment and the victim could get compensation promptly. After all, getting those 'concrete' benefits like money or a lighter sentence is much more significant for them, I believe.
>
> Yet we will definitely respect their opinions. If they do not want to accept it after we have tried to persuade them, we will not insist on that.
>
> In the criminal reconciliation meeting, the agents of both parties will discuss the compensation agreement.

Lawyer L's account sounded as though the lawyer viewed criminal reconciliation as beneficial for both parties so that he assisted the officials to facilitate this programme. But he also talked about the problems with this programme, which made the benefits regarding compensation of questionable value.

Importantly, lawyer L's account implies that rather than challenging public power, the lawyers acted as 'go-betweens' to get their clients to accept the offer of 'reconciliation,' and this further facilitated the officials' 'persuasion.'[80] Although it was understandable considering the dilemma the lawyers might face – the potential adverse results their clients might get if they 'offended' the officials and the fact that their clients found it hard to get compensation through the normal procedure,

---

[79] Interview with lawyer L in Xi'an in August 2010.

[80] Joshua Rosenzweig, Flora Sapio, Jiang Jue, Teng Biao and Eva Pils 'The 2012 Revision of the Chinese Criminal Procedure Law: (Mostly) Old Wine in New Bottles' at http://www.law.cuhk.edu.hk/research/crj/papers.php (last accessed on 7 January 2013).

this process was an erosion of the adversarial and rights-centred conceptions of justice underlying earlier reform efforts.[81]

5.3.2 Some Lawyers' Comments on Criminal Reconciliation

Lawyer L expressed the view that the problems of criminal reconciliation arose mainly from its focus on compensation.[82]

> I have been the agent in about five criminal reconciliation cases; they were all traffic accident related crime cases. As to the process of criminal reconciliation, it is mainly bargaining over compensation. Often the officials would simply connect the degree of the suspect's/defendant's regret with the amount of compensation he/she would be willing to pay in criminal reconciliation.
>
> I find that the parties might fight with each other when they meet at the beginning of the criminal reconciliation meeting. But the situation changes after the criminal reconciliation agreement on compensation is reached. In particular, the victim changes his/her attitude of anger when he/she gets the money.
>
> However, I think that criminal reconciliation is an unfair system. It readily conveys the impression that criminal law or penalty is just for poor people who cannot afford paying compensation. I do not know how to resolve this problem as a lawyer. Maybe poor people will just have to accept this unfairness resulting from wealth disparity? It is really disappointing.

Therefore, in the opinion of lawyer L, although compensation in criminal reconciliation was advantageous for both parties, it led to unfairness. Yet of course, concerning the specific clients in one case, he would try to make criminal reconciliation successful since it was good for his clients.

Another lawyer interviewed, Z, also commented on the importance and the problem of compensation in criminal reconciliation.[83]

> I noticed that the victim's (or his/her family's) economic circumstances mattered crucially for whether or not the parties could reach a criminal reconciliation agreement. Often, victims from families in good economic circumstances would refuse to enter into a criminal reconciliation process.

Lawyer Z further talked about the problem of unfairness and coercion in criminal reconciliation from the perspective of the judge's power.[84]

---

81 Ibid.
82 Interview with lawyer L in Xi'an in August 2010.
83 Interview with lawyer Z in Xi'an in August 2010.
84 Ibid.

> The most serious problem with criminal reconciliation, in my opinion, is that the judge's discretionary power is unreasonably great. It is thereby easy for them to do some under-the-table things.
>
> According to my own experience, in some cases, the defendants cannot get the expected lighter sentence after the enforcement of the compensation agreement. When that happens, it is really unfair. And the defendant would in such a case think that the judge must have gained something from the other party. However, reducing the sentence after the defendant has paid compensation is just a way of taking into account an extenuating circumstance in sentencing (*zhuoding liangxing qingjie*) as provided in the Criminal Procedure Law, rather than a statutory one (*fading liangxing qingjie*). It is totally up to the judge's discretionary power. So it is hard for the defendant to challenge such an outcome.
>
> In this regard, in criminal reconciliation programmes, defendants in the same kind of crime may get different sentences because of the judge's discretionary power. Such differential treatment will give the impression that law is unfair.
>
> Moreover, since in the current system mediation and reconciliation are directly connected with the judges' own interests coming from their internal performance assessment system, it is possible that they would use their discretionary power to put pressure on the parties during the process of criminal reconciliation to make it successful. And it is easy for them to make it successful as it is hard for the parties to offend the judge who will judge their cases afterwards.
>
> As for ways to resolve this problem, we as lawyers have to 'communicate' well with the judges to help our clients obtain a reasonable and expected outcome.

Lawyer Z's account substantiated the discussion of the officials' dominant role in the process. It seemed that the officials' dominance in criminal reconciliation largely came from their very great discretionary power in this programme. As a result, the parties (and their agents) faced much uncertainty concerning the outcome of the case in criminal reconciliation, while the lawyers could only resort to ways outside the legal system, like building a good personal relationship with the officials, to resolve this uncertainty in the outcome of the case. Thus, the officials and the parties (and their agents) would have much personal contact in criminal reconciliation which was likely to produce some under-the-table trade. This was exactly what prosecutor L from the People's Procuratorate worried about, as shown in the first section.

5.4 THE ROLE OF OTHER PARTICIPANTS IN CRIMINAL RECONCILIATION PROGRAMMES

5.4.1 Serving Officials' Purposes

The term 'other participants' refers to those people who participated in the criminal reconciliation programmes apart from the parties and the responsible officials. They included the victims' or the suspects'/defendants' parents, teachers, employers, leadership (*lingdao*), peers such as their schoolmates, and some officials observing the criminal reconciliation meeting (i.e. the police officer responsible for the case and the officials from the local Justice Bureau).[85]

As we have seen, except for observing the criminal reconciliation meeting, these people, especially the parties' parents, teachers, employers, leadership, assisted the responsible prosecutors/judges in the criminal reconciliation programmes. Specifically, they helped the officials in getting the parties' agreements to participate in criminal reconciliation, making the parties reach criminal reconciliation agreements, and supplying updated information regarding the suspects'/defendants' performance in the follow-up programmes to the responsible officials.

Nonetheless, as noted in Chapter 4, such assistance might have constituted coercion impairing the parties' voluntariness in criminal reconciliation. For instance, they helped the officials to persuade repeatedly the parties to give their 'voluntary participation' in circumstances where it was hard for the parties to offend these people. And the extensive observation of the criminal reconciliation meeting in itself was likely to make the parties feel uncomfortable or unhappy.

In addition, it was found in the interviews with the juvenile parties' parents that they largely took it for granted that they could represent their children in the criminal reconciliation process. They appeared to believe that they could express the emotions and stands expected to be shown

---

[85] Article 41 of the 2010 Opinions of the Supreme People's Court on Implementing the Criminal Policy of Combining Severity with Leniency [最高人民法院关于贯彻宽严相济刑事政策的若干意见] mentions the role of these participants in mediation: 'We shall make full use of the roles of the defendant's and the victim's work units, basic level community organizations, defence lawyers, legal representatives and relatives in the process of mediation of collateral civil disputes and coordinate these [persons' or entities'] efforts in the process of mediation, to try to eliminate the dispute and promote harmony through getting the parties to reach an agreement on civil compensation and allowing the defendant to obtain the victim's and his family's forgiveness.'

from the parties in criminal reconciliation like voluntary participation, remorse about the alleged crime and satisfaction with the criminal reconciliation programmes.

All these activities of the other participants further lowered the status of the directly involved parties and lessened the parties' intentions in criminal reconciliation programmes. In this sense, those other participants also assisted the officials in terms of marginalizing the parties in this programme.

5.4.2 Other Participants' Comments on Criminal Reconciliation

All the other participants interviewed expressed their zealous enthusiasm for criminal reconciliation and high opinions of this programme. For instance, in case no. five in location A (a theft case), the juvenile parties' teacher, W, who had helped the responsible prosecutor arrange the criminal reconciliation meeting with extensive observation by the parties' teachers and schoolmates, talked about his welcome to this programme.[86]

> When the responsible prosecutor F contacted me about resolving the case through criminal reconciliation, I expressed my strong support immediately and promised to help F to persuade the suspect and victim to accept this offer, because I believed that it was beneficial for the suspect and the relationship between the two parties as classmates.

He further evaluated this programme highly:[87]

> First, it resolved the contradiction between the suspect and the victim caused by the case; second, it gave both parties a chance to learn more about law; third, as many student delegates from other classes also attended the meeting, it had a great educational meaning to more students.

At this point, the author asked whether or not such an extensive participation might embarrass the parties, especially the suspect. W did not share this opinion by saying that it surely would not since he had told the victim, C, before the meeting that attending a meeting observed by his schoolmates and teachers was the right way to face the mistake, and rumour or judgements concerning him could only be eliminated through such a public channel.[88] Thus, C himself agreed to that type of meeting.

---

[86] Interview with W in May 2008 in the People's Procuratorate of D district in Changzhou.

[87] Ibid.

[88] Ibid.

In case no. nine in location A (an intentional injury case), the parties' coach also talked about her activities and thoughts in the criminal reconciliation process in the interview.[89]

> My husband and I have lived with these children for many years as their coaches. We know these children very well that they are all good youngsters; this case happened just because youngsters are always impetuous.
>
> After the incident had happened, we were anxious about (the victim) C's injury and worried about the awful influence the case might bring to the three suspects too. We knew that a criminal trial and sentence would not only badly affect the suspects' current performance on the training programme, but also affect their future. So we felt glad when the responsible prosecutor F approached us to introduce criminal reconciliation. We thought that it was good since according to F's introduction, firstly there would be no criminal record for the suspects, and secondly the victim could get compensation quickly.
>
> Then we helped prosecutor F to suggest the use of this programme to the parties' parents and the young parties. The suspects' parents were willing to participate for they did not want their children to be prosecuted and have a criminal record. As for the victim's parents, getting compensation promptly through criminal reconciliation to cover the operation fee was the most attractive point, so they also agreed to participate.

In the first criminal reconciliation meeting, the two parties could not reach an agreement on compensation. This coach even helped them to reach an agreement via consulting a judge she was acquainted with about the sum of compensation after the failure of the first meeting.[90] She then conveyed the information given by that judge to the victim's parents, which led to the victim's parents' compromise in the second criminal reconciliation meeting and the parties' coming to an agreement.[91] At the end of the interview with her, she also praised criminal reconciliation as 'a good way to handle criminal cases since the result benefited both parties.'[92]

It seemed that these people thought it a really good chance for the parties (especially the suspect/defendant perhaps), so that the parties should take the opportunity. However, it might also be possible that these people assisted the officials because they did not want to offend the officials. They might be concerned that they would still have to deal with

89 Interview with the coach Y in May 2008 in Changzhou.
90 Ibid.
91 Ibid.
92 Ibid.

those officials in the future and it would be adverse to them if they offended the people with power.

5.5 SUMMARY

This chapter further addressed the role of the official, the lawyer, the parties and the other participants in criminal reconciliation, as well as their comments and feelings about this programme through their accounts in interviews, in an attempt to shed some light on the questions raised in Chapters 3 and 4.

It was found that, contrary to the claimed goal that criminal reconciliation would empower the parties to resolve their cases mainly by themselves, it was the officials who played the leading and dominant role during the process of criminal reconciliation. The parties, by contrast, could play only a somewhat passive role. The officials could arbitrarily disregard the procedural regulations or guidelines during the process of criminal reconciliation for the purpose of meeting the various requirements set in the internal performance assessment system. So in fact, it was not the procedural regulations or guidelines, but the performance assessment system, that guided the officials' conduct in this programme. The unrestricted power of the officials facilitated this outcome. The lawyers' assistance and the other participants' assistance in criminal reconciliation, possibly out of their consideration of the benefits of criminal reconciliation or their personal wish to keep good relations with the officials, further facilitated the officials' dominant and leading role in this programme. This weakened the parties' role in the criminal reconciliation processes with the result that the parties were usually passive and employed by the officials as a 'tool' to meet their own goals.

In this context, it was not surprising that the officials and the other participants mostly commented positively on criminal reconciliation as having achieved the claimed goals, and the official case files drew a positive and uncritical picture of this programme. Some of the parties also rated criminal reconciliation highly at interview. It might be because they indeed participated in this programme voluntarily, while it might be also because the interviews with them were conducted under official observation. However, two victims explicitly expressed negative comments and their distress out of somewhat coercive participation caused by the officials and their teachers or leaderships. This showed the significance of voluntary participation in criminal reconciliation on the one hand, and the coercion coming from the repeated persuasion of the officials and their teachers or leaderships on the other hand.

The interviewees' accounts also illustrated difficulties some of the officials met in criminal reconciliation. Some officials felt uncertain about the structure of the programme in the absence of clear regulation. Additionally, criminal reconciliation took too much of their time and energy, which conflicted with some other requirements set in the performance assessment system. The lawyers felt uncertain in criminal reconciliation processes since the official's power was too strong, possibly causing unfairness to the parties. For the parties, the main difficulty came from the absolute focus on compensation in this programme. For one thing, it brought heavy pressure on the suspect/defendant; for another, it actually could not do much to redress the victim.

To sum up the findings shown in Chapters 3 to 5, it emerged from the case file examination and interviews that criminal reconciliation practices in the three studied locations differed from the accounts in public sources. The parties did not have power in this programme to resolve the case mainly by themselves. This programme was still controlled and led by the officials to serve interests arising out of the performance assessment system. The parties' rights and voluntariness were easily harmed by the officials' unrestricted power during this process. In addition, in many cases, the predicted goals of criminal reconciliation such as redressing the victim's damage, educating the suspect/defendant, restoring the parties' relationship, bringing 'closure' were not achieved, which placed in question the end of 'promoting a harmonious society.' As the interviews showed, the focus of this programme was actually on compensation. But such a focus led to unfairness and the parties' discontent and difficulties, all of which further impeded the criminal reconciliation's achievement of those purported goals.

Although the fieldwork for the present study was small-scale, two arguments may further support the author's findings shown in Chapters 4 and 5.

First, concerning the limited access to research samples, since the author's access was restricted to those cases 'selected' by the officials as 'good examples' and the parties' accounts might have been affected by the officials' presence in the interview, the real picture can only be worse.

Second, increasing public reports from a variety of locations in China have also demonstrated problems with criminal reconciliation of the kind the author found in the empirical study. For example, a news report published in April 2012 disclosed that the suspect of an alleged crime of illegal confinement, Niu Hao, who was the deputy director of the housing bureau of Zhaolin district of Luohe city in Henan province, had signed a compensation agreement with the victims through 'reconciliation' to resolve this case.[93] According to their 'agreement,' as an 'exchange' for the payment of the compensation, the victims needed to express their forgiveness, ask the Public Security Bureau not to investigate the suspect's liability and cooperate with the Public Security Bureau in order to make sure of this outcome, and the 'reconciliation' should mean a 'closure' to the matter.[94] At first, the victims had fully complied with the 'agreement.' What finally irritated the victims and made them reveal this matter was the suspect Niu Hao's further 'requirement' to ask them to change their testimony at the Public Security Bureau before he paid the last instalment of the agreed compensation.[95] According to the victims, Niu asked them to say that they had not been beaten by Niu; their wounds were caused by their own fall.[96]

This case implies that criminal reconciliation mainly revolves around compensation, and how easy it is for the rich and powerful to use this process to impose coercion (on the other party) and avoid punishment. What the officials did (or failed to do) in this process further infringed the weaker party's rights and harmed justice. This might indicate that, as argued in this chapter, under pressure or from personal interests to meet the internal performance assessment criteria, what the officials care about most in criminal reconciliation is compensation.

---

93 Lai Yang [来扬] 'The Expert Talked about the Incident Where the Deputy Director Beat the Journalist and Said "Private Resolution" with the Exemption from Criminal Liability Is Invalid [专家谈副局长持枪打记者事件称免刑责的私了无效]' at http://www.chinanews.com/fz/2012/04-09/3803624.shtml (last accessed on 24 April 2012).

94 Ibid.

95 Ibid.

96 Ibid.

6. Understanding wider problems with the Chinese criminal justice system through the lens of criminal reconciliation

The preceding three chapters have provided an account of criminal reconciliation practices in Changzhou, Chongqing and Xi'an on the basis of case files and interviews with people who experienced this process.

The discussion thus far indicates that criminal reconciliation in the places studied is led and dominated by officials. The officials implement this programme in ways routinely contravening procedural rules and guidelines. As a result, the parties' access to justice, the suspects'/defendant's right to be presumed innocent until proven guilty and the principle of voluntary participation by all parties to a criminal reconciliation process may be compromised. As argued in Chapters 3 to 5, these problems are caused, on the one hand, by the problematic design of the rules guiding criminal reconciliation (henceforth, these rules will include the relevant Articles of the Criminal Procedure Law) and the conflict among the predicted goals of criminal reconciliation. On the other hand, they also result from the officials' motivation to initiate these programmes arising from the internal 'performance assessment (*jixiao kaohe*) system.'

If we regard criminal reconciliation as part of a wider system, the specific problems observed and analysed in previous chapters turn out to reflect problems with the wider Chinese criminal justice system. Three problems are taken to be fundamental in the context of the present study. First, legal rules are ignored, in part counteracted by internal regulations and in part supplanted by 'hidden rules' (*qian guize*) in practice. As noted in Chapters 4 and 5, prosecutors and judges flaunting legal rules could be understood to do this, because they possess unrestricted power. Nevertheless, as argued in this chapter, 'hidden rules,' rather than showing the officials' great power, reveal their weakness in the face of various external and internal pressures. The pressure comes from, for instance, the Political-Legal Committees (*zhengfa wei*), the Public Security

Bureaus, People's Congresses, local governments and the internal performance assessment systems. Second, the criminal process reflects an authoritarian approach to education aimed at thought reform. Third, by evading the real problems leading to difficulty in enforcement (*zhixing nan*), the government fails to take sufficient responsibility for protecting the victims' rights to get compensation in civil litigation collateral to criminal proceedings. A closer analysis of these problems of the general criminal justice system is provided below.

6.1 CONTRADICTORY RULES AND 'HIDDEN RULES' (*QIAN GUIZE*)

Chapter 4 shows that in the cases observed, procedural regulations and guidelines on criminal reconciliation were disregarded in various ways by the officials thereby compromising the parties' rights and interests. For example, judges and prosecutors used unfair criteria such as household registration (*hukou*) and ability to compensate to exclude some suspects/defendants from participating in criminal reconciliation. The procedural regulations and guidelines compulsorily required the suspects'/defendant's admission of guilt before initiating this process. Yet in some cases, the officials simply initiated this process when the suspect/defendant had not admitted guilt and tried to 'make them realize their guilt and fault through criminal reconciliation.'[1] In some cases, officials used undue pressure to get other parties to engage in this process when they were actually reluctant to participate thus compromising the principle of voluntary participation. Also, the regulations or guidelines asked for both parties' (direct parties) attendance in criminal reconciliation meetings. However, in some cases, the suspect/defendant was absent from the meetings because they were under detention. In many criminal reconciliation meetings, there was no communication about the case between the parties as there should have been under the regulations or guidelines; the parties' communication involved little more than bargaining over the amount of compensation.

In fact, the disregard for written rules is not unique to criminal reconciliation; it is a general problem with the Chinese criminal justice system. As argued by Chen Ruihua, in Chinese criminal justice practice, 'hidden rules' (*qian guize*) have in reality largely replaced written rules.

1 Interview with prosecutor H in Chongqing in June 2008.

6.1.1 The Prevalence of 'Hidden Rules' and 'Parallel Systems'

According to Chen, 'in amending the PRC Criminal Procedure Law, we should not focus on further improvements of the written rules concerning issues such as individual rights protection and reallocation of the power among the Public Security Bureau, the People's Procuratorate and People's Court.'[2] In his view, 'the fundamental problem with the PRC Criminal Procedure Law' is not the imperfection of the written rules, but the disregard for these written rules in practice, which leads to the 'malfunction of the Criminal Procedure Law.'[3]

Chen argues that officials in the criminal justice process, although expected to abide by or even enforce rules contained in statutory law, in particular the Criminal Procedure Law, use 'hidden rules' (*qian guize*), which are designed by themselves, to replace the written rules.[4] For example, according to Chen, the 1996 Criminal Procedure Law has provided the lawyer with rights to meet their clients at the investigation stage,[5] but this right is usually restricted or simply denied by investigators in practice.[6] A lawyer revealed that normally the investigators would simply put off the lawyers' application to meet their clients. For this purpose, they might avoid encounters with the lawyers under various pretexts.[7] A survey conducted by the Beijing Lawyers Association in 2005 indicated that at the investigation stage, about 38 percent of lawyers' applications to meet with their clients were rejected, and no reason was provided in 45.3 percent of the rejection cases.[8]

Long Zongzhi, another scholar, describes three main 'hidden rules' in the Chinese criminal justice practice: the first relates to the collection of evidence. According to Long, the 1996 Criminal Procedure Law makes

---

[2] Chen Ruihua [陈瑞华] 'An Initial Research on the Malfunction of Criminal Procedure [刑事程序失灵问题的初步研究]' (2007) 6 *China Legal Science* [*中国法学*] 141–2.

[3] Ibid, 141.

[4] Ibid, 141–2.

[5] Article 96 of the 1996 Criminal Procedure Law.

[6] Supra note 2, 143.

[7] Chen Shihe [陈世和] *The Embarrassment of Law* [*法律的尴尬*] Beijing, Law Press [法律出版社] 2011, 325–6.

[8] Mike McConville *et al*, *Criminal Justice in China: An Empirical Inquiry* Cheltenham, UK and Northampton, MA, USA, Edward Elgar Publishing 2011, 172.

certain forms of gathering of evidence illegal.[9] Article 43 of the 1996 CPL says that 'judges, procurators and investigators must, in accordance with the legally prescribed process, collect various kinds of evidence ... [I]t shall be strictly forbidden to extort confessions by torture and to collect evidence by threat, enticement, deceit or other unlawful means.'[10] However, Long argues that, in practice, it has been normal to use 'irregular' (*bu guifan*) or illegal ways to collect evidence.[11] The second 'hidden rule' is that when the defendant claims that his/her confession was induced by torture, the judge is inclined to simply deem the claim as a fabrication and accordingly ignores it.[12] Third, Article 162 of the 1996 CPL stipulates that 'if the evidence is insufficient and thus the defendant cannot be found guilty, he/she shall be pronounced innocent accordingly.'[13] Yet in practice, according to Long, the court is rarely prepared to acquit the defendant despite the lack of evidence; normally, in such cases, the defendant is instead given a 'lenient' sentence (*sic*) or a suspended sentence.[14] Some research has shown that the acquittal rate in China 'remains less than one percent.'[15]

6.1.2 Internal and External Pressures as the Reason for 'Hidden Rules' and 'Parallel Systems'

Chen Ruihua provides five causes for the malfunction of written rules and the prevalence of 'hidden rules' in the Chinese criminal justice practice. In general, these five reasons, according to the author, can be categorized into two sorts – first, deficiencies of the institutional design, which is somewhat in conflict with his argument that 'the fundamental problem with the PRC Criminal Procedure Law is not the imperfection of the written rules.' The author believes that it obscures a fundamental

---

9 Long Zongzhi [龙宗智] '"Hidden Rules" in Legal Practices [法律实践中的"潜规则"]' at http://www.yadian.cc/paper/21974/ (last accessed on 7 April 2012).

10 See the English translation of this Article at http://www.cecc.gov/pages/newLaws/criminalProcedureENG.php (last accessed on 7 April 2012).

11 Supra note 9.

12 Ibid. This has been evidenced by empirical observation of trials: Mike McConville *et al*, supra note 8.

13 See the English translation of Article 162 at http://www.cecc.gov/pages/newLaws/criminalProcedureENG.php (last accessed on 7 April 2012).

14 Supra note 9.

15 Sida Liu, Terence Halliday 'Recursivity in Legal Change: Lawyers and Reforms of China's Criminal Procedure Law' (2009) Vol. 34 No. 4 *Law and Social Inquiry* 935.

reason causing the officials' disregard for written rules. Second, the officials' enormous power lacks effective supervision (*jiandu*). Consequently, according to Chen, the officials can always calculate the costs and benefits of implementing legal rules and can always substitute those written rules leading to low efficiency, possibly harming their interests, or counteracting goals and targets set for them by higher authorities with 'hidden rules.' In this respect, Chen argues that the lack of an effective implementation system (*youxiao de zhixing jizhi*) is one reason for the ineffectiveness of restrictions on officials' power. Yet to the author, lack of checks on official power is not the fundamental reason for the officials' disregard for written rules. This is because, in essence, these 'hidden rules' result from prosecutors' and judges' weakness in the face of strong external and internal pressures. The internal pressure, as also noted by Chen Ruihua, comes from the various internal assessment criteria; the external pressure takes the form of interventions from the Party and other State authorities. The external and internal pressures mean that in the Chinese legal system, prosecutors and judges can hardly execute their power independently, which is the basis for the argument that their adoption of 'hidden rules' is because of their unrestricted power. Therefore, the author argues that 'hidden rules' are a sign of the prosecutors' and judges' weakness rather than of their power. While 'supervision by the media and public opinion' (*yulun jiandu*), are now popularly regarded as the most effective ways of curbing the abuse of power, the current system in fact continues to rely heavily on 'supervision' by other Party-state authorities. (Public opinion, moreover, is itself under the supervision of the Party-state.) Such 'supervision' amounts to interference with the procuratorates and courts, and further harms the already flawed judicial independence.

Conflicting ideologies or power struggle?

According to Chen Ruihua's more detailed account of the argument outlined above, the primary reason for 'hidden rules' is that there are fundamentally conflicting ideologies in the Chinese criminal justice system.[16] For instance, according to Chen, the 1996 CPL has stressed the suspect's/defendant's right to legal counsel, which would include the right to plead not guilty.[17] Additionally, Article 43 says that 'it shall be strictly forbidden to extort confessions by torture and to collect evidence

---

[16] Ibid, 147–8.
[17] Ibid, 151.

by threat, enticement, deceit or other unlawful means.'[18] This, as argued by Chen, indicates the 1996 Criminal Procedure Law's intention to protect the voluntariness of the suspect's/defendant's statements under interrogation.[19] However, meanwhile, the 1996 CPL also stipulates the responsibility to answer the interrogators' questions truthfully (*rushi gongshu*) for the suspect/defendant.[20] The suspect's/defendant's attitude (i.e. whether or not to answer the interrogator's questions truthfully, whether or not to admit guilt) can also affect the sentence afterwards, according to a long-standing ideology as well as a criminal policy 'to be lenient with those who confess and severe with those who refuse to' (*tanbai congkuan, kangju congyan*).[21]

Such an internally conflicted design of the Criminal Procedure Law, according to Chen Ruihua, originates from the in-depth conflicts between different legal values, which are legal values transplanted from Western jurisdictions on the one hand, and based on native legal traditions on the other.[22] In this regard, Chen argues that the prevalence of 'hidden rules' also shows the unsuitableness of those values transplanted from Western jurisdictions.[23] The example just given illustrates this: on the one hand, the CPL has recognized the principle of 'no one should be forced to incriminate himself,' while on the other hand, 'finding out the (substantive) truth of a case' and viewing confession as 'the most critical evidence' are still strong in the 'Chinese legal culture.'[24]

This author acknowledges Chen's realization of the conflicting provisions in the statutory laws. Yet the conflict in legal rules, such as the one causing the regular use of torture in getting a confession, is not mainly due to different legal cultures or values. The difference in cultures between China and Western countries may have been cited too often as the explanation, or excuse, by some domestic scholars (and practitioners) to exclude the mechanisms protecting the parties' rights to criminal justice processes.

Actually, as observed by some scholars, the process of revising the CPL is like a power game among the various state authorities as well as

---

[18] The 1996 PRC Criminal Procedure Law at http://www.cecc.gov/pages/newLaws/criminalProcedureENG.php (last accessed on 7 April 2012).

[19] Supra note 2, 151.

[20] Supra note 2, 151–2.

[21] Supra note 2, 152.

[22] Ibid.

[23] Ibid.

[24] Ibid.

a game of power and rights.[25] Sida Liu and Terence Halliday reviewed the lawmaking processes of the 1979 and 1996 CPL and described them as 'power struggles' of the various state authorities with 'conflicting interests.'[26] According to Liu and Halliday, the 'contradictory concepts and ideologies incorporated in the final version' (of the 1996 CPL) are the result of compromises of the state authorities taking part in the lawmaking process.[27] Such a process also played out in the latest revision of the CPL in 2012.[28] On the second main revision of the CPL in 2012, Chen Guangzhong commented that 'the investigators, in particular the police, are under great burden to solve cases,' so 'they are inclined to have great power and little restriction during this process,' and this has also been shown in the new CPL, effective in 2013.[29] Taking into account the obvious power imbalance between the Public Security Bureau, the People's Procuratorate and the People's Court, the conflicting provisions in the CPL are in essence a sign of this power structure as well as the result of their power struggles, instead of conflicts among Western and Chinese legal values.

Pursuing own interests or pressure from the quota system?

Second, according to Chen Ruihua, in implementing legal rules, the officials normally engage in a cost–benefit calculation.[30] Hence, if a programme or a system would lead to marked increases of cost but only a little improvement of benefit, namely an overall decrease of efficiency, they will be inclined to circumvent such programmes or systems,[31] and adopt programmes or systems that have higher efficiency through the creation of hidden rules.[32] An example for this is the gradual shift away

---

[25] Zhao Jiayue [赵佳月] 'The Revision of the Criminal Procedure Law: A Game Between Power and Rights [刑诉法修改： 权力与权利的博弈]' at http://nf.nfdaily.cn/nfrwzk/content/2011-09/13/content_29780011.htm (last accessed on 6 May 2012).

[26] Supra note 15, 927.

[27] Ibid, 929.

[28] See: e.g. Ye Doudou [叶逗逗] Wang Heyan [王和岩] 'Major Revisions to the Criminal Procedure Law: The Advance and Retreat of Public Powers [刑诉法大修：公权力进退]' at http://china.caixin.com/2012-03-12/100367126.html (last accessed on 23 May 2012).

[29] Supra note 25.

[30] Supra note 2, 142.

[31] Supra note 2, 144–5.

[32] Ibid.

from collegiate judicial panels[33] to one-person adjudicators in charge of handling criminal cases, in reaction to judges' rising workloads.[34]

Furthermore, according to Chen Ruihua, if strictly observing the legal rules would damage the officials' interests or lead to disciplinary measures, criminal punishment or a bad evaluation under the internal performance assessment (*jixiao kaohe*) system explained in Chapter 1, it is much easier for the officials to just circumvent these rules.[35]

Carl Minzner has also argued that internal quotas can replace legal rules in judicial practice. According to Minzner, Chinese bureaucracy 'relies on internal responsibility systems' to manage the judicial system just like any other bureaucratic system.[36] Yet quotas and requirements set out under these internal systems, 'translating' *some* legal rules, are not always consistent with legal rules.[37] As a result, 'aims and goals expressed in national law that have not been reduced to hard targets, or are not capable of being so reduced, may fade in importance' and then be ignored by officials.[38]

The abovementioned practice that judges do not acquit when they ought to according to Article 162 of the 1996 CPL is an example in point. Because under the procuratorates' internal performance assessment system the prosecutor would be disciplined if there was an acquittal in a case where he/she had initiated prosecution, the prosecutor would try every means to avoid acquittal in the court.[39] For example, they might communicate with the adjudicating judge(s) to persuade, pressurize or bribe them. This might result in judges suggesting to prosecutors that the

---

33 Article 10 of the Organic Law of the People's Courts of the People's Republic of China.

34 Nowadays, criminal cases are growing so judges face a heavy burden in resolving cases. Making one single judge to resolve as many cases as possible and as fast as possible, rather than putting three judges or a jury in one case as required in the collegiate judicial system, is markedly costing less and raising efficiency. The avoidance of the collegiate judicial system can also make the internal assessments on (judges') performance and the imposition of liability on judges much easier and more efficient. Therefore, as argued by Chen, the collegiate judicial system is inclined to be avoided in judicial practice. See: supra note 2, 144–5.

35 Ibid, 147–9.

36 Carl Minzner 'Judicial Disciplinary Systems for Incorrectly Decided Cases: The Imperial Chinese Heritage Lives On' (2009) Vol. 39 *New Mexico Law Review* 84.

37 Ibid, 85.

38 Ibid.

39 Ibid, 85.

charges be withdrawn, or in judges giving a 'lenient' (*sic*) sentence.[40] This is, of course, a serious violation of the suspect/defendant's rights.

This problem also gives rise to the other two abovementioned 'hidden rules.' As noted in Chapter 1, resolving cases (*po'an*) is a crucial criterion used by the Public Security Bureaus in China to assess the performance of the police;[41] and as observed in Chapter 4, in China, the relationship between the Public Security Bureau, the People's Procuratorate and the People's Court is like a 'production line.'[42] In this production line, according to Chen Ruihua, the three state authorities are largely working together to meet the various quotas set in their performance assessment systems, so they are prone to abandon legal rules obstructing their achievement of these quotas and to adopt 'hidden rules' facilitating fulfilment of the quotas.[43] For instance, as discussed by Chen, the number of arrests approved by the procuratorates is normally a criterion the Public Security Bureau uses to assess the police. The number and rate of cases not prosecuted is a criterion to evaluate the performance of the police and the prosecutor to the extent that they are in charge of approving arrests. The conviction rate, in turn, is used to assess the performance of the police and the prosecutors.[44] This means that the various quotas set in the internal performance assessment systems, which are directly connected with the officials' interests, are not only a source of stress but they are also incentives for the officials to ignore some written rules and adopt 'hidden rules.'

Lack of supervision or lack of independence?

Why can officials follow 'hidden rules' at the cost of the written rules protecting the parties' rights? Chen Ruihua states that the officials' power is too strong and lacks effective 'supervision' (*jiandu*), and that the Chinese criminal procedure itself lacks adequate mechanisms for effective implementation, which 'innately leads to avoidance and disregard for such procedures.'[45]

---

[40] Supra note 2, 144–5.

[41] Ibid.

[42] Chen Ruihua [陈瑞华] 'The Main Problems with the Chinese Criminal Justice System [中国刑事司法制度的主要问题]' at http://article.chinalawinfo.com/Article_Detail.asp?ArticleID=19991&Type=mod (last accessed on 22 June 2011).

[43] Chen Ruihua [陈瑞华] 'Sentence with Flexibility [留有余地的判决]' at http://xinjin.xxlnm.fyfz.cn/art/910367.htm (last accessed on 27 April 2012).

[44] Ibid.

[45] Supra note 2, 142.

Lack of effective supervision might be the most widely cited problem in domestic China, offered as an explanation for power abuses infringing individual rights. In this specific discussion related to the empirical study of criminal reconciliation practices, the focus is the power the prosecutors and judges possess.

The People's Procuratorate in China was established in accordance with the model of the Soviet institution, which is characterized by its taking on two roles – public prosecutor and supervisor (of other state authorities).[46] The People's Procuratorate also possesses discretionary power over some cases – according to Article 142 of the 1996 CPL, 'with respect to a case that is minor and the offender need not be given criminal punishment or can be exempted from it according to the Criminal Law, the People's Procuratorate *may* decide not to initiate a prosecution.'[47]

The People's Courts, according to the PRC Constitution, are the judicial organs of the State and 'shall, in accordance with the law, exercise judicial power independently and are not subject to interference by administrative organs, public organizations or individuals.'[48] Yet scholars such as Chen Ruihua say that because of the undue emphasis on exploring the substantive truth (*shiti tanzhi*) in handling cases in Chinese criminal procedure, the judge has been granted great discretionary power which calls for effective supervision.[49]

Scholars who regard a lack of supervision as the main problem are inclined to focus on institutional checks upon the prosecutors' and the judges' power. For instance, according to Cai Guoshan, supervision of the People's Procuratorate comes 'mainly from inside the Procuratorate.'[50] It consists in supervision conducted by the procuratorial committee (*jiancha weiyuanhui*), the People's Procuratorate of the higher level, as well as the disciplinary inspection departments set up within the People's

---

[46] Stanley Lubman 'Studying Contemporary Chinese Law: Limits, Possibilities and Strategy' (1991) Vol. 39 *The American Journal of Comparative Law* 300.

[47] The English translation of the 1996 CPL at http://www.cecc.gov/pages/newLaws/criminalProcedureENG.php (last accessed on 27 April 2012).

[48] Articles 123 and 126 of the PRC Constitution at http://www.cecc.gov/pages/newLaws/constitutionENG.php. (last accessed on 27 April 2012).

[49] Chen Ruihua [陈瑞华] 'Three Traditions of the Chinese Criminal Justice System [中国刑事司法制度的三个传统]' at http://www.procedurallaw.cn/xsss/zdwz/200905/t20090518_220963.html (last accessed on 23 June 2012).

[50] Cai Guoshan [蔡国山] 'Who to Supervise the People's Procuratorate? On the Improvement of the People's Supervision System [谁来监督检察院？：兼论人民监督员制度之完善]' (2011) 4 *Law and Economy* [*法制与经济*] 169.

Procuratorate.[51] However, Cai argues that this kind of supervision means 'letting one supervise oneself,' which is in itself highly suspect.[52] For example, the decision not to prosecute is made by the chief prosecutor (*jiancha zhang*) or after discussion by the procuratorial committee (*jiancha weiyuanhui*).[53] The internal supervision is supposedly undertaken by the procuratorial committee as well, and therefore actually allows the supervisor to supervise and examine itself.[54]

Chen Ruihua's argument about the officials' disregard for written rules is concerned with the ineffectiveness of the supervision system as well. According to Chen, if we want a set of procedural rules to be implemented well, there ought to be a tribunal mechanism (*caipan jizhi*) to deal with any alleged violations of procedure, and an annulment mechanism (*xuanbu wuxiao jizhi*), attributing responsibility for violations of procedure.[55] Yet neither of these two mechanisms has been properly established in the Chinese Criminal Procedure Law.[56] In the judicial system, Chen says, the courts cannot review the police and the prosecutors' conduct, because on the one hand, they do not play a role at any stage before trial, and on the other hand, there is no tribunal mechanism to appraise the official's illegal conduct (violating the procedure even during trial).[57]

The violation of the lawyer's right to meet their clients and the suspect's/defendant's right to apply for a change of enforcement measures (*qiangzhi cuoshi*) are taken by Chen as instances resulting from this problem.[58] The statutory laws do not impose any adverse consequence or legal liability on officials infringing these rights and rules. Nor do they provide any opportunity for the lawyers or suspects/defendants to lodge appeals (to the courts) when they encounter such infringements; the investigators can easily restrict and even deprive the lawyers and the suspects/defendants of such rights in practice.[59]

With regard to supervision of the courts, the PRC Constitution provides that the People's Procuratorate shall supervise the People's

---

51 Ibid.

52 Ibid.

53 Articles 288 and 289 of the 1999 PRC Criminal Procedural Regulation of the People's Procuratorate [人民检察院刑事诉讼规则].

54 Supra note 50, 169.

55 Supra note 2, 142.

56 Ibid.

57 Ibid, 155.

58 Ibid, 143.

59 Ibid.

Court and the Public Security Bureau. As stipulated in the Criminal Procedure Law, the People's Procuratorate can lodge a protest (*kangsu*) if it discovers any mistake in the Court's verdict. It can also present comments concerning any illegal conduct on the part of the People's Court in hearing cases. Nevertheless, according to Chen Ruihua, in practice, the Procuratorate is very reluctant to conduct supervision of the People's Court due to its assumption of two conflicting roles, namely supervision and prosecution.[60] The role of supervision, according to Chen, asks for neutrality while the role of prosecution (and investigation in certain 'crimes') asks for the prosecutor's proactive involvement.[61] Under the current stress on 'cracking down against crime,' the Procuratorate is inclined to ignore its role as a supervisor and pays much more attention to prosecuting 'crime.'[62]

In addition, supervision of the People's Procuratorates and People's Courts can come from the People's Congress. Article 3 of the PRC Constitution provides that 'all administrative, judicial and procuratorial organs of the state are created by the People's Congresses to which they are responsible and under whose supervision they operate.'[63] Yet Cai Guoshan says that, according to the statutory laws, supervision from the People's Congress is only general and *ex post*.[64] For example, Article 10 of the Organic Law of the People's Procuratorates has stipulated that the People's Procuratorates only need to 'report their work to the People's Congresses and their Standing Committees.' So does the Court. In fact, even though this 'general and *ex post*' supervision may constrain prosecutors and judges, any constraints arising from People's Congress supervision are difficult to justify by reference to genuine democratic legitimacy of the People's Congresses or by the argument that the Congresses are better qualified than prosecutors and judges to make these decisions.

In sum, in the opinion of scholars such as Chen Ruihua and Cai Guoshan, prosecutors' and judges' regular usage of 'hidden rules' in practice which infringes upon the parties' rights results from their great power without effective supervision. However, if there are tribunal and annulment mechanisms in the institutional design, as argued by Chen,

60 Chen Ruihua [陈瑞华] 'Who to Supervise the Supervisor [谁来监督监督者]' at http://article.chinalawinfo.com/Article_Detail.asp?ArticleId=34869 (last accessed on 28 April 2012).

61 Ibid.

62 Ibid.

63 Article 3 of the 2004 PRC Constitution.

64 Supra note 50, 170.

can the People's Courts properly implement them to reduce the force of 'hidden rules' adopted by other state authorities violating the parties' rights?

According to the view taken here, further supervision mechanisms are unlikely to be effective, because the origin of the officials' adoption of 'hidden rules' does not lie in written laws nor the lack of the Court's role in written laws, nor the ineffectiveness of the supervision system. Rather, for prosecutors and especially for judges in China, the real problem is that neither can exercise their power independently. As shown in the following, they have to subject themselves to instructions from the Party and other State authorities, such as the Public Security Bureaus, the People's Congresses and local governments, as they are subject to the various internal quotas as shown above.

Party control takes the form of direct interventions from the Political-Legal Committee (*zhengfa wei*) in the general operation of the procuratorates, as well as in the handling of individual cases. The Political-Legal Committee, according to the definition of the Chinese Communist Party, is the department set up by the Party at the central and all local levels 'to lead and manage political-legal affairs.'[65] It has been given the responsibility, among other things, 'to unify the conduct and thinking of all the political-legal departments,' 'to supervise and coordinate each political-legal department,' 'to conduct research and coordination in important and complicated cases' and 'to organize and maintain social stability.'[66] The 'political-legal departments' include the Public Security Bureau, the People's Procuratorate, the People's Court, the State Security Bureau and the prison.[67] This definition by the Party shows that the Public Security Bureau, the People's Procuratorate and the People's Court are all supposed to operate under the leadership of the Political-Legal Committee. The enormous power of the Political-Legal Committee also stems from the fact that, according to Party custom, the head of the Political-Legal Committee is also a member of the Party Committee (*dangwei*)[68]

---

[65] Lan Wuyou [蓝无忧] 'The Twist and Destroy of Rule of Law by the Political-legal Committee [政法委对法治的扭曲破坏]' at http://www.chinainperspective.com/ArtShow.aspx?AID=15187 (last accessed on 26 April 2012).

[66] Ibid.

[67] Ibid.

[68] The Party Committee, or *dangwei*, is the short name of the Committee of the Communist Party of China or *dang de weiyuanhui*. It is set at central level, which is called the Central Committee of the Communist Party of China (*zhongguo gongchandang zhongyang weiyuanhui*), and all the basic levels

(central or local), while normally the presidents of the People's Procuratorate and the People's Court are not committee members.[69]

Moreover, since usually the director of the Public Security Bureau is also the head of the Political-Legal Committee in most locations in China, in essence, the procuratorates and the courts are led and directed by the Public Security Bureaus.[70] A widespread phrase captures the powerfulness of the Public Security Bureau and the weakness of the Procuratorate and Court: 'big Public Security Bureaus; little Courts; dispensable Procuratorates' (*da gong'an, xiao fayuan, keyoukewu jianchayuan*).[71] As noted by Jerome A. Cohen, this leads to the problem that, on the one hand, the Procuratorate is 'without incentive to self-monitor,' while on the other hand, it is 'even less likely to intervene in investigations by the Public Security Bureau, whose investigators generally outrank the Procuratorate counterparts in the Party's political pecking order.'[72]

Recently, there has been discussion about a possible decline of the powers and statuses of the Political-Legal Committee and the Public Security Bureau in the Chinese political-legal system (*zhengfa xitong*). As observed in some places, the police chiefs no longer necessarily become the heads of the Political-Legal Committees, and the heads of the Political-Legal Committees are not members of Party committees.[73] Yet

---

including provisions, cities, municipalities and autonomous regions (*zhongguo gongchandang jiceng weiyuanhui*)). About the responsibilities and work of the Party Committee, see the Constitution of Communist Party of China at http://news.xinhuanet.com/english/2007-10/25/content_6944738.htm (last accessed on 20 July 2012).

[69] Zhang Hui [张辉] 'The Obstacles of Judicial Independence in China: On the System of Political-legal Committee's Harmfulness to Judicial Independence and Violations of Human Rights [中国司法独立的障碍: 兼论政法委体制对司法独立的侵害及其对人权的侵犯]' at http://boxun.com/news/gb/china/2011/01/201101240023.shtml (last accessed on 26 April 2012).

[70] Jin Xiaogang [金晓刚] 'The Origin of Unjust Cases: The Appeal to "Abolish the Political-legal Committee" Is Increasing [制造冤案的祸源 "取消政法委" 呼声涨]' at http://www.aboluowang.com/2012/0331/241072.html (last accessed on 26 April 2012).

[71] Ibid.

[72] Jerome A. Cohen 'Law in Political Transitions: Lessons from East Asia and the Road Ahead for China' at http://www.cecc.gov/pages/hearings/072605/Cohen.php?PHPSESSID=b63a0066ec44bfc7e52470d7373a8916 (last accessed on 26 April 2012).

[73] See e.g. *The Economist* 'China's Security State: Guarding the Guardians' at http://www.economist.com/node/21557760 (last accessed on 23 July 2012), Dui Hua 'Taming Police Influence in Politico-legal Committees' at http://

to what extent such changes would affect their powers in reality is debatable – as argued by some scholars, China remains an authoritarian state relying on coercive forces, especially the police, to maintain its political stability.[74]

For a long time, the institution of the Political-Legal Committee has been criticized for its adverse effects on judicial independence and the administration of justice. Chen Guangzhong has argued that many cases are in fact decided by the Political-Legal Committee and that 'the Public Security Bureau, the People's Procuratorate, and the People's Court' are routinely 'coordinated' (*xietiao*) by the Political-Legal Committee to handle cases according to its own decision.[75] Lawyer Chen Youxi has gone so far as to comment that 'almost all the unjust and wrongly decided cases disclosed in recent years could find direct interventions from the Political-legal Committee.'[76] That is to say, very likely the injustice of a case lies in the Political-Legal Committee's 'coordination' and directions, not in the Court, the Procuratorate or even the Public Security Bureau.

The 'Zhao Zuohai case'[77] is an example of the potentially harmful role of the Political-Legal Committees. In this case, the People's Court originally thought that this case should not be sentenced due to serious flaws in

---

www.duihuahrjournal.org/2011/11/taming-police-influence-in-politico.html (last accessed on 23 July 2012) and Yazhou Zhoukan [亚洲周刊] 'Competitive Election Adopted in the Party Committee of Guangdong Province: Head of the Political-legal Committee Is No Longer a Member Which Implies Its Decreasing Status 廣東省委換屆推差額選舉 政法委不是常委地位下降]' at http://www.yzzk.com/cfm/Content_Archive.cfm?Channel=bc&Path=2447308872/21bcc.cfm (last accessed on 23 July 2012).

[74] See e.g. Fu Hualing 'Zhou Yongkang and the Recent Police Reform in China' (2005) Vol. 38 No. 2 *The Australian and New Zealand Journal of Criminology* 241–51; He Weifang 'The Police and the Rule of Law: Commentary on "Principles and Secret Agents"' (Sep 2007) *The China Quarterly* 671–3.

[75] Chen Baocheng [陈宝成] '刑事诉讼法学家陈光中建议取消地方政法委拍板权 [The Criminal Procedure Law Expert Chen Guangzhong Advised to Abolish Local Political-legal Committees' Power to Make Final Decision]' at http://nf.nfdaily.cn/nfdsb/content/2010-05/15/content_11945697.htm (last accessed on 26 April 2012).

[76] Supra note 69.

[77] See the general introduction and discussions of the Zhao Zuohai case at e.g. Clifford Coonan 'Zhao Zuohai: Beaten, Framed and Jailed for a Murder that Never Happened' at http://www.independent.co.uk/news/world/asia/zhao-zuohai-beaten-framed-and-jailed-for-a-murder-that-never-happened-1973042.html (last accessed on 26 April 2012); Dui Hua 'Zhao Zuohai Case Provokes Responses on Legal Protections from Chinese Public, Government' at http://www.duihuahr

evidence; the People's Procuratorate held the same opinion and asked the Public Security Bureau to further investigate while the Public Security Bureau could not find any new evidence.[78] However, later, the Shangqiu Political-Legal Committee intervened and ordered the three organs to resolve it since it was murder.[79] In this situation, under the pressure from the Political-Legal Committee, the People's Court gave a suspended death penalty sentence to the alleged defendant Zhao Zuohai, who was later found to have been tortured to extract his 'confession' and to have been wrongfully convicted and sentenced, because the person alleged to have been killed by him reappeared alive.[80] There is no mechanism at all for investigating the Political-Legal Committee's accountability in handling and directing cases even of this extreme nature.[81] If any misconduct in handling a case is disclosed afterwards, only the police, prosecutors or judges (in charge) may take responsibility.[82]

Judicial independence has been especially eroded in a variety of ways. In addition to pressure and interventions from the Party's Political-Legal Committee, as analysed by Carl Minzner, the People's Courts at all levels also face pressure from the Party policies such as maintaining social stability or preventing large-scale citizen protests.[83] As also observed by Benjamin Liebman, the speech concerning establishing 'socialist rule of law' by Luo Gan, head of the Central Political-Legal Committee in 2006, characterized 'following the leadership of the Party' as a requirement for the legal system (including the People's Procuratorates and People's Courts) in order to 'guarantee the political colour and loyalty to the

---

journal.org/2010/06/zhao-zuohai-case-provokes-responses-on.html (last accessed on 26 April 2012). Ira Belkin 'China's Tortuous Path Toward Ending Torture in Criminal Investigations' (2011) Vol. 24 No. 2 *Columbia Journal of Asian Law* 274–6; Tomas Stutsman 'The Use of Demonstration Projects to Advance Criminal Procedure Reform in China' (2011) Vol. 24 No. 2 *Columbia Journal of Asian Law* 344; Margaret K. Lewis 'Controlling Abuse to Maintain Control: The Exclusionary Rule in China' (2011) Vol. 43 *International Law and Politics* 630–31.

78 He Weifang [贺卫方] 'Nothing Has More Reformational Characteristics than Judicial Reform [没什么比司法改革更具改良特色]' at http://blog.sina.com.cn/s/blog_488663200102dufm.html (last accessed on 26 April 2012).

79 Ibid.

80 Ibid.

81 Ibid.

82 Ibid.

83 Supra note 36, 84.

Party.'[84] These general policies, according to Minzner, are crucial to the People's Courts and have been adopted as requirements and tasks more significant than the legal rules for the Courts and judges.[85]

Yet these political requirements have weakened judicial independence and produced awkward situations, which result in the officials' violation of written rules protecting the parties' rights. For example, as discussed in Chapter 1, since 2000, the Party has highlighted judicial mediation as an effective way to address social conflicts and unrest and thereby to achieve 'harmony' in society. In this context, according to Randall Peerenboom and He Xin's report, 'judges may be caught between solving cases in an efficient manner and the political requirement of a higher mediation rate.'[86] Under this political pressure and tension, judges use methods such as pleading and even forcing the parties to make mediation consume less time and energy.[87] This analysis fits the observation of criminal reconciliation practices as well – the officials' violations of the procedural rules as shown in Chapters 4 and 5 can also be seen as largely caused by pressure coming from the Party's policies of 'promoting a harmonious society,' which has been transformed into the internal performance assessment criteria.

Obstacles from local government, widely characterized as 'local protectionism,' are another problem leading to weakness of the People's Procuratorates and People's Courts in executing their authority. As argued by Zhang Hui, the administrative structure in China as stipulated by the Constitution has decided that the personnel and finance of the local People's Procuratorates and the People's Courts are subject to the local People's Congresses and local governments, so the Procuratorates and Courts are one community of beneficiaries with local governments and the People's Congresses.[88] This structure gives local People's Congresses and local governments power to interfere with the People's Courts and Procuratorates – they may face retaliatory budget cuts if they tried to exert independence in such cases.[89]

---

[84] Benjamin L. Liebman 'China's Courts: Restricted Reform' (Sep 2007) *The China Quarterly* 627–8.

[85] Supra note 36, 84.

[86] Randall Peerenboom, He Xin 'Dispute Resolution in China: Patterns, Causes, and Prognosis' at http://www.fljs.org/uploads/documents/Peerenboom_He%20Xin%231%23.pdf (last accessed on 16 July 2012).

[87] Supra note 69.

[88] Ibid.

[89] Ibid.

In sum, while there are a multitude of officially recognized 'supervision' mechanisms, these mechanisms are ineffective, largely because of the Procuratorates' and Courts' weakness vis-à-vis the Party, the Public Security Bureau and local governments. For instance, scholar Yu Jianrong recalls being told by a judge that in fact 'the judges are conscientious but have no strategies,' since 'the secretary (of the Party) controls their position; the mayor controls their salary; and the Political-Legal Committee controls their case.'[90] Since the People's Procuratorates and People's Courts are ultimately subject to these entities, the violation of rights perpetrated by the Procuratorates and Courts may be more appropriately viewed as power abuse of the Procuratorates and Courts by these entities.

It is therefore very problematic to call for more supervision (*jiandu*) of the Procuratorates and Courts. According to the view taken here, rather than addressing the problem of rights' violations, more supervision results in more potentially harmful interference with the People's Procuratorates and People's Courts.

The expansion of the People's Congress' supervision in recent years could be referred to as an example here. Following the thought that more supervision is needed, the People's Congress has 'expanded the Standing Committees' power,' albeit without any statutory basis, to undertake 'supervision' in individual cases (*ge'an jiandu*). Yet, this expansion of power, as argued by Cai Dingjian, has actually constituted a form of intervention rather than supervision of the People's Procuratorates and Courts.[91] As conceded by Randall Peerenboom, interventions from the People's Congress also cause 'awkward situations' for judges, since they sometimes 'receive conflicting advice from different People's Congresses.'[92]

Moreover, the effects of supervision from the media and the public, widely called '*yulun jiandu*,' which is increasingly referred to as another potentially effective supervisory mechanism, are also in question. On the

[90] In Chinese, 书记管着帽子，市长管着票子，政法委管着案子, see: Yu Jianrong [于建嵘] 'What Has Stability Overwhelmed? [稳定压倒了什么?]' at http://www.gscn.com.cn/pub/critique/sdgc/2011/11/02/1320226193705.html (last accessed on 26 April 2012).

[91] See the summary of Cai Dingjian's talk and views at the conference 'Legal Reform in China: Problems and Prospects' held by the Carnegie Endowment for International Peace and the Asia Foundation in Washington, DC on 18 April 2005 at http://www.carnegieendowment.org/files/panel2_summary.pdf (last accessed on 26 April 2012).

[92] Randall Peerenboom 'Judicial Independence and Judicial Accountability: An Empirical Study of Individual Case Supervision' (Jan. 2006) No. 55 *The China Journal* 78.

one hand, against the background that there is no freedom of speech in China, the media are still controlled and supervised by the Party.[93] In 2004, *yulun jiandu* has been explicitly defined by the Chinese government as 'an official form of Party supervision stipulated in the Internal Supervision Regulations of the Communist Party of China.'[94] In this sense, Li-Fung Cho argues that 'this [tight supervision by the Party] was by far the clearest indication that China's *yulun jiandu* should not be seen to correspond to the Western press theory of the "Fourth Estate," which implied that the press has powers independent of the government to criticize state policies.'[95]

On the other hand, as argued by Benjamin Liebman, in China today, public opinion, more appropriately defined as 'cheap speech' rather than 'free speech,' has in fact formed 'populist pressures' on the People's Courts, especially in the context of the Party's highlighting of 'social stability' and 'harmony.'[96] This, according to Benjamin Liebman and Tim Wu, has already produced a 'new type of Party-state intervention,' which is characterized by quick response to public opinions, even sacrificing legal rules.[97] Thus, Liebman and Wu say that:

> When criticism is used as a political weapon against an already weak judiciary it does not improve governance but endangers progress toward a rule of law system. At its worst, and when supported by the state, cheap mass criticism can cause judges to become unwilling to make decisions that run the risk of inflaming the public thereby causing a surrender of judicial authority to the vicissitudes of public opinion.[98]

To sum up, more supervision – *jiandu* – would not be likely to prove effective in addressing the problem of hidden rules, and would pose the risk of more undue interference with the People's Courts and the People's Procuratorates. Courts and Procuratorates need to be strengthened not further weakened by additional layers of supervision.

---

[93] Li-Fung Cho 'The Emergence of China's Watchdog Reporting' in David Bandurski and Martin Hala (eds) *Investigative Journalism in China* Hong Kong, Hong Kong University Press 2010, 169.

[94] Ibid.

[95] Ibid.

[96] Supra note 84, 633.

[97] Benjamin L. Liebman, Tim Wu 'China's Network Justice' (2007) Vol. 8 No. 1 *Chicago Journal of International Law* 285.

[98] Ibid, 261.

6.1.3 Preliminary Conclusions

All the problems leading to the malfunctioning of the system discussed by Chen Ruihua can also be found in criminal reconciliation as a sub-system implemented in the general framework of criminal justice. To that extent, the criminal reconciliation system may be said to replicate problems also found in the wider criminal justice system. For example, concerning the lack of an implementation mechanism for the (criminal) procedure, as shown in Chapter 1, those local rules or guidelines for criminal reconciliation chiefly provide a set of procedures governing this programme and the officials' conduct (power) in this process. Judicial review of this process and legal liability imposed on the officials cannot be found in these regulations and guidelines. It is not included in Articles 277 to 279 of the 2012 CPL either. Also, there are conflicts in rules governing criminal reconciliation. For example, as argued in Chapter 3, the procedural regulations and guidelines emphasize the parties' *voluntary* participation in this process. However, they also provide that many other people such as the parties' employers, 'leadership' or teachers could also attend criminal reconciliation meetings. This, it was observed, may put pressure on the parties and impair the voluntariness of their decisions.

As argued in this section, the fundamental problems leading to the prevalence of 'hidden rules' in judicial practices are internal and external pressures on the police, prosecutors and judges coming from the internal performance assessment systems and various other entities. These problems were further aggravated in criminal reconciliation processes.

Internal pressures, as shown in Chapter 5, were increased by procedural regulations and guidelines for criminal reconciliation and the internal performance assessment systems taking these specific rules into account. As discussed in Chapter 5, officials could be expected to make certain choices; it would be natural for them to evade time-consuming programmes like criminal reconciliation. Nevertheless, they could not simply give up on this programme since it had been set as a task in the internal performance assessment system. The performance assessment system often involved requirements regarding the number of criminal reconciliation cases, whose handling was time intensive, yet at the same time required officials to dispose of a high number of cases with complete closure. The officials might be disciplined or at least their bonus and promotion might be affected if they could not fulfil the various tasks imposed by the performance assessment system. Therefore, it might be simpler in this case for them just to abandon 'complicated' and 'time-consuming' procedures. Avoiding such procedures would be much easier when there were no effective checks on their power, and where there were no other adverse consequences.

External pressures impeding the prosecutors' and judges' independent exercise of power, as noted in Chapter 4, resulted from the fact that the decision not to prosecute in criminal reconciliation is always made by the procuratorial committee (*jiancha weiyuanhui*), not the prosecutor in charge. In the People's Court, as noted in Chapters 3 and 4, in criminal reconciliation, the People's Procuratorate could present 'sentencing suggestions' (*liangxing jianyi*) to the People's Court, and given the weakness of the People's Court as a part of the 'production line,' it could be expected to subordinate itself to the Public Security Bureau and the People's Procuratorate.

Indeed, as shown in Chapter 1, there are officially recognized and endorsed practices of collaboration (*liandong*) and cooperation (*duijie*) in criminal reconciliation, whereby a case could, or in fact should, be reconciled cooperatively by the three state authorities. This explicit endorsement of cooperation further strengthens the three organs' connection and mutual reliance as a 'production line.' It further harms judicial independence, as well as the prosecutors' independent exercise of power.

In addition, in the current context, criminal reconciliation is being strongly promoted by the Party as a mechanism embodying the policy of 'combining severity with leniency' and helpful for 'promoting a harmonious society.' According to the analysis in this section, however, the strong promotion of this mechanism by the Supreme People's Court and the Supreme People's Procuratorate, and the quotas set for criminal reconciliation cases only put pressure on the procuratorates. Under such pressure, the system is unlikely to achieve genuinely harmonious resolution of cases.

6.2 CRIMINAL JUSTICE THROUGH 'CORRECTION' (*JIAOZHENG*) AND 'THOUGHT REFORM' (*SIXIANG GAIZAO*)

'Educating and correcting (*jiaozheng*) the suspect/defendant' is one of the officially stated aims and functions of criminal reconciliation. In order to achieve this aim, as shown in the empirical study discussed in Chapters 4 and 5, the officials paid special attention to education, particularly in cases involving juvenile offenders. In such cases, responsible officials would deliver educational statements during, before or after criminal reconciliation meetings.[99] They would, in some cases, arrange for follow-up programmes such as 'teaching and help' projects.

There are two prominent features of the concept of *jiaozheng* in criminal reconciliation.

First, education and correction in criminal reconciliation processes are characterized as focusing on changing the suspects'/defendants' thought and improving their moral character. For instance, in the follow-up programmes, the person in charge (i.e. the juvenile suspects'/defendants' teachers, or the responsible officials) provided help focusing particularly on the suspect's/defendant's thought and moral character. The suspect/defendant was required to submit so-called 'thought reports' (*sixiang huibao*) to the officials regularly.

Second, education and correction not only targeted the suspect/defendant; rather, the officials intended to involve the public in this process. For instance, as shown in Chapter 5, a judge highlighted criminal reconciliation's significance in 'propagating legal knowledge' (*pufa*). In some cases, criminal reconciliation meetings were arranged by the officials in such a way that the suspect's/defendant's schoolmates and teachers could observe and participate, with an apparent expectation that they, too, would be educated.

'Education' and 'correction' is not a particular aim set for criminal reconciliation. Rather, they are general goals the Chinese ordinary criminal justice process is expected to achieve. In the ordinary process, just like in criminal reconciliation, education targets individual (perceived) offenders and/or immediate parties to a dispute, as well as a wider public, as discussed below.

6.2.1 The Concept of 'Correction' in the Wider Criminal Process

Education and correction are officially regarded as important features of the normal (adjudicative) criminal trial process. The scholar Li Changsheng has recently proposed a way of understanding the trial process by reference to its educational aims. According to the PRC Criminal Procedure Law, the normal criminal trial process (in the first instance trial) includes the formal stages of opening a court session (*kaiting*), court investigation (*fating diaocha*), court debate (*fating bianlun*), the defendant's final statement (*zuihou chenshu*), assessment

[99] As indicated in Chapter 4, these statements are just a formality including asking the suspects/defendants to 'study hard' or 'listen to their parents' and so on.

(*pingyi*) and sentence announcement (*xuanpan*).[100] Li Changsheng, however, proposes to think of the trial process as involving four stages, namely declaration of attitude (*biaotai*), revelation (*zhanshi*), education (*jiaoyu*) and remorse (*huiguo*). Li has thus characterized the Chinese trial as 'educational ("formative" or "educational" trial' (*jiaohua xing tingshen*).[101]

Li's account amounts to a creative and deeply perceptive reinterpretation of the criminal justice process. At the stage of opening a court session, that is, at the stage of 'declaring one's attitude,' the defendant is required by the Court to show his/her attitude towards the charges that have just been presented by the prosecutor – normally, the defendant is requested to admit guilt or plead not guilty.[102] In practice, according to Li, most defendants would admit guilt at this stage.[103]

In the ensuing stage of the trial hearing, which among other things involves the Court's examination of the evidence, the prosecutor makes the defendant 'reveal' the crime he/she has been charged through examining (putting questions to) the defendant.[104] Nevertheless, as observed by Mike McConville *et al*, the questions raised by the prosecutors are chiefly 'clarifications, or merely observations, or even a statement confirming the contents of the documentary evidence under consideration' rather than 'challenging.'[105] Li Changsheng observes that, at this stage, the prosecutors may even use strategies to 'coerce' or 'induce' the defendant, who often[106] does not have a defence lawyer, to *illustrate* the alleged crime collaboratively with the prosecutor.[107] Such a process also shows that the trial system set up in the 1996 CPL is not adversarial in practice and that defendants' rights to criminal justice processes are heavily compromised.

---

[100] Hao Yinzhong [郝银钟] 'On the First Instance Trial [第一审程序论]' in Zhang Jun [张军] Hao Yinzhong [郝银钟] (eds) *刑事诉讼庭审专题研究* [*Research on the Criminal Trial*] Beijing, Renmin University of China Press [中国人民大学出版社] 2005, 169.

[101] Li Changsheng [李昌盛] 'The Chinese Pattern of Criminal Trial: *Bildung* Trial [刑事庭审的中国模式: 教化型庭审]' (2011) 1 *Science of Law (Journal of Northwest University of Political Science and Law)* [*法律科学(西北政法大学学报)*] 131.

[102] Ibid, 132.

[103] Ibid.

[104] Ibid.

[105] Supra note 8, 248.

[106] Mike McConville *et al* found that in 46% of cases the defendant was not legally represented (ibid, 293).

[107] Supra note 100, 132.

The following, in Li Changsheng's view, crucial stage of court debate provides a platform for the prosecutor to present 'prosecution opinions' (*gongsu yijian*).[108] From the perspective of the formal characterization of the trial, prosecution opinions mainly serve the purpose of presenting an argument to the Court – for instance, a legal argument for the defendant's guilt. According to Li, however, they in fact serve an educational purpose, and education is based on feelings and reason (*qing li*) – this characterization draws on a widely used conceptual triad of 'law, reason, and feelings' but notably makes no explicit mention of 'law.' For instance, a report provided by the People's Court of Xishan district in Wuxi city shows that they have adopted four methods to educate defendants during trial: (i) reflection through identification with the other (*huanwei sikao*), a method which seeks to make the defendants feel the victims' hurt and thereby to 'step out of his/her narrow and wrong sense of values';[109] (ii) 'reform through familial affection' (*qinqing ganhua*), which, according to this official report, tries to make the defendant repent and is to 'rebuild the defendant's rationality through family bonds';[110] (iii) 'criticism and condemnation,' a method only used when the previous two cannot take effect and the defendant 'refuses to admit guilt when the evidence is sufficient'[111] so as to 'use law and evidence to make the defendant realize his/her criminal conducts as well as the harm';[112] (iv) the fourth method is called 'balancing benefits and costs' (*quanheng libi*), a method trying to make the defendant 'form a rational and wise attitude towards life' through the realization that 'committing a crime is not worth it.'[113]

As further shown by Li Changsheng, some People's Procuratorates even formally require prosecutors to state the goal of educating the defendant to 'become a new person' (*gai guo zi xin*) and 'propagating legal knowledge to the defendant and other citizens [sitting on the trial]'

---

[108] Ibid.

[109] Chen Min [陈敏] Wang Wei [王伟] 'The Effects of Deepening the Moral Reform Work for the Defendants: The Experience of the People's Court of Xishan District in Wuxi City [深化刑事被告人道德教化显成效:无锡锡山法院刑事审判经验材料]' at http://www.dffy.com/fazhixinwen/sifa/200907/20090723154611.htm (last accessed on 9 May 2012).

[110] Ibid.

[111] Ibid.

[112] Ibid. This is supplementary to other methods based on 'feelings and reason.'

[113] Ibid.

should be 'necessary components' in their plea at trial.[114] Li also says that, in practice, the prosecutor often expresses moral condemnation of the defendant during this process of 'education.'[115] In the setting of the Chinese trial, in which there is no jury or judge to persuade of the defendant's guilt, because the defendant is de facto already presumed guilty, the purpose of the moral condemnation is to educate the defendant (as well as other people attending the trial), not to win debate in court, according to Li.[116] In the same vein, Pang Zheng shows how the prosecutor delivered moral condemnation to the defendant of an alleged fraud crime at the stage of court debate:[117]

> We think the crime originated from two wrong ideas of the defendant: the first one is the intention to reap without sowing. In our city, a number of people are creating wealth and maintaining their life through their own hard work. Thus, no matter how humble their social status was, they are worthy of our respect. Yet the defendant Chen intended to reap without sowing and to take others' wealth through fraud. This was a base way of making a living.
>
> The second one is to take chances. The defendant Chen defrauded others to obtain their wealth on so many occasions, yet he naively thought of this as creditor-debtor relationships. However, the mills of God grind slowly but surely and law is always the last ditch of conscience in our society.
>
> In sum, the prosecutor hopes that the defendant could draw lessons from this crime, and we want to caution those eager to have a try.

Such statements, as argued by Pang, show that the prosecution statement has two contradictory functions – on the one hand, it is to prove that the defendant has committed the alleged crime; yet on the other, it has to presume that the defendant has committed the alleged crime.[118]

The last stage is the defendant's final statement. At this stage, the defendant is expected to express explicitly his/her remorse towards the crime he/she is charged with, which might bring about some leniency in sentencing.[119] Standard ways of expressing repentance, according to Li's empirical study, were: 'I admit guilt, I hope (the judge) will sentence me leniently, taking into account my child'; 'I did make mistakes in my work and hope that the Court will sentence me leniently'; 'I admit guilt and

[114] Supra note 100, 132.
[115] Ibid.
[116] Ibid.
[117] Pang Zheng [逄政] 'Education in the Court [法庭上的教化]' (2008) 10 *Fang Yuan Fazhi* [*方圆法治*] 60.
[118] Ibid, 61.
[119] Supra note 100, 133.

feel very regretful towards my conduct. I hope the Court will give me another chance. I was too greedy and flouted the law and rules of discipline in committing the crime, but I really hope the judge will sentence me leniently considering that my family is so poor.'[120] Li says that in practice, considering the potential benefits in sentencing, almost all defendants (some 86 percent) would grab this 'final opportunity' to show their remorse, which is (taken by the officials as) also a sign of the success of the whole trial process as actually an education process.[121]

Education also plays a critical role in the Chinese system of correction and punishments *post* conviction, which involves prisons and schools of discipline and education for juvenile offenders (*shaonianfan guanjiao suo*).[122] Article 3 of the 1994 PRC Prison Law lays down 'combining punishment with reform, combining education with labor' as a principle of the prison system in China.[123] Article 62 further stipulates that 'thought education' should be carried out with regard to principles, legal knowledge, morals, current affairs, and politics. According to Victor Shaw, education about 'principles' covers political ideas such as socialism, communist leadership and a subject called 'Marxism-Leninism and Mao Zedong Thought.'[124] 'Legal education' focuses on the PRC Criminal Law, Criminal Procedure Law and Prison Law.[125] Moral education often covers 'collectivism, civility, social ethics and worldviews.'[126] Education about current affairs is about the Party's current policies and government agendas.[127]

In addition to 'thought education,' education through (typically manual) labour also plays a role. In the context of ordinary prisons with

---

[120] Li Changsheng [李昌盛] 'The "Defendant Talking" Style Trial which Lacks Defense [缺乏对抗的被告人说话式审判]' at http://www.docin.com/p-26284336.html?bsh_bid=85286478 (last accessed on 10 May 2012).

[121] Ibid.

[122] The school of discipline and education for juvenile offenders or *shaonianfan guanjiao suo* is an institution especially for juvenile criminals. According to Article 74 of the PRC Prison Law, criminal punishments to juvenile delinquents shall be executed in the school of discipline and education for juvenile offenders. See: Victor N. Shaw 'Corrections and Punishments in China: Information and Analysis' (2010) Vol. 26 No. 1 *Journal of Contemporary Criminal Justice* 55.

[123] See the English translation at LawInfoChina: http://www.pkulaw.cn/fulltext_form.aspx?db=chl&gid=10917 (last accessed on 9 May 2016).

[124] Victor N. Shaw, supra note 122, 60.

[125] Ibid.

[126] Ibid.

[127] Ibid.

inmates serving criminal sentences, this is known as 'reform through labour (*laodong gaizao*).'[128] In the context of China's so-called 're-education through labour (*laodong jiaoyang,* RETL)' system, those to be educated have not been convicted in a trial process, but are deemed guilty on the basis of a decision made by the police.[129] According to Article 3 of 'the Ministry of Public Security's Trial Methods for Implementing Re-education Through Labor' issued in 1982, the principle of RETL is education, saving and reforming; education and reform are first and foremost, and production and labour are second.[130] Paragraph 2 of the 'Decision of the State Council on Re-education Through Labor' issued in 1957 also says that 'rehabilitation through labour is a measure whereby education and reform are mandatorily imposed on persons who are

---

[128] Reform through labour or *laodong gaizao* is an enforcement measure imposed on criminals in China. It mainly aims to reform criminals through physical labour and education. The place to conduct *laodong gaizao* involves prison, detention house, and so on. See: the explanation by Yang Tao on Xinhua Net [新华网] 'Is "Reform Through Labour" the Same with "Reeducation Through Labour"? ['劳动教养' 就是 '劳动改造' 吗?]' at http://news.xinhuanet.com/banyt/2004-05/12/content_1464763.htm (last accessed on 2 July 2011) and the brief introduction of this system by Ramin Pejan 'Laogai: "Reform Through Labor" in China' at http://www.wcl.american.edu/hrbrief/07/2laogai.cfm (last accessed on 2 July 2011).

[129] Re-education through labour or *laodong jiaoyang* is an administrative measure imposed on people violating laws who should not be punished by the criminal law. It is conducted in the administration house of re-education through labour (*laodong jiaoyang guanlisuo*) or schools of re-education through labour (*laodong jiaoyang xuexiao*) and is decided by the administration committee of re-education through labour built in every city or province. See the explanation by Yang Tao, supra note 128 and by Human Rights Watch 'Reeducation Through Labor in China' at http://www.hrw.org/legacy/campaigns/china-98/laojiao.htm (last accessed on 2 July 2011). This system has been widely criticized for its violation of the Constitution and human rights. See e.g. Human Rights Watch 'Reeducation Through Labor: A Summary of Regulatory Issues and Concerns by Human Rights in China' at http://hrichina.org/public/PDFs/Reports/HRIC-RTL.pdf; 'The Appeal Lodged by 69 Chinese Scholars to the National People's Congress about Initiating Unconstitutional Review on the System of Reeducation through Labor' at http://review.jcrb.com/ljzd/index.htm (last accessed on 2 July 2011). On 28 December 2013, the Standing Committee of the National People's Congress passed the decision to abolish this system.

[130] The Ministry of Public Security's Trial Methods for Implementing Re-education Through Labor [国务院关于转发公安部制定的劳动教养试行办法的通知] (1982) at http://www.cecc.gov/pages/selectLaws/criminalJustice/trialMethods.php (last accessed on 2 July 2011).

interned for rehabilitation through labour, and is also a measure to resettle them and provide employment for them.'[131] 'Help shall be given to them in cultivating their consciousness of loving the country, abiding by the law and regarding work as a matter of honour, in learning skills of labour and production, and in fostering a habit of loving manual labour so that they may be turned into working people who take part in socialist construction and who support themselves by their own labour.'[132] The requirement that persons incarcerated in prisons or RETL facilities should perform physical labour, according to Shaw, is related to the socialist (or Marxist) idea of transformation of consciousness as well as, more recently, to the Confucian idea that 'mind can be best exercised and reformed by labour.'[133]

Even assuming, for a moment, that those incarcerated really were in need of education, the goals, methods and real outcomes of these various 'education' programmes are dubious. This point has been made by Chinese scholars, domestic and international rights defenders, and several human rights organizations.[134] Moreover, through examining the history of China's RETL system since 1955, Fu Hualing argues that the RETL system nowadays serves 'multifold functions,' one of which is the political function of controlling and suppressing political dissidents.[135]

The experience of Ye Jinghuan provides good insights into how RETL works in ordinary – as opposed to unusually cruel – cases through depicting her miserable experience in the Beijing RETL institution. Ye

---

[131] Decision of the State Council on Re-education Through Labor [国务院关于劳动教养问题的决定] (1957) at http://www.novexcn.com/rehibilitation_t_labour.html (last accessed on 2 July 2011).

[132] Ibid.

[133] Victor N. Shaw, supra note 122, 62. See also: Mao Zedong's talk 'Where Do Correct Ideas Come From?' [人的正确思想是从哪里来的?] in May 1963, which says 'where do correct ideas come from? Do they drop from the skies? No. Are they innate in the mind? No. They come from social practice, and from it alone; they come from three kinds of social practice, the struggle for production, the class struggle and scientific experiment' at http://art-bin.com/art/omao22.html (last accessed on 12 May 2012).

[134] See e.g. the report 'Reeducation Through Labor in China' by Human Rights Watch at http://www.hrw.org/legacy/campaigns/china-98/laojiao.htm (last accessed on 2 July 2011) and the report 'Re-education Through Labor Abuses Continue Unabated: Overhaul Long Overdue' by Chinese Human Rights Defenders (CHRD) at http://docs.law.gwu.edu/facweb/dclarke/public/CHRD_RTL_Report.pdf (last accessed on 2 July 2012).

[135] Fu Hualing 'Re-education Through Labour in Historical Perspective' (Dec. 2005) No. 184 *The China Quarterly* 829–30.

describes her own experience as 'virtual torture' and writes of insults by officials of the institution. In terms of the manual work, Ye says that people under re-education through labour have to work continuously for 14 to 15 hours per day, almost without rest or breaks.[136] With regard to 'education,' Ye describes various 'rules.' These include: RETL detainees must lower their heads before guards; they must beg the officials to be allowed to eat, go to the restroom, and so on; on certain occasions, they must bow or kneel in front of officials; and they may be required to produce written 'self-criticisms' if they do not perform well. Moreover, they are subjected to a system of mutual surveillance and collective responsibility for good conduct called '*bao jiao*.' Under this system, detainees assigned to oneself will monitor and report on one's every action.[137] Based on her own experience, Ye concludes that, actually, the 'manual work' is exploitation and the 'education' is mental torture. Exploitation and torture are designed, according to Ye, to 'strike your dignity, ruin your soul, debase your personality and to harm your health.'[138]

Although pre-trial defendants are not, at least not according to the principles laid down in the CPL, supposed to be educated, elements of 'thought education' are present in the regimen for pretrial detainees as well. They are not subjected to the same kind of 'thought education' and 'education through labour' that is used for persons at trial or after conviction. However, the Detention House Regulation promulgated by the State Council in 2012 says that 'the detainee should receive education.'[139] Article 21 of this regulation further stipulates that 'the detention house should provide legal and moral education for detainees, and organize appropriate recreational and sporting activities.'[140]

A number of online reports give an impression, albeit anecdotal, of the practice of 'moral and legal education' in detention centres. For example, an official account of the detention centre in Zezhou county in Shanxi province states that all the detainees received at least ten hours of legal education in total.[141] The police also organized education on current

---

136 Ye Jinghuan [野静环] *A Rewarding Trip: Report on Life in the Beijing Transferring Institution of Reeducation Through Labor* [*不虚此行: 北京劳教调遣处纪实*] (unpublished draft on file with author).

137 Ibid.

138 Ibid.

139 Article 3 of the Detention House Regulation [拘留所条例].

140 Ibid, Article 21.

141 Chao Xuku [晁绪库] 'The Detention House in Zezhou County Strengthened Education Work to Facilitate the Detainees' Reform [泽州县拘留所

affairs and 'heart-to-heart' conversation sessions for the detainees.[142] The detention house in Putian city in Fujian province was prepared to establish a drug prevention education centre in order to promote the ability of the detainees, who were deemed a 'high-risk group,' to quit drugs.[143] In addition, this detention house was intended to establish a psychological education centre to carry out psychological consultation and 'correction' of detainees.[144]

In sum, an 'educational' mindset in the sense just outlined characterizes a suspect's experience from the moment they are detained, and this is of obvious relevance to the practice both of the ordinary criminal justice system and of criminal reconciliation. As shown in Chapter 5, some officials interviewed even commented on the bad conditions in the detention centre as an opportunity for the suspects/defendants to reflect seriously and change to be 'good guys' (after being shocked by the bad conditions there).[145]

The effect of such 'educational' experiences is further reinforced by practices designed to educate the wider public while exposing the suspect to public censure and shame. As shown in criminal reconciliation, the goals of education and thought reform set for the Chinese criminal process are not limited to suspects/defendants/inmates either; they target the public, the ordinary people in society, as well. This is dramatically shown in 'open trial (*gong shen*) meetings' and 'open sentencing (*gong pan*) rallies,' rituals essentially the same as 'parade and public exposure' (*youxing shizhong*), a way of punishment that prevailed in the Cultural Revolution (1966–76)[146] and still practised in China today.[147] For

---

加强教育促进被拘人员转化]' at http://jc.jcnews.com.cn/jincheng_content/2012-04/24/content_162200.htm (last accessed on 10 May 2012).

[142] Ibid.

[143] Xu Aiqiong [许爱琼] 'The Detention House in Putian City Is the First in the Province to Establish a Drug Control Propaganda and Education Centre [莆田市拘留所将建禁毒宣传教育基地全省首创]' at http://news.66163.com/2012-04-10/622023.shtml (last accessed on 10 May 2012).

[144] Ibid.

[145] Interview with prosecutor L in the People's Procuratorate of B district in Xi'an in September 2010.

[146] According to the brief introduction by the BBC, the 'Great Proletarian Cultural Revolution was a ten-year political campaign – a social experiment aimed at rekindling revolutionary fervor and purifying the party. Mao Zedong and his wife, Jiang Qing, directed popular anger against other members of the party leadership.' 'While others were removed from office, Mao was named supreme commander of the nation and army.' 'Ideological cleansing began with

example, it was reported that in 2012 in Xianyang city in Shaanxi province, in order to educate secondary students, the police escorted juvenile criminals into the school to 'tell their stories' in public.[148] In 2010, it was reported that 32 individuals were declared formally detained as criminal suspects and 20 defendants were convicted and sentenced in a 'public arrest and sentencing rally' (*gongbu gongpan dahui*) in Loudi city in Hunan province.[149] Over 6,000 people attended this rally, and all the suspects and defendants were paraded across the city with their names written on white boards hanging round their necks.[150] To anyone who had lived through it, this would have vividly recalled the Cultural Revolution when such techniques were common.

6.2.2 The Ideology of 'Thought Reform' underlying 'Correction'

The most direct reason for 'educating and correcting' the criminals' (suspects and defendants included) thought lies in the idea that 'crime' is closely connected or even directly results from problems in a person's moral consciousness, resulting from capitalism, or bad class influence. So consciousness can be transformed to make criminal motivation disappear. This idea goes back to the Mao era, the idea of 'false consciousnesses' from which people had to be freed, as developed by Marx and Engels and elaborated on by Mao Zedong. Mao said in the article 'Where Do Correct Ideas Come From?' in 1963 that:

---

attacks by young Red Guards on so-called "intellectuals" to remove "bourgeois" influences.' 'Millions were forced into manual labour, and tens of thousands were executed.' 'The result was massive civil unrest, and the army was sent in to control student disorder.' 'At the 1977 11th Party Congress, the Cultural Revolution was declared officially to have ended with the arrest of the Gang of Four.' See: BBC News 'The Cultural Revolution' at http://news.bbc.co.uk/hi/english/static/special_report/1999/09/99/china_50/cult.htm (last accessed on 12 March 2012).

[147] Jiang Shigong [强世功] *Punishment and the Rule of Law: The Emergence of the Modern Rule of Law (1976–1981)* [*惩罚与法治：当代法治的兴起 (1976–1981)*] Beijing, Law Press [法律出版社] 2009, 173.

[148] *Beijing Times* [*京华时报*] 'Juvenile Offenders Were Escorted into the School to Educate 3000 Students with Legal Knowledge in Xianyang, Shaanxi Province [陕西咸阳少年犯被押解进校向3000学生示众说法]' at http://news.sohu.com/20120105/n331275818.shtml (last accessed on 8 January 2012).

[149] The discussion of this case on a Chinese BBS at http://bbs.anhuinews.com/thread-493688-1-1.html (last accessed on 12 March 2012).

[150] Ibid.

> it is man's social being that determines his thinking ... It is therefore necessary to educate our comrades in the dialectical materialist theory of knowledge, so that they can orientate their thinking correctly, become good at investigation and study and at summing up experiences, overcome difficulties, commit fewer mistakes, do their work better, and struggle hard so as to build China into a great and powerful socialist country and help the broad masses of the oppressed and exploited throughout the world in fulfillment of our great internationalist duty.[151]

A number of scholars have noticed and commented on the continuity of the ideology and practices adopted in the Maoist time and China today. For instance, Stanley Lubman observed that judicial practices in criminal processes in the Mao era deeply influenced judicial activities in criminal as well as non-criminal areas in the 1990s.[152] Elizabeth Perry argued in a broader context that the 'revolutionary past' in the Maoist period had been 'succeeded' by post-Mao leaders, and 'the Cultural Revolution was the most dramatic, but not the last expression' of the various Maoist approaches such as 'mobilizing the masses' and 'dividing society.'[153]

Jiang Shigong argues that punishment methods used in the Cultural Revolution were largely attributable to the very close perceived relationship between or the conflation of deficient moral consciousness and crime.[154] Furthermore, according to Jiang, since there was no clear distinction between criminality and innocence and the relationship between crime and moral consciousness was complicated but direct, almost anyone could end up being labelled a criminal.[155]

> There was no clear and fixed distinction between criminality and innocence during the Cultural Revolution – crime was defined mainly as the result of reactionary, feudal or bourgeois, or corrupting and uncivilized thoughts, as well as the degeneration of morality and the frailty of willpower. In this sense, crime was not understood as an act; rather, it was a matter of ideological quality, personality and attitudes toward life. Accordingly, punishment and correction should directly touch the criminal's soul and thought, and should permeate a person's daily life.

---

151 毛泽东 [Mao Zedong], 人的正确思想是从哪里来的? [Where do correct ideas come from] at http://omeublog.grupolusofona.pt/futurocomhistoria/files/2012/02/Postcolonial-Predicament.pdf (last accessed on 12 May 2012).

152 Stanley B. Lubman *Bird in a Cage: Legal Reform in China after Mao* Stanford, Stanford University Press 1999, 71.

153 Elizabeth J. Perry 'Studying Chinese Politics: Farewell to Revolution?' (Jan. 2007) No. 57 *The China Journal* 9–10.

154 Supra note 147, 16–17.

155 Supra note 147, 20.

Therefore, according to Jiang, the goal of punishment at that time was neither retribution nor prevention; rather, educating and reforming the criminal into 'a new person' (*chongxin zuoren*) were the goals of punishment.[156] That is to say, the Cultural Revolution view of punishment seemed to be also motivated by the idea of rehabilitation – yet since its conception of crime included mere 'thought crime' (or criminal thought), it was widely different from the narrow justifications of criminal punishment associated with rehabilitation in liberal Western systems.

Methods of punishment and re-education ranged from measures mainly targeting the criminal's 'soul and thought' such as writing 'thought reports' (*sixiang huibao*) to activities also involving the wider public in society such as 'criticism and denouncement' (*pidou*), parade and public exposure (*youxing shizhong*), 'study class' (*xuexi ban*) and singing 'revolutionary songs.'[157] Therefore, according to Jiang, punishment was not supposed to target merely a particular wrongdoer; education and thought reform were crucial to – needed by – everybody in society. It was related to everyone in the sense of eliminating problematic thoughts from everyone's minds, which carried political significance to 'accomplish the republic's mission.'[158] As a result, as argued by Jiang, the entire country became at the same time a 'school' to educate each person and a 'prison' to reform their 'selfish ideas,' which were viewed as 'corrupt remains of feudalism, capitalism or revisionism.'[159] The ideology underlying punishment popularly used in the Cultural Revolution like 'parade and public exposure' as analysed by Jiang Shigong may shed some light on the strong stress on education in the criminal justice system and the use of 'open trial meetings' and 'open sentencing rallies' in China today.

The current situation in China is widely different from the Cultural Revolution, during which legal institutions had been denounced and almost entirely destroyed. The officially stated function of 'education' of the kind discussed above has accordingly changed. It is today dominated by the goals of 'special prevention' and 'general prevention' of crime.[160]

Many scholars have commented on this point and discussed how this ideology influences the use of public, open trials (*gongkai shenli* or

---

[156] Supra note 147, 19.

[157] Ibid.

[158] Supra note 147, 19.

[159] Ibid.

[160] Jerome A. Cohen, *The Criminal Process in the People's Republic of China 1949–1963: An Introduction* Cambridge, MA, Harvard University Press 1968, 81.

shenpan), a requirement for the majority of cases in criminal, as well as civil and administrative, procedure nowadays.[161] For example, as observed by Mike McConville *et al*, the Chinese trials served the function of educating the defendant and the public.[162]

> Historically, one purpose of trials in China has been educative not only of the defendant but also more generally of the community by seeing justice in action and hearing at first hand the sentencing homily as a cautionary example to all. In addition, the presence at trials of members of the public is one important mechanism by which society as a whole may be given accurate knowledge.

Li Changsheng also described the educational function of open trials in China today as:[163]

> On the one hand, the judicial officials 'implant' legal values and rules as well as moral values to the defendant in order to make them realize their faults and take active responsibility for them. On the other hand, through setting 'negative examples,' officials can educate other people to comply with the law, which is beneficial for the maintenance of social stability.

The emphasis on education or crime prevention, nevertheless, changes the function of public trials in the Chinese criminal justice system compared to its function according to liberal criminal justice theory, which sees it as a significant mechanism to restrict the judge's power and to protect the defendant's rights.[164] It is recognized as one of the most fundamental safeguards for judicial justice.[165] That is to say, the value to the State, namely educating the defendant as well as the public, has surpassed the value to individual rights protection in public trial in China. As argued by Jerome A. Cohen, following the Soviet model, in China,

---

[161] According to the CPL, cases of first instance in a People's Court shall be heard in public. However, cases involving state secrets or private affairs of individuals shall not be heard in public. No cases involving crimes committed by minors who have reached the age of 14 but not the age of 16 shall be heard in public. Generally, cases involving crimes committed by minors who have reached the age of 16 but not the age of 18 shall also not be heard in public.

[162] Supra note 8, 193.

[163] Supra note 101, 132.

[164] Wang Xiaoxian [王效贤] 'On Open Trial [论公开审判]' at http://article.chinalawinfo.com/Article_Detail.asp?ArticleId=41580 (last accessed on 11 May 2012)

[165] Chen Ruihua [陈瑞华] *Justice Can Be Seen* [*看得见的正义*] Beijing, China Law Press [中国法制出版社] 2000, 77.

law is used mainly to discipline people and to reach the State's goals.[166] In other words, the criminal justice system, as well as all the participants in this system, ranging from the officials to the parties, is viewed by the authorities as a tool to serve political ends. In this regard, Donald Clarke and James V. Feinerman described Chinese trial as mainly serving 'a propaganda effort, directed at the citizens, to condemn vice and praise justice,' so it is 'any trial with an audience.'[167] Although Mike McConville *et al* found in an empirical study of the criminal process that only few trials had an audience consisting of persons other than the defendant's and victim's families and friends,[168] this may still not essentially weaken its educative intention. Because, as noted by Liebman and Wu, a variety of channels including State-controlled media and internet have been increasingly used to serve educational ends.[169]

6.2.3 A Critique of Thought Reform

With regard to the '*educational* trial' in the ordinary criminal process, Li Changsheng criticized it as an important factor rendering 'presumption of innocence' impossible.[170] According to Li, since the trial is designed to serve the goal of 'educating the defendant' to make him/her repent and 'become a new person' (*gai guo zi xin*), the basic premise is that the defendant has committed the crime he or she is accused of.[171] This shifts the responsibility of finding out if the defendant has committed the crime to earlier stages, such as arrest or prosecution, and to the Public Security Bureau and the People's Procuratorate.[172]

Moreover, according to Li, in a trial designed in such a way, the defendant who expresses objection to the accusation or keeps silent at trial would be deemed as a recalcitrant that cannot be educated, which might result in some more serious punishment afterwards.[173] As noted in the first section, the 1996 Criminal Procedure Law has stipulated that the suspects have an obligation to answer truthfully (*rushi gongshu*), which

---

[166] Supra note 160, 69.

[167] Donald C. Clarke, James V. Feinerman 'Antagonistic Contradictions: Criminal Law and Human Rights in China' in Stanley Lubman (ed) *China's Legal Reforms* Oxford, Oxford University Press 1996, 140.

[168] Supra note 8, 193.

[169] Supra note 97, 294.

[170] Supra note 101, 133.

[171] Ibid.

[172] Supra note 101, 134.

[173] Ibid.

was in the 2012 revision. Consequently, the measures provided for the purpose of protecting the defendant's rights, such as the now-stipulated right against self-incrimination,[174] the procedure for summoning a witness to appear before the court, and generally getting a strong defence, cannot be fully realized in practice because these protective rules and procedures are in conflict with the premise of the 'presumption of guilt' and might impede the officials' education work.[175] Li's criticism is in accordance with the observation made by Donald Clarke and James V. Feinerman that in the Chinese criminal trial the issue of whether the suspect was guilty or not guilty had been decided prior to trial.[176] Trial was the place to 'educate, not to confuse.'[177]

The ideas of moral education and character reform, nevertheless, indicate a more in-depth problem with the Chinese criminal justice system. Another scholar, Yi Yanyou, argues that the central idea of moral education and character reform shows that the Chinese State regards criminals (suspects and defendants included) as people who are not free, for instance because they have been controlled by their passion, or have lost their willpower due to irritation or have been seduced by some temptation.[178] Therefore, the State believes that the system of corrections and punishments has the function of liberation from such bad influences.[179] This idea, according to Yi, suggests that the Chinese government holds the doctrine that 'the government [State] can compulsorily make citizens more free.'[180]

Yi argues that this doctrine confuses two different kinds of freedom – 'inner freedom' and 'individual freedom.'[181] Referring to Hayek's use of these concepts in 'the Constitution of Liberty,' Yi takes 'inner freedom' to mean that 'a person could act on his own deliberation, will, brief, and ration, instead of on impulse or passion, which are regarded as

---

[174] This right had not been provided for at the time of publication of Li's article, but it has been laid down in the 2012 CPL.

[175] Supra note 101, 134.

[176] Supra note 167, 139.

[177] Ibid.

[178] Yi Yanyou [易延友] *Chinese Criminal Procedure and Chinese Society* [*中国刑诉与中国社会*] Beijing, Peking University Press [北京大学出版社] 2010, 38.

[179] Yi Yanyou 'Can a Government Compulsorily Make Her Citizens More Free? Revisiting Non-judicial Detentions under the People's Republic's Administrative Regulations and Their Justifications' (2010) Vol. 2 *Tsinghua China Law Review* 398.

[180] Ibid. 398–9.

[181] Ibid.

irrational.'[182] Accordingly, a criminal suspect may be viewed by the State as an unfree person, in need of liberation from passions, impulses or other disturbing factors.[183] Thus, the government is entitled to take measures to liberate this unfree person.[184]

This type of freedom is essentially different from what Yi terms personal or individual liberty, which, according to Yi, asks for 'a person's choices or adherences without being compelled by others' will.'[185] Personal freedom or individual liberty is the underlying value of the Constitution.[186] Adopting the idea of 'inner freedom,' the Chinese State has deprived individuals of their personal or individual liberty, and thus has violated the Constitution.[187]

According to the view taken here, the 'inner freedom' approach at its core is an expression of authoritarianism. Yi's analysis resonates with Isaiah Berlin's famous account of 'two concepts of liberty' as developed in a lecture delivered in 1958, and Berlin's work can help us better understand the connection between thought reform and authoritarianism, and between authoritarianism and China's criminal justice system. In this work, Isaiah Berlin also discussed two liberties – 'positive liberty' and 'negative liberty.' According to Berlin, 'negative liberty' is concerned with the question of 'what is the area within which the subject – a person or group of persons – is or should be left to do or be what he is able to do or be, without interference by others.'[188] It is 'freedom from something.' According to Berlin, liberal thinkers hold that there should be 'frontiers of freedom' in society that no one (the government or public power or social control) is allowed to cross; in other words they support negative liberty.[189]

By contrast, 'positive liberty' deals with the question of 'what, or who is the source of control or interference that can determine someone to do, or be, this rather than that';[190] it can be usefully, if simplistically, understood as 'freedom to.' As also in Hayek and Yi, this conception of liberty uses the notion of a 'lower self' that can influence a higher self

---

[182] Ibid.

[183] Ibid.

[184] Ibid.

[185] Ibid.

[186] Ibid.

[187] Supra note 178, 41.

[188] Isaiah Berlin, *Four Essays on Liberty* Oxford, Oxford University Press 1969, 121–2.

[189] Ibid, 126, 164.

[190] Ibid, 132.

(through passions, desires, and so on), and implicitly assumes that the 'real' or 'ideal' or 'higher self' must be liberated to become its own 'master.'[191] Berlin is critical of this idea, arguing that it 'splits a person into two personalities' – 'the transcendent, dominant controller and the empirical bundle of desires and passions to be disciplined and brought to heel.'[192] The predominant controller can be further 'inflated into a super-personal entity,' ranging from a group to a state.[193]

Taking this insight and applying it to Yi's analysis, it appears that the problem with the rhetoric of 'liberation' of criminals and other targets of thought education is not merely that it justifies infringements of the rights of individual, negative liberty. In essence, Berlin's 'positive liberty' concept is a concept that can be employed by an authoritarian state seeking to justify its use of power in the name of 'liberating' its subjects.[194] Some other scholars have commented on the characteristic of the Chinese criminal justice system as an authoritarian system. For example, Børge Bakken discusses the reasons why the Chinese criminal justice system is linked so closely to the public, arguing that this is due to its significance in controlling people – by means of not only 'punishing the already deviant minority,' but also and mainly 'frightening (*zhenshe*) the majority.'[195] Yet, according to Bakken, these are just 'outward signs of control' (*zhibiao*), and 'moral and ideological education were the basis of control (*zhiben*).'[196] In a more vague and indirect way, Li Changsheng has also mentioned that the '*educational* trial' implied that the criminal process in China follows the 'family model,' which is based on the trust in state power or authorities and in the good morality of officials to educate the suspect/defendant and to change their 'bad' morality.[197]

6.2.4 Preliminary Conclusions

The emphasis on educating the suspect/defendant, present both in ordinary criminal justice processes and in criminal reconciliation, helps to explain why there is no 'presumption of innocence' in the practice of

[191] Ibid, 131–2.
[192] Ibid, 134.
[193] Ibid.
[194] Ibid, 133.
[195] Børge Bakken, *The Exemplary Society: Human Improvement, Social Control, And The Dangers Of Modernity In China* New York: Oxford University Press 2000, 87.
[196] Ibid.
[197] Supra note 101, 131.

criminal reconciliation. Absence of the suspect's/defendant's 'admission of guilt' (*renzui*) or 'repentance' (*huizui*) can be ignored as an impediment to carrying out 'criminal reconciliation' by the responsible official. The suspects/defendants were from the outset regarded as 'criminals' that needed to be educated and corrected through criminal reconciliation. This not only denied suspects and defendants access to a proper criminal justice process in which the presumption of innocence could be upheld and their rights could be protected. It also made it virtually impossible for their participation in criminal reconciliation to be genuinely voluntary. It is perhaps noteworthy in this context that, although Articles 277 to 279 of the 2012 CPL require the voluntary participation of the victim, they do not mention voluntary participation of the suspect or defendant as a procedural requirement for 'reconciliation' to be carried out. The 2012 CPL only requires their admission of guilt. While this absence of a requirement pertaining to suspects and defendants may better reflect the current reality of criminal procedure, it turns criminal reconciliation even more clearly into a mechanism in which the accused person's rights can be infringed.

What is worse, criminal reconciliation may serve a 'better' or more convenient channel for the officials and the State to conduct authoritarian education. This is because firstly, criminal reconciliation is formally based on the suspects'/defendant's admission of guilt, which, according to the government's ideology, indicates that they are 'bad' or 'unfree' people in need of education and reform. Secondly, as noted in Chapter 1, mediation since the Mao era has been characterized by mediators' exploring both parties' thoughts and using 'faults' in *both* parties' thoughts to facilitate mediation settlements.[198] Consequently, the authoritarian approach to education as discussed in this section can be delivered more easily and explicitly in criminal reconciliation processes compared to the normal trial process.

[198] Examples and detailed analysis can be seen in Gao Qicai [高其才] Zuo Ju [左炬] Huang Yuning [黄宇宁] *Political Judiciary: The People's Court of Hua County in 1949–1961* [*政治司法：1949–1961年的华县人民法院*] Beijing, Law Press [法律出版社] 2009, 560–68.

6.3 THE STATE'S FAILURE TO ENFORCE VICTIMS' CLAIMS TO COMPENSATION THROUGH CIVIL LITIGATION

As shown in Chapters 4 and 5, criminal reconciliation has become a programme with an exclusive focus on compensation: the ability to compensate was a compulsory pre-requirement for the suspect/defendant to enter into this programme and to obtain a lenient outcome. The suspect/defendant unable to afford paying compensation was simply excluded from the programme, even though all the other circumstances (i.e. admitting guilt or showing remorse) met the pre-requirements stipulated in the local regulations or guidelines.

Compensation was also the most important or even the only topic discussed in the criminal reconciliation meeting. For example, the juvenile victim of case no. nine in location A (a juvenile intentional injury case) said in the interview that he had not heard the other parties' apology in and after the criminal reconciliation meeting; what the meeting involved was merely bargaining over compensation between the two parties' parents. In some cases, the officials repeatedly held criminal reconciliation meetings merely to let the parties bargain over the compensation amount. In some other cases where the parties had already reached agreements privately, the official did not hold a criminal reconciliation meeting at all. Since compensation was the most crucial issue in the criminal reconciliation meeting, it seemed that the officials were inclined to think that there was no need for the defendant or parties to attend the meeting. For instance, as shown clearly in case no. five in location C (a juvenile robbery case), the criminal reconciliation meeting proceeded without the presence of the juvenile defendant, as he was still detained at that point.

Compensation also played a very significant role in the official's decision following the criminal reconciliation meeting. For example, as shown in Chapter 4, in the 'internal guideline' issued by the B district People's Court in location C, the amount of compensation was directly connected with how much reduction of sentence the defendant could get. Furthermore, according to some officials in the interview, in their views, the amount of compensation the suspect/defendant paid bore a close relationship with the degree of the victim's satisfaction and the suspect's/defendant's attitude towards the alleged crime as well as his/her harmfulness to society.

Criminal reconciliation can lead to infringement of the victim's rights stipulated in statutory laws. According to Article 77 of the 1996 CPL, 'if a victim has suffered material losses as a result of the defendant's criminal act, he has the right to file an incidental civil action during the course of the criminal proceeding.'[199] Article 36 of the PRC Criminal Law provides that 'if a victim has suffered economic losses as a result of a crime, the criminal shall, in addition to receiving a criminal punishment according to law, be sentenced to pay compensation for the economic losses in the light of the circumstances.'[200] As noted by Mike McConville *et al*, complaints and petitions after the trial result from the fact that the victim's rights to get civil compensation are not well protected.[201]

However, as observed by some scholars, the problems with enforcing civil litigation decisions have existed for more than 30 years,[202] and are regarded as a 'regular feature' of the Chinese judicial system.[203] In relying on the bait of sentence reduction or a decision not to prosecute to 'enforce' private law obligations owed by an alleged perpetrator to the victim, the State effectively forces the victim to trade his or her consent for what he/she has a legal right to already under private law (often, under tort law), namely, civil compensation. According to the view taken here, this allows the State to avoid tackling wider problems urgently awaiting resolution through judicial reform.

6.3.1 The Reasons Leading to the Problem with Enforceability

The reasons leading to this problem have been addressed a lot in academia. Many have noticed that the fundamental problem lies with the People's Court, or the system, not the defendants.

---

199 http://www.cecc.gov/pages/newLaws/criminalProcedureENG.php (last accessed on 9 March 2012).

200 Ibid.

201 Supra note 8, 199.

202 Tang Weijian [汤维建] 'The Rational Reflection on Solving the Problem with Enforcement: Focusing on the Establishment of An Independent Enforcement System [关于破解"执行难"的理性反思: 以执行体制的独立化构建为中心]' (2007) 5 *Study and Exploration* [*学习与探索*] 90.

203 Donald C. Clarke 'The Execution of Civil Judgments in China' in Stanley Lubman (ed) *China's Legal Reforms* Oxford, Oxford University Press 1996, 67. Yet there are reports saying that the enforcement problem is better than in even some rich countries like the U.S. and the U.K., ranking 20th out of 178 in the 'Doing Business 2008 Survey' by the World Bank. And the situation is becoming better along with the improvement of China's economy. See: Randall Peerenboom, He Xin 'Dispute Resolution in China: Patterns, Causes, and Prognosis' at http://www.fljs.org/uploads/documents/Peerenboom_He%20Xin%231%23.pdf (last accessed on 16 July 2012).

For instance, Donald Clarke argued that due to local protectionism and the lack of judicial independence, what the Court could do is very limited – as also discussed in the first section of this chapter – in China, the People's Court is always subject to various authorities including local government, Party committees and local People's Congresses.[204] Stanley Lubman also acknowledges this as the most serious obstacle to execution. Consequently, according to Lubman, the Courts sometimes have to 'solicit or seek instructions from local Party and governments' in execution.[205] In addition to the direct intervention or resistance from these powerful authorities, as further analysed by Clarke, it is very hard for the Court to get cooperation even from the banks in execution (especially banks located in places other than where the Courts are), as some local governments have issued rules 'forbidding the forcible transfer of funds from local parties to outside parties.'[206]

Chen Ruihua argues that it is very problematic to make the People's Court undertake 'dual tasks' of adjudication and execution.[207] Adjudication and execution are two powers different in nature – adjudication belongs to judicial power, which should be by nature passive and neutral, while execution belongs to administrative power, which asks for the Court's proactive efforts in taking enforcement measures on behalf of the creditor (namely, the victim in the civil litigation collateral to criminal cases).[208] Yet, as argued by Chen, making a judicial institution assume administrative work innately decides the powerlessness of the Court in enforcement.[209]

In the same vein, Tang Weijian also recognizes this flawed system in the Court as the main obstacle for enforcement. Tang says that the Constitution only empowers the People's Court to exercise jurisdiction, which means that all the other powers such as execution that the People's Court possesses should be subordinate to jurisdiction.[210] Thus, judges would input their efforts mainly to adjudication, not execution.[211] Donald Clarke also notices the subordinate position of execution in the People's

---

[204] Ibid, 71–2.
[205] Supra note 152, 268.
[206] Donald C. Clarke, supra note 203, 78–9.
[207] Supra note 165, 157.
[208] Ibid.
[209] Ibid, 159.
[210] Supra note 202.
[211] Yuan Jianping [袁建平] 'The Problem with Enforcement and Its Resolution from the Perspective of Judicial Justice [司法公正视角下的执行难及其矫治]' (2010) 7 *Journal of Socialist Theory Guide* [*理论导刊*] 68.

Court. According to Clarke, it is the tradition of the Chinese courts that execution is not their main concern, as demonstrated by the Court's internal organization:[212]

> The president [of the Court] takes charge of criminal adjudication, the vice-president takes charge of civil adjudication, and the vice-president's assistants take charge of execution. When the adjudication committee discussed cases … problems in executing judgments come last – if there is any time left.

Since the main reason leading to the enforceability problem lies with the Court, it is hard to imagine reconciliation and mediation resolving this problem. Actually, as indicated by Randall Peerenboom and He Xin, there have been studies showing that mediation agreements are not more easily enforced as compared to courts' sentences.[213] Moreover, mediation was sometimes used by the parties as a strategy to delay enforcement, which further aggravated the enforceability problem.[214]

It is noteworthy that, in 2014, some places started implementing a new system, called Criminal Reconciliation Aid Association,[215] which was reportedly a social organization established jointly by corporations and individuals under the authorities' instruction and management. According to the report, this association would sign an agreement with the suspect/defendant participating in the criminal reconciliation programme to lend them money, and the suspect/defendant would need to repay within an agreed period. Otherwise, the suspect/defendant will be held to civil accountability. This is propagandized by the authorities as a terrific way to address the unfairness problem with criminal reconciliation. Nevertheless, the vague standard of selecting some economically weak suspects/defendants to sign this agreement is in itself leading to more unfairness. Moreover, the voluntariness of corporations and individuals in contributing to this system imitated by the authorities, which still evades its responsibility with the State Compensation System, is highly dubious.

---

212 Supra note 203, 70.

213 Supra note 86.

214 Ibid.

215 In Chinese, 刑事和解救助协会. See e.g. the report of it in Jiangsu province 'Suzhou Closed 1,342 Criminal Reconciliation Cases [苏州办结刑事和解案一千三百四十二起]' by Ding Guofeng [丁国锋] and Ma Chao [马超] at http://js.legaldaily.com.cn/content/2014-07/15/content_5668159.htm?node=34636 (last accessed on 18 March 2015).

6.3.2 Preliminary Conclusions

To sum up the analysis above, the promotion of criminal reconciliation as a means of boosting the enforceability of tort and other private law claims held by victims against perpetrators of crime rests on a deeply flawed argument. The already-discussed problem of unfairness towards economically weak defendants resurfaces in the context of the 'enforceability' argument, only in reverse form. Indirectly, the enforceability argument suggests that responsibility for solving the problem of enforceability may be legitimately shifted from the State to the defendant. Criminal reconciliation may also lead to a risky confusion of the State's 'claim' to punish crime and private person's claims for compensation. Furthermore, while any claims the victims hold ought to be enforceable, in their full amount without any requirement for concessions such as may occur in a negotiation process, the fact that they may obtain even more than what they can get according to law, may make criminal reconciliation a mechanism that undermines and contravenes the suspects'/defendants' interests.

7. Conclusion

This book has examined 'criminal reconciliation' (*xingshi hejie*) as a 'new' criminal process. There are three main findings.

First, at the level of institutional design according to statutory law and official regulations, the roles given to officials in the Public Security Bureaus, the procuratorates and the courts, parties, and lawyers (in the relatively rare cases in which they are involved) in the process of criminal reconciliation are different when compared to their roles in the normal criminal process.

The procedure of criminal reconciliation designed in the local regulations and guidelines, and now in Articles 277 to 279 of the 2012 CPL, suggests that criminal reconciliation is intended to be a non-adversarial process. Criminal reconciliation is supposed to be based primarily on communication between the parties, and to take place only once a suspect or defendant has admitted guilt, so that the principle that the guilt of the suspect can be determined only through a trial, which is supposed to play a dominant role in the ordinary criminal process, can be abandoned. Since the premise of criminal reconciliation is the suspect's/defendant's admission of guilt, education and correction of this 'guilty' participant become the focus of the reconciliation process. The criminal reconciliation procedure purports to give the parties a dominant role in the criminal reconciliation process, and officials are expected to respect the voluntary nature of their participation. Special rules purportedly imposing restrictions on public power under the more adversarial ordinary process do not apply in criminal reconciliation, since the officials are supposed to be secondary to the parties. The role of criminal defence lawyers, too, is virtually eliminated. Officials are mainly expected to *facilitate* the parties' communication and reconciliation. Such a change in the roles of the parties and officials in criminal reconciliation, compared to the adversarial adjudication process, is officially claimed to be this process's main advantage. It is purported to help bring 'closure' to criminal cases and to satisfy both parties, a result unlikely to be reached, and not aimed at, in the normal criminal process.

Second, the empirical study presented in this book shows that while the formal roles of the actors in criminal reconciliation are indeed different from the roles of actors in the ordinary criminal process according to this process's institutional design, differences are not what procedural law, regulations, guidelines and official claims would lead one to expect. In other words, while criminal reconciliation is supposed to be widely different from the normal criminal process 'on paper,' as elaborated in Chapter 6, a certain degree of convergence between criminal reconciliation and the ordinary criminal justice process can be observed in its operation.

In practice, and despite the promise of the formal procedure, the officials of the criminal justice system, not the parties in criminal cases, still dominate the process and control its outcome. The great discretion and unrestricted power given to the officials in this process do not serve the purported function of merely enabling and facilitating the parties' reconciliation based on the voluntariness of their participation. On the contrary, as shown in Chapters 4 and 5, the discretion and unrestricted power can facilitate official abuse of power to infringe the parties' voluntariness and rights in criminal reconciliation. Local regulations and guidelines governing the criminal reconciliation procedure, which are designed to protect the parties' voluntary participation, can be simply discarded by some prosecutors and judges. The study has moreover shown institutional reasons motivating officials to abandon the rules, including in particular their desire to meet official performance evaluation criteria.

The parties are further marginalized in criminal reconciliation processes. As shown in Chapter 5, the parties become tools for the officials to fulfil their own tasks as defined by the internal assessment system. Officials in charge of criminal reconciliation operate under outcome-oriented pressures identified in Chapter 6, and have incentives to coerce the parties to 'reconcile.' In this case, as observed by Carl Minzner, 'alternative dispute resolution' mechanisms such as mediation and reconciliation are not truly an 'alternative to litigation'; rather, they are conducted under the condition that 'litigation channels are shut.'[1] Violations of the suspect's/defendant's right to be presumed innocent until proven guilty, and the principle of voluntary participation by all parties to a criminal process, and the parties' 'legally protected' interests may be obscured by the very fact that what is taking place is styled as 'reconciliation' or 'mediation,' and purports to 'empower the parties to resolve disputes.' This designation of the procedure as a voluntary,

1 Carl F. Minzner 'China's Turn Against Law' (2011) Vol. LIX No. 4 *The American Journal of Comparative Law* 963.

parties-led one therefore easily leads one to ignore the fact that the parties are still weak in the face of public power, and that power can still easily infringe the parties' voluntariness in the process of reconciliation and mediation. Given the conflict between the formal rules in the books and the informal organizational rules related to audits and outcome targets, this study reinforces the observations of other researchers that informal rules are readily given primary importance in practice notwithstanding that the outcomes achieved are reported in terms of compliance with the formal rules.[2]

The change of role of any lawyer, who becomes involved in this process, as shown in Chapter 5, further facilitates the infringement of individual rights by public power. So far as the role of lawyers is concerned, there is no institutional expectation of lawyers becoming involved in the process at all, and it appears that lawyers play a role in only a small percentage of cases. Since the two parties are expected to come together for a mutual goal – reaching a reconciliation agreement with each other – and the officials are 'deemed' to play the role of friendly facilitators in this process, any lawyers hired by either party are normally expected by the officials to act as their 'assistants' to facilitate the 'reconciliation' process. In some cases, indeed, as shown in Chapter 5, the lawyers are fully aware that their clients' rights and 'legally protected' interests would be harmed in criminal reconciliation. Yet in so far as they believe that their clients' interests as to getting a just (or good and satisfactory) result for the case would also be harmed if they refused the officials' 'offer' of criminal reconciliation, they have reasons for considering criminal reconciliation a comparatively better option for their clients. A lawyer quoted in Chapter 5 commented aptly that it was paramount to 'maintain a good relationship' with the officials to allow their clients to get 'good results' in the criminal reconciliation process.[3] This remark not only further testifies to the plight the lawyers were facing, but also to the weakness of the parties and the strength of public power in this process. In all these characteristics, criminal reconciliation practice replicates difficulties also affecting the ordinary, supposedly adversarial criminal justice process, with the further disadvantage of reducing the role of lawyers, who have no clearly defined role in criminal

---

[2] Amitai Etzioni *A Comparative Analysis of Complex Organizations* New York, Free Press of Glencoe, 1975; Malcolm M. Feeley 'Two Models of the Criminal Justice System: An Organizational Perspective' (1973) Vol. 7 No. 3 *Law & Society Review* 407.

[3] Lawyer Z's account in Chapter 5.

reconciliation and, indeed, do not even get a mention in the relevant rules of the CPL.

Third, in practice, criminal reconciliation operates unfairly in respect of economically weak parties. This unfairness is mainly due to an almost exclusive focus on compensation. This focus on monetary compensation not only leads to unfairness among suspects/defendants, but also results in criminal reconciliation failing to address the victims' needs through obtaining psychological redress arising from the 'crime.' Coerced by the public power to participate in such a process, victims are in fact re-victimized. The feelings of anger, hurt or helplessness some interviewees expressed indicate that criminal reconciliation does not really bring about 'closure' in their cases. Instead, this 'reconciliation' process mainly served the purpose of suppressing conflict at the cost of individual rights.

In sum, criminal reconciliation in practice does not operate according to its institutional design in the way that many official, as well as academic assessments of this mechanism, might lead one to expect. Instead of empowering the parties, it is actually controlled by the officials. Instead of being based on the 'voluntariness of the parties,' it is based on coercion (by public power) and rights' violations. Instead of a 'panacea' for bringing about 'closure' and 'harmony,' it actually suppresses conflicts.

In the socio-legal scholarship, Malcolm Feeley comes up with 'Two Models of the Criminal Justice System.' Viewing the criminal justice system as an institutionalized organization requiring the actors (i.e. the victim, the suspect/defendant and the judicial officers) to 'follow highly defined rules' in order to reach a common goal of 'processing arrests,' Feeley discusses two models in depicting and explaining this system – the goal model and the functional-systems model.[4] The goal model, according to Feeley, adopts an objective approach to 'contrast observed behaviors with the formally stated goals' in assessing the effectiveness of the criminal justice system.[5] Criticizing this model as ignoring other equally important factors shaping the actors' behaviours, Feeley applauds the functional-systems model in terms of taking into account causes and various conditions leading to behaviours not adhering to those formally stated goals, and thereof argues that it is just unreasonable and unrealistic to expect the actors' adherence.[6]

---

[4] Malcolm M. Feeley, supra note 2, 408.
[5] Ibid, 411.
[6] Ibid, 421.

Analysing the causes and conditions of the actors' behaviours in criminal reconciliation like the functional-systems model though, the author tries to take a different approach – despite an acknowledgment of these factors, the discussions of this book further question the actors' behaviours in the sense of injustice, unfairness, and violations of the individual rights in criminal reconciliation, and argue that such a shift of judicial reform, leading to those violations and results, should not be a proper route to take. The criminal justice system should be reformed to eliminate the institutional obstacles impeding the compliance with regulations and rules protecting the parties' rights and access to justice.

How the local regulations and guidelines operate under the 2012 CPL might be a question for further study. In any case, considering the prevalence of contradictory institutional expectations and 'hidden rules' in Chinese judicial practice and the other problems with the Chinese criminal justice system, as discussed in Chapter 6, without changes to the general system and those more fundamental problems, the future operation of criminal reconciliation is unlikely to differ substantially from the practice shown in this book.

Through showing the problems with criminal reconciliation, this research sheds some light on the heated debate over judicial reforms in China since the 2000s. As discussed in Chapter 1, the debate mainly revolves around whether or not the current judicial reforms that are characterized by the wider use of mediation and reconciliation in the judiciary are a proper way 'with Chinese characteristics' to address social conflicts and build a 'harmonious society.' The author's research findings imply that this judicial reform is unlikely to produce the positive effects predicted. The so-called 'harmonious judiciary' to be built through increased use of mediation and reconciliation mechanisms may rather be a type of judiciary based on infringement of the parties' rights.

The new leadership under Xi Jinping has announced its commitment to building 'the rule of law *with Chinese characteristics*' at the 4th Plenary Session of the 18th Central Committee of the Chinese Communist Party in 2014, in the context of tightening its control of the judiciary and blatant suppression of civil society though. The author's research on criminal reconciliation may present a microcosm of this big picture – the ruling Party tries to resort to tradition and its alleged uniqueness in an attempt to maintain its authoritarian rule, while on the other hand, it tries to cover it up with terms such as 'rule of law' facing citizens' increasing awareness of rights and the rule of law elements. However, this paradox, bringing about more contradictions and dissatisfaction in society, will ultimately endanger the Party's authoritarian rule.

Appendix

Table A.1 Sentencing normalization form of the Criminal Division of B District People's Court [in Xi'an]

Case: No.:

Relevant [personal] information	Name	Gender	Date of birth
	Ethnicity	Household registration	Education level
	Time of criminal detention	Time of arrest	Previous criminal record
Brief description of case			
[Possible] sentence [for offence(s) charged] stipulated in the Criminal Law (*fading xing*)			

Sentence after considering the harm caused by the crime to society (*ji zhun xing*)	Crime					
	Minimum stipulated sentence					
	Sentence without taking into account relevant circumstances (*ji zhun xing*)					
Sentence announced (*xuangao xing*)	Adjustment in accordance with the circumstances affecting sentencing (*liangxing qingjie*)	Circumstances affecting sentencing	Degree of sentence reduction in accordance with provisions of the Supreme People's Court	Degree of sentence reduction as confirmed by the People's Court of B district	Degree of sentence increase in accordance with provisions of the Supreme People's Court	Degree of sentence increase as confirmed by the People's Court of B district
	Proposed sentence to be announced					
	Sentence factually announced					
Conviction						
Any other issues for clarification						

Collegial panel member: Person in charge:

Date of discussion:

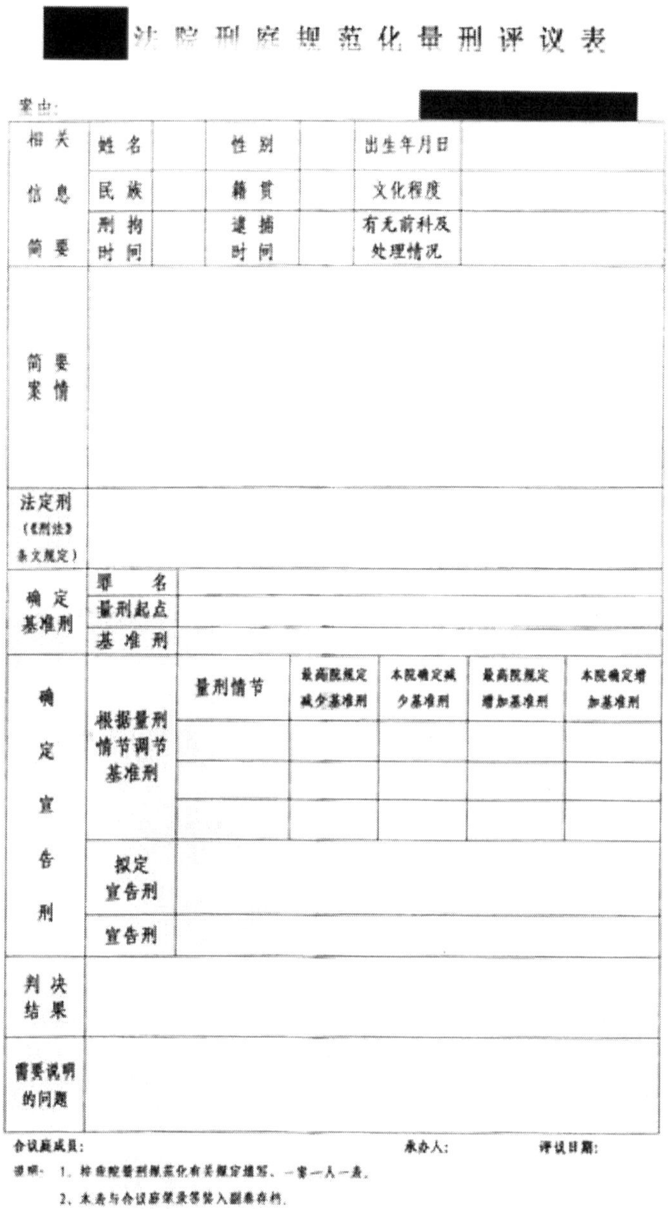

[redacted]法院刑庭规范化量刑评议表

案由： [redacted]

相关信息简要	姓名		性别		出生年月日	
	民族		籍贯		文化程度	
	刑拘时间		逮捕时间		有无前科及处理情况	
简要案情						
法定刑（《刑法》条文规定）						
确定基准刑	罪名					
	量刑起点					
	基准刑					
确定宣告刑	根据量刑情节调节基准刑	量刑情节	最高院规定减少基准刑	本院确定减少基准刑	最高院规定增加基准刑	本院确定增加基准刑
	拟定宣告刑					
	宣告刑					
判决结果						
需要说明的问题						

合议庭成员： 承办人： 评议日期：

说明：1、按本院量刑规范化有关规定填写，一案一人一表。

2、本表与合议庭笔录等装入副卷存档。

Figure A.1 Sentencing normalization form of the Criminal Division of B District People's Court [in Xi'an]

Bibliography

LAWS AND REGULATIONS

Laws

Law of the People's Republic of China on Guarding State Secrets [中华人民共和国保守国家秘密法] (2010)
Law of the People's Republic of China on Public Security Administration Punishments [中华人民共和国行政处罚法] (1996)
Law of the People's Republic of China on Road Traffic Safety [中华人民共和国道路交通安全法] (2003)
The Civil Servant Law of the People's Republic of China [中华人民共和国公务员法] (2005)
The General Principle of the Civil Law of the People's Republic of China [中华人民共和国民法通则] (1986)
The Organic Law of the People's Courts of the People's Republic of China [中华人民共和国法院组织法] (2006)
The Organic Law of the People's Procuratorates of the People's Republic of China [中华人民共和国检察院组织法] (1983)
The Organic Law of the Urban Residents Committees of the People's Republic of China [中华人民共和国城市居民委员组织法] (1989)
The Organic Law of the Villagers' Committees of the People's Republic of China [中华人民共和国村民委员会组织法] (2010)
The PRC Constitution [中华人民共和国宪法] (2004)
The PRC Criminal Law [中华人民共和国刑法] (1997)
The PRC Criminal Procedure Law [中华人民共和国刑事诉讼法] (1996) and the newly revised 2012 version
The PRC Judges Law [中华人民共和国法官法] (2001)
The PRC Lawyer Law [中华人民共和国律师法] (2007)
The PRC Prison Law [中华人民共和国监狱法] (1994)
The PRC Prosecutors Law [中华人民共和国检察官法] (2001)

Administrative Legislation

Decision of the State Council on Re-education Through Labor [国务院关于劳动教养问题的决定] (1957)

The Ministry of Public Security's Trial Methods for Implementing Re-education Through Labor [国务院关于转发公安部制定的劳动教养试行办法的通知] (1982)
The Organic Regulation of the Sub-district Office [城市街道办事处组织条例] (1954)
The PRC Detention House Regulation [拘留所条例] (2012)
The Regulation on Foundation Administration [基金会管理条例] (2004)
The Regulations on Registration and Administration of Social Organizations [社会团体登记管理条例] (1998)
The Temporary Regulations on Registration and Administration of Non-profit Non-government Organizations [民办非企业单位登记管理暂行条例] (1998)

Department Rules

Opinions on Improving the Establishment of Urban Community issued by the Ministry of Civil Affairs [民政部关于在全国推进城市社区建设的意见] (2000)
Provisions on the Handling Procedures for Road Traffic Accidents [道路交通事故处理程序规定] (2008)
Provisions on the Procedure of Handling Traffic Accidents [交通事故处理程序规定] (2009)

Judicial Interpretations

Opinions of the Supreme People's Procuratorate on the Handling of Minor Criminal Cases when the Parties Have Reached Reconciliation [最高人民检察院关于办理当事人达成和解的轻微刑事案件的若干意见] (2010)
Opinions on Fully Implementing the Criminal Policy of Combining Severity with Leniency in Procuratorial Work issued by the Supreme People's Procuratorate [最高人民检察院关于在检察工作中贯彻宽严相济刑事司法政策的若干意见] (2006)
Opinions on Further Implementing the Working Principle of 'Giving Priority to Mediation and Combining Mediation with Judgment' [最高人民法院关于进一步贯彻'调解优先、调判结合'工作原则的若干意见] (2010)
Opinions on Implementing the Criminal Policy of Combining Severity with Leniency [关于贯彻宽严相济刑事政策的若干意见] (2010)

Opinions on Reforming and Improving the Judicial Committee of the People's Court issued by the Supreme People's Court [最高人民法院关于改革和完善人民法院审判委员会制度的实施意见] (2010)

Opinions on Reforming and Improving the Judicial Committee System of the People's Court [关于改革和完善人民法院审判委员会制度的实施意见] (2010)

Opinions on Several Issues concerning the Regulation of Sentencing Recommendation (Trial Implementation) [关于规范量刑程序若干问题的意见(试行)] (2010)

Provisions on Several Issues Concerning the Civil Mediation Work of the People's Court [关于人民法院民事调解工作若干问题的规定] (2004)

Several Opinions of the Supreme People's Procuratorate on Handling Petty Criminal Cases Where the Parties Have Reached Reconciliation issued by the Supreme People's Procuratorate [最高人民检察院关于办理当事人达成和解的轻微刑事案件的若干意见] (2011)

The Criminal Procedural Regulation of the People's Procuratorates [人民检察院刑事诉讼规则] (1999)

The Judicial Interpretation on CPL issued by the Supreme People's Court [最高人民法院关于执行《中华人民共和国刑事诉讼法》若干问题的解释] (1998)

The Organic Regulation of the Procuratorial Committee of the People's Procuratorate [人民检察院检察委员会组织条例] (2008)

The Supreme People's Court, the Supreme People's Procuratorate, the Ministry of Public Security, the Ministry of Justice: Opinions on the Nationwide Trial Implementation of Community Correction [最高人民法院、最高人民检察院、公安部、司法部关于在全国试行社区矫正工作的意见] (2009)

Documents of the Chinese Communist Party

Constitution of Communist Party of China [中国共产党章程] (2007)

Opinions on Deeply Promoting the Resolution of Social Conflicts, the Innovation of Social Management, and the Fairness and Integrity of Law Enforcement issued by the CCP Central Political and Judicial Committee and the CCP Central Leading Group of Stability Maintaining Work [中央政法委、中央维护稳定工作领导小组关于深入推进社会矛盾化解、社会管理制度、公正廉洁执法的意见] (2010)

BOOKS

Bakken, Børge *The Exemplary Society: Human Improvement, Social Control and the Dangers of Modernity in China* New York, Oxford University Press 2000

Berlin, Isaiah *Four Essays on Liberty* Oxford, Oxford University Press 1969

Bian, Jianlin [卞建林] Wang, Li [王立] (eds) *Criminal Reconciliation and an Alternative Procedure* [*刑事和解与程序分流*] Beijing, The Chinese People's Public Security University Press [中国人民公安大学出版社] 2010

Braithwaite, John *Crime, Shame and Reintegration* Cambridge, Cambridge University Press 1989

Cai, Guoqin [蔡国芹] *Research on Criminal Mediation System* [*刑事调解制度研究*] Beijing, The Chinese People's Public Security University Press [中国人民公安大学出版社] 2010

Chen, Ruihua [陈瑞华] *Criminal Proceedings: The Chinese Model* [*刑事诉讼的中国模式*] Beijing, Law Press [法律出版社] 2008

Chen, Ruihua [陈瑞华] *Justice Can Be Seen* [*看得见的正义*] Beijing, China Law Press [中国法制出版社] 2000

Chen, Ruihua [陈瑞华] *Leading Issues in Criminal Proceedings* [*刑事诉讼的前沿问题*] Beijing, China Renmin University Press [中国人民大学出版社] 2005

Chen, Shihe [陈世和] *The Embarrassment of Law* [*法律的尴尬*] Beijing, Law Press [法律出版社] 2011

Cohen, Jerome A. *The Criminal Process in the People's Republic of China 1949–1963: An Introduction* Cambridge, MA, Harvard University Press 1968

Di, Xiaohua [狄小华] Liu, Zhiwei [刘志伟] (eds) *The Theory and Practice of Restorative Justice in Juvenile Cases* [*恢复性少年司法理论与实践*] Beijing, People Publishing [群众出版社] 2007

Elrod, Preston, Ryder, R. Scott *Juvenile Justice: A Social, Historical, and Legal Perspective* Sudbury, Massachusetts, Jones and Bartlett Publishers 2005

Etzioni, Amitai *A Comparative Analysis of Complex Organizations: On Power, Involvement, and Their Correlates* New York, Free Press 1975

Fan, Yu [范愉] *Research on Alternative Dispute Resolution* [*非诉讼纠纷解决机制研究*] Beijing, Renmin University of China Publishing [中国人民大学出版社] 2000

Fan, Yu [范愉] *The Theory and Practice of Dispute Resolution* [*纠纷解决的理论与实践*] Beijing, Tsinghua University Press [清华大学出版社] 2007

Gao, Qicai [高其才] Zuo, Ju [左炬] Huang, Yuning [黄宇宁] *Political Judiciary: The People's Court of Hua County in 1949–1961* [*政治司法：1949–1961年的华县人民法院*] Beijing, Law Press [法律出版社] 2009

Ge, Lin [葛琳] *On Criminal Reconciliation* [*刑事和解研究*] Beijing, The Chinese People's Public Security University Press [中国人民公安大学出版社] 2008

Jiang, Shigong [强世功] *Punishment and the Rule of Law: The Emergence of the Modern Rule of Law (1976–1981)* [*惩罚与法治: 当代法治的兴起 (1976–1981)*] Beijing, Law Press [法律出版社] 2009

Leng, Shao-chuan, Chiu, Hungdah *Criminal Justice in Post-Mao China: Analysis and Documents* Albany, State University of New York Press 1985

Li, Jianshu [李剑书] 'Three Bottle-necks in the Establishment of the Criminal Reconciliation System in China [中国刑事和解制度构建的三重瓶颈]' in Bian Jianlin [卞建林] and Wang Li [王立] (eds) *Criminal Reconciliation and an Alternative Procedure* [*刑事和解与程序分流*] Beijing, The Chinese People's Public Security University Press [中国人民公安大学出版社] 2010

Liebmann, Marian *Restorative Justice: How it Works* London and Philadelphia, Jessica Kingsley Publishers 2007

Lubman, Stanley B. *Bird in a Cage: Legal Reform in China after Mao* Stanford, Stanford University Press 1999

Ma, Mingliang [马明亮] *Negotiated Justice: A New Procedural Idea* [*协商性司法：一种新程序主义理念*] Beijing, Law Press [法律出版社] 2007

Marshall, Tony F. *Restorative Justice: An Overview* Minnesota, Centre for Restorative Justice & Mediation 1998

McConville, Mike *et al Criminal Justice in China: An Empirical Inquiry* Cheltenham, UK and Northampton, MA, USA, Edward Elgar Publishing 2011

Peerenboom, Randall *China's Long March Toward Rule of Law* Cambridge, Cambridge University Press 2002

Sharp, Susan *Restorative Justice: A Vision for Healing and Change* Alberta, Edmonton Victim Offender Mediation Society 1998

Song, Yinghui [宋英辉] *Empirical Research on Criminal Reconciliation* [*刑事和解实证研究*] Beijing, Peking University Press [北京大学出版社] 2010

Song, Yinghui [宋英辉] Yuan, Jinbiao [袁金彪] (eds) *The Theory and Practice of Criminal Reconciliation in China* [*我国刑事和解的理论与实践*] Beijing, Peking University Press [北京大学出版社] 2009

Sun, Qin [孙勤] *An Analysis of the Values of Victim–Offender Reconciliation* [*刑事和解价值分析*] Beijing, The Chinese People's Public Security University Press [中国人民公安大学出版社] 2009

The Central Commission of Comprehensive Governing [中央社会治安综合治理委员会办公室] (ed) *Strategies for the Long-term Peace and Stability* [*长治久安之策*] Beijing, Chang'an Press [中国长安出版社] 2009

Trevaskes, Susan *Courts and Criminal Justice in Contemporary China* U.K., Lexington Books 2007

Van Ness, Daniel W., Morris, Allison, Maxwell, Gabrielle 'Introducing Restorative Justice' in Morris, Allison, Maxwell, Gabrielle (eds) *Restorative Justice for Juveniles* Oxford, Hart Publishing 2003

Wang, James C.F. *Contemporary Chinese Politics* New Jersey, Prentice Hall 1995

Wang, Yijun [王一俊] *Criminal Reconciliation* [*刑事和解*] Beijing, China University of Politics and Law Publishing [中国政法大学出版社] 2010

Wu, Hongyu [武红羽] *The Process of Judicial Mediation: From the Perspective of the Relationship Between Judicial Mediation and Judicial Realm* [*司法调解的生产过程: 以司法调解与司法场域的关系为视角*] Beijing, Law Press [法律出版社] 2010

Wu, Xiaofeng [武小凤] *Conflict and Compromise: On Criminal Reconciliation* [*冲突与对接: 刑事和解刑法制度研究*] Beijing, The Chinese People's Public Security University Press [中国人民公安大学出版社] 2008

Wu, Zhiming [吴志明] Lin, Huabin [林化宾] Wu, Junying [吴军营] (eds) *The General Mediation System: The Eastern Experience of Responding to Social Conflicts* [*大调解: 应对社会矛盾凸显的东方经验*] Beijing Law Press [法律出版社] 2010

Ye, Jinghuan [野静环] *A Rewarding Trip: Report on Life in the Beijing Transferring Institution of Reeducation Through Labor* [*不虚此行: 北京劳教调遣处纪实*] (unpublished draft on file with author)

Yi, Yanyou [易延友] *Chinese Criminal Procedure and Chinese Society* [*中国刑诉与中国社会*] Beijing, Peking University Press [北京大学出版社] 2010

Zehr, Howard *Changing Lenses* Ontario, Herald Press, 1990

BOOK CHAPTERS

Braithwaite, John, Mugford, Stephen 'Conditions of Successful Reintegration Ceremonies: Dealing with Juvenile Offenders' in Declan Roche (ed) *Restorative Justice* England, Dartmouth Publishing Company 2004

Brown, Jennifer Gerarda 'The Use of Mediation to Resolve Criminal Cases: A Procedural Critique' in Declan Roche (ed) *Restorative Justice* London, Ashgate Publishing 2004

Chen, Guoqing [陈国庆], Chen, Ruihua [陈瑞华], Wang, Jiangcheng [汪建成], Zhang, Zhiming [张志铭] *et al* 'Theoretical Basis of Criminal Reconciliation [刑事和解的理论基础]' in Song Yinghui [宋英辉] Yuan Jinbiao [袁金彪] (eds) *The Theory and Practice of Criminal Reconciliation in China* [*我国刑事和解的理论与实践*] Beijing, Peking University Press [北京大学出版社] 2009

Chen, Qi [陈颀] 'The Incentive Mechanism of "Reducing Punishment with Money" ["赔钱减刑" 的激励机制]' in Su Li [苏力] (ed) *Law and Social Sciences* [*法律和社会科学*] Beijing, Law Press [法律出版社] 2009

Chen, Ruihua [陈瑞华] 'Theoretical Reflection on Detention [未决羁押的理论反思]' in Chen Ruihua [陈瑞华] (ed) *An Empirical Study of the Detention System* [*未决羁押制度的实证研究*] Beijing, Peking University Press [北京大学出版社] 2004

Cho, Li-Fung 'The Emergence of China's Watchdog Reporting' in David Bandurski, Martin Hala (eds) *Investigative Journalism in China* Hong Kong, Hong Kong University Press 2010

Clarke, Donald C. 'The Execution of Civil Judgments in China' in Stanley Lubman (ed) *China's Legal Reforms* Oxford, Oxford University Press 1996

Clarke, Donald C., Feinerman, James V. 'Antagonistic Contradictions: Criminal Law and Human Rights in China' in Stanley Lubman (ed) *China's Legal Reforms* Oxford, Oxford University Press 1996

Di, Xiaohua [狄小华] 'Restorative Justice and Criminal Mediation [复合正义和刑事调解]' in Wang Ping [王平] (ed) *Forum on Restorative Justice* [*恢复性司法论坛*] Vol. 2005 Beijing, Qunzhong Publishing [群众出版社] 2005

Fu, Hualing 'Challenging Authoritarianism Through Law' in Jean-Philippe Béja, Fu Hualing, Eva Pils (eds) *Liu Xiaobo, Charter 08 and the Challenges of Political Reform in China* Hong Kong, Hong Kong University Press 2012

Fu, Hualing, Gullen, Richard 'From Mediatory to Adjudicatory Justice: The Limits of Civil Justice Reform in China' in Margaret Y.K. Woo and

Mary E. Gallagher (eds) *Chinese Justice: Civil Dispute Revolution in China* Cambridge, Cambridge University Press 2011
Hao, Yinzhong [郝银钟] 'On the First Instance Trial [第一审程序论]' in Zhang Jun [张军] Hao Yinzhong [郝银钟] (eds) *刑事诉讼庭审专题研究* [*Research on the Criminal Trial*] Beijing, Renmin University of China Press [中国人民大学出版社] 2005
Horwitz, Allan V. 'Diversion in the Juvenile Justice System' in Günter Albrecht, Wolfgang Ludwig-Mayerhofer (eds) *Diversion and Informal Social Control* Berlin, Walter de Gruyter 1995
Hoyle, Carolyn, Young, Richard 'Restorative Justice: Assessing the Prospects and Pitfalls' in Mike McConville and Geoffrey Wilson (eds) *The Handbook of the Criminal Justice Process* Oxford, Oxford University Press 2002
Kang, Huaiyu [康怀宇] 'The Current Situation and the Future: An Investigation on People's Mediation from the Microscopic Perspective [现状与前瞻: 人民调解的微观考察]' in Zuo Weimin [左卫民] (ed) *Dispute Resolution in the Age of Transformation* [*变革时代的纠纷解决*] Beijing, 北京大学出版社 [Peking University Press] 2007
Li, Site [李斯特] 'The Context of the People's Judiciary and the Mass Line [人民司法群众路线的谱系]' in Su Li [苏力] (ed) *Law and Social Science* [*法律和社会科学*] *Vol. 1* Beijing, Law Press [法律出版社] 2006
Liu, Guangan [刘广安] Li, Cunpeng [李存捧] 'People's Mediation and Rights Protection [民间调解与权利保护]' in Xia, Yong [夏勇] (ed) *Towards an Age of Rights* [*走向权利的时代*] Beijing, China University of Political Science and Law Press [中国政法大学出版社] 1995
McCold, Paul 'Primary Restorative Justice Practice' in Allison Morris, Gabrielle Maxwell (eds) *Restorative Justice for Juveniles* Oxford, Hart Publishing 2003
Palmer, Michael 'The Revival of Mediation in the People's Republic of China: (1) Extra-judicial Mediation' in W.E. Butler (ed) *Yearbook on Socialist Legal Systems* New York, Transnational Publishers 1987
Pils, Eva 'The Dislocation of the Chinese Human Rights Movement' in Stacy Mosher, Patrick Poon (eds) *A Sword and a Shield: China's Human Rights Lawyers* Hong Kong, China Human Rights Lawyers Concern Group 2009
Research Group of 'Empirical Study of Restorative Justice and the Reform of the PRC Criminal Procedure Law' ['恢复性司法与中国刑事诉讼法改革实证研究' 课题组] 'An Overview of the Current Implementation of Criminal Reconciliation in China [我国刑事和解适用现状之概览]' in Song Yinghui [宋英辉] Yuan Jinbiao [袁金彪] (eds) *The Theory and Practice of Criminal Reconciliation in China*

[*我国刑事和解的理论与实践*] Beijing, Peking University Press [北京大学出版社] 2009

Song, Yinghui [宋英辉] 'Empirical Report on the Implementation of Criminal Reconciliation by the People's Procuratorates in Four Provisions [四省检察机关适用刑事和解调查报告]' in Song Yinghui [宋英辉] (ed) *Empirical Research on Criminal Reconciliation* [*刑事和解实证研究*] Beijing, Peking University Press [北京大学出版社] 2010

The People's Procuratorate of Wuxi City in Jiangsu Province [江苏省无锡市人民检察院] 'A Summary of Restorative Justice Work in The People's Procuratorates of Wuxi City [无锡市检察机关恢复性司法工作总结]' in Song Yinghui [宋英辉] Yuan Jinbiao [袁金彪] (eds) *The Theory and Practice of Criminal Reconciliation in China* [*我国刑事和解的理论与实践*] Beijing, Peking University Press [北京大学出版社] 2009

The Research Office of the People's Procuratorate in Jiangsu Province [江苏省检察院研究室] The Research Office of Wuxi City People's Procuratorate [无锡市检察院研究室] 'Innovating Judicial Ideas and Exploring Criminal Reconciliation [创新司法理念探索刑事和解]' in Bian Jianlin [卞建林] Wang Li [王立] (eds) *Criminal Reconciliation and an Alternative Procedure* [*刑事和解与程序分流*] Beijing, The Chinese People's Public Security University Press [中国人民公安大学出版社] 2010

Walgrave, Lode 'Imposing Restoration Instead of Inflicting Pain: Reflection on the Judicial Reaction to Crime' in Andrew von Hirsch, Julian Roberts, Anthony E. Bottoms, Kent Roach, Mara Schiff (eds), *Restorative Justice & Criminal Justice: Competing or Reconcilable Paradigms?* Oxford, Hart Publishing 2003

Walgrave, Lode 'On Restoration and Punishment: Favorable Similarities and Fortunate Differences' in A. Morris and G. Maxwell (eds), *Restorative Justice for Juveniles* Oxford, Hart Publishing 2001

Wu, Jianxin [吴建新] 'Confusions and Thoughts during the Transplant of Restorative Justice in China [恢复性司法中国化中的困惑与思考]' in Wang Ping [王平] (ed) *Forum on Restorative Justice* [*恢复性司法论坛*] *Vol. 2007* Beijing, China Procuratorial Press [中国检察出版社] 2007

Zehr, Howard, Mika, Harry 'Fundamental Concepts of Restorative Justice' in Declan Roche (ed) *Restorative Justice* England, Dartmouth Publishing Company 2004

Zhang, Zhaoxia [张朝霞] Xie, Caineng [谢财能] 'Criminal Reconciliation: Misunderstanding and Clarification [刑事和解: 误读与澄清]' in Bian Jianlin [卞建林] Wang Li [王立] (eds) *Criminal Reconciliation and an Alternative Procedure* [*刑事和解与程序分流*] Beijing, The

Chinese People's Public Security University Press [中国人民公安大学出版社] 2010

JOURNAL ARTICLES

Belkin, Ira 'China's Tortuous Path Toward Ending Torture in Criminal Investigations' (2011) Vol. 24 No. 2 *Columbia Journal of Asian Law*

Cai, Guoshan [蔡国山] 'Who to Supervise the People's Procuratorate? On the Improvement of the People's Supervision System [谁来监督检察院？：兼论人民监督员制度之完善]' (2011) 4 *Law and Economy* [*法制与经济*]

Chen, Ruihua [陈瑞华] 'An Initial Research on the Malfunction of Criminal Procedure [刑事程序失灵问题的初步研究]' (2007) 6 *China Legal Science* [*中国法学*]

Chen, Ruihua [陈瑞华] 'Private Cooperation in Criminal Proceedings: The Emergence of Criminal Reconciliation in China [刑事诉讼的私力合作模式： 刑事和解在中国的兴起]' (2006) 5 *China Legal Science* [*中国法学*]

Chen, Weidong [陈卫东] 'Several Opinions on Criminal Reconciliation [关于刑事和解的几点看法]' (2009) 3 *Chinese Laws* [*中国法律*]

Chen, Yufan [陈玉范] Qu, Guangchen [屈广臣], 'Thoughts on "Private Resolution" ["私了" 问题的法律思考]' (1995) 1 *Modern Legal Science* [*当代法学*]

Choukroune, Leïla, Garapon, Antoine 'The Norms of Chinese Harmony' (2007) 3 *China Perspectives*

Clarke, Donald C. 'Dispute Resolution in China' (1991) Vol. 5 No. 2 *Journal of Chinese Law*

Ding, Guofeng [丁国锋] Ma, Chao [马超] 'Suzhou Closed 1,342 Criminal Reconciliation Cases [苏州办结刑事和解案一千三百四十二起]' at http://js.legaldaily.com.cn/content/2014-07/15/content_5668159.htm?node=34636 (last accessed on 18 March 2015)

Du, Yu [杜宇] '"Criminal Conciliation": Critics and Preliminary Response ["刑事和解": 批评意见与初步回应]' (2009) 8 *Chinese Criminal Science* [*中国刑事法杂志*]

Feeley, Malcolm M. 'Two Models of the Criminal Justice System: An Organizational Perspective' (1973) Vol. 7 No. 3 *Law & Society Review*

Fu, Hualing 'Criminal Defence in China: The Possible Impact of the 1996 Criminal Procedural Law Reform' (Mar. 1998) No. 153 *The China Quarterly*

Fu, Hualing 'Re-education Through Labour in Historical Perspective' (Dec. 2005) No. 184 *The China Quarterly*

Fu, Hualing 'The Politics of Mediation in a Chinese County: The Case Study of Luo Lianxi' (2003) Vol. 5 No. 2 *Australian Journal of Asian Law*

Fu, Hualing 'Zhou Yongkang and the Recent Police Reform in China' (2005) Vol. 38 No. 2 *The Australian and New Zealand Journal of Criminology*

Ge, Lin [葛琳] 'An Analysis of the Practical Predicament of Criminal Reconciliation [刑事和解的现实困境解析]' (2010) 5 *Justice of China* [*中国司法*]

He, Weifang 'The Police and the Rule of Law: Commentary on "Principles and Secret Agents"' (Sep. 2007) *The China Quarterly*

He, Weifang [贺卫方] 'The Reform of the Chinese Court and Judicial Independence: Observation and Reflection of a Participant [中国法院的改革与司法独立：一个参与者的观察与反思]' (2003) 3 *Zhejiang Social Sciences* [*浙江社会科学*]

He, Yongjun [何永军] 'On Legitimacy and Legalization of Criminal Reconciliation [论刑事和解的合法性与合法化]' (2009) 3 *Journal of Kunming University of Science and Technology (Social Science)* [*昆明理工大学学报（社会科学版）*]

Hong, Dayong [洪大用] 'An Initial Research on the Poverty Relief Work by Chinese Non-governmental Organizations [中国民间组织扶贫工作的初步研究]' (2002) 2 *Jianghai Academic Journal* [*江海学刊*]

Hudson, Barbara 'Restorative Justice and Gendered Violence: Diversion or Effective Justice? (2002) Vol. 42 No. 3 *The British Journal of Criminology*

Lewis, Margaret K. 'Controlling Abuse to Maintain Control: The Exclusionary Rule in China' (2011) Vol. 43 *International Law and Politics*

Li, Buyun [李步云] Liu, Zhiwei [柳志伟] 'Several Issues Relating to Judicial Independence [司法独立的几个问题]' (2002) 3 *Legal Research* [*法学研究*]

Li, Changsheng [李昌盛] 'The Chinese Pattern of Criminal Trial: *Bildung* Trial [刑事庭审的中国模式：教化型庭审]' (2011) 1 *Science of Law (Journal of Northwest University of Political Science and Law)* [*法律科学(西北政法大学学报)*]

Li, Hong [李宏] 'On Judicial Justice and Independent Trial [论司法公正与审判独立]' (2010) 5 *Legal System and Society* [*法制与社会*]

Li, Hongjiang [李洪江] 'The Implementation of Criminal Reconciliation Should be Slowed Down' [刑事和解应缓行] (2006) 5 *Chinese Prosecutors* [*中国检察官*]

Li, Lianfeng [李连峰] Shang, Shumin [尚淑敏] 'On the Construction of Criminal Reconciliation System: On the Basis of "Private Resolution" among the People [论我国刑事和解制度的构建：以民间“私了”传统为基础的构建模式]’ (2009) 12 *Academic Exchange* [*学术交流*]

Liang, Genlin [梁根林] ‘Ten Falsification in Using Criminal Reconciliation in Death Penalty Cases [死刑案件被刑事和解的十大证伪]’ (2010) 4 *Legal Science* [*法学*]

Liang, Ping [梁平] ‘The Establishment of a Diverse Dispute Resolution System [多元化纠纷解决机制的制度构建]’ (2011) 3 *Contemporary Law Review* [*当代法学*]

Liao, Huanguo [廖焕国] Zeng, Xiangsheng [曾祥生] ‘The Interactive Between the Civil Law and Criminal Law: Conflicts and Coordination of the Tort Law and Criminal Law [民刑互动：侵权责任法与刑法的冲突与协调]’ (2010) 3 *Wuhan University Journal (Philosophy & Social Science* [*武汉大学学报(哲学社会科学版)*]

Liebman, Benjamin L. ‘China’s Courts: Restricted Reform’ (2007) 191 *The China Quarterly*

Liebman, Benjamin L. ‘Legal Reform: China’s Law-Stability Paradox’ (2014) Vol. 143 No. 2 *Daedalus Spring*

Liebman, Benjamin L. ‘Leniency in Chinese Criminal Law? Everyday Justice in Henan’ (2014) *Columbia Public Law Research Paper*

Liebman, Benjamin L., Wu, Tim ‘China’s Network Justice’ (January 2007) *Chicago Journal of International Law*

Liu, Lingmei [刘凌梅] ‘Introduction and Assessment on Criminal Reconciliation in Western Jurisdictions [西方国家刑事和解理论和实践介评]’ (2001) Vol. 23 No. 1 *Modern Law Science* [*现代法学*]

Liu, Sida, Halliday, Terence ‘Recursivity in Legal Change: Lawyers and Reforms of China’s Criminal Procedure Law’ (2009) Vol. 34 No. 4 *Law and Social Inquiry*

Liu, Sida, Wang, Zhizhou ‘The Fall and Rise of Law and Social Science in China’ (2015) Vol. 11 *Annual Review of Law and Social Science*

Lü Gang [闾刚] ‘The Analysis of the Judicial Function and Process of Restorative Justice [恢复性司法功能和过程分析]’ (2005) 1 *Journal of Anhui Vocational College of Police Officers* [*安徽职业警官学院学报*]

Lubman, Stanley ‘Bird in a Cage: Chinese Law Reform after Twenty Years’ (2000) *Northwestern Journal of International Law & Business*

Lubman, Stanley ‘Dispute Resolution in China after Deng Xiaoping: “Mao and Mediation Revisit”’ (1997) Vol. 11 No. 2 *California Law Review*

Lubman, Stanley ‘Mao and Mediation: Politics and Dispute Resolution in Communist China’ (1967) Vol. 55 No. 5 *California Law Review*

Lubman, Stanley 'Studying Contemporary Chinese Law: Limits, Possibilities and Strategy' (1991) Vol. 39 *The American Journal of Comparative Law*

Ma, Congcong [马丛丛] 'An Examination of the Idea of Restorative Justice Embodied in the Customary Tibetan Law [藏族习惯法之现代恢复性司法理念审查]' (2011) 7 *Business Culture* [*商业文化*]

Ma, Jinghua [马静华] 'The Theoretical Basis of Criminal Reconciliation and the Construction of this System in China [刑事和解的理论基础及其在我国的制度构想]' (2003) 4 *Legal Science* [*法律科学(西北政法大学学报)*]

Ma, Zhangmin [马章民] 'Combination and Conflict Between the Tort Law and Criminal Law [侵权责任法与刑法的衔接与冲突]' (2010) 9 *Legal System and Society* [*法制与社会*]

Minzner, Carl F. 'China's Turn Against Law' (2011) Vol. LIX No. 4 *The American Journal of Comparative Law*

Minzner, Carl F. 'Judicial Disciplinary Systems for Incorrectly Decided Cases: The Imperial Chinese Heritage Lives On' (2009) Vol. 39 *New Mexico Law Review*

Minzner, Carl F. 'Xinfang: An Alternative to Formal Chinese Legal Institutions' (2006) Vol. 42 *Stanford Journal of International Law*

Miu, Weihui [缪伟辉] '刑事和解的价值提取 [The Values of Criminal Reconciliation]' (2010) 10 *Legal System and Society* [*法制与社会*]

Pang, Zheng [逄政] 'Education in the Court [法庭上的教化]' (2008) 10 *Fang Yuan Fazhi* [*方圆法治*]

Peerenboom, Randall 'Judicial Independence and Judicial Accountability: An Empirical Study of Individual Case Supervision' (Jan. 2006) No. 55 *The China Journal*

Peerenboom, Randall 'What Have We Learned about Law and Development? Describing, Predicting and Assessing Legal Reforms in China' (Spring 2006) Vol. 27 *Michigan Journal of International Law*

Perry, Elizabeth J. 'Studying Chinese Politics: Farewell to Revolution?' (2007) No. 57 *The China Journal*

Pils, Eva 'Taking Yuan Seriously: Why the Chinese State Should Stop Suppressing Citizen Protests Against Injustice' (2011) No. 2 *Temple International and Comparative Law Journal*

Shaw, Victor 'Corrections and Punishments in China: Information and Analysis' (2010) Vol. 26 No. 1 *Journal of Contemporary Criminal Justice*

Song, Yinghui [宋英辉] 'An Empirical Analysis of Criminal Reconciliation in China [我国刑事和解实证分析]' (2008) 5 *China Legal Science* [*中国法学*]

Stutsman, Tomas 'The Use of Demonstration Projects to Advance Criminal Procedure Reform in China' (2011) Vol. 24 No. 2 *Columbia Journal of Asian Law*

Sun, Wanhuai [孙万怀] 'Do Death Penalty Cases Need Reconciliation and Can They Be Reconciled? [死刑案件可以并需要和解吗?]' (2010) 1 *China Legal Science* [*中国法学*]

Tamanaha, Brian Z. 'The Primacy of Society and the Failures of Law and Development' (2009) Vol. 44 *Cornell International Law Journal*

Tan, Zelin [谭泽林] Zhao, Qiusheng [赵秋生] 'Problems and Improvements of Laws Accordingly in Implementing Criminal Reconciliation in China [我国刑事和解实施中的问题与相应实体、程序法完善]' (2009) 9 *Politics and Law* [*政治与法律*]

Tang, Weijian [汤维建] 'The Rational Reflection on Solving the Problem with Enforcement: Focusing on the Establishment of An Independent Enforcement System [关于破解"执行难"的理性反思: 以执行体制的独立化构建为中心]' (2007) 5 *Study and Exploration* [*学习与探索*]

Teng, Biao 'Rights Defence (*weiquan*), Microblogs (*weibo*), and the Surrounding Gaze (*weiguan*): The Rights Defence Movement Online and Offline' (2012/3) French Centre for Research on Contemporary China

Trevaskes, Susan 'The Shifting Sands of Punishment in China in the Era of "Harmonious Society"' (2010) Vol. 32 No. 3 *Law & Policy*

Wang, Xiang [王向] 'An Analysis on the Social Welfare Policy to the Floating Population [流动人口社会保障政策分析]' (2003) 4 *Information of Economics and Law* [*财经政法资讯*]

Wang, Zhixiang [王志祥] Zhang, Weike [张伟珂] 'On the Legitimacy of Criminal Reconciliation in Capital Cases [死刑案件中刑事和解的正当性探究]' (2011) 4 *Northern Legal Science* [*北方法学*]

Xia, Min [夏敏] 'Closure: A Not Easy Task in Trial [案结事了：一个不轻松的审判课题]' (2007) 2 *China Trial* [*中国审判*]

Xiang, Chaoyang [向朝阳] Ma, Jinghua [马静华] 'The Establishment of the Values of Criminal Reconciliation and Its Chinese Pattern [刑事和解的价值构造及中国模式的构建]' (2003) 6 *Chinese Legal Science* [*中国法学*]

Xiao, Shiwei [肖仕卫] '"The Third Realm" in Criminal Justice: An Analysis of the Structural Position and Function of Criminal Reconciliation in China [刑事法治的"第三领域"：中国刑事和解制度的结构定位与功能分析]' (2007) Vol. 19 No. 6 *Peking University Law Journal* [*中外法学*]

Xiao, Shiwei [肖仕卫] Ma, Jinghua [马静华] 'The Unique Function of Criminal Reconciliation in China: From the Perspective of Resolving the Problem of "Solving Criminal Cases Privately" [中国刑事和解的独特功能：以刑事案件"私了"问题之解决为起点的分析]' (2010) 2 *Criminal Science* [*中国刑事法杂志*]

Xu, Yang [徐阳] 'Harmfulness of and Safeguard Against Power Abuse in Criminal Reconciliation [刑事和解中权力过度推进之危害及其防范]' (2009) 6 *Legal Review* [*法学评论*]

Yao, Li [姚莉] 'An Analysis of the Essentials of Judicial Justice [司法公正要素分析]' (2003) 5 *Legal Research* [*法学研究*]

Yi, Yanyou, 'Can a Government Compulsorily Make Her Citizens More Free? Revisiting Non-judicial Detentions under the People's Republic's Administrative Regulations and Their Justifications' (2010) Vol. 2 *Tsinghua China Law Review*

Yu, Jingyao [俞静尧] 'An Structural Analysis of Judicial Independence and Legal Reform [司法独立结构分析与司法改革]' (2004) 3 *Legal Research* [*法学研究*]

Yuan, Jianping [袁建平] 'The Problem with Enforcement and Its Resolution from the Perspective of Judicial Justice [司法公正视角下的执行难及其矫治]' (2010) 7 *Journal of Socialist Theory Guide* [*理论导刊*]

Zhang, Fuxiong [张孚雄] 'Thoughts on the Use of Criminal Reconciliation in Serious Crimes [重罪案件刑事和解的理论思考]' (2011) 2 *Law and Economy* [*法制与经济*]

Zhang, Shuqin [张书琴] 'Treating Criminal Reconciliation Rationally [理性对待刑事和解]' (2007) 3 *Hebei Law Science* [*河北法学*]

Zhou, Shixiong [周世雄] 'On Criminal Reconciliation: Taking the Exploration of Criminal Reconciliation in Hunan Province as an Analytic Sample [也论刑事和解制度：以湖南省检察机关的刑事和解探索为分析样本]' (2008) 3 *Law Review* [*法学评论*]

ELECTRONIC SOURCE MATERIALS

'An Introduction of the Thought Report System in the Chinese Communist Party [党员思想汇报制度]' http://www.whci.gov.cn/whjszx/shownews_dj.asp?newsid=20 (last accessed on 27 January 2011)

'An Introduction of the Thought Report System in Universities in China [学生党员思想汇报制度]' http://www.csust.edu.cn/pub/wfxy/xsgz/xsdj/t20081121_83308.htm (last accessed on 27 January 2011)

Bai, Quanmin, 'Opinions,' interview of the spokesman of the Supreme People's Procuratorate at http://www.lianghui.org.cn/2011/2011-03/12/content_22119264_2.htm (last accessed on 15 March 2011)

BBC News 'The Cultural Revolution' http://news.bbc.co.uk/hi/english/static/special_report/1999/09/99/china_50/cult.htm (last accessed on 12 March 2012)

Beijing Times [*京华时报*] 'Juvenile Offenders Were Escorted into the School to Educate 3000 Students with Legal Knowledge in Xianyang, Shaanxi Province [陕西咸阳少年犯被押解进校向 3000 学生示众说法]' http://news.sohu.com/20120105/n331275818.shtml (last accessed on 8 January 2012)

Braithwaite, John 'Crime, Shame and Reintegration' http://www.ciaj-icaj.ca/english/publications/DP1999/braithwaite.pdf (last accessed on 20 January 2008)

Cai, Dingjian, at the conference 'Legal Reform in China: Problems and Prospects' held by the Carnegie Endowment for International Peace and the Asia Foundation in Washington, DC on 18 April, 2005 http://www.carnegieendowment.org/files/panel2_summary.pdf (last accessed on 26 April 2012)

Chao, Xuku [晁绪库] 'The Detention House in Zezhou County Strengthened Education Work to Facilitate the Detainees' Reform [泽州县拘留所加强教育促进被拘人员转化]' http://jc.jcnews.com.cn/jincheng_content/2012-04/24/content_162200.htm (last accessed on 10 May 2012)

Chen, Baocheng [陈宝成] '刑事诉讼法学家陈光中建议取消地方政法委拍板权 [The Criminal Procedure Law Expert Chen Guangzhong Advised to Abolish Local Political-legal Committees' Power to Make Final Decision]' http://nf.nfdaily.cn/nfdsb/content/2010-05/15/content_11945697.htm (last accessed on 26 April 2012)

Chen, Chunlong [陈春龙] 'The Current Situation and Reform of China's "Hukou System" [中国"户口制度"的现状与改革]' http://www.iolaw.org.cn/showArticle.asp?id=1729 (last accessed on 6 December 2010)

Chen, Min [陈敏] Wang, Wei [王伟] 'The Effects of Deepening the Moral Reform Work for the Defendants: The Experience of the People's Court of Xishan District in Wuxi City [深化刑事被告人道德教化显成效：无锡锡山法院刑事审判经验材料]' http://www.dffy.com/fazhixinwen/sifa/200907/20090723154611.htm (last accessed on 9 May 2012)

Chen, Ruihua [陈瑞华] 'Criminal Reconciliation: A Conversation Between Legal Experts and Legal Scholars [刑事和解：法律家和法学家的对话]' http://www.procedurallaw.cn/xsss/zdwz/200807/t20080724_51763.html (last accessed on 24 October 2011)

Chen, Ruihua [陈瑞华] 'Sentence with Flexibility [留有余地的判决]' http://xinjin.xxlnm.fyfz.cn/art/910367.htm (last accessed on 27 April 2012)

Chen, Ruihua [陈瑞华] 'The Main Problems with the Chinese Criminal Justice System [中国刑事司法制度的主要问题]' http://article.chinalawinfo.com/Article_Detail.asp?ArticleID=19991&Type=mod (last accessed on 22 June 2011)

Chen, Ruihua [陈瑞华] 'Three Traditions of the Chinese Criminal Justice System [中国刑事司法制度的三个传统]' http://www.procedurallaw.cn/xsss/zdwz/200905/t20090518_220963.html (last accessed on 23 June 2012)

Chen, Ruihua [陈瑞华] 'Who to Supervise the Supervisor [谁来监督监督者]' http://article.chinalawinfo.com/Article_Detail.asp?ArticleId=34869 (last accessed on 28 April 2012)

Chen, Xuan [陈暄] '4243 Cases Resolved "Privately": The Enforcement Rate of Criminal Reconciliation in Hunan Reached 99.5% [4243件案子"私了"：湖南刑事和解案件赔偿履行率达 99.5%]' http://hn.rednet.cn/c/2009/12/13/1871544.htm (last accessed on 27 July 2010)

Chinese Human Rights Defenders (CHRD) 'Re-education Through Labor Abuses Continue Unabated: Overhaul Long Overdue' http://docs.law.gwu.edu/facweb/dclarke/public/CHRD_RTL_Report.pdf (last accessed on 2 July 2012)

Chun'an Court Research Group [淳安法院课题组] 'Fieldwork on the Application of Criminal Reconciliation Procedure: Using Chun'an Court's Judicial Practice as a Sample [关于刑事和解程序适用问题的调研：以淳安法院司法实践为样本]' http://www.hzcourt.cn/art/2015/6/3/art_51_12392.html (last accessed on 27 July 2010)

Clarke, Donald C. 'Choice of Dispute Resolution Mechanisms in China' http://lawprofessors.typepad.com/china_law_prof_blog/2011/08/choice-of-dispute-resolution-mechanisms-in-china.html (last accessed on 11 September 2011)

Cohen, Jerome A. 'China's Legal Reform at the Crossroads' http://www.cfr.org/china/chinas-legal-reform-crossroads/p10063 (last accessed on 17 May 2015)

Cohen, Jerome A. 'Law in Political Transitions: Lessons from East Asia and the Road Ahead for China' http://www.cecc.gov/pages/hearings/072605/Cohen.php?PHPSESSID=b63a0066ec44bfc7e52470d7373a8916 (last accessed on 26 April 2012)

Cohen, Jerome A. 'The PRC Legal System at Sixty' http://www.eastasiaforum.org/2009/10/01/the-prc-legal-system-at-sixty/ (last accessed on 9 March 2012)

Coonan, Clifford 'Zhao Zuohai: Beaten, Framed and Jailed for a Murder that Never Happened' http://www.independent.co.uk/news/world/asia/zhao-zuohai-beaten-framed-and-jailed-for-a-murder-that-never-happened-1973042.html (last accessed on 26 April 2012)

Dui Hua 'Dui Hua Estimates 4,000 Executions in China, Welcomes Open Dialogue' https://sna.etapestry.com/prod/viewEmailAsPage.do?databaseId=DuiHuaFoundation&mailingId=22213781&personaRef=11073.0.152691&jobRef=2967.0.31681565&memberId=789166155&erRef=11073.0.152697&key=e2eacaff46787bfeefcaa24cf35264c7 (last accessed on 1 March 2012)

Dui Hua 'Taming Police Influence in Politico-legal Committees' http://www.duihuahrjournal.org/2011/11/taming-police-influence-in-politico.html (last accessed on 23 July 2012)

Dui Hua 'Zhao Zuohai Case Provokes Responses on Legal Protections from Chinese Public Government' http://www.duihuahrjournal.org/2010/06/zhao-zuohai-case-provokes-responses-on.html (last accessed on 26 April 2012)

Equality and Human Rights Commission 'The Right to a Fair Trial' http://www.equalityhumanrights.com/advice-and-guidance/before-the-equality-act/guidance-for-service-users-pre-october-2010/criminal-justice-system/the-right-to-a-fair-trial/ (last accessed on 6 March 2012)

Fei County of Linyi City in Shandong Province [山东省临沂市费县] 'Measures on Establishing Collaboration Between Criminal Reconciliation and People's Mediation [关于建立刑事和解与人民调解对接机制的实施办法]' http://fxzfw.cn/News_View.asp?NewsID=438 (last accessed on 25 October 2011)

Feng, Liqiang [封利强] Cui, Yang [崔杨] 'Experience and Problems of Criminal Reconciliation: An Investigation on the Implementation of Criminal Reconciliation in Chaoyang District in Beijing [刑事和解的经验与问题：北京市朝阳区刑事和解现状]' http://article.chinalawinfo.com/Article_Detail.asp?ArticleID=42834 (last accessed on 24 October 2011)

Feng, Renqiang [冯仁强] Xie, Meiyin [谢梅因] 'Definition and Disposition of the "Repentance" in Criminal Reconciliation [刑事和解"反悔"行为的认定与处理]' http://www.procedurallaw.cn/xsss/zdwz/200902/t20090227_185404.html (last accessed on 25 June 2011)

Fu, Hualing 'Access to Justice in China: Potentials, Limits, and Alternatives' (draft) http://papers.ssrn.com/sol3/papers.cfm?abstract_id=1474073 (last accessed on 9 July 2015)

Guo, Songmin [郭松民] 'The Embarrassment of the Enforcement Agency [法院执行局的尴尬]' http://news.sina.com.cn/c/2005-09-20/18087819132.shtml (last accessed on 18 June 2011)

He, Weifang [贺卫方] 'Amendments on the PRC Court Organic Law and Judicial Independence [中国法院组织法的修改与司法独立]' http://article.chinalawinfo.com/Article_Detail.asp?ArticleID=33871&Type=mod (last accessed on 28 October 2010)

He, Weifang [贺卫方] 'Nothing Has More Reformational Characteristics than Judicial Reform [没什么比司法改革更具改良特色]' http://blog.sina.com.cn/s/blog_488663200102dufm.html (last accessed on 26 April 2012)

Hua, Rui [华蕊] 'The "Fuqing Discipline Inspection Commission Explosion Case" Unresolved for Ten Years Will Be Heard Recently [十年不决的'福清纪委爆炸案'二审于近日开庭]' http://blog.boxun.com/hero/201104/chrd/106_1.shtml (last accessed on 14 June 2011)

'Huang Songyou Answered Journalists Questions Regarding "Provisions of the Supreme People's Court about Several Issues Concerning the Civil Mediation Work of the People's Court" [黄松有就《关于人民法院民事调解工作若干问题的规定》答记者问]' at http://www.china.com.cn/chinese/PI-c/661957.htm (last accessed on 12 May 2015)

Human Rights in China 'Reeducation Through Labor: A Summary of Regulatory Issues and Concerns' http://hrichina.org/public/PDFs/Reports/HRIC-RTL.pdf (last accessed on 2 July 2011)

Human Rights Watch 'Reeducation Through Labor in China' http://www.hrw.org/legacy/campaigns/china-98/laojiao.htm (last accessed on 2 July 2011)

Jiang, De [蒋德] Wan, Zhong [万众] 'Criminal Reconciliation Has Been Introduced into Prison: The Judge Says that It Is Not Illegal Leniency [狱内伤害案引入刑事和解：检察官称绝非法外施恩]' http://news.sohu.com/20090721/n265364272.shtml (last accessed on 22 July 2009)

Jiang, Ping [江平] Guo, Daohui [郭道晖] Li, Buyun [李步云] 'Review: Further Discussions on Rule of Law and Rule of Man [温故：再谈法治与人治大讨论]' http://www.aisixiang.com/data/80806.html (last accessed on 3 November 2011)

Jin, Xiaogang [金晓刚] 'The Origin of Unjust Cases: The Appeal to "Abolish the Political-legal Committee" Is Increasing [制造冤案的祸源"取消政法委"呼声涨]' http://www.aboluowang.com/2012/0331/241072.html (last accessed on 26 April 2012)

Kunming Daily [*昆明日报*] 'The Organic Law of the Sub-district Office over "50 Years Old" Was Banned, yet New Responsibility Has Not Been Clear yet: The Sub-district Office Is More and More Embarrassed ["50 多岁"的《城市街道办事处组织条例》已被废止，但新职责依

然不明确: 街道办身份越来越尴尬]' http://szcg.km.gov.cn/ggxx/news.aspx?id=5371 (last accessed on 28 March 2011)

Lai, Yang [来扬] 'The Expert Talked about the Incident Where the Deputy Director Beat the Journalist and Said "Private Resolution" with the Exemption from Criminal Liability Is Invalid [专家谈副局长持枪打记者事件称免刑责的私了无效]' http://www.chinanews.com/fz/2012/04-09/3803624.shtml (last accessed on 24 April 2012)

Lan, Wuyou [蓝无忧] 'The Twist and Destroy of Rule of Law by the Political-legal Committee [政法委对法治的扭曲破坏]' http://www.chinainperspective.com/ArtShow.aspx?AID=15187 (last accessed on 26 April 2012)

Li, Changsheng [李昌盛] 'The "Defendant Talking" Style Trial which Lacks Defense [缺乏对抗的被告人说话式审判]' http://www.docin.com/p-26284336.html?bsh_bid=85286478 (last accessed on 10 May 2012)

Li, Keji [李克杰] 'A Contradictory System of Quality and Task and Its Gap from the Reality [素质与任务的矛盾制度与现实的断裂]' http://epaper.timedg.com/html/2010-07/12/content_492444.htm (last accessed on 20 December 2010)

Li, Ming [黎明] 'The 'All-about-Money' Criminal Reconciliation Is Damage [要钱的刑事和解是祸水]' http://news.ifeng.com/opinion/society/detail_2009_08/18/1303072_0.shtml (last accessed on 5 November 2011)

Li, Ping [李萍] Liu, Yu [刘宇] 'Discussion on the Establishment of Criminal Reconciliation System in Juvenile Cases in the People's Procuratorate [检察机关构建未成年人刑事和解制度探讨]' http://www.shjcy.gov.cn/njcgyd2007/llsj/t20070809_33593.htm (last accessed on 12 February 2011)

Li, Yinfang [李银芳] Li, Jinfu [李金富] 'Reasons and Strategies of Petitioning Related to Judicial Cases [涉法上访案件的成因及对策]' http://www.dffy.com/fayanguancha/sh/200409/20040916085512.htm (last accessed on 8 February 2012)

Liu, Dehua [刘德华] Wang, Li [王莉] Jian, Hua [简华] 'The Victim Can Nominate National People's Congress Deputy to Participate in the Criminal Reconciliation Process [哪位代表介入刑事和解? 被害人点名]' http://news.china.com.cn/rollnews/2010-07/05/content_3023494.htm (last accessed on 28 July 2010)

Long, Zongzhi [龙宗智] '"Hidden Rules" in Legal Practices [法律实践中的"潜规则"]' http://www.yadian.cc/paper/21974/ (last accessed on 7 April 2012)

Ma, Jing [马竞] Cao, Tianjian [曹天健] 'Hebei Police Successfully Mediated 3438 Minor Injury Cases in Nearly One Year [河北警方

试水轻伤害案件调解处理，近一年成功调解3438起]' http://www.criminallaw.com.cn/article/default.asp?id=2146 (last accessed on 27 July 2010)

Mao, Zedong 'On the Correct Handling of Contradictions among the People' http://www.peopleofcolororganize.com/wp-content/uploads/pdf/poco/contradictions.pdf (last accessed on 9 July 2015)

Mao, Zedong 'Where Do Correct Ideas Come From? [人的正确思想是从哪里来的？]' at http://art-bin.com/art/omao22.html (last accessed on 12 May 2012)

Marshall, Tony F. 'Restorative Justice: An Overview' http://library.npia.police.uk/docs/homisc/occ-resjus.pdf (last accessed on 16 February 2008)

Ouyang, Fang [欧阳芳] 'The Police of Ji'an City in Jiangxi Province Experimentally Conducted Criminal Reconciliation to Promote Social Harmony [江西吉安公安局试行刑事和解制度.促社会和谐]' http://www.chinapeace.org.cn/zhzl/2009-08/24/content_82878.htm (last accessed on 27 July 2010)

Peerenboom, Randall, He, Xin 'Dispute Resolution in China: Patterns, Causes, and Prognosis' http://www.fljs.org/uploads/documents/Peerenboom_He%20Xin%231%23.pdf (last accessed on 16 July 2012)

Pejan, Ramin 'Laogai: "Reform Through Labor" in China' http://www.wcl.american.edu/hrbrief/07/2laogai.cfm (last accessed on 2 July 2011)

Rosenzweig, Joshua, Sapio, Flora,Jiang, Jue, Teng, Biao and Pils, Eva 'The 2012 Revision of the Chinese Criminal Procedure Law: (Mostly) Old Wine in New Bottles' http://www.law.cuhk.edu.hk/research/crj/papers.php (last accessed on 7 January 2013)

San Xiang Municipal Newspaper [*三湘都市报*] 'Hunan Tried Criminal Reconciliation: Minor Criminal Cases Can Be Reconciled Privately [湖南试行刑事和解制：轻微刑事案件可私下和解]' http://www1.china.com.cn/policy/txt/2006-11/22/content_7393033.htm (last accessed on 11 February 2011)

Shan, Shibing [单士兵] 'The "Illusion of Harmony" behind Criminal Reconciliation [刑事和解背后的"和谐幻觉"]' http://gb.cri.cn/9083/2006/11/23/2165@1317252.htm (last accessed on 24 February 2012)

Smith, Jennifer and Gompers, Michael 'Realizing Justice: The Development of Fair Trial Rights in China' http://www.law.upenn.edu/journals/ealr/articles/volume2/issue2/SmithGompers2ChineseL.&Pol%E2%80%99yRev.108(2007).pdf (accessed on 10 January 2010)

Song, Yinghui [宋英辉] 'Empirical Analysis on Criminal Reconciliation in Public Prosecution [公诉案件刑事和解的实证分析]' http://www.sqxb.cn/blog/blog.aspx?id=309&zuozeid=83 (last accessed on 27 July 2010)

Southern Weekend [*南方周末*] 'A Shooting Case Resulting in Three Judges' Death in Yongzhou, Hunan Province: The Murder Has an Incurable Disease [湖南永州致三法官死枪击案： 凶手身患绝症]' http://www.infzm.com/content/45861 (last accessed on 15 November 2010)

Southern Weekend [*南方周末*] 'The Fourth "Strike Hard" Campaign: The More We Gain, the More Horrible It Is [第四次全国"严打"成果越大越可怕]' http://news.qq.com/a/20100702/000470.htm (last accessed on 21 March 2012)

Southern Weekend [*南方周末*] 'The Fourth Strike Hard: Can It Be Like the Previous Ones? [第四次严打： 能像过去一样打吗?]' http://nf.nfdaily.cn/epaper/nfzm/content/20100701/ArticelB10005FM.htm (last accessed on 29 November 2010)

Strang, Heather 'Restorative Justice Programs in Australia: A Report to the Criminology Research Council' http://www.criminologyresearchcouncil.gov.au/reports/strang/qld.html (last accessed on 7 April 2015)

Su, Li [苏力] 'Deliberative Justice and the Big Mediation System [关于能动司法与大调解]' http://article.chinalawinfo.com/Article_Detail.asp?ArticleId=53760 (last accessed on 9 March 2012)

Sun, Ming [孙明] 'My Views on the Judge's Private Meeting with the Parties and Their Lawyers [法官私自会见当事人及委托律师之我见]' http://www.dffy.com/sifashijian/sw/200601/20060104221654.htm (last accessed on 9 April 2011)

Sun, Yu [孙瑜] Chen, Lei [陈磊] 'Solving Criminal Cases Privately: Moving on in Debates [刑事案件私了： 在争议中前行]' http://news.sina.com.cn/c/l/2007-03-21/160612576540.shtml (last accessed on 26 August 2008)

'The Appeal Lodged by 69 Chinese Scholars to the National People's Congress about Initiating Unconstitutional Review on the System of Reeducation through Labor' at http://review.jcrb.com/ljzd/index.htm (last accessed on 2 July 2011)

The Economist 'China's Security State: Guarding the Guardians' http://www.economist.com/node/21557760 (last accessed on 23 July 2012)

The Justice Bureau of Haishu District [海曙区司法局] 'Haishu District Has Reached Perfect Collaboration Between Criminal Reconciliation and the People's Mediation [海曙区实现刑事和解与人民调解工作无缝对接]' http://www.zjsft.gov.cn/art/2011/8/8/art_61_31321.html (last accessed on 25 October 2011)

The People's Court Daily [人民法院报] 'From Controversy to Harmony: The Transplant of Restorative Justice to China [从对抗走向和谐：恢复性司法的本土移植]' http://news.xinhuanet.com/legal/2007-05/10/content_6080026.htm (last accessed on 2 March 2012)

The People's Procuratorate of Wuhua District in Kunming City [昆明市五华区检察院] '"Cooperation Among Departments and Between the People's Procuratorate and the People's Court" Promotes Criminal Reconciliation in Our Court [我院"部门联动检调对接"积极促进刑事和解]' http://www.kmwh.gov.cn/kmwh/web/jwb/j5/jcy/showdoc.jsp;jsessionid=Ot51m9BDkebtjnp8RzU7mU9Qmv9bnuDjlMTimcwXMvfFgfOVXroz!742181009?docid=D105138&fieldid=F3792 (last accessed on 25 October 2011)

Wang, Chengduo [王成铎] 'Yantai: On the Way of "Peaceful Judiciary" [烟台: 走在"平和司法"的大道上]' http://www.jcrb.com/n1/jcrb904/ca477942.htm (last accessed on 24 October 2011)

Wang, Dong [王栋], Zhao, Bin [赵斌], 'Main Problems Facing Criminal Reconciliation and Strategies [刑事和解面临的主要问题与对策]' http://www.hongfan.org.cn/projects.php?optionid=377&auto_id=29 (last accessed on 7 August 2015)

Wang, Feiling [王飞凌] 'The Transformation of China's Hukou System [中国户口制度的转型]' http://www.chinaelections.org/newsinfo.asp?newsid=185108 (last accessed on 6 December 2010)

Wang, Xiaoxian [王效贤] 'On Open Trial [论公开审判]' http://article.chinalawinfo.com/Article_Detail.asp?ArticleId=41580 (last accessed on 11 May 2012)

Wang, Xuetang [王学堂] 'Popular Identification on Criminal Reconciliation: An Empirical Analysis Based on Three News Reporting [刑事和解的民众认同： 基于三起新闻事件的实证分析]' http://www.dffy.com/faxuejieti/ss/201101/20110110150022.htm (last accessed on 19 December 2011)

'Work Allocation in Tianjin No. 2 Intermediate People's Court [天津市第二中级人民法院审判庭业务划分]' at http://www.huanglawyer.net/Article/ShowArticle.asp?ArticleID=435 (last accessed on 27 October 2011)

Wu, Aiying [吴爱英] 'Sparing No Effort to Make Judicial Organs Maintain Social Stability [全力做好司法行政机关维护社会稳定工作]' http://www.gov.cn/gzdt/2012-10/23/content_2249495.htm (last accessed on 9 July 2015)

Wu, Yingzi [吴英姿] '"Mediation First": Reform Pattern and Legal Interpretation ["调解优先"：改革范式与法律解读]' http://article.chinalawinfo.com/ArticleHtml/Article_78723.shtml (last accessed on 20 June 2015)

Xia, Jianzhong [夏建中] 'The Concept of Community and the Establishment of Community in Urban China [社区概念与我国城市社区建设]' http://www.ccpg.org.cn/Article/ShowArticle.asp?ArticleID=272 (last accessed on 8 December 2010)
Xiao, Zhiyun [肖之云] 'Huangmei: "Two Fast One Trial" Criminal Reconciliation Are Effective [黄梅：'两快一审'刑事和解显成效]' http://www.hbjc.gov.cn/ssjd/201509/t20150907_714579.shtml (last accessed on 1 November 2015)
Xinhua Net [新华网] 'Is "Reform Through Labour" the Same with "Reeducation Through Labour"? ['劳动教养'就是'劳动改造'吗?]' http://news.xinhuanet.com/banyt/2004-05/12/content_1464763.htm (last accessed on 4 January 2011)
Xinhua Net [新华网] 'Interpret Decisions of the Sixth Plenary Session: Implement Criminal Justice Policy of Combining Severity with Leniency [解读六中全会决定：实施宽严相济的刑事司法政策]' http://news.xinhuanet.com/legal/2006-12/09/content_5459413.htm (last accessed on 7 April 2011)
Xinhua Net [新华网] 'The Supreme People's Court Raised Idea of "Harmonious Judiciary" for the First Time [最高法院首次提出"司法和谐"理念]' http://news.163.com/07/0107/11/347SD32N000122EH.html (last accessed on 9 March 2012)
Xinhua News Agency [新华社] 'Mediate When It Can, Adjudicate When It Should, Fuse Trials and Mediation, Bring Closure [能调则调，当判则判，调判结合，案结事了]' http://www.gov.cn/2007lh/content_549985.htm (last accessed on 3 November 2011)
Xu, Aiqiong [许爱琼] 'The Detention House in Putian City Is the First in the Province to Establish a Drug Control Propaganda and Education Centre [莆田市拘留所将建禁毒宣传教育基地全省首创]' http://news.66163.com/2012-04-10/622023.shtml (last accessed on 10 May 2012)
Xu, Bin [许斌] 'Laws and Regulations Should Be the Products of Open Game [法律法规应该是公开博弈的产物]' http://www.china.com.cn/news/comment/2010-07/30/content_20607709.htm (last accessed on 6 March 2012)
Xu, Chi [许驰] Liu, Xiaohan [刘晓晗] 'Ming Guangchao: Lighting Up the Light in Juvenile Delinquent's Heart [明广超：点亮失足少年心中的灯]' http://js.jcrb.com/rwgs/201010/t20101014_454600.shtml (last accessed on 19 March 2012)
Yan, Jun [严峻] 'The Debates Triggered by "Avoiding Punishment with Money" ["赔钱减刑"引发的是非争议]' http://www.zj.xinhuanet.com/magazine/2007-05/08/content_9972222.htm (last accessed on 4 March 2011)

Yan, Xiaoguang [闫晓光] 'Criminal Reconciliation Conducted by the People's Court of Foshan City of Guangdong Province Triggered Debates: It Was Criticized as "Avoiding Punishment with Money" [广东佛山法院刑事和解引争议：被指"'以钱买刑"]' http://news.163.com/10/0730/00/6CQ5UU5R0001124J.html (last accessed on 23 July 2010)

Yang, Mengchen [杨孟辰] Zhang, Shuyang [张舒阳] '北京朝阳检察院十年刑事和解工作当事人满意率 100% [Beijing Chaoyang Procuratorate Implemented Criminal Reconciliation for Ten Years 100 Percent of Parties Satisfied]' http://legal.people.com.cn/n/2012/0926/c42510-19110709.html (last accessed on 1 November 2015)

Yazhou, Zhoukan [亚洲周刊] 'Competitive Election Adopted in the Party Committee of Guangdong Province: Head of the Political-legal Committee Is No Longer a Member Which Implies Its Decreasing Status [廣東省委換屆推差額選舉 政法委不是常委地]' http://www.yzzk.com/cfm/Content_Archive.cfm?Channel=bc&Path=2447308872/21bcc.cfm (last accessed on 23 July 2012)

Ye, Doudou [叶逗逗] Wang, Heyan [王和岩] 'Major Revisions to the Criminal Procedure Law: The Advance and Retreat of Public Powers [刑诉法大修: 公权力进退]' http://china.caixin.com/2012-03-12/100367126.html (last accessed on 23 May 2012)

Yu, Jianrong [于建嵘] 'What Has Stability Overwhelmed? [稳定压倒了什么?]' at http://www.gscn.com.cn/pub/critique/sdgc/2011/11/02/1320226193705.html (last accessed on 26 April 2012)

Zhang, Guochen [张国臣] 'The People's Courts in Our City Implemented Criminal Reconciliation Actively to Resolve Social Conflicts [市法院充分运用刑事和解: 积极化解社会矛盾]' http://www.alt.gov.cn/Article/ShowArticle.aspx?ArticleID=44190 (last accessed on 27 October 2011)

Zhang, Hui [张辉] 'The Obstacles of Judicial Independence in China: On the System of Political-legal Committee's Harmfulness to Judicial Independence and Violations of Human Rights [中国司法独立的障碍: 兼论政法委体制对司法独立的侵害及其对人权的侵犯]' http://boxun.com/news/gb/china/2011/01/201101240023.shtml (last accessed on 26 April 2012)

Zhang, Huihua [张辉华] Wang, Yuan [王媛] 'On the Introduction and Implementation of Criminal Reconciliation in China from the Perspective of Restorative Justice [从恢复性司法看刑事和解在我国的引入和应用]' http://www.chinacourt.org/html/article/200411/02/137288.shtml (last accessed on 22 July 2008)

Zhang, Jie [张洁] '"Restorative Justice, Criminal Reconciliation, Community Correction": Three Crucial Systems in Juvenile Justice System

['恢复性司法、刑事和解、社区矫正':少年司法中的三项重要制度]' http://www.yffz.org/E_ReadNews.asp?NewsId=1249&page=2 (last accessed on 13 February 2011)

Zhang, Xingchuan [张星川] 'An Initial Analysis of the Problems and Strategies for the Current Criminal Reconciliation Work [浅议当前刑事和解工作中存在的问题及对策]' http://www.jcrb.com/jcpd/jcll/201008/t20100803_394537.html (last accessed on 12 December 2011)

Zhang, Yinghong [张英红] 'The Commission of Politics and Law Impedes Judicial Independence [政法委妨碍司法独立]' http://www.chinaelections.org/NewsInfo.asp?NewsID=26678 (last accessed on 22 April 2011)

Zhao, Jiayue [赵佳月] 'The Revision of the Criminal Procedure Law: A Game Between Power and Rights [刑诉法修改: 权力与权利的博弈]' http://nf.nfdaily.cn/nfrwzk/content/2011-09/13/content_29780011.htm (last accessed on 6 May 2012)

GOVERNMENT PUBLICATIONS

Almanac of Xinbei District, Changzhou City 2003–2005 http://www.cznd.gov.cn/nj2005/zfrw/4.htm (last accessed on 15 November 2010)

Almanac of Xinbei District, Changzhou City 2006–2008 http://www.cznd.gov.cn/nj2008/Templates/zhengfa/html5-6.html (last accessed on 15 November 2010)

Statistical Bulletin of the National Economic and Social Development of Dadukou District of Chongqing in 2007 http://www.ddktj.gov.cn/wwweb/sjck/tjgb/20091223/1950.html (last accessed on 7 February 2011)

Statistical Bulletin of the National Economic and Social Development of Dadukou District of Chongqing in 2008 http://www.ddktj.gov.cn/wwweb/sjck/tjgb/20091223/1951.html (last accessed on 7 February 2011)

The Community Correction Office of Jiangsu Province http://www.jssf.gov.cn/xxgk/jgsz/nsjg/200810/t20081028_18928.html (last accessed on 6 December 2010)

Index